Routledge Revivals

SUDANESE MEMOIRS

SUDANESE MEMOIRS

Being mainly translations of
a number of Arabic Manuscripts relating to
the Central and Western Sudan

H. R. PALMER

THREE VOLUMES IN ONE

First published in 1928 by Frank Cass and Company Limited

This edition first published in 2018 by Routledge
2 Park Square, Milton Park, Abingdon, Oxon, OX14 4RN
and by Routledge
52 Vanderbilt Avenue, New York, NY 10017, USA

Routledge is an imprint of the Taylor & Francis Group, an informa business

© 1928 by Taylor and Francis

All rights reserved. No part of this book may be reprinted or reproduced or utilised in any form or by any electronic, mechanical, or other means, now known or hereafter invented, including photocopying and recording, or in any information storage or retrieval system, without permission in writing from the publishers.

Publisher's Note
The publisher has gone to great lengths to ensure the quality of this reprint but points out that some imperfections in the original copies may be apparent.

Disclaimer
The publisher has made every effort to trace copyright holders and welcomes correspondence from those they have been unable to contact.
A Library of Congress record exists under ISBN: 11022641

ISBN 13: 978-0-367-17818-5 (hbk)
ISBN 13: 978-0-367-17820-8 (pbk)
ISBN 13: 978-0-429-05784-7 (ebk)

SUDANESE MEMOIRS

CASS LIBRARY OF AFRICAN STUDIES

GENERAL STUDIES

No. 47

Editorial Adviser: JOHN RALPH WILLIS

SUDANESE MEMOIRS

Being mainly translations of
a number of Arabic Manuscripts relating to
the Central and Western Sudan

H. R. PALMER

THREE VOLUMES IN ONE

FRANK CASS & CO. LTD.
1967

Published by
FRANK CASS AND COMPANY LIMITED
67 Great Russell Street, London WC1
by arrangement with the Federal Government of Nigeria

First edition	1928
New impression	1967

Printed in Great Britain by
Thomas Nelson (Printers) Ltd., London and Edinburgh

SUDANESE MEMOIRS

VOLUME ONE

PREFACE

The MSS which are translated in these volumes have been obtained at different times and in different places in the Western Sudan during the past twenty-four years.

The text of the "Kanem War of Idris Alooma" is the one procured by the traveller Barth in 1853 and sent by him to the British Foreign Office, as was its companion MS "A History of the First Twelve Years of the Reign of Mai Idris Alooma."(1)

Many of the others are anonymous and some may be said to represent merely oral tradition.

I am much indebted to Mr. J. R. Patterson, both for correcting the proofs and for two maps, which illustrate the texts, prepared by him, also to Mr. A. E. V. Walwyn for permission to print his "Notes on the History of Daura."

H. R. PALMER.

Kaduna, April 2, 1927.

---

(1) Government Printer, Lagos, 1926.

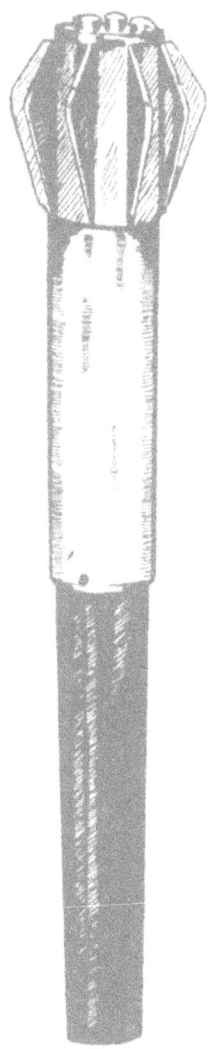

$\frac{3}{8}$ actual size

Sceptre of the Mais of Bornu.

The Sceptre of the Mais of Bornu. (Kan. babu).

INTRODUCTION TO KANEM WARS OF MAI IDRIS ALOOMA.

THE expeditions to Kanem which form the subject matter of this work and continue the account of Mai Idris Alooma's reign given by Imam Ahmed ibn Fartua in his "The first twelve years of the reign of Mai Idris Alooma," represent rather the struggles of rival branches of an originally homogeneous dynasty, the Magumi or Saifawa, for dominion over Kanem, than any racial hostility between the peoples of Kanem and those of Bornu. At N'gazargamu as capital, the rightful line of Sultans or Mais had established itself about 1470 A.D. after they had wandered about since the end of the preceding century, when Mai Umr Idrisimi finally left the old capital at N'jimi in Kanem and went West.

Mai Idris Katagarmabe, the grandfather of Mai Idris Alooma, had, as this work records, first re-entered N'Jimi in the year 1505, one hundred and twenty-two years after the first expulsion of the Saifawa Mai Daud Nigalemi from it. Idris Katagarmabe was succeeded in 1526 by his son Muhammad, who was able firmly to maintain his authority over Kanem and secure the respect of the Bulala, so much so that when he was succeeded by his brother 'Ali, about 1545, the latter married a Mairam (Princess) of the Bulala, who gave birth to Idris Alooma as his posthumous son.

According to present-day tradition, this Bulala Mairam, Aisa Kili N'girmaram, who afterwards became the Magira or Official Queen Mother, had great difficulty in preserving Idris' life from his cousin Mai Dunama N'Gumaramma, and the son of the latter, Mai Abdullah, but on the death of Abdullah she became Regent, and is said to have built the brick palace and mosque at Gambaru on the Komadugu, the ruins of which still remain, in order that Idris might not be corrupted by the manners of the capital N'gazargamu or Birni, which lies some fifteen miles to the south of Gambaru.

The affection which, as the narrative states several times, Idris felt for the Bulala Sultan Muhammad ibn Abdullahi was thus, no doubt, due to the fact that Muhammad was his own maternal uncle, or otherwise closely connected with Magira Aisa Kili.

As a good deal of misapprehension and confusion has existed with regard to this Bulala Kingdom since the days of the Arab geographer Idrisi, owing to a confusion between the name of its original capital Ga'u, just north of Lake Fitri and east of the present Yawo, with the Gao or Gaoga which succeeded Kaukau or Kukia in the Niger Valley as capital of the Songhay Empire, it will be convenient here to record certain Kanuri songs which have reference to the Bulala Mais and also certain other facts and traditions.

Though, as Barth states, the actual Sultans or rulers of the Bulala were a branch of the Saifawa of Kanem, their first Sultan being known as Mai Jil Sukumami, the rank and file of the Bulala were not Magumi but Kayi or Keyi, from the Wadai region, who intermarried with the N'gizim or Kuku tribes of the Fitri region, the Dajo.

The name Bulala is connected with the salutation bestowed on them in songs " Ye Kilalan " (Kiyi-ilala) which, among the Kanembu, means " O exalted Kiyi or Kayi," and with the Tamashek terms for " noble " or " freeman " Ili, Ilili, Illela, Lilloa, and Illam. In Bornu, the Bulala are commonly called " Kayi Bulala."

The precise date and relationship of Jil Sukumami* is rather obscure, but he was a contemporary of the Mais Idris and Daud Nigalemi, and thus he flourished about the middle of the 14th century—1350-1380.

On the other hand, it appears evident both from the songs which will be given below and other facts, that he was not descended from Dunama Dabalemi or even from Umme Jilmi, but from the Mais Biyuma (Wayama) and Bulu, who lived before the Bornu Muslim era, which began with Umme Jilmi, circa 1086.

The centre of power of these Mais, as we learn from Idrisi's notice of Kanem, was not N'jimi, but the region of Madan or Madam (Idrisi's Matan) *i.e.* the south-eastern part of Kanem in the region of the modern Bâri and N'guri extending east to Lake Fitri.

Here was situated the original Biyo or Waiyo, whence comes the name Biyuma or Wayama, from which the Kanuri and Bulala rulers are by the Bagarmians called respectively Biyo and Biyo Bulala.

According to the Chronicles and Girgams, Bulu was the son of Biyoma or Waiyama. The descendants of Bulu are the Buluwa or Bulwa, who in the narrative are mentioned as almost synonymous with Idris' enemies in this region, and whose name compounded with the Tamashek " ilala " (nobles) is responsible for the name Bul-ilala =Bulala, and on the other hand, is the same name as the name Bolewa, which is applied to a ruling caste in the region of Fikka which formed part of one of the so-called Kororafa migrations into Nigeria at a very early period, and that of the sea port on the east of Lake Chad still called Bol.

To the immediate south of Lake Chad also lay Gamtilo one of the earliest Barbar settlements, and Balagi or Balge, an ancient capital which lay about five hours journey east of Gamtilo.

The following Tebu traditions current at Bulma concerning the Oasis of Kawar and neighbouring part of the Sahara are given by Captain Buchanan.†

"The first people of Kawar were Sos (giants) from the Fezzan. Legend declares they were a very big race, while it is still claimed by the natives that the skeletons of these giants, and the great houses where they lived, are even yet to be seen in the Fezzan near Tejerri. These giants were as tall as twenty elbows.

* Sukuma denotes in Kanuri a woman all of whose children but one have died.

† " Sahara " by Angus Buchanan, M.C., F.R.G.S.
John Murray, London, 1926.

"In due course the Sultan of the Beri-Beri came to Bulma and asked the Sultan of the Sos for permission to settle there with his people. Whereupon the giant king, answering nothing, took a wand and, extending it, turned slowly round so that he formed a mighty circle, the edge of which extended to Yeggeba, in northern Kawar and to Dibbela in the south (a diameter of 100 miles or more); and within that area the Beri-Beri were permitted to live".

"The Sos were at that time settled in the oasis in the valley of Bulma, the rainfall of which was coming from Jado, and going to Fachi and Termit*".

After this legendary time it is said that: "In 800 A.D. there was a great invasion of Beri-Beri, who were Muslims. They came from Yaman in Arabia by way of the Fezzan and Kawar, and continued to the country of Mao (Kanem territory) leaving in their passage some people who thought the country of Bulma attractive and suitable to settle in."

"In this way the foundation was laid of Jado, Siggidim, Dirku, and Bulma."

"Furthermore all oases † between Bulma and Chad were colonised by Beri-Beri. Some of them were already occupied, but the inhabitants were ejected by the Beri-Beri. The original people were a tribe named Koiyam and representatives of the race are still to be found in Bornu."

"When the Tebu came to the region they found the Beri-Beri had already been in occupation of Kawar for a long time. The first Tebu came from Termit, and it is claimed that the tribe originated from lawless people who had committed murder in their own countries to the south, and were obliged to flee and become lawless. Later in their history, when the Tebu were an established race in Tibesti, the first of the tribe to discover Kawar chanced across it by accident when in pursuit of strayed camels. This adventurer found the country promising to live in, and returned to Tibesti with the news. As a consequence of this discovery a number of Tebu crossed to Kawar with their families to settle."

"In this way Ashenumma, Arrigi, Tiggumama, N'gassar, and Chimmidur were founded."

"In time the Tebu grew in strength and gained supremacy over the Beri-Beri, who became subject to them."

"Later on the Tuareg of Air came to Bulma and Fachi, and took them over as colonies, exacting tax, which for a long time was paid to the Sultan of Agades. But the Tuwareg never occupied the country."

"The three oldest towns in Kawar are: Bulma, Dirku, and Gazbi. Of these Bulma is by far the most important because of its prolific salt-pits."

"As a place of outstanding fame in the Sahara it is naturally rich in local history. At various periods the town has occupied

---

* An extremely interesting geographical observation, for no watercourse exists along that line to-day; it suggests evidence of physical change and decay in the Sahara.

† Another observation of particular interest. Wells, at places, are all that remain along that line of territory at the present time.

three different situations. The site of the oldest town, known to the natives as Birabirn, is about a quarter of a mile south of the Bulma of the present."

With regard to the ancestry of the Saifawa or Magumi who, as has been seen, were the " Magge " or Royal " Clan " both of the rightful Mais of Kanem and of the Bulala, the Bornu legend set forth more than once in these pages, is that their paternal ancestor was Saif ibn Dthi Yazan of Yaman.

Saif is a historical personage and, round the regions where he lived, Yaman and Adan (Aden), there centres much myth not unmixed with history.*

According to Arab tradition Bilkis, Queen of Sheba, came from Saba in Yaman, the " Arabia Felix " of the Romans, which lies to the north and west of Aden, and embarked at Aden for her visit to King Solomon. Cain, also, after killing his brother, was, it is believed, tempted by Iblis, the common enemy of mankind, to become a fire-worshipper, as his brother Abel had been, with the words " Be thou also a worshipper of fire, and the sovereignty of the earth of which thou hast been deprived shall be restored to thee and thy progeny." Cain and his progeny are supposed to have erected their first fire altar at Aden. In the 23rd verse of the 27th chapter of Ezekiel, Aden is described on equal terms with Sheba in its commercial relations with ancient Tyre.

The history of the people of Aden is bound up with that of the people of Yaman. The earliest inhabitants of Yaman were those of the other parts of Southern Arabia bordering the Red Sea and beyond. The evidence of the Bible and of tradition is that the Kushites were the first known race who peopled those tracts. How long they lasted cannot be conjectured, but Ibn Khaldun, the Arab historian, states that they were succeeded by a tribe who were the descendants of Sham, *i.e.* Semites, from which the inference is that the Kushites were non-Semitic. The first Semites did not remain long in southern Arabia, but migrated northwards along the west coast. They left behind them the tribe of 'Ad, of whom Sheddad, son of 'Ad is said to have built, not far from Aden, a wonderful palace.

The next invasion of Southern Arabia differed from previous ones in that it came from the west, when the Amalekites of the Bible, called the Bani 'Amar, overran the country. It is supposed that in course of time the Bani 'Amar, became amalgamated with the Sabaeans and formed the Himyarites; but, however evolved, there existed a line of Himyarite rulers of Aden and Yaman for several hundreds of years before the birth of Christ. The Himyarite power declined and finally disappeared in the destruction wrought by the Roman expedition to Yaman under Elius Gallus, Prefect of Egypt, in the reign of Augustus in about A.D. 110. With eighty ships of war, 130 transports, and 10,000 Roman infantry, this Roman general made incursions into Arabia and left traces of Roman civilization behind him, although he did not penetrate as far as Sana'a.

It was, perhaps, in the centuries before and after the birth of

* For fuller accounts of Aden *see* Journal of Central Asian Society 1927-1928.

Christ that Aden attained its second period of greatness. It became a great market. Spikenard, alabaster, and frankincense were much in demand not only in Europe, but also in India and China. Merchants and their ships crowded the ports of the Red Sea, where these and other luxuries were obtained. The harbour of Aden was full of ships either passing up the Red Sea with the products of Arabia and Eastern Africa, or waiting for a favourable wind which would blow them to the Gulf of Cambay in India, whence also they would be blown back to Aden by the return monsoon.

It was only about half a century after the birth of Christ that the unknown author of the "Periplus" placed on record the prosperity of Aden in his book of mercantile jottings. He calls the place "Eudaimon Arabia" and tells us that it " is a village by
" the shore, having convenient anchorages and watering-places
" sweeter and better than those at Ocelis (the modern Sheikh Saad,
" near Perim); it lies at the entrance of a bay, and the land recedes
" from it. It was called 'Eudaimon' because, in the early days
" when the voyage was not yet made from India to Egypt, and
" when sailors did not dare to sail from Egypt to the ports across
" this ocean, all came together at this place. It received the
" cargoes from both countries, just as Alexandria now receives the
" things brought both from abroad and from Egypt. But not long
" before our own time Charibael (*i.e.* a Yamanite king) destroyed
" the place."

After the destruction of the town of Aden, referred to in the "Periplus," there is no historical mention of the place for two or three hundred years. Christianity began to supplant other creeds in Europe. The Emperor Constantine sent Christian embassies to many places, and among them one to Aden, where a church was erected in 342 A.D. But Christianity did not flourish in Aden, although it met with more success in the Yaman proper. Its spread ended in a massacre, crushing out the new religion. A few survivors of this massacre fled to Abyssinia, where they induced the Najash, who was a Christian, to take up arms to avenge the fate of their brethren. The Najash agreed to the suggestion, and despatched an army of 70,000 men, under the command of his son Aryat. This force landed at Aden, and marched into Yaman, after Aryat had burnt his transports to show his troops that for them the question was one of death or glory. This happened about 525 A.D. The Abyssinians after routing the Jew authors of the Christian massacre, and after driving the Himyarite ruler, Dthu Nowas, to die by a voluntary jump over a cliff to avoid being taken, remained in the land they had captured.

But Saif ibn Dthi Yazan, the descendant of the Himyarite kings, seeing the people turning against the Abyssinians by reason of their cruelty and oppression, sought aid to regain the kingdom of his fathers, and applied first to Byzantium and then to Kosroes Parwiz, King of Persia. There were four Abyssinian kings of Yaman, and it fell to the last of them, Masruk, to meet the new invaders. At first Kosroes had refused to entertain the request of Saif, but the latter changed his ground when he saw that his appeal to sympathy was likely to be ineffective. He described the wealth of his lawful possessions, and played upon the cupidity of the Persians with better effect. Finally, Kosroes collected an army of 3,600 men—mainly prisoners and condemned criminals—and despatched them by sea to Aden with the remark: "If they conquer these regions, it will add to my kingdom; if they perish, they but suffer the just punishment of their crimes." Saif himself led this force, which fought its first battle just outside Aden. Masruk was killed, and the Persians established their dominion over Yaman, where Saif ruled as a Persian Viceroy. This was in about the year A.D. 575.

The last Persian Viceroy, Badan, became a follower of Muhammad, and after his death in A.D. 632, Aden and Yaman passed into Muhammadan hands, and were governed by the house of Ummayya until A.D. 749, when they passed into the possession of the Abbaside Caliphs, Daud ibn Abd al Majia being appointed Governor of Aden. In A.D. 932, Yaman threw off its allegiance, and its rulers became independent under the style and title of Imam. It is a remarkable fact that many of the rulers of Yaman after Badan bore Persian names.

El Bekri, the Arab writer who lived towards 1050 A.D., states that in his day the people of Kanem were idolaters but that princes of the fugitive Beni Ummayya of Damascus were in the country. The Bornu writers also speak of the Caliphate shifting to Bornu after the death of the Ummayyad Caliph Umr ibn Abd ul Aziz, but it is doubtful whether El Bekri's statement should be taken too literally, while again, the fact that the Ummayyads did rule Yaman for a time and that the Bornu people claimed descent from Saif ibn Dthi Yazan may well have led to such an inference.

The Timbuctu authors also state that the kings of both Bornu and Songhay came from the "army of the Caliph Umr ibn Abd ul Aziz."

A much better authority, however, is Yakubi who states definitely that the rulers of Kanem were of the Barbar tribe of Zaghawa while Leo Africanus states that they were of the Libyan tribe of Bardoa.

The fact is that while it is probable that some travelling Arab chief, possibly an Ummayyad, or possibly a Himyarite, married into the Zaghawa or Kayi, his sons who succeeded made good their claims to rule not through him but through their mothers.

To all intents and purposes both Saif ibn Dthi Yazan and his son Ibrahim are a myth, and the first real Mai of Kanem was Mai Dugu Bremmi, who succeeded because he was the "Dugu" or son of the chief's daughter or sister.*

He was followed by Mai Fune, *i.e.* a Kayi (Kindin) or Zaghawi Mai, who wore a litham or mouth covering (fune) like the Tuwareg, of whom the Zaghawa were a branch.

---

* In Tamashek—Tegasi.

Introduction.

As regards this succession by the sister's son in the Sudan there is a relevant passage in MacMichael's History of the Arabs of the Sudan, Volume I, page 138: "At first the king of Nuba attempted to repulse them (the Guhayna) but they failed: then they won them over by giving them their daughters in marriage. Thus was their (i.e. the Nuba) Kingdom disintegrated on account of their mother, according to the custom of the infidels as to the succession of the sister's son."

These early Barbar chiefs of Kanem were nomads as appears from Yakubi's (891 A.D.) notice of Kanem (a term which denoted the Sudan in general to the south of Tibesti) as also from Ibn Khaldun's extract from the work of Ibn Said; but whereas Dugu may perhaps have lived mainly in the region between Lake Fitri and Borku, and from there made his famous expedition to Yari Arbasan near the Sanaga River in the Congo Basin, his successor Fune, according to the consensus of the different records, died in Kanem, where his people (called Funiyawan in one Girgam) had at least a grazing ground in the regions which lay towards the south-east corner of Lake Chad or on the Bahr-ul-Ghazal.

Barth gives to the place where Fune died, the name of Malana: most Girgams give N'galan Bute or N'gala M'bute; one reads Muli Funiyawan.

It seems however that the variant readings all denote the same region, and that probably the best reading of all is Malan, i.e. Idrisi's Manan, or Matan (Madan) which in his day (1150), was the most important part of Kanem. This Manan or Malan possibly denoted the region called Kuluwan or Kuluwa in the Arabic Lists where Funi's second successor Katuri died. It was in the Kulu region where, in the chronicle translated below, the Bulala made their big stockade to accommodate all their followers in Kanem. The place is now called Mowal Kulkulma.

The settlement or even semi-settlement of this ruling family of Magumi in this region would naturally result in their kindred on their mother's side, other Kayi or Kindin, following in their wake.

That they did so hardly needs proof, especially as there is no doubt that the Bulala were the result of intermarriage between Kayi (Kindin) and the N'gizim or Kuka tribes of the Fitri region. The latter, according to tradition, supported to some extent by notices in Arab authorities, were in part of Kushite or Gara extraction, for they were apparently pastoral people (Fellata) who possessed sheep and goats, if not cattle.

The origin of the Bulala is however put beyond doubt by the following extracts from their songs concerning their Magumi Mais.

Extracts from Bulala Songs.	Translation.

1

Bula Jil, Ye Kiyi-ilâla:	O town of Jil: O noble Kiyi:
Maina Jil, Kafe, Salmami,	Prince Jil: He whose path is open as the plain: Son of Salma,

Extracts from Bulala Songs.	Translation.
Sikumami, Adamami,	Son of Sikuma, son of Adama,
Kanje bula N'jimibe.	The Smoke of the town of N'jimi.
2	
Karumarammi,	Son of the daughter of the Gara (Kara)
Abdul Karim Lefiami Dunamarammi;	Abdul Karim, son of Lefia the daughter of Dunama;
Yange sube jeye n'zu libillabe.	Who has greaves of iron tied with a girdle of silver.
Abdul Karim Lefiami,	Abdul Karim son of Lefia,
Lefia Dunamarambe.	Lefia daughter of Dunama.
Karadin Kasaga Kimewa;	In the palm of his hand he holds a red spear;
Bibien laya Kimewa;	On his arm is a charm covered with red leather;
Tata n'girma Kimelan;	A boy (he is) mounted on a red war-horse;
Jibchia, Kilusu Kimelan.	When he dismounts he alights on a red carpet.
Wayye kuru chigurosko,	Presently, (he says) I shall seek council of God,
Allah chiworin:	He asks God if it will be propitious (to go to war);
Yalan Kindin Yisoro,[1]	The Kindin have come against the North.
Allah Chiworin;	He asks God if it will be propitious (to go to war);
Futen Magumi Saifu chiguduro,	In the west the Magumi of Saif ibn Dthi Yazan descend like rain,
Allah chiworin;	He asks God if it will be propitious (to go to war);
Karima Mairammi,	Abdul Karim, son of a princess,
Mairam Wadairambe,	The Princess of Wadai,
Andi Kirigu fanden'de dugo	If we go not forth to war
Kutu faniyen.	We shall be unhappy.
Allah Yalan Bohadi chiguduro,	God has sent the Buhadi (Fezzanis) like rain on the North,
Allah Chiworin;	Yet he asks God if it will be propitious (to go to war).

1. The meaning from this point to the end of the poem appears to be that the singer is inciting Abdul Karim to go to war and finding excuse for his doing so.

Extracts from Bulala Songs.	Translation.
3	
Buluwari Bulama, Hadijami;	Chief of the land of the Bulwa, son of Hadija;
Kâ sube,	Whose staff is of iron
Kirkiron'zu libillabe[1]:	Spiralled with silver:
Bula Wayo Futemi.	His town Wayo (Biu) in the west.
Ye Kiyi-ilâla, Kwa Wayoma;	O noble Kiyi, warrior and ruler of Wayo;
Falmatami Dunamarammi.	Son of Falmata the daughter of Dunama.
Kagil subewa:	Owner of[2] an iron anvil.
Madama Futemi,	At Madama in the west,
Ali Adamami Bundirambe	Ali son of Adama the daughter of a lion.
Bula Madamin kargo.	At the town of Madama lies.
4	
Kukade[3] Aminami;	Owner of the town of Kuka, son of Amina;
Kuguma Hauwami;	Owner of the fiddle[4], son of Hauwa.
Kugun'zu libillabe:	Whose fiddle was of silver:
Bula Kukaden kargo.	He lies in the town of Kuka.
5	
Bula Ferum, ye Kiyi-ilâla,	O town of Ferum, O noble Kiyi.
Fiema Aisami,	Fiema son of Aisa,
Bula Ferumnin kargo.	He lies at Ferum.
6	
Kwa Idrisu	The warrior Idris,
Idrisu Aisami	Idris son of Aisa,
Fefeturam duniabe	Whose protecting wings[5] spread over the world,
Bula Fefelan Kargo.	He lies at the town of Fefe.

1. Kirkirno = lit., to mix, mould, with a turning movement. Here the word evidently means the metal binding a spear shaft.
2. Translating the postfix -wa = in possession of.
3. or ? Kukabe.
4. "Kugu" = goge (H) = fiddle. So in following line.
5. Fefeto " wing." The idea apparently is of protection.

Extracts from Bulala Songs.	Translation.
7	
Am Jihad, ye Kiyi-ilâlam	Am Jihad (town), O noble Kiyi,
Aji Fantami, Aji Lilawan Fantami,	Hajj son of Fanta, Hajj son of Fanta of Lilawa,
Aji, kuduwan, Fantami,	Hajj, of many towns, son of Fanta,
Aji, tumbal deguwa, Fantami;	Hajj with four clan drums, son of Fanta;
Aji Mairam Barimarambe;	Hajj son of the Princess of Bari;
Aji jibturam deguwa,	Hajj with four halts,
Jibturam fal Wasuri Buhadibe,	One halt among the Wasuri Buhadi,
Jibturam fal Kindin ikilanbe;	One halt among the slaves of the Kindin,
Jibturam fal Magumi Saifube,	One halt among the Magumi of Saif,
Jibturam fal Wadai Kwodeyibe:	One halt among the Kodok of Wadai:
Haji, yaji, Fantami,	Hajj the little, son of Fanta,
Lilawan Mairammi,	Son of the Princess of Lilawa,
Kwâ Barima, Bukr Zeinambe.	Warrior, ruler of Bari, Bukr son of Zeinam.
Ni dugu kime	You are the red grandson of a king,
Fune chilimwa	With the black mouth-veil
Karau kau chilimwa	And armlets of black stone.
8	
Amaramma, ye kelalan	Owner of Amaram, O noble Kiyi,
Kwâ, Tahir Hauwami,	Warrior, Tahir son of Hauwa,
Hauwa Budumarambe,	Hauwa daughter of the Buduma.
Mairam Kelu Budumarammi,	Son of Princess Kelu of the Buduma,
Mairam Aisha Budumarammi	Son of Princess Aisha of the Buduma
Kwâ Buduma Fannami	Warrior, a Buduma, son of Fanna,
Yirimarammi	Son of the daughter of the Yirima,
Mai Bula Yelabe	A king whose town is in the North.

Introduction.

It will be observed that in spite of the fact that their Mais were descended from the early Magumi Mais, and in spite of the fact that they distinguish as enemies not only the Magumi Saifu but the Wasuri (Buhadi) of Fezzan and the Kindin, the singers address the Bulala in general as " Ye Kelalan " which latter is merely a lengthened form of Keyi or Kayi, *i.e.* people who are *imoshagh* in Tamashek.

Bulala, as the name of a people, was a compound of their tribal name Bulwa or Bul, and " ilala " plural of " ili " meaning " free men " or " nobles " in the Tuwareg languages.

To this same general type of population we must also assign the Kananiyya mentioned in this history. In the text their ethnic affinity is not definitely stated, but from the location of their habitat (the north of Kanem), as well as the general description of them and, in particular, the fact that they were large cattle owners, it does not appear that they were primitive pagan negroes. The theological abuse showered on them further indicates that they were probably not racially unconnected with the Kanuri, as indeed might also be inferred from the position of their towns.

Had they been of Teda or Tubu affinity, they would have been part of the Bulala confederation which apparently they were not. The inference is therefore that, whether they were Hadadi or Bongo (Blacksmiths) in part, as Barth suggested, they were of Barbar or Tuwareg connection, and not dissimilar from the Ikli whom Barth discusses with them (vol. ii, p. 277). Ikli or Takili is the Tamashek term for slaves as a caste or grade of society, and not primarily a place name.

In the days of Makrisi (circa 1400), there obviously were communities of Ikli resident in Kanem, and it seems therefore highly probable that these Kananiyya were Ikli who had remained in Kanem throughout the civil war between the Saifawa and Bulala.

But apart from these considerations, the name Kananiyya or otherwise Kinaniyya, may be connected with both the general Kanuri words for Barbar Tuwareg, Kindin (Kinin), and Amakitan on the one hand, and on the other, with the place names Kanan (district south of Bauchi), Kwana, Gwana and Kana, which latter terms were used by the Kanuri to denote the so-called Kwararafa who were akin to themselves, and dominated Eastern Nigeria from about 1300 to 1750 A.D.

Similarly the name Kananiyya seems to bear a relation to the half forgotten Barbars of Kordofan, called Anag or Abu Gonaan (Kanaan). The fact that these Ikli were still a numerous people in Kanem as late as 1570 is interesting as showing that, before the civil war which began about 1370 A.D. the Teda or Tubu had not penetrated Kanem in any considerable numbers.*

Moreover, as these Ikli were a branch of the Zaghawa from whom the ruling dynasty were drawn, it would seem to follow that the connection between the Kwana (Kwararafa) and the Kanuri is that they were both in origin Zaghawa Barbars.

A consideration of the ethnological data set forth above leads to the conclusion that from possibly 900 A.D. onwards to the time of

---

* *See* also the Tubu accounts given by Capt. Buchanan quoted p. 3 *supra*.

the Kanem Civil War towards 1400 A.D. and, as this history shows, even after it, a very large proportion of the population of Kanem, apart from the so-called Saifawa or Magumi themselves (the ruling house), was of the caste which in the Sahara is called Imghad, *i.e.* they were the product of Sudanese women by Barbar or Kindin (Kayi) men. As the number increased and they split into communities and septs they were in many cases called Ikli, strictly speaking " slaves ", though naturally all acknowledged the authority of the Magumi Mais who were *imoshagh, i.e.* descended from a Kayi woman who had married an Arab and thus acknowledged by the Ikli as their noble or governing caste.

In Wadai, too, a Wadaian Chronicle, from which extracts are appended, shows that the case was very similar there also during the period in question. Northern Wadai was ruled by Kindin (Beli) or Kayi, with whom the rising Kayi-Magumi are said to have had battles in the deserts to the north of Masrub on the road to Dongola.

It is probably impossible to arrive at an accurate ethnic description of the tribes which inhabited Kanem when these invading Barbars first came there from the east towards 800 A.D. but it is evident that at this period Kushite races had been long established and were in fact the dominant factor in the tribal organisations that obtained in those regions.

The leading tribe or confederation was that of the N'gal-agha whose traditional origin brings them first from Yam or Yayambal (on the Nile) but ultimately from " Bagdad " *i.e.* Mesopotamia, or southern Arabia.

N'gal (the tribal) and N'gala (the place name) however, are but variants of the common Barbar name which was almost universal in the Sudan for the Kushite races, *i.e.* N'gala, Gara, Kara, Kola or Kolli, Gola and other metatheses between K and G and L and R with variant medial vocalisation. These names meant to the Kayi-Kanuri and to all other Barbars, the " servile Hamites " or Kush, whom they conquered, as opposed to the negroes proper, to which terms such as Dam-Dam, Dama, N'yam-N'yam, etc., were applied.

That these Kushite tribes lay, generally speaking, to the west of the Kindin or invading Barbars, is shown by the old Bornu title N'gal-ti-ma (Galladima), *i.e.* " ruler of the land of the N'gal ". The Galladima's sphere of action was always the western segment of an arc resulting from theoretical lines drawn through the capital city as centre, north-west to south-east, and north-east to south-west. Just as the N'gal-ti-ma ruled the west so the Kagha-ma (Kaigamma) ruled the south, and the Yeri-ma the north, while the east being their own country had to take its ruler's title from the name of a town such as Mastur (Mastrema).

It therefore hardly admits of doubt that in the period of the Christian era prior to the Kayi invasion of Wadai and Kanem, these Barbars (Kindin) were domiciled to the east of Wadai, *i.e.* in northern Kordofan or the region called Mâkida which the Magumi records claim to have been their ancestral home.

Agha or ara means servile peoples or strangers.

The period in question is however the period roughly 1-800 A.D., when the dominant power in that region was the people called Blemmyes. It is then so probable as to be almost certain that Kindin, Blemmyes, and Tuwareg are much the same people.

Moreover, since during the period of Roman ascendancy in Egypt, Saharan Gara races called Nobatae (Nuba) had, with Roman assistance, driven the Blemmyes west into the desert and Fezzan where they reappear as Hawara, Hawaza, Buhadi, Uzlan or Illam, it will be apparent why the Magumi and Kayi called the Kushite Gara of Fitri, with whom they first came in contact at a very early date, by the name of Nuba. The name Nuba has stuck to them ever since though they have other tribal names for themselves which are entirely different.

The text from which this translation has been made is, in the main, that of the manuscript which Barth obtained from the Wazir Haj Bashir in 1853 and sent home to the Foreign Office.

There exists, however, in Bornu, a manuscript here called manuscript (A) which belonged to the late Maina Gumsumi, the senior representative of the Saifawa. This manuscript, however, is imperfect for at page 53 it skips about seventy pages and proceeds straight to the final exordium about the Kuraish and Beni Saif.

Though in the parts which are common to both, the sense of the two manuscripts is identical or almost so, they differ in diction in places, as is natural with scribes who regard the *ipsissima verba* of an ordinary author as in no way sacred, but rather as statements which they are at liberty to amplify or adorn in any way their taste indicates.

In general, therefore, Barth's manuscript has been followed and minor verbal differences ignored, save, in such passages as seemed to convey either different information or further information not in Barth's manuscript, a translation of the text of manuscript A has been added in brackets after the translation of the text in Barth's manuscript.

These passages are however few in number, the only one of importance being the final exordium.

Appended to this translation of Imam Ahmed's Kanem Wars of Idrisi Alooma, are a number of translations of Arabic documents relating to the history of Bornu and Wadai which are still extant in Bornu and of which I have copies.

For the acquisition of copies of these old manuscripts, which are now difficult to obtain, I am indebted to many of the present day Bornu Chiefs, from the Shehu downwards, and particularly to Galladima Kashim, a descendant of the last real Mai—Mai Dunama Lefiami.

I am also greatly indebted to Mr. P. G. Butcher and Captain R. C. Abraham of the Nigerian Political Service for their very great assistance in preparing independent translations of much of the second half of the 'Kanem Wars', which have been of great service in the final revision of the whole work.

CHRONOLOGY OF THE EXPEDITIONS TO KANEM.

With an inconsistency or lack of exactitude not unusual among Sudanese writers, the Imam Ahmed makes in his preface statements about the season at which the respective expeditions took place which, in strictness, do not tally with his text.

The discrepancy however is caused by the fact that, evidently, when writing his preface, the Imam regarded the fighting expeditions as five in number with a final visit, six in all, whereas, in the succeeding pages, seven distinct visits are mentioned.

Clearly the expedition numbered V in the text, was the expedition made in the *saif*, or hot season, whence it follows that the ensuing one, VI, was the one made in the *kharif* (wet season).

The following dates appear to fit the circumstances:—

Sec. 12. *Expedition i.*—Set out on the last day of Sha'aban and celebrated 'Id ul Saghir at Aghafi, *i.e.* set out on 19th December, 1571.

Sec. 35. *Expedition ii.*—Beginning of the cold season. Celebrated 'Id ul Saghir at Shami, winter of 1572-73.

Sec. 48. *Expedition iii.*—In the hot season. The 'Id is not mentioned. Winter of 1573-74, presumably after 24th January, 1574, the date of the 'Id.

Sec. 55. *Expedition iv.*—In the early date season of the year 1574.

Sec. 69. *Expedition v.*—When the height of the cold season had passed after the 'Id ul Saghir. Not long after the 14th January, 1575, the date of the 'Id ul Saghir.

Sec. 103 *Expedition vi.*—Set out on Thursday, 15th Jumada al Ula. The expedition took place in the *kharif* (rainy season). It took place in August-September 1575, (8th August was 1st Jumada al Ula).

It would appear that after Idris' return from this expedition to Kanem, he set out on the expedition against Amsaka in Mandara, which is related in " The first twelve years of the reign of Idris Alooma ", for Amsaka apparently fell on the 4th December, 1575.

Sec. 117 *Expedition vii.*—In Shawwal. This final expedition probably took place in December or January, 1576.

The Kaigamma, " General of the South " of Bornu.
(Kaigamma Kakami).

THE KANEM WARS.

By Imam Ahmed ibn Fartua.

In the name of God, the Merciful, the Compassionate. May the blessing of God be upon our Lord and Prophet Muhammad, the chosen and perfect apostle, the Seal of the prophets, the Imam of the pure, and upon his relations and his companions, the god-fearing, and those who follow them righteously, until the day of meeting and recompense. Praise be to God in his mightiness and greatness. His mightiness transcends the how and where and other conceptions of man. He is the Guide of him who does His will in reading His book which embraces all wisdom and which exalts His people, the Muslims, above all other people, setting forth all in due order with proofs, rousing the conscience to the passing of days and of nights.

God sent our Prophet, our Lord and Master Muhammad, the greatest of the prophets and messengers, upon whom be the highest blessing and peace. He sent him to the whole of creation. Before him Infidelity struck its flag, idols and fetishes became his slaves, wrong-doing and ignorance rose and went off to the most distant lurking places.

He did not cease striving in Jihad with tongue and lance and pitiless sword, giving good-tidings and warning, a missionary in the path of peace, until truth appeared, emerging from error just as morning comes out from the darkness of night. A king is among the things most desired by men; his position is conspicuous to fame whereas an enemy of the Faith dwells nigh to the rivers of error and insolence and sin, even though, there is in fact, no holy war.

Even so the King, the great King, acts in His kingdom according to the desires of His heart, without asking help or hindrance or remorse.

May the blessing of God and peace be upon the Prophet and upon his relations and companions of proved nobleness, everlasting blessing, and peace without ceasing.

We have undertaken to write of the Kanem Wars which were waged by our Sultan, the Commander of the Faithful, the vice-gerent of the Lord of the Worlds in this land of Bornu; Al Hajj Idris, ibn Ali, ibn Idris, ibn Ali, ibn Ahmad, ibn Othman, ibn Idris, ibn Nikale, ibn Ibrahim, ibn Ahmad, ibn Salma, ibn Bikuru, ibn Biri, ibn Dunama, ibn Umme, ibn Abdul Jalil, ibn Huwa, ibn Rike, ibn Bulu, ibn Wayama, ibn Katuri, ibn Arsu, ibn Fune, ibn Duku, ibn Ibrahim, ibn Saif, ibn Dthi-Yazan, of the Himyar of the Kuraish.

He waged five wars against Kanem, three in the cold season, the fourth in the hot season, and the fifth in the season of the rains.

The Sultan Ibrahim son of Saif, mentioned above, so we have heard from the lips of our elders, buried his father in the land of Yaman in the valley of Sana'a and then migrated from Yaman by slow stages till he came to the land of Sima in Kanem. He settled there, he and his son and grandson. Years passed, till the time of Daud ibn Nikale.

MS. Page 3. Before the time of Sultan Daud, there was no discord, or quarrel in any of the four quarters of the realm, and everyone was under the authority and protection of the Mais of Kanem.

We have heard from learned Sheikhs that the utmost extent of their power in the east was to the land of Daw and to the Nile in the region called Rif; in the west their boundary reached the river called Baramusa. Thus we have heard from our elders who have gone before. What greatness can equal their greatness, or what power equal their power, or what kingdom equal their kingdom.

Far away! Far away!

The author of the book 'Ifrikiya', relates that the people of Himyar son of Ghalib are the successors of the Bani Hashim, successors whose title is undisputed, Hashim being of the seed of Luwai son of Ghalib. They are therefore brothers. We have mentioned their affairs above. Luwai ibn Ghalib was ruler of Hijaz. Himyar ibn Ghalib was king of Yaman and enjoyed the power that his brother Luwai ibn Ghalib gave him. The Amalik came from the seed of Himyar; and from the seed of the son of Ghalib came every excellence, and nobleness, and the Prince of the Prophets. (The blessing of God and peace rest on him and them all).

MS. Page 4. This is all far away! We saw in the book 'Ifrikiya' that Himyar conquered the world, and had a magnificent kingdom. He built between Kufra and Irak one thousand houses of crystal, and placed in every house a bed with eight legs of silver, each leg gilded with gold, and on each bed was a slave of the daughters of the kings. Himyar was the brother of Luwai ibn Ghalib and Luwai was the ancestor of the Kuraish.

We have seen also written in the above mentioned book that when the Bani Hashim and the Himyar obtained booty in war they divided it since the Himyar were the heirs of the Bani Hashim. So we read in 'Ifrikiya.'

We have seen also in the book 'Fatuhu Sham' that one of the kings of Yaman named Saif ibn Dthi Yazan foretold our Prophet's coming, since God inspired him with wisdom and eloquence so to do.

Let him who reflects take heed to the words we have quoted from the book 'Ifrikiya' and the book 'Fatuhu Sham', that he may know the ancestry of our Sultan Al Hajj Idris ibn Ali (may God ennoble him) for he is of the exalted race. Truly his descent is traced back to the Kuraish and such is not the case with many people.

Let us now return to the story of Sultan Daud.

During his reign as Khalifa mischief sprang up and evil doing, by the power of God most high and mighty, in his absolute foreknowledge.

Thus God caused men of the tribe of Bulala and of the people of Fitri and Madama to enter Kanem. They settled down in Kanem and could not be expelled until the time of the pious, just, and courageous Sultan, Commander of the Faithful, Idris ibn Ali ibn Ahmad, may the blessing of God rest on his posterity till the blast of the horn.

When Idris ibn Ali (Katagarmabe) was made Khalifa of the land of Bornu he assembled his many armies, red and black, and went to the land of Kanem.

He reached Garni Kiyala, and there ensued a battle between him and Sultan Dunama ibn Salma. Sultan Idris gained a great victory, and Sultan Dunama and his army fled and retired to the borders of a far country.

Then the Sultan Idris ibn Ali went to Sima (N'jimi) famous for the kings of the dynasty of Saif ibn Dthi Yazan and stayed there to his great delight.

We heard from the Sheikh Dunama ibn Rusku that between the date of Daud's quitting Sima and the date of the Sultan Idris's entry, there was an interval of 122 years exactly. The Sultan Idris ibn Ali then stayed at Sima as long as God willed, and returned to Bornu.

He had not yet planned to return a second time when news came to him from Kanem that Sultan Dunama ibn Salma was killed and that his brother Adam ibn Salma had been made Emir. This did not deter him from going to Kanem. He marched to Kanem as he did before, and reached the town of Jugulgul. A battle took place between him and Sultan Adam. God helped him, and gave him victory and Adam's army fled, and did not stop till they were far from Kanem—very far.

Then Sultan Idris went to N'jimi as he did the first time, and remained there as long as God willed. The story goes that afterwards Sultan Idris ibn Ali ordered Adam to come to Kanem with all due ceremony and made him swear an oath of fealty in the name of God most high and mighty.

The Sultan Idris ibn Ali returned to Bornu with his wrath appeased, and delighted with his good fortune, and lived in his country till he met the end that God (exalted be He) willed for him.

He died at Walamma. May God have mercy upon him.

After Idris's death his son Muhammad ibn Idris ibn Ali was made Khalifa in the land of Bornu. He reigned long. The Bulala Sultan Kadai ibn Abdul Jalil came to Bornu. We have heard that between his coming and the installation of Sultan Muhammad ibn Idris there was only an interval of forty days. The Sultan Kadai was killed at a place called Lada; so we have heard from our venerable Sheikhs.

From that time Sultan Muhammad ibn Idris ibn Ali found no one to oppose him in Kanem, till the ordained end of his days. May God have mercy upon him.

He was succeeded by his full brother Ali ibn Idris the Khalifa and he dwelt long in power, feared as was his brother, Sultan Muhammad ibn Idris, his predecessor. No one in Kanem refused to follow and obey him, till the end which God had decreed for him on the tablet came to him. May God have mercy upon him. Then Dunama ibn Muhammad became Khalifa.

Discord arose between him and Sultan Abdul Jalil ibn Kadai until Abdul Jalil invaded Bornu. The above mentioned Sultan Dunama ibn Muhammad met him with his army and a battle took place in Bornu. God gave our Sultan Dunama a great victory and Abdul Jalil returned in flight.

MS. Page 8. Sultan Dunama then went to Kanem; gained a second victory, and returned to Bornu, after killing Chiroma Biri and his peers such as Kagutima Doniyo and others of the Bulala.

After that time the Sultan Abdul Jalil made no more attacks on Sultan Dunama, but he made forays in Bornu without intending to fight. Every time he came to raid in Bornu, he ran away with great haste and did not stand for fear Sultan Dunama might catch him at his secret designs, and conquer him.

The Sultan Abdul Jalil continued to act thus, till the death of Sultan Dunama, who predeceased him.

Afterwards Sultan Abdul Jalil died.

Abdul Lahi ibn Dunama was made Khalifa in Bornu while Sultan Abdul Jalil was still alive.

Thereupon Abdul Jalil ibn Kadai made a raid in person, with his people, and emirs, and chiefs. They continued to make forays into Bornu day and night, as they formerly had done in the time of Sultan Dunama ibn Muhammad, and did not cease from this detestable habit till Sultan Abdul Jalil died.

His son Abdul Lahi was made Khalifa of the Bulala kingdom in the time of our Sultan Abdul Lahi ibn Dunama. They never had a real battle but constant raiding went on as before, till Sultan Abdul Lahi Dunama died.

MS. Page 9. To him succeeded, our just, God-fearing and noble lamp, dispelling darkness; pilgrim to the two illustrious cities; Idris ibn Ali ibn Idris (may God ennoble his face). He deterred the people of Bornu from wrongdoing, impurity, and all kinds of iniquity, and Truth and Right came by their own, and shone in the land of Bornu.

Evil went and hid her footsteps and the path of righteousness was plainly established without let or hindrance, or deviation, so that all the notable people became Muslims except atheists and hypocrites and malevolent persons. For such there is no remedy. God will count them and requite them on the Last Day.

We learn (for to God belongs what He has concealed and to us what He has revealed) that when justice reigned in the days of Hajj Idris ibn Ali in Bornu east and west and south and north, the Muslims were no longer troubled with the Bulala raids, or the N'gafata or Tatala or other similar bandits.

The Bulala had advanced and had occupied the towns of Tal, and Gatiga. Between these two towns and Kanem there was constant raiding day and night which was hurtful to our land of Bornu.

When our Sultan Hajj Idris ibn Ali ibn Idris (may God ennoble him in both worlds) became Mai, the Bulala returned to Kanem, and on the Bornu side there was no desire to raid or wage war for a single day. Persons who entered the country did so openly and after asking leave, and presenting themselves to the Sultan. Peace and friendship were established between our Sultan Hajj Idris and the Sultan of Kanem Abdul Lahi ibn Abdul Jalil, so that they even became related by marriage. A written pact of friendship was made between the two towns above mentioned after duly consulting the notables and chiefs of Kanem and Bornu. Thus was the matter concluded.

There was neither hatred, nor offence, nor grievance, between the people of Kanem and Bornu except in the matter of three towns which the people of Kanem had seized in days gone by at the time of the fighting between Sultan Ahmad (Dunama) ibn Muhammad and Sultan Abdul Jalil ibn Kadai.

MS. Page 10.

After the latter laid hands on the three towns, Tal called Kali, Guguti, and Bulugi, they never sent any messenger to Bornu, and the people of Bornu on the other hand always wished to regain them till the death of the Sultan Abdul Lahi ibn Abdul Jalil.

When his son Sultan Muhammad ibn Abdul Lahi succeeded, he neither hindered the towns coming in to Bornu nor yet handed them over. But this proud, envious, and evil people then dethroned him for no reason at all, and made his paternal uncle Sultan Abdul Jalil ibn Abdul Jalil their Khalifa.

He it was who abandoned the friendly relations which had been established between the Sultans Abdul Lahi and Idris and between Sultan Muhammad and our Sultan, and cast them away in contempt.

When the matter of the three towns was mentioned to him, he took no notice, and did not show any good will at all. Sultan Idris then proposed to him and his chiefs and emirs to submit the matter to the Shari'a and arbitration, but they were unwilling to follow the Sunna.

MS. Page 11.

A second time when our Sultan proposed to have the matter settled by the Courts, they wrote a letter and sent it to him. When he opened it he found its argument based on " forcible seizure "— to the effect that these towns had been taken from us by Sultan Salma " by force " in the past, and why therefore should they return them.

We saw the contents of the letter. Sultan Hajj Idris was astonished at their being so illogical and wanting in perception, and their failure to realise that our Sultan had, after the death of their Sultan (Salma) visited Kanem twice, and taken over Kanem and all the country under it, after putting to flight the two Sultans,

Dunama and his brother Adam, sons of Salma. He was also astonished and we also, at their argument for another reason; namely that "forcible seizure" only holds good as an argument for possession where infidels are concerned.

EXPEDITION I.

MS. Page 12. Then our Sultan Idris ibn Ali made up his mind to go to Kanem himself. He assembled his notables in council, his emirs and his captains and his chiefs and others and they all agreed that a rapid expedition should be made.

Idris then left his capital called Birni and halted at Gambaru. Thence he moved to Zantam, then to Kasimwa, in the west.

After he had been there a few days, the son of Hajj Birki, called Hajj Lefia, came on behalf of Sultan Abdul Jalil ibn Abdul Jalil, in the capacity of an ambassador. But our Sultan would not discuss with him the question of "forcible seizure" at all, and he was obliged to return to Kanem.

Then our Sultan Hajj Idris left Kasimwa and went east, and again halted at Zantam some few days and nights.

From Zantam he went to Ghotuwa, and thence onwards by easy stages in the midst of his own land till he came to Bari which lies round about the stockade of Gatiga, which is a town well known to all the inhabitants of Bornu, who from near or far visit Kanem, as a grazing ground for camels.

MS. Page 13. Hajj Idris stayed there a few days, three or so, to concentrate his army, and moved forward at the end of the month Rajab. Some people however said it was the 1st of Sha'aban, as there was the usual dispute about seeing the moon on the twenty-ninth day.

The Sultan passed Sakala, continued marching past Gayawa and spent the heat of the day at Furtu with a huge army. His emirs, and chiefs, and captains, amused themselves with much talk by the way. It was on that day that Asiyama Ali ibn Fuguma Thani died; a Thursday.

The Sultan and his army were at Furtu three days awaiting reinforcements both horse and foot, bearers of shields and archers, from all directions till the number of the people became very great.

The Sultan left Furtu on the Sunday. Our Bornu people knew this place by three different names. Some called it Ikli, others called it Galjadu, while others again called it Furtu, the name adopted in this book.

The big drum (Tobol) was beaten, and the force moved to the east on the Sunday morning, and marched on to Alali, where it bivouacked.

MS. Page 14. In the morning the drum sounded. The army got ready, saddled up, and went east with the Sultan to N'gibiwa-Kanjewa, thence to Digala, Burum, Ruru, Kasuda, Gumami, Sulu, Mulighim, Kuru, and the stream called Malahe. From there to Rimbawa and Ma'o—a town well known to all the people of Kanem.

Sultan Hajj Idris was fourteen days marching between Furtu and Maʻo, without halting for two days. He reached Maʻo on a Saturday before midday, and remained there nine days without being attacked by Sultan Abdul Jalil except one day on which detachments of the Bulala and Bornu armies met. This was caused by Abdul Jalil ibn Bi coming in the evening from the town of Yitukurma where the Sultan Abdul Jalil ibn Abdul Jalil had resided. This Abdul Jalil ibn Bi who has been mentioned and his people came to where we were, and slept behind our position. In the morning they went to the west and to the north with the idea of surprising us.

The Wazir Idris ibn Harun had gone out with his force to look for the camel-men in a northerly direction.

When Abdul Jalil ibn Bi and his men saw the dust of the Wazir's force on the plain they fled in fear from them into the bush. The Wazir at first did not see what was afoot.

But when Abdul Jalil ibn Bi had retired to a distance, he found a few men belonging to the Bornu army who had got separated from the Wazir by carelessness or forgetfulness. The Bulala wrought havoc among them, except for those whom God saved by flight.

The son of Kajalma Abdullahi ibn Hawa was killed.

Then a report reached the Wazir Idris ibn Harun that Abdul Jalil ibn Bi was inflicting loss on Bornu people near our camp, and that there was only a dune between him and the scene of the action.

He advanced at once with all speed. Maidalla Muhammad ibn Fatima joined forces with him and came forward and placed himself before his uncle in the advance.

When the Bulala nearest to them saw them, they fled into the bush, putting spurs to their horses and galloping away, for fear Maidalla and his men should come up with them.

Maidalla took up the pursuit in front and the Wazir Idris followed on his nephew's tracks. The three chiefs went on like this till they had covered a considerable distance. Maidalla then stopped the pursuit, as also the Wazir Idris ibn Harun, and they returned to our camp—the Bulala having retired a long way in flight into the bush, since God had afflicted them with great fear. They returned to their Sultan and informed him of what had happened. So we heard.

The Muslims accepted the flight as a favourable augury for a great victory over the Bulala. Their cowardly retreat was a sign from God that He had strengthened us and given us the victory, and made them weak and feeble.

So matters went on between them and us till God gave us a great victory over them on a Monday, the last day of the month Dthu'l' Kiida, by His strength and munificence, for on God do the Faithful rely, and lean on Him in every contingency.

We will relate the origin of the fight, God (exalted be He) being willing, at the end of this book.

Let us return to the original story concerning **Ma'o** and Yitukurma. Not one of the captains and emirs of the Bulala came out against us after Abdul Jalil ibn Bi came out against the stragglers of our people on one day only, until our Sultan Al Hajj Idris ibn Ali left Ma'o after nine days. The distance between **Ma'o** and Yitukurma is a half day's journey for a strong man.

The Sultan was an accomplished diplomatist and was conversant with correct procedure and methods of negotiation. God most high had endowed him with knowledge. As has been said before in this book:—

"There is no forbidding what God has given,
"Nor can that be given which God has forbidden."

This maxim Idris, with the wise political instinct which, as we have noted, he was endowed, followed in sending an embassy with a note to the Sultan of the Bulala and his captains and his emirs and his chiefs. The ambassador was Fuski ibn Kilili of the tribe of Kayi.

MS. Page 17.

The note ran as follows:—

"If my note reaches you in safety, and you read it at leisure, know that my desire is that you should send to me an upright and sensible man to hear what I have to say about the true reason of our coming here, and return to you."

Such was the tenor of our Sultan's letter to the Bulala.

When it reached them, and they had read the contents in the presence of their people, they became very angry and positively refused to send anyone. They sent a letter written by Hajj ibn Dili, but sent no representative though they had plenty of sensible men to send to us even as we had sent to them.

The contents of their letter were to the effect that they could not understand our action, in that "you have burnt our houses on your way, and done evil in our land. You have done it and that is all."

MS. Page 18.

That is what they said. When we saw their letter we were utterly astonished, and saw that their action was that of men puffed up with pride, and that none would return answer like this save people confident in their power and strength over all. Had matters been as they thought and argued and supposed, we should have remained at home in our country. Alas! Alas! the matter was not as they thought. Sultan Idris left Ma'o on a Monday after being there nine days. When his people mounted and got under way, the dust arose and spread to the four quarters of heaven, so that no one could see the road. A short halt was therefore called for the dust to settle while the men stood still, but at that moment the wind sprang up and cleared away the dust through the beneficence of God towards our Sultan and his army; a blessing which will never cease. Under these conditions the Sultan divided his army into two divisions, one of which was under the leadership of the Wazir Idris ibn Harun and was on the west of the line of advance, and the other under the Sultan's personal command on the east.

Both the divisions advanced to the north of Kanem making for Wasami. All the sick and the baggage followed behind the Sultan.

Thus they marched till they reached the town Wasami about midday. At Wasami water is plentiful. The army halted here and every one built himself a hut. They halted on Monday and Tuesday there.

News then came in that the Bulala and their Sultan had come to Kirsila, and were threatening Wasami, so all our people armed, put on mail, mounted, and moved off to the east of Kirsila where the Bulala army and their Sultan were.

After passing a hill our Sultan and his army halted to await the attack of the Bulala, but they saw nothing; so after the two o'clock and four o'clock prayers had been observed there, they returned to their quarters.

In the evening of that day the Ramadan moon was seen, and that was Wednesday night (Tuesday night) following the last day of the month of Sha'aban. The people spent the night preparing for the Ramadan fast.

In the morning the Sultan commanded the people to move off and to leave none behind. So they moved off and went towards Kirsila to give battle. We marched from early morning till about 9 o'clock, when we saw a body of Bulala drawn up in five parties, each party remaining stationary awaiting our approach.

When we had advanced to about bow shot from them or perhaps rather further, they fled to the east, and putting spurs to their horses, scattered. Our people followed them a long way, and then returned to our Sultan Hajj Idris (may God give him victory). The big drum was then beaten as a sign of victory, as our enemies had fled in fear.

On this day we saw the one and only beautiful egg fall near the head of one of the Bulala, when they turned in flight. Kulaima Muhammad ibn Kina took it. From this every intelligent man knows of their cowardice and fear on that day.

The Sultan returned from pursuing the enemy, and advanced to the south of Kanem arriving at Manmana in the afternoon or evening on a Thursday. The Sultan slept there with his army, and in the morning moved to Tusa. It was a Friday. On this day there was such a violent sand storm, that no one could see in front of him and so we had to feel our way. Thus we reached Tusa about midday. The Sultan halted near a well to water the horses and the people who were thirsty as they had found no water at Manmana where they had slept. Of the people some stayed near the well like the Sultan to get water, while others followed the drum with the intention of camping; but the Sultan ordered the drummers to mount a hill to the west and pile the baggage there. When the press of people round the well became great, the majority followed the drums and deposited the baggage at the camping place, to save it and rest their tired animals. Only a few men remained with the Sultan.

MS. Page 21. Thereupon our enemies the Bulala on the Thursday knowing with certainty that we had been a day and night without water, returned from fleeing and followed us in large numbers, with the intention of attacking us. They came suddenly on the town of Tusa while we were all unheeding from thirst and unaware. When the Bulala saw the two separate parties at Tusa, they fell upon those who were with the Sultan in force, and advanced nearly to our encampment. Those who were there, however, soon heard of the attack, and came out in large numbers towards the Bulala, under Siyakama Saka, Farkama Muhammad ibn Bint Fatima, Asiyama ibn Marghi, and others of the chiefs, emirs, and captains, men at arms, and shield-bearers. Also the people of the north who sided with us came in large numbers under the Wazir and others from north of the camp to attack the enemy, as well as the people from the south whose names we have mentioned above.

MS. Page 22. When the people of Kanem (Bulala) saw our people come out to fight, and how numerous they were on all sides, their hearts turned and they fled incontinently without pause. Our army pursued, killing and wounding, with swords and spears and whips, till they were tired of it. The enemy's cavalry spurred their horses, and left the infantry behind like a worn-out sandal abandoned and thrown away, and there was no means of safety for those on foot save the providence of God, or recovery from a wound after crouching in the darkness.

No one knows how many of the enemy's foot soldiers were killed save God, most High. The only man killed on our side was Arjinoma Ali or Dunama Ali ibn Gabiya (may God have mercy upon him). On the other hand four men were wounded by spear thrusts Yuroma Nasar, Fukabu of Dilikni, Sunuma ibn Dabua, and Shattima ibn Tasala. Fukabu of Dilikni died at Tusa a day later. Yuroma Nasar lived eleven days, and went to Sima, where he died on a Monday (may God have mercy upon him). We think that he did not die of his wound, for he was as a man who dies of some sickness, or who dies suddenly while in apparent health. Sunuma and Shattima ibn Tasala recovered from their wounds by the goodness of God and His help.

MS. Page 23. The Sultan remained at Tusa eight days, and leaving on a Saturday, proceeded to Sima, where the great Sultans of past times lived, till in the time of Sultan Daud ibn Nikale, as has been related above in this book, Sima was cut off. His desire was to reunite Sima to Bornu. May we be benefited by his return there.

When he marched off, the dust rose in all the four quarters of heaven, as we have related it did when he left Maò.

Such was his return, and thus he reached Sima before midday. On arrival there we found the well destroyed by the Bulala so that it would be impossible for our people to get water.

The people were mad with thirst when they found the well destroyed. The Sultan commanded them to dig another well near the destroyed one. So every man started well digging, that many wells might be dug. Verily this treacherous act of the enemy was beyond the pale and availed them nothing. When the people heard the command from above they all obediently set to work digging, as they had done at Tusa and at Gamira previously, when the Sultan Abdul Jalil and his host fled in panic.

Within two days, plenty of excellent water was found for men and animals to drink. This was on Saturday and Sunday.

On Monday morning the Sultan went to visit the tombs of the great Sultans, his ancestors, with his captains, and emirs, and ulema. He and his people read the Kur'aan three times, and prayed to God, and gave alms of minor offerings and many horses and oxen, seeking after God, Exalted and Mighty. The people then went to their quarters.

MS. Page 24.

On that day Yuroma Nasar died (may God have mercy upon him). It was eleven days between the day he received his wound and his death, as we have mentioned.

After the death of Yuroma, the Sultan only remained four days at Sima.

On the Friday morning he gave the order to move and go to the town of Aghafi, where was a stockade of the Bulala. When he moved, the dust rose to the sky. The people were very weary as happens often on the march, as we have said before.

We heard of it from Limam ibn Aiyesha who was near the Sultan on that day, for we actually would have been ignorant of the Sultan's march, had it not been for the dust in the sky like smoke. It was a long way from where we were to the camp of Sultan Abdul Jalil.

O people who have sense, judge, compare, and note—where shall be found the like of our Sultan, whose setting forth from our land is accompanied by great clouds of dust? Hard it is, grievous is his absence! May God bless our Sultan, in his kingdom, his sons and relations, with the fullness of blessing, which shall never end till the day of judgment, by the grace of our Lord Muhammad.

When we reached the road to Aghafi, the Sultan put all the feeble on to the animals with the coats of mail and arms as a precaution, so that he would be free from anxiety. He marched on till he arrived at the stockade in the afternoon, and camped to the south of the stockade with the whole of his great army.

MS. Page 25.

While our Sultan was in Aghafi the Sultan Abdul Jalil came that night (Friday night) and camped near our Sultan with evil design, in case the water there had not been plentiful and sufficient.

On the Saturday morning the Sultan called all his captains, and emirs and chiefs and all who were fit and strong, so that the whole army might go out against the Bulala. Every soldier hastened to obey his command. Then the Sultan Abdul Jalil made a movement with his army, the Bulala, and went towards Shami. Jalil's army, to bring about an engagement.

The Sultan Hajj Idris ibn Ali (may God ennoble him in both worlds) had already advanced to the high ground which was extensive. In this commanding and conspicuous position he could watch the enemy, and find an opportunity to attack them.

MS. Page 26. When the Bulala saw the Amir ul Muminin and Sultan of the Muslims, King Hajj Idris clearly visible like the sun at noon, they became cowards utterly, and were afraid for their lives. They broke in flight and put spurs to their horses. The pursuit continued far; some were slain, others captured. The Wazir only returned from the pursuit at evening.

The Wazir Idris ibn Harun found among the captives two noble youths of the Bulala royal house of Sultan Kadai and of Sultan Abdul Jalil. He brought them to our Sultan in a state of great fear thinking they would be executed. When a ransom was settled, the Sultan released them owing to his tender heart and pity for all men, and forgiving nature. Otherwise he would not have released these two. He then followed up the tracks of the enemy himself with the cavalry but without the heavily armed troops. The pursuit continued to the end of the day.

Then certain scouts of Sultan Abdul Jalil saw the army of our Sultan Hajj Idris ibn Ali, and ran towards the place where their Sultan was to inform him of the rapid approach of our Sultan. Our men pursued them but did not catch them till night intervened.

When the scouts reached their Sultan Abdul Jalil in the town of Sandu, and gave the news that we had come, the Bulala set spurs to their horses and fled, though they had previously made all preparations to pass the night there. From all that we gathered from those who saw the place where they had encamped, they must have fled in a panic, as they left behind an ox they had slaughtered for meat. They fled a long way.

MS. Page 27. Our Sultan Hajj Idris ibn Ali came to the spot in the evening, and stayed the night there. In the morning all the horses were watered in the open country, and the pursuit of Abdul Jalil was resumed, and continued till evening. We saw indications that the Bulala had prayed in the early morning in a place we came to, and after that we gave up hope of catching them. This was in front of their town of Ikima on the Shami side of Ikima. We followed on to Ikima in the evening about sunset and camped for the night to the south of Ikima towards the western side of it. In the morning we arose with our Sultan, and went in search of the place where we had left our sick people and baggage at Aghafi. We reached it at midday, and there were mutual congratulations between our Sultan and those whom he had left there. He himself slept at Ikima, and released all those whom Sultan Abdul Jalil had bound. The prisoners thus set at liberty were delighted.

Let us now return to the story of Aghafi. When the Sultan Hajj Idris reached the stockade of Aghafi after his expedition, he remained there and celebrated the 'Id As-Saghir' there, and at the end of Ramadan when the moon of Shawwal was seen, the great drum was beaten and all other ceremonies observed throughout the night, as was the custom in Bornu, till day-break. When the sun shone the drum was beaten. The people watched the sun rise, and the 'Id' was celebrated. What joy could be greater than this, or what Sultan greater than our Sultan; to have the drum beaten in Kanem at the stockade of Aghafi, even as it is beaten in our land of Bornu in the ancient manner which is so well known.

After the 'Id' the Sultan set off again to seek Sultan Abdul Jalil in the evening. He pushed on till night fall. A halt was made for the evening prayer, and then the men mounted and marched throughout the night without sleep, only halting an hour for the night prayer and to feed the horses.

They arrived at Fifisi, a well known town. The men who first arrived at Fifisi in the early morning were Koyam, and they found Abdul Jalil and his army watering their horses. They at once turned off in the direction of the bush which lies towards Shami from Fifisi. All galloped back, and told Sultan Hajj Idris.

When Sultan Abdul Jalil and his army saw the Koyam approaching the town of Fifisi they too had fled. Our Sultan then wheeled in the direction they had taken, and left Fifisi, ordering the Wazir Idris ibn Harun to make a reconnaissance. The Wazir set out in front with all speed; the Sultan pressed on behind him, and both did their utmost to come up with the Bulala. They continued the chase till a little past midday when the horses gave out through lack of water and owing to the pace. The horses of the Bulala on the other hand did not need water, since they had watered them at Fifisi in the night, as we have related above. But our horses had had no water, since the evening before at Aghafi, till nearly midday on Monday. This was the reason we did not come up with the Bulala. Also, as a second reason, flight to save one's life is more rapid than the chase of those who follow a fleeing enemy.

For these two reasons they were able to get well away. The Sultan Hajj Idris then halted with his troops, for it was evident that, if the pursuit continued, our horses would suffer badly, which would not conduce to safety.

The Sultan then returned with his whole army to the town of Fifisi, and did not return to his camp till midday. As for the army which scattered on the plain, they took much booty on that day, camels, oxen, and a good deal of other property. They were however unable to quench their thirst till evening.

The Sultan moved to a place to the south on the outskirts of the town and camped for the night.

In the morning the force moved back to the stockade of Aghafi, where we had a permanent camp.

We reached Aghafi on the third day about eight o'clock in the morning. Our Sultan received news that Sultan Abdul Jalil and his army had gone towards Shami from Aghafi and had halted in the town of Gasiku, where his mother Bi, the daughter of Gurgur lived, till the day of her death. When this news was noised abroad, our Sultan left the stockade of Aghafi at the hour of the evening prayer, and marched with his army to N'jimi (Sima) where he arrived early in the night. The men got what sleep they could. The Sultan then arose and set off again before day-break. The army marched past Malima and halted at a place near Gasiku, called 'Midday Halt', for the night.

Though Sultan Abdul Jalil came to Gasiku he did not stay there long, but departed in haste into the bush with all the corn he could find.

MS. Page 30. Sultan Hajj Idris only heard of this after leaving Sima and before arriving at 'Midday Halt'. Had we heard this before, we should have gone straight on to Gasiku. As it was we camped near there for the day and the following night.

In the morning we entered Gasiku before midday and remained there for two or three days. We found in the vicinity such booty and useful things as God provided for us, but we could not come up with the Sultan Abdul Jalil, for the Bulala went far from their homes into the bush to save themselves, and stayed in a thirsty place.

Hence we returned to our permanent camp.

When we were ready to return, we left Gasiku after sunrise, and marched to Malima, where we halted during the heat. After the two o'clock prayer, we moved rapidly on to Sima, which was reached in the evening. After passing the night there, we reached the stockade of Aghafi and stayed there until we found the people we had left there to collect information, well and enriched with booty. The Sultan thenceforward rested in the stockade of Aghafi and made no attempt to follow Sultan Abdul Jalil.

Captains and emirs and chiefs among the Bulala however came over to our Sultan and also the Arab tribes and the people of Fitri and other people.

MS. Page 31. All who came were handed over as guests to the learned Sultan Muhammad ibn Abdul Lahi to be sworn on the "Kura'an" to be of good behaviour, except such as wished to follow our Sultan back to Bornu to settle.

The number of Muhammad ibn Abdul Lahi's followers thus became very numerous, and were assigned duties, after renouncing their allegiance to Sultan Abdul Jalil. They remained with their Sultan Muhammad in the stockade of Aghafi, whereas our Sultan Hajj Idris remained outside.

We thus remained with Sultan Muhammad ibn Abdul Lahi for some time, until 'alfa' grass was not obtainable for the camels and horses, except at a distance.

When Sultan Hajj Idris sought to depart, Sultan Muhammad rose and preceded him on a Thursday to the south to Gamtilo. On the Friday Sultan Hajj Idris also came to Gamtilo, which is the town where the learned and God-fearing Sultan Biri ibn Dunama died. Our Sultan with his chiefs and learned men read the Kur'aan there to gain merit with God. The Sultan then returned to his camp before the time of the two o'clock prayer.

On the Saturday morning the big drum was beaten and the Sultan moved south to Balagi. But the Imam Al Kabir Ahmad ibn Sofia, the writer of this book, went off before the Sultan left, to the west of the stockade of Aghafi accompanied by the Imam al Saghir Muhammad ibn Ayesha and their people wishing to make a pilgrimage to the Musjid (mosque) of Armi. They reached the mosque and looked at it, and meditated on it knowing it to be indeed the mosque of Armi, and so gave praise to God. They passed on to Balagi, and only arrived there after two o'clock when the Sultan had pitched camp.

O Muslims, consider the journey of these two Imams in a wide circle and their return to their Sultan who, by his might, had terrified the land of Kanem and put it in subjection.

On this day came news to Balagi that the learned Sultan Muhammad ibn Abdul Lahi had seized his paternal uncle Biri ibn Sikama and his brothers and cut off their hands.

In the morning our Sultan went towards the river in the south, and camped at Fisla. He remained there a few days. While he was there, there came in to him foreign tribes of Arabs, and Kuka, and people of Fitri, just as they did at Aghafi.

When they had all saluted him, the Sultan went west with all among the tribe of Buluwa who wished to go to Bornu and others who desired to emigrate.

Thus they marched until they reached the town of Diawa and stayed there a short time for the people to rest and allay their thirst and hunger. When the Amir-ul-Muminin had relieved their distress, he moved to N'gala, and on to Auno for the night.

Thence he marched to Dilwa, and then to N'gala, where he camped, and to Madagam. At this latter town Sultan Muhammad ibn Abdul Lahi and his forces met our Sultan Hajj Idris ibn Ali (may God ennoble his face).

All the chiefs of both Sultans, who were present themselves, held a long meeting. So long did they sit into the night, that the people thought they had gone to sleep over their lengthy discussions. Then the Bornu people and the Bulala separated, and went back to sleep at their respective camps.

Towards morning there came a report that the Sultan Abdul Jalil ibn Abdul Jalil was threatening the town of Yitukurma, and wished to attack Sultan Muhammad ibn Abdul Lahi. In consequence of this our Sultan Hajj Idris turned to the east, and encamped close to the town of N'gala with the intention of attacking Sultan Abdul Jalil. But though he remained there till morning nothing more was heard of Sultan Abdul Jalil's movements.

The Sultan turned west once more and camped near Madagam and continued travelling towards Bornu till he came to Sulu and Kagusti and Siki Dananma.

**MS.
Page 34.**

He then delimited the boundary between Bornu and Kanem. The big drum was beaten on this spot, and the boundary made so clear that there could be no dispute.

From thence our Sultan passed to the land of the Sugurti, and the towns of Bulugi, Guguti and Bari; which latter place is famous as the place where people going from Bornu to Kanem assemble, and where they separate and go their several ways on the journey to Bornu.

No sooner had the Sultan reached Bari than reliable information came in that Sultan Abdul Jalil had moved to attack Sultan Muhammad ibn Abdul Lahi; that the two forces had actually engaged in fierce battle near the town of Yitukurma; and that Sultan Muhammad ibn Abdul Lahi was in full flight towards Bornu, after both sides had suffered heavy losses. We heard that one Ali, called Fado, was killed in this fight. He was the rival of Sultan Muhammad ibn Abdul Lahi, and had married Bi, the daughter of Yarima.

To return to the main story. The Emir of the Faithful heard the news of the fight between the two Sultans and that the Sultan Muhammad had retired in the Bornu direction to the town Bari, and in a speech to hearten, encourage, and fire his people and army had declared that they intended to go back to Kanem and would return to Kanem if God willed.

**MS.
Page 35.**

Our people were of two minds. Some were all for escorting and supporting Al Hajj Idris, while others were for returning to their homes for lack of provisions. Subsequently all the chiefs, emirs and captains agreed to return to Kanem.

EXPEDITION II.

When the season of the rains had passed by, and all preparations had been completed, our Sultan set out for Kanem again. He set out at the beginning of the cold season and advanced with his army to the stockade of Gatiga where reinforcements arrived. He continued his march thence to Guguti, Bulugi, Kitati, Kagusti, Ririkmi, and finally to Garni Kiala.

He then selected his best men and horses and made a forced marched by night to Yisambu to try and catch Kaloma Dunama and his brother Abdul Jalil ibn Bi. Then he journeyed in the belly of the night towards Yisambu, leaving the baggage and sick behind.

On his reaching Yisambu after sunrise, Kaloma and his brother fled precipitately, so that he failed to find them, though he took some spoil.

The Sultan returned and camped at the town of Wasami with his army for the night.

**MS.
Page 36.**

At dawn he put a chief named Yuroma Yagha in charge of the sick who had been left behind with the baggage, while he with all the horsemen who were efficient, marched out and halted at Malima towards midday and watered the horses. From Malima he turned east, and reached Sima in the evening. After a short halt in the night, the Sultan and his men marched on to the stockade of Aghafi, but when they arrived there towards dawn, they found nothing.

They followed the tracks of the fugitive army to the east and did not rest nor halt. They came up with the escort provided for the harîm of Sultan Abdul Jalil, and captured them together with Gumsu and Bi and all the other women whom God did not save.

Our Sultan then returned to Aghafi and then to N'jimi, where he remained. He sent a messenger to Yuroma Yagha, whom he had left behind as Khalifa over the sick and the baggage. The day the Sultan left Wasami for Sima, the Sultan's Khalifa, the Chief Yuroma whom we have mentioned, stayed the night at Wasami, and on the Monday went to the district of Shami.

He camped at the village of Diru with his force to await authentic news of the Sultan.

It was not long however before a messenger from the Sultan arrived at Diru with the good news that our Sultan had indeed captured Sultan Jalil's harîm. After the messenger had delivered this news, he added that the Sultan wished the Yuroma's force to meet him at N'jimi.

The Khalifa left with his people to go to N'jimi. They stopped at Madima and slept there. In the morning of Friday reached Sima at about eight o'clock. The two contingents met and saluted one another rejoicing in the reunion.

The Sultan remained at Sima during Friday and Saturday, and on Sunday set off on an expedition leaving four big chiefs in charge of the camp, Kaigama Bukr, Chiroma Biri, son of the Sultan, Dalatu N'gizimma, and Hiruma Yagha, and their following with them. He also left with them the shield-bearers, gun-men and bow-men, who could not go with him for lack of transport to carry their food. They were a very great number.

Then the Amir ul Muminin Hajj Idris ibn Ali (may God ennoble his face and grant him might; and bless him to the end of time) set forth on Sunday to the east towards the land of Kawal, which we reached about eight o'clock on Monday morning. We found nothing there, and spent the heat of the day and the night there.

At a little before or after midnight the Sultan mounted with his horsemen and went in a southerly direction at first but when the sun rose and he had observed the morning prayer he moved eastwards and then towards Shami.

At about eight o'clock he celebrated the Id Al-Saghir. When on this Tuesday we had celebrated the Id Al-Saghir, the Sultan and his men mounted their horses and made an attack on our enemies among the Tubu. Many of them were killed, and many camels, sheep, oxen and slaves were captured.

The Sultan then returned to Kawal with all speed, and men and animals had their fill of water.

The Sultan mounted the hill to the west of Kawal and there was gathered before him the whole army and all their captives and spoils.

They spent the night there. On Wednesday morning the Sultan went west to Sima, where he had left his troops. He marched all that day except for halts for prayer, till towards evening, the army came to the town of Saghi about sunset, where the watering of the thirsty horses went on till night.

The Sultan slept in this town with all his force.

On Thursday morning the Sultan and his chiefs, and emirs, mounted after the early prayer, before sunrise, and went on their way to Sima without halt or pause. They passed Ikima and Gurfala, and were close to Sima, when a report spread that Sultan Abdul Jalil and his people, had moved on to Sima to attack the people we had left there with the four Khalifas whom we have mentioned above.

This report was not confirmed, but we approached Sima with caution. When we were very near, some of our people saw the tracks of Bulala camels, and thus it became evident that the report was true.

MS. Page 39. The Sultan sent out three leaders of whom one was the chief of the shield-bearers by name Yisimi, another the Imam Al-Saghir, Muhammad ibn Aiyesha, and the third Hano, chief of the gun-men. Two of them, the Imam and the chief of the shield-bearers reached our people in Sima.

When Hano saw the dust which was caused by the fugitive Bulala, he returned in haste to the Sultan, who, on hearing his news, said "Do not go into Sima, but hasten to the north of Sima, for, perchance you will find traces of the Bulala there."

When Hano heard the Sultan's words, he spurred his horse and went off with his contingent to the north. The Imam al Kabir Ahmad ibn Sofia, the author of this book, with his friend Mu'alim Hajji, chief of the town of Faya, galloped after the Sultan as he turned his horse towards the enemy. Among the retreating Bulala, of those who were on foot or mounted on camels, many were killed. Only those mounted on horses escaped.

Let us return to the story of Sultan Abdul Jalil and his army.

MS. Page 40. When Abdul Jalil who was on the road to Bagarmi heard for certain that Sultan Hajj Idris had arrived in Kanem and had captured his people and even his wife Gumsu on the march, and afterwards gone to N'jimi and further east to attack the Tubu, leaving his sick at N'jimi, he made up his mind to go to N'jimi with his army. In conceiving this plan he was guided by the advice of his chiefs and emirs. They quickly moved up and reached N'jimi on the Wednesday night. We heard from one of them that on this night not one of them lit a fire in the camp. On

Thursday morning they moved round on to the road to the east, the route by which the Sultan had gone to attack the Tubu. This they did, so that the Bornu people should not think that they were Bulala.

And when our Bornu people at Sima did become aware of their presence, they did think that it was the Sultan Al Hajj Idris coming. Many of the shield-bearers of the people of Guguti, of the tribe of Tumagira, went out to meet their Sultan first, before the other people, in order that their prestige in his eyes might be enhanced.

But when they drew close to the Bulala about the distance of a horse's charge, they saw from their array that matters were not as they thought.

Of the four captains who had been left at Sima as Khalifas, only one went out, to wit Dalatu N'gizimma, who followed the shield-bearers with his men outside the camp.

Then, so we have heard, sighting these few horsemen and shield-bearers, the Bulala paused, in fear and trembling, for they thought that this must be part of a large force about to come out and attack them. But when they looked behind the people who had come out, they saw no one. Then they became rabid to surround the men who were coming out; and kill them. When the shield-bearers saw a charge imminent, they fled and sought the inside of the camp. The Bulala spurred after them close on their heels, and the only shield-bearers who survived the charge were those whom God preserved and whose end God postponed.

MS. Page 41.

As for Dalatu N'gizimma, he took up a position outside the camp, and on recognising the Bulala, stood firm and faced them, till a contingent of Bulala came up with him. When he made up his mind to fight, he knew that the Bulala horsemen were many. He could not stand his ground however, and he and his force were obliged to retire.

The Bulala followed them as they had followed the shield-bearers. Then one of the Bulala horsemen, so people say, caught hold of the coat of mail of Dalatu who was making for the camp, with the idea of pulling him back over the quarters of his horse; but Dalatu perceived his intention, and bent down on the saddle and spurred his horse, till he felt the strength of his own horse and the weakness of the horse of Bulala. Hence he was able to effect his escape, and the man who was holding his coat of mail let go in haste. Dalatu then distanced them, and with his people gained the inside of the camp.

Some of the Bulala got into the camp in their pursuit of Dalatu, but most of them stopped and did not enter, paying due regard to their personal safety.

Two parties of our enemies however did come in; of these some were killed together in one place, while others made their escape in safety.

The three Khalifas whom the Sultan had left, behaved well as I shall describe, from what I heard from the people in the camp.

MS. Page 42.

The leader, Kaigama Bukr ibn Abdul Lahi, stood to arms alone on the edge of the camp after his people had all dispersed. Chiroma Biri ibn Sultan Idris remained in the midst of the camp with all his people and faced the Bulala with the resolute determination of holding out, till they retired in flight.

Yuroma also remained in the camp with his company like Chiroma.

We have already described in detail the behaviour of Dalatu.

Let us return to the story of our Sultan Hajj Idris. After driving off the Bulala, our Sultan returned to Sima, and entered the camp in the late afternoon. All were delighted to see the Sultan so soon, and their fears were at an end.

On that day there died the Bulalai Yuroma ibn Ahmad though their drum was beaten the whole night to conceal the fact.

On our side we lost three men Mitrama Liyatu, Malagalma Abdul Lahi ibn Abdul Lahi, and Junoma Muhammad Al-Saghir ibn Junoma. They died of their wounds. May God have mercy upon them. We buried Mitrama Liyatu and Junoma Muhammad Al-Saghir at Sima, and Malagalma Abdul Lahi at the town of Satum.

The Sultan then left Sima and moved to Gimara, thence on a Monday he moved in the direction of Yaman and camped at Satum near the town of Yitukurma. Malagalma Abdul 'Lahi died there of his wound, may God have mercy upon him.

MS. Page 43.

At this place it was reported that Sultan Abdul Jalil was at Dagalu and the report proved correct.

The Sultan therefore ordered his Wazir Idris ibn Harun to act as his Khalifa in charge of the baggage and sick, while he himself with the sound horses and camels went to Dagalu to seek out Sultan Abdul Jalil.

On his approach to Dagalu, Sultan Abdul Jalil fled into the thirsty bush with his force. Though the Sultan followed he could not catch him, and so returned with the considerable amount of booty he had captured. He and the Wazir met in the region called Karga Simsim.

The Wazir Idris had, after the Sultan departed to Dagalu, moved on the Monday towards Simsim, and reached it on the Tuesday, after camping one night at the town of Bâri where he found a number of strangers of the " Ahel Armi " with the chief " Ga'uma." Some captures were made and goods taken.

To return to the Sultan. After returning from his expedition and meeting the Wazir at Simsim, he found there an Arab tribe, and also Tubus, and much discussion ensued.

The Tubus wanted to go to Bornu, and actually did so, but the Arabs remained in Kanem after formal promises and undertakings had been made between them and the Sultan.

MS. Page 44.

But our Sultan did not stay in this place long. He went with his army back in the direction of Shami and camped at Bâri, thence on a Monday, to Mandu, from which point he turned north to follow up Sultan Abdul Jalil.

He caught sight of him and his army west, and followed them till he reached Kitaki.

When Abdul Jalil heard that Sultan Hajj Idris and his army were on his tracks, and were not likely to give up the chase, he turned about and fled into the desert, the thirsty desert, as he usually did.

The Sultan therefore halted at Kitaki to wait for the part of the army which was with Maidalla ibn Fatima. Maidalla ibn Fatima slept at the town of Mandu, after the Sultan had left it. It was here that Dalatu Turga died, may God have mercy upon him.

In the morning Maidalla ibn Fatima our Sultan's Khalifa left Mandu after burying Dalatu. He then advanced towards Ma'o, sending forward the shield-bearers and mailed horsemen slowly in front to see that all was well, until he had passed Ma'o and had halted in some other place near by.

[O Muslims, know ye not that every one acted according to his judgment and good sense, great and small, rich and poor; thus also we see the good judgment of Maidalla on this day, in sending on ahead the shield-bearers and following with the horsemen slowly himself till he reached the town of Ma'o.]

At Ma'o a messenger came to us from the Sultan saying that the whole force was to be sent to him at the town of Yira, but that Maidalla's march and dispositions had been excellent, he being an astute tactitian and bold to seize an opportunity.

MS. Page 45.

In the morning therefore by the power of God most high, the Khalifa ibn Fatima arose, and gave the shield-bearers the order to mount. Thus he marched in the same order as before. The force slept at Yikima before reaching Yira after enduring severe thirst till about midday. After a good night the three chiefs assembled at the lodging of the Imam Al Kabir Ahmad ibn Sofia, to take counsel, to wit Kaigama ibn Abd ul Lahi, Yarima Ali ibn Ghuwa, and Kalifa Maidalla Muhammad ibn Fatima.

They consulted about what was to be done in the absence of news of the Sultan and the Bulala, and as a result they resolved to stay where they were, and make a big zariba round the camp. They therefore built a fence of thorns of sufficient height and width.

The people had not been arguing about the wisdom of this counsel long, before a definite message came from the Sultan to say that he was established in the town of Shitati, that the Sultan Abdul Jalil had fled very far away, and that he wished our force to join him. Thus we heard from the messenger.

The Khalifa Maidalla ibn Fatima then ordered the force to make ready. They arose, and mounted, leading the baggage animals.

MS. Page 46.

The shield-bearers went in front of the cavalry as usual, and they marched in force to Shitati.

Here we saw Al Hajj ibn Musa on the road, coming to meet us sent by the Sultan to show us a good road.

When we met him, our people were filled with exceeding joy.

We reached the Sultan and his army before midday, and the men went off to see their friends with the good news.

At this meeting the people found two causes for rejoicing; the first that all had rejoined the Sultan in safety, and the other in that there was no lack of food; for we found that the people with the Sultan had the plenty of autumn and there was nothing lacking.

All the people went off to ask for food, millet and the like, and the Sultan stayed there two full days.

Then the Sultan left the town of Shitati, after the big drum had been beaten as the signal for the march. He went west to Bornu with all his people, the shield-bearers, the archers, and emirs and captains complete, leaving none behind.

He halted at Shitati, and there the Arabs who were with the Sultan turned back, after being granted permission to do so.

The Sultan continued his march west slowly, till he came to Bari.

MS. Page 47. Here the Sultan commanded the public crier to proclaim to all who had made captives, that they should bring them to the Sultan's "Fâsher", and that any Muslim who concealed anything was guilty of rebellion against God and His Prophet. Straightway every one brought all his captures, free or slave, without concealing a single one, to the house of the Sultan as was ordered.

The Sultan first gave orders that the free should be separated from the slaves. He made this division irrespective of sex. Afterwards he assembled all the free and sent them to their relatives, friends, or tribes. He set apart the slaves to be divided.

This act of our Sultan Hajj Idris was in accord with the fairness, greatness, and excellence with which God (exalted be He) endowed him, and in accord with his high principles, able judgment, goodness and unselfishness. Albeit he remembered the doings of the Sultans of the Bulala in olden times. When they invaded the land of Bornu, they never released the free men whom they captured, and a female, free or slave, was alike to them, as was a male slave and a free man. Such was their conduct in past days.

Our Sultan followed the path of truth, and in matters of conduct his character made him choose the best, as we have mentioned at the beginning of this book. The attributes of excellence are many, nor can a doubter be excellent. May God (exalted be He) place us and all Muslims among the number of those who excel, those who are remarkable in their striving for the Faith and for the Victory of Virtue with its seal of prosperity and fortune and beneficence. He is the Hearer of prayers and the Accomplisher of hopes.

[Our Sultan's character may be likened to that in the Shar'ia in the Hadith of Maath ibn Jabal (may the blessing of God rest on them and on all the prophets, the best of Thy creation for man), or again we may compare with it the saying of Abu Muhammad Abdul Lahi ibn Abi Zeid in the Risalah:—

> "He who is truly noble, will pardon him who has done him wrong; will give to him who holds off from him, and approach him who shuns him."

Such was the character of our Sultan in very truth: otherwise he would never have acted as he did towards the people of Kanem at Bari and other towns, knowing full well and clearly all that the Bulala had done aforetime. Such forgiveness is indeed hard for mortals, unless God create in them the power so to act.

Know ye not what the Mighty saith in His Great Book, where He praises His prophet:—

"Verily they are exalted by their greatness of conduct."

We have also seen in the book called Bahr Al Hasîs concerning prayer:—

"Allahhuma, as Thou has fashioned me nobly make me to be of noble conduct."

Again in the Hadith of the author of the Shar'ia (may the blessing of God rest on him and on all the prophets), we find "the first thing that will be put into the scale is nobility of conduct." For what is more important than this, my brother Muslims!]

Let us now return to our story. After Sultan Hajj Idris had of his generosity released all the people of Kanem who were of free status at the town of Bari without ransom, he ordered his army to disperse and go to their homes, after he had given them advice about the journey, and good counsel about transport, arms, and stores necessary for warlike expeditions in the future. The Sultan omitted nothing in his speech to the troops.

The Mighty in His Great Book said "take all precautions" and following this saying the Sultan gave all his people the best advice.

Thus all the chiefs, and emirs and captains separated to their several homes and abodes.

EXPEDITION III.

They had been but a short time in their homes, before news came that Sultan Abdul Jalil was close to the town of Buluji, with his army, and was beating the big drum as he went, as might have been expected of him.

When Sultan Hajj Idris heard of it, he tried to get to them but they veered off to the north and went to Kara and Jitku, where they stayed sometime. At the moment the Wazir Idris ibn Harun was at the town of Butti near to Kara and Jitku. The Bulala dare not attack the Wazir Idris ibn Harun, though he was near them, because they knew his reputation for valour and wariness and experience in war. Thus they remained for some days.

Now when our Sultan Hajj Idris (may God bless his sons and posterity throughout the ages) heard of this, he could not rest tranquil at Gambaru, but felt he must go to the Wazir.

He therefore set out on a Wednesday evening, and marched to Milu and next morning to Lada where he arrived about eight o'clock.

He went on from there to Bari and Gayawa. He and his Wazir Idris met at Gayawa. Afterwards the Sultan and his army marched to Sugurti in the evening. On this day the people were very weary, and news came that Sultan Abdul Jalil had returned from Jitku to the east, and had encamped at Ikrima.

The Sultan therefore advanced to Alma Al-Ahmar. He did not follow the straight road by Sulu, but turned off with his army to the north making for the town mentioned above, Ikrima. He marched fast, and about noon reached a well where there was plenty of water to water his horses.

After the two o'clock and five o'clock prayers, the Sultan moved off. On that day there were two wing commanders to the army, Kaigama and Yarima, so we have heard from the chief emirs.

The Sultan moved forward rapidly till evening. Then after the evening prayer, the army mounted and pushed forward till they reached the well with the big mouth and plenty of water, from which the corn in the farms is watered. The name of the well is Rubku.

MS. Page 50. The Sultan and his people stayed there and watered their horses easily and rapidly; then all went round about and collected grain which they put on their horses. They remained till about a third or half the night had passed. Some of them collected fodder for their horses.

The Sultan then mounted and his people with him and marched till sunrise found them still marching. The Sultan dismounted for the morning prayer, as did the rest, and they continued on their way to Ikrima. Eight o'clock passed, and it got near midday. The dust from our army rose sunwards and grew and covered the earth, till Sultan Abdul Jalil's people who had gone out foraging saw it, and galloped back in haste to inform him.

Then indeed the big drum was beaten with short rapid beats to summon in haste the men who had scattered in the bush that morning. The drummers went on beating with frantic rapidity and without pause.

We heard that the drum is beaten by the Bulala in two ways.

If they hear bad or terrible news, the drum is beaten with short rapid beats without pause. On the other hand if the news is good the drum is beaten slowly and deliberately without hurry or quickening. Thus the people of Kanem informed us.

To return to the original story of the Bulala.

MS. Page 51. When the Bulala saw the dust of our host mounting up to the sky, they were utterly terrified. They went out of their senses with panic. Their army trembled and was paralysed. Some ran away on their feet, others on horses or camels. They fled like donkeys attacked by a lion, or sheep and goats which rush away blindly in flight. Such was their plight.

The Sultan's army spurred forward and followed them till midday. We could not catch their horsemen, but we caught a number of camels, and all the captured cattle which were in their hands. We also found all their possessions thrown about in confusion on the ground. Of their fine cloths and adornments and other effects, there was nothing we did not capture, and not a single one of their women got away.

When the sun grew hot, our Sultan returned to the well which was on the edge of their camp, and watered the horses and camels.

Most of the chiefs and emirs on seeing that the Sultan had returned from pursuit, returned also to the well, but the distinguished chief Idris ibn Harun did not return from the pursuit till about two o'clock and only then returned because his horses failed through thirst. Had it not been for that, he would have followed them further.

MS. Page 52.

When the well became insufficient for the press of people, our Sultan ordered his army to dig many wells in order to have the benefit of sweet water. They did so and drank their fill, and then watered the camels and horses.

The Sultan then went to the Bulala camp, and alighted at the lodging of Abdul Jalil. So also the emirs went to the houses of the Bulala emirs, till nothing was left.

When all traces of the camp had been obliterated, the people all went into the bush to sleep. The Imam Al Kabir Ahmad ibn Sofia, the writer of this book, entered on that day the dwelling of the Wazir Bikoru.

The people and Sultan stayed in this place two full days to rest in their great delight and joy.

At about two o'clock on the Tuesday the Sultan ordered his people to prepare to march, the drum was beaten, and they marched off to Rubku. They were two days on the road. On the third day they reached Rubku about 8 a.m. before midday, thence we went to Bari.

MS. Page 53.

Then the Sultan commanded the people that were with him, to make haste and not delay, because of the approach of the rains when the dates were ripening.

Hajj Idris left Bari after two o'clock evening prayer, and went to the south; he marched very rapidly and reached Kabuwa at eight in the evening; he went on to Kikari the following midday. Thence he and his army marched on to Dabubu which they reached in the evening about eight o'clock. On that day heavy rain fell. This was the first rain that fell before the end of the hot season.

When the day dawned upon us, Sultan Al Hajj left Dabubu and halted at the town of Ruwaya and passed the day there. The people were at rest in spirit for they were close to the town of Gambaru.

Then the Emir of the Faithful, Sultan Hajj Idris ibn Ali (may God strengthen him and give him victory and aid him) left the town of Ruwaya after the midday and evening prayers had been said, and went with his army towards Gambaru and halted there the next evening.

MS.
Page 54.

The people of the great city Birni left with the Fuguma Ali ibn Garu and his people and others also of the reds and blacks, rejoiced at the arrival of our Sultan who had accomplished their hopes and desires and had put Sultan Abdul Jalil and his people to flight from the town of Ikrima. He brought with him as booty their baggage and property as well as their provisions. The people welcomed the army and shook hands and embraced them because of the return of the Sultan with his troops in safety after a mighty victory.

Then the Sultan ordered his people to make haste and prepare for another expedition, and to return to Kanem at an early date lest the time of the dates should pass before they arrived there. Our Sultan (may God bless him and his sons and his descendants until the day of judgment) gave them this excellent counsel and good advice because he knew that the dates are a very profitable business for the people of the land of Kanem, and the purpose of his proposed further expedition at the time mentioned, was to do them as much damage as possible. In addition the people and their beasts would live in great comfort there on account of the great quantity of grass and water and green fodder. This was the best time of the year there. The captains, and the emirs, and the chiefs prepared to go to Kanem at once.

EXPEDITION IV.

MS.
Page 55.

The people assembled together from the east, and from the west, from the north and from the south, at the appointed time, in the town of Gatiga except those who dwelt to the east, like the people of Guguti and others also in the east who remained in their towns waiting for our coming.

When the people had collected before him in the town of Gatiga, Idris arose from there after the beating of the big drum and went towards Kanem, marching along the waters of Chad. He did not cease travelling till he came to Guguti, then Buluji, then Sugurti, and close to Ruru. In this place the Sultan counselled his people to send in advance a strong party of horsemen to Kanem, and for that purpose he commanded them to obtain provisions for the journey.

He then appointed Hiruma Yagha to be Chief of the people whom he left behind with the goods and baggage, and the shield-bearers who lacked strength.

He gave orders to march to the town of Garni Kiyala which is the famous town where a battle was fought between Sultan Idris ibn Ali ibn Ahmad, and Sultan Dunama ibn Salma until God (exalted be He) gave victory to Sultan Idris (Katagarmabe) over his enemies.

Then the greatest of our Sultans, Sultan Hajj Idris rose up in the morning at the rising of the sun and went on with the chiefs of the people whose fighting power and whose strength he knew, who cared for no one, and feared not criticism nor blame and would not exceed instructions.

So he arrived at the town of Kamisino in the early morning and halted, passing midday there. After the two o'clock and four o'clock prayers had been observed he made a rapid march with his army and halted at the town of Laba in the evening a little before sunset. This is a famous town for, as we have heard, the people in it farm their farms even when there is no rain.

When we had spent the night there and the stragglers had come up safely in the morning, Idris arose and led the army eastwards travelling to reach the town of Garni Kiyala in two or three days. Here he halted when the sun had sometime risen. The people rested there a little and gave water to their animals.

When the two o'clock and four o'clock prayers had been observed, the men mounted their horses, climbed the steep hill close to the well, and travelled eastwards seeking the town of Yisambu and so on until the setting of the sun.

We halted in the desert to feed the people and nosebags were tied on to the horses. But eating in this place was only possible with great difficulty, for cooking was always done by the women and girls slaves and could not be well done by men and men slaves. On this journey not one girl could come with us. For this reason cooked food was very difficult to obtain and very expensive.

We stayed a little. Then the Sultan and his people mounted and travelled all night. When dawn broke and the morning prayer had been observed they mounted, and riding quickly, passed by the town of Wasami which is near Yisambu. We had only gone past the town a short distance when we saw the enemy's standard raised in the open.

Thereupon our people wished to make a rush, but Sultan Hajj Idris prevented them from doing so, until we were close to them. The Sultan ordered the Wazir Idris ibn Harun and Farkoma Muhammad ibn Bint Fatima to spy out the lodgings of Abdul Jalil ibn Bi and the rest of the army to spy out Kulluma Dunama ibn Bi. So the horsemen turned at once towards the lodgings I have mentioned.

Every soldier arrived at his appointed place, but Kulluma Dunama ibn Bi had gone from the town far away with all his people, so our men came upon his house empty and found nothing in the town at all except what was in outlying hamlets.

Abdul Jalil ibn Bi fled and escaped, fearing our armies. He had left his wife, the daughter of Yarima, in his house, turning from her when he saw the dust of our armies rising to the skies. For he was certain that the safety of a man himself is better for him than the safety of his wife. So he fled, deserting his wife, since personal necessity is more compelling than the lack of a wife, as the author of the book Ifrikiya has said.

Our people were scattered to the north and south looking for prisoners. They gained great booty. On this day was taken the daughter of Chiroma Abdul Jalil, son of the Sultan, the wife of

Abdul Jalil ibn Bi. The people ceased not to go through the midst of the land of Kanem taking prisoners, until the sun was near its setting.

The Sultan returned to the west in search of water. All the army went with him after they had tired themselves out with running, and had exhausted themselves and their horses.

They arrived at the town of Dalli where is much fruit and great plenty. The Sultan watered his horses as did also the people theirs.

Then the Sultan mounted the hill which is to the west of the town of Dalli and came down from it into the midst of the hijlij trees. The people divided themselves in search of shade in which to rest from the heat of the sun. Our men mightily ill-treated the men of this town and cut the fruit in flower half-formed and nearly ripe. As for the young dates they were busy cutting them down for they were of great use to eat.

The people stayed in this place two days. When the rearguard came up in the morning, the Sultan mounted, and all mounted with him and went to the west, looking for the place where the soldiers were whom he had left with Yuroma Yaga, looking to find him where He who is exalted should please to bring about their meeting.

MS. Page 59. Then fresh news came to us that the Tubu had assembled on the road between us and our people. They were nomads from the bush. The news was true and the Sultan believed it. When he was certain of its truth, he ordered the chiefs, and emirs, and captains of the Wazir Idris ibn Harun, and of Arjinoma Abdu Lahi ibn Said, and of the other chief leaders to advance and advance towards these Tubu.

Thereupon they went quickly to catch the brigands. The Sultan followed in their tracks slowly without galloping that he might know of a certainty what befell.

Before he came up with them a man returned and brought him news that the chiefs whom he had sent on ahead towards the Tubu had got into touch with them. All the people of the Tubu had ranged themselves in battle array with their shields and spears waiting for the fight with the chiefs. This was true and no falsehood. Sultan Hajj Idris ibn Ali (may God grant him might and victory) galloped forward on his horse, and, with the emirs and chiefs who were with him, went boldly on till they reached the Tubu drawn up in battle formation.

Each of the emirs began to kill the enemy in front of their Sultan without ceasing. The battle waxed too mighty for the Tubu and they were driven away in flight. All our horsemen followed after them, killing the men and making the women captives. Not one of them escaped except him whom God (exalted be He) granted escape in His ordained providence.

The Sultan continued following them as far as the distant desert. Every one who came near, was speared and laid rolling about in his blood. The Sultan ordered them to be finished off and killed. Not one that we saw with our eyes escaped.

Death that day smote them like a plague and that day became fatal to them like the day of destruction of the people of 'Ād in the wind of sickness as our Lord has told us in His Book which explains all.

After the annihilation of the enemy whom we were following, our Sultan returned in search of a deep well in which was much water so that he could water his horses and his troops. The men found the well for which they were hoping and watered their animals there without stint. They scattered into the shadows and rested a little. Some drank a draught of water once and twice. Others of them were able to do so once only. Then Sultan Hajj Idris (may God strengthen him and give him victory), in his unerring judgment gave marvellous counsel and wonderful advice.

He rose up from this place and went towards Garni Kiyala to meet his people whom he had left with his Khalifa and lieutenant Hiruma. Then there stood up before him and his army the guide who had shown the people the path to Garni. He was a warrior among the defeated Tubu whom our army had left alive. His life they had spared when they killed his fellow tribes-men so that they might take him as guide for the road on our return. The life of this man was spared by the foresight of our excellent Sultan. Had it not been for this guide, our people would have lost the traces of the road to Garni. This Tubu went before the army until he brought them to the town without once losing their way or getting off the road.

We watered the horses and camels to the last one. Then we climbed up to the east of the well of Garni and halted on a hill. Every horseman dismounted from his horse and every man made his camel kneel with the intention of stopping there and resting, until the sick who were with Chiroma Biri, the son of the Sultan, and Hiruma Yagha came up. We were waiting for the dawn, when true news came to us that the troops who were with the Khalifa were very near Garni. All the people who were with the Sultan and those with the Khalifa, rejoiced at their meeting and assembling together in one camping place.

Sultan Hajj Idris ibn Ali (may God who is exalted ennoble him) sent at once messengers to the Khalifa and those who were with him, ordering them to halt on the hill west of the town of Garni and giving them permission to stay there or come up to him. They therefore halted. Between us and them was the fortified town of Garni only. When our Sultan, the Emir of the Faithful Hajj Idris left the Khalifa and the sick on the day he set out for Yisambu, he had said as an order to all the people who were going with him, "Take provision for eight days." He then went with them in the direction of Yisambu.

He returned to Garni. Between the arrival of the Sultan on his return and the arrival of the Khalifa there passed only seven days neither more nor less. It was for this reason that the Sultan had ordered the Khalifa and his men to halt, since he had enjoined on his own following the time limit of the eight days mentioned in the orders. This estimate was shown to be an accurate forecast by the way in which matters befell. A thing like this is very rare.

When we were halted at Garni in the state I have mentioned, and the allotted eight days were completed, the Sultan, the Emir of the Faithful Hajj Idris ibn Ali (may God who is exalted ennoble him and bless his children and posterity for ever and ever from age to age, for God who is exalted hears prayers and brings to pass hopes) left the town of Garni we have mentioned and ordered the Khalifas also to move.

The Sultan went on with his army in advance of the Khalifa and the Khalifa went on with his army in the tracks of the Sultan. Thus they travelled eastward seeking places with fruit in them. Idris found a place in which to rest from the midday heat and then halted in one of the neighbouring towns.

Then the Khalifa came forward with his men and every man found quarters among his own people. Then were completed the eight days of which he had told them. They passed the night in this town. When day dawned, the Sultan travelled on with all his army not leaving one man behind. They all kept together until they halted at the well known town of Yedi. Yedi is a town in which there is much fruit, and the fruit was hanging down on the stalk. The people scattered. Every man was busy cutting dates for his use; great and small scattered to cut dates down for the horses and camels and donkeys and oxen.

Of the people some pounded the dates until they became like a paste; others ate them as they were; others scattered them on purpose on the sand when they had eaten their fill; others threw them under the palms; others would only cut the fresh dates, before they were ripe and before they had coloured, and throw them on the sand. Thus with effort and toil they destroyed the fruit on every side until nothing was left at Yedi, and Dabaku, and other towns besides these two which had fruit in them.

They stayed here only for a few days until there was no fruit left in all the country. It was as if a mighty storm of wind had come from the heavens.

Affairs being as above, our Sultan arose with his people and went to the south of the land of Kanem and camped in a town where was much fruit, called Foga. There they destroyed all the fruit as they had done in Yedi and Dabaku and other towns.

Very heavy rain fell in this town after the Sultan had halted in it. He rose up from thence with his army and went on and halted near the town of Dalli after he had passed by it.

The army did not cease from marching to the south of Kanem, day after day, until they arrived at Auno or near it where they spent two or three days.

They left Auno and pushed on towards Dagalu, a town which is famous among the people of Kanem. At this time it was inhabited by people who had great wealth.

When we had passed by Dalmi, our people saw some spies of the people of Dagalu and wished to catch them, but they fled back. Our people followed after them with all speed, but could not catch them because of the quantity of water in the marshes which were full at that time. For this reason our people abstained from searching for them. Also the heat of this day was overpowering.

The Sultan and his army halted in this place with the intention of passing the night. When the dead of the night had passed and dawn was near, Sultan Hajj Idris and his men mounted and continued their march towards Dagalu. The prayer of dawn was observed on the road. They rode on, pressing forward through much water until about eight o'clock. They found the town empty; the people having fled by night when the spies had given them information that we were seeking them.

Thereupon our people were of different opinions; some of them went to the south and some to the east. Our camel drivers who were of the Koyam tribe and some others, came upon the tracks of the fugitives before they arrived at Dagalu and saw them plainly running away to the north. They caught up the fugitives and seized great booty from them.

As for the people who had gone in other directions they obtained little except what God had decreed for them.

The Sultan passed the night there. God (exalted be He) being with us, we arose safely in the morning.

The Sultan gave his orders to the people by the beating of the drum and turned west towards Bornu. The Sultan thus went a very long way from Sultan Abdul Jalil.

When Sultan Idris the Emir of the Faithful came to the land of Kanem in the rainy season, Sultan Abdul Jalil fled into the uttermost parts of the desert.

We have heard that when our Sultan arrived at Yisambu on his journey, Sultan Abdul Jalil fled from Ago. The people who were with him scattered. As for Abdul Jalil ibn Bi, he fled to the remotest part of the desert of Itnawa and elsewhere, and did not come near to the land of Kanem until our Sultan Hajj Idris had gone away from Dagalu into Bornu. Thus also did all the chiefs of Sultan Abdul Jalil; like him they fled a long way from the land of Kanem.

When Sultan Al Hajj came to Yedi at the time when the people were busy with their dates, Abdul Jalil also came stealthily close to Yedi and stole a few camels. By night he fled into the desert. Neither Abdul Jalil nor any of his people appeared after that until the Emir of the Faithful Haj Idris ibn Ali (may God ennoble him in both worlds) had returned to Bornu.

To return to our subject; when our Sultan had reached Dagalu the chiefs spread out into the outlying parts of the town in search of captives. He only passed one night there marching on from Dagalu in the early hours of the day. Thus he came to N'gala and the district of N'gala and the vicinity of Tatanu.

Near Tatanu he found our people with plentiful supplies of food. Their hunger was appeased and they had plenty of millet and milk and condiments. Fresh green food was available when needed. The result was that the condition of our people changed from being mutinous to contentment.

The Sultan continued marching towards our country of Bornu very slowly, making halts during the day and at night until he arrived at Ruru with the army. The morale of the army gave no cause for anxiety, nor had they aught of which to complain save the weariness of marching, which was, indeed, a kind of torment.

The day dawned upon us in Ruru; the army wishful to go to Bornu. The Sultan appeared before his people and enjoined on them to prepare provisions for three days. They heard what he said, obtained what would suffice them for three days, and returned quickly to him.

He then arose and went with them to the north towards the town of Siru travelling night and day. Then the second day dawned. When our people had gone forward a short distance they saw a great quantity of cattle and sheep which they took as booty. They found sufficiency of everything except camels of which they found very few. They passed that day full of great joy for what God (who is exalted) had sent to them. Then the third day came. This was the end of the allotted time of which the Sultan Hajj Idris (may his Lord ennoble him) had spoken.

He returned to the Khalifa's camp. We went with him and arrived there at sunset. The two armies, that which had done the fighting and that which was left behind, rejoiced and welcomed and greeted each other with shaking of hands and embracing. After that the order was given to move forward at the beating of the drum. The Sultan and people mounted and marched on day after day till they halted at Limara and spent two or three days there.

Our Emir Hajj Idris on his return march did not incline towards Gatiga or Bari, but when he reached Gayawa turned on to the road which led us to Dilara and left the path which goes to these two towns.

When he left Dilara, the people divided, some going to camps far from the Sultan and some to camps near him, until they halted with him at Gambaru on the bank of the river.

From there the chiefs and the captains and the emirs separated to their various dwellings. The Sultan Hajj Idris had made them an eloquent speech and enjoined that provision, when required for another journey to Kanem, should be neither too great nor too small. They listened to his words with obedience and consent and returned to their villages, nor were they negligent or idle, but exerted themselves industriously in finding animals for the journey as well as spears, shields, horses and provisions for general use.

Thus the people stayed in Bornu until the rainy season was past and the cold season had set in.

EXPEDITION V.

When the height of the cold season had passed and the people had observed the 'Id Al-Saghir, the Sultan set forth on the journey he had spoken about, the journey to Kanem. He set forth on the first day of the month 'Shawwal' from the town of Gambaru and halted at Zantam.

The people heard of his setting forth and came out from their dwelling places and went to him, some meeting him in Zantam, and others in more distant places; but the Imam Al-Kabir Ahmad ibn Sofia, the author of this book, joined the Sultan at Dabubu, having himself no animals for the journey. The Sultan continued marching with his army until he halted in Itnawa; thence to Gatiga where the army increased and became much larger.

From Itnawa, the Sultan arose and travelled eastwards towards Kanem, near the time of the entering in of the hot season, with his captains and emirs until they reached Guguti, then Sugurti, then Ruru, then Kasuda. From there he took the road to Siki and left the Gumani road. From Siki he marched to Ririkmi, then to Wagam, and continued travelling till the army reached Wasami, then Ma'o, then Gamira, then the great town known as N'jimi.

When Sultan Hajj Idris ibn Ali (may God ennoble him in both worlds) halted in Gamira he sent Farkuma ibn Bint Fatima to the town of Balagi as his emissary to spy out the state of the country and to find with certainty what people were in it and to bring to him news that was of a certainty true.

After the Sultan had left the town of Gamira and arrived at the great city Sima and passed a day there, the above mentioned captain Farkuma Muhammad came in from his journey, after his investigation and examination of the land, and gave the Emir true information concerning the news of the town Balagi.

The Sultan only remained in Sima two or three days before moving on. He had issued instructions to the army to equip themselves with water according to their usual custom when they heard the order to do so given. Accordingly when the order was given to fill all the water pots, both great and small, they hastened to comply. When the preparations were complete, and all the people had taken what sufficed them, the Sultan moved off with his people after the two o'clock and four o'clock prayers. They travelled at a great rate till they halted at the town of Aghafi a little before sunset on the second day.

They spent the night there. When the third day dawned, the Sultan arose intending to go to Garku. Half way there, we heard shouts from the east and when we asked what it was, were told that it was the spies of Sultan Abdul Jalil who had ridden over to see our ranks and our condition. When they had gained the information they sought they turned back quickly on their swift horses. At any rate that was our people's opinion about them.

Having halted at Sima on the journey which we are now writing about, we had found little water in the wells because of their age, so that the army had been divided into two parts; one of which stayed by the wells to dig and to water their animals slowly with the very little water they found there, while the other scattered in search of water.

It was reported that when the people of the great chief known as Jerma ibn Ammat Allah went to the bush in search of water and food, the spies of Sultan Abdul Jalil came upon them in the desert and took from them horses and camels, the numbers of which we do not know for certain.

MS. Page 72.

Our Sultan decided to leave Sima on Monday, and ordered the Wazir Idris ibn Harun to take his army in the direction of our enemy. The Wazir set off in the morning of that day. The Sultan the Emir of the Faithful Hajj Idris ibn Ali (may God grant him victory) set out in the evening of that day in a southerly direction and halted at the town of Aghafi.

The Wazir Idris, as above mentioned, went towards the enemy and came in site of them on the Monday whilst the Sultan was in Aghafi. The Sultan set out on the Tuesday and halted with his army in Ganjaya about midday. The Wazir did not come to the Sultan. We observed the two o'clock prayer and at about four o'clock the head of our column was amazed at the dust rising up from the direction of the enemy. The people who were in the neighbourhood of our camp cried out when they saw it for the people who were with the Sultan thought that the dust was the dust of the Bulala.

When the dust became great, the people who were close to the Sultan in the middle of the camp saw to it that the due preparations for fighting were made. They rose up, put on their armour, girded on their swords, and mounted their picked horses clad in their coats of mail in the twinkling of an eye. They moved forward quickly in the direction of the dust. But when they came

MS. Page 73.

out from within the 'zariba' of the camp, they saw that the dust was the dust of the Wazir Idris ibn Harun returning to us. So the army returned to the camp and the Wazir came and halted in his usual camp.

The Sultan passed the night there. When the rear-guard came up (by God's favour and help) in safety, the Sultan Hajj Idris gave orders to all his people about the journey so that they hastened to bring in their animals and to put on them their saddles.

Then spies appeared from the direction of Sultan Abdul Jalil to spy upon us. They returned with news of us to him, even as the Wazir had gone to spy on them in the first place. Thus each side was trying to spy on the other and the parties often missed the right place. In the end the Sultan the Emir of the Faithful Hajj Idris ibn Ali (may God who is exalted ennoble him) moved off from Ganjaya on Tuesday with his army to Garku where there occurred the fight with the enemy in the night. The Sultan ordered our horsemen to march cautiously and very slowly. In like manner he ordered the shield-bearers to exercise discretion and circumspection, qualities with which God in the fullness of his foreknowledge, had endowed Idris. The wise man is he who forestalls events before they happen.

MS. Page 74.

So we arrived at Garku by slow stages. When we reached it and halted there, every man with great caution as had been ordered, the people began to cut down the thorn trees to protect the Sultan's camp, every man according to his share, according to the custom of our people which was initiated by our Sultan Hajj Idris (may God ennoble him in the time of his power).

When he halted with his army at any camp whatsoever, he used to order the people to divide up their camping place into sections so that every chief and captain should have his share of it, and should live in it, and make a fence for its enclosure. Thus the circumference of the 'zariba' was finished with great speed and rapidity. It comprised a large area, so great that everyone could find his share of dwelling space.

It was in this very town of Garku that fighting broke out at night between us and between our enemies. They rushed upon us unexpectedly though its perimeter was fortified in the same way as other places.

In the building of these stockades, which the experienced thought and sound prudence of our Sultan had established, there was great advantage and usefulness. Firstly in that it obviated the need of tying up animals, so that they could be allowed to roam about in the midst of the camp. The horses and other animals also were unable to stray away. Then again it prevented thieves from entering for infamous and evil purposes, for they were frustrated and turned back. Again it prevented any one from leaving the camp on errands of immorality, debauch or other foolishness. Again when the enemy wished to force an entrance upon us either by treachery or open fighting he was obliged to stand up and occupy himself with the defences before he reached us. If we had taken many captives and much booty and put them inside, we could sleep restfully and the night hours were safe: also if the male or female slaves wished to run away from the camp, they were afraid to go out. The advantages of a stockade cannot be numbered.

There was no early warning that the Bulala would make a surprise attack on the Sultan's camp. Their onset only became known after the evening prayer. Some did not know until the night, and some did not even know until the enemy had entered the camp or had come close to it. Had there been a stockade there would not have been fighting and slaughter on this occasion between the Bulala and our Sultan Hajj Idris ibn Ali (may God enoble him and bless him in his children and descendants for ever and ever by the grace of the Lord of creation, our master Muhammad the chosen, and his house, upon whom be blessing—Amen).

The Sultan went to Kanem four times before this journey in which there was fighting between us and them openly night and day. In this fighting he ravaged the three great and famous valleys until they were like vast empty plains: one of them the great town Ikima, the second the stockade of Aghafi, and the third the town of Ago.

When the Sultan laid waste these three valleys, there resulted to the inhabitants great misfortune, in that he laid waste the whole country. Then too the people who lived in Kanem were removed to the land of Bornu, including the people who lived at Kulu to the south and were riverain peoples. There did not remain in Kanem any branches of the tribes which went to Bornu. They did not however move to Bornu of their own will or desire, but impressed by the news of the conqueror, and the fear he inspired.

Had it not been for the Tubu, who wished to support Sultan Abdul Jalil and be his subjects, we had only gone to Kanem once.

God knows best the truth about character, and how He richly endowed Sultan Idris, by His grace, and abundant beneficence, and strengthened him, so as to be a terror to his many enemies, and, what time he gained the mastery over the Bulala Sultan, who relied on the Tubu, to go out to battle against them all.

Is it not stated in the account we have heard from our Sheikhs and elders who have gone before us that the Tubu attacked Sultan Dunama ibn Dabale, the son of Sultan Salma, son of Bikuru openly so that a state of war ensued, and lasted between the Tubu and Sultan Dunama for seven years seven months and seven days, raising fires of hate which lasted for all that time?

Thus we have heard from trustworthy sources; but there was no tribe of Bulala in those days.

MS. Page 78. We heard too from Wunoma Muhammad Al-Saghir ibn Tuguma in his life time, when he was telling us about the early Sultans (he was learned in ancient history) that the number of the horsemen of Sultan Dunama ibn Dabale was 30,000. Thus we heard from him, nor are we ignorant of, nor have we forgotten what he told us, since the day he told us.

But the war of Sultan Dunama ibn Dabale was with the tribe of the Tubu.

Whereas our Sultan fought the Bulala and Tubu and other people of different tribes, whose origin is unknown, and fought them all patiently, relying on God, and going forward trusting Him, till he vanquished them, and put them to flight.

We shall talk of this plainly in what follows, if God wills.

The Bulala, after our Sultan had destroyed all their towns in the land of Kanem, even the town of Ikima and the stockade of Aghafi, wished to build up the old town of Ago and to return to it. They dwelt in it still, as we have heard. Whilst they were sojourning with the intention of settling there, they heard the news of our Sultan Hajj Idris, what time he came to Yisambu in the rainy season on a military expedition and halted in Dalli.

MS. Page 79. When they heard of his coming, they were afraid with a very great fear, and left the town of Ago; leaving it altogether and not returning to it. The people were amazed and stupified throughout the villages and towns of Kanem, for they were certain that Sultan Hajj Idris ibn Ali would not cease from coming to Kanem so long as Sultan Abdul Jalil was there as ruler.

They therefore abandoned this town of Ago, and left it empty as the desert so that the troops of our Sultan should not surprise them there. Their women, however, daughters of the royal house, sent to Sultan Abdul Jalil and his army whom they knew were utterly cowed, to say that they did not love them and were bewildered. So the Bulala became even more terrified, and planned to build a stockade at Kiyayaka. In fact they built huts and sheds and found all that they needed as supports for these buildings.

We heard from trustworthy persons who had entered the country of Sultan Abdul Jalil that the towns of Yaki and Makaran and Kurkuriwa were inhabited. We were told that the Bulala said they would never move from this region.

As the Poet says:—
"My master wept when he saw the road behind him, and felt that we should never find Kaisira. I said to him weep not, we will change the seat of power or we will die, and seek help from God."

Thus they built on the borders of this region which was contiguous to the river near the town of Kulu. They built at the town which had the largest perimeter, stockades on all sides but one, *i.e.* the south. When they had finished building they set about moving the people so that the town should be filled.

Every one they saw in Kanem was sent to their new fortress, except the people of Tatalu, and Afaki near by, or those whose villages were afar off and difficult of access. As for the Tubu they removed them to the town of Kiyayaka mentioned above, as for instance the tribe of Kasharda. There were no Tubu tribes in the remotest parts of the land of Kanem which did not come in *en masse* without leaving anyone behind. All who came willingly or unwillingly built grass huts in which they dwelt with their families, until there was gathered together in the above-mentioned place a great number of people. God (who is exalted) alone knows the number of them. They took their stores and grain supply as food. Between them and the people of the south there was made a pact of friendship and alliance and concord. Traders in foodstuffs were constant in coming and going between this region and the south to buy and sell. They sold food in exchange for cattle and clothes and other articles.

Trading did not cease between the Bulala and the owners of foodstuffs until the Emir of the Faithful camped at Garku, the Emir Hajj Idris ibn Ali (may God who is exalted ennoble him and bless him in his children and posterity until the end of the ages).

Now let us return to the story of the Bulala. They came towards our army by night, reaching them on Wednesday the fifth day of the sacred eleventh month of God (be He exalted) according to that which we found true without any mistake.

They took the road which was between us and them, which is the one leading from Kiyayaka to Garku. After they had observed the two o'clock and four o'clock prayers they advanced towards us. Their chiefs and nobles pushed on the common people, and inspired them with the hope of booty and much wealth that their bodies might be made strong for the fight and their courage raised by the desire for wealth. This speech excited them and made them move on till they came near our camp.

News of this reached our Sultan and then the scouts came in and told him. But in the event the enemy came in a very different way from that which the news-teller had said.

What the scouts said was that the Bulala army was coming towards us from the town of Kiyayaka and that it was divided into four divisions intended to enter our camp from the four gates separately. So our people were informed.

When the Sultan heard this news, he took counsel with his people after he had collected them together. They came to the decision that every chief and captain should stand to in the place in which he was, everyone of them to guard his side of the encircling defences near his camping place.

They had only a little while to wait before the enemy came rushing in extended order upon the camp like a swarm of locusts. The Sultan rode forth and met them with a small body of men from the forces in the camp, attacking them heavily and killing the drummer at the outset. This strong counter attack repulsed them and the Sultan drove them out of the camp.

Then they began to deny that they were of the tribe of the Bulala. Thus when our Sultan Hajj Idris charged down upon one of them and said to his people after he had smitten down his enemy: "This man is a Bulala". The man denied his origin vigorously and said "I am not a Bulala" Then he leant back over the hinder part of his saddle and fled towards his town galloping on without ever once looking back.

When the Sultan returned from outside the camp to the interior of it, others of the enemy entered with the big drum from the other gate, beating the drum and frightening the weaklings among our people.

MS. Page 83. They burnt the tents and grass so that the people left the camp. And they ham-strung the beasts, both horses, camels and bulls and committed the evil deeds and atrocities ordained by God in His Book.

Now our enemies were divided into three groups; the first, those who snatched up by way of plunder whatever they could lay hands upon, living or dead, animals or stores, where and whenever they could lay hands on them and then returned to the place from which they had set out; the second, those who went into battle, following the only drum which was left to them; the third, who wandered at random in the camp until death overtook them, wandering aimlessly without the slightest idea in which direction to go. Now our people, the people of Bornu, were similarly divided into three sections; the first group warriors and fighters like our Sultan and these at that time were few; the second, those who remained behind the palisades and did not venture into battle but remained hidden from view as if cloaked in the veil of God: among these were the Koyam; the third group were the type of people who wander about the inside and outside of a camp and are unskilled in the arts of war.

Our Sultan Al Hajj Idris ibn Ali (to whom may God give a mighty victory) after returning from without the camp to the interior and after having driven the enemy back towards their own country, came upon the drummers in charge of the enemy's sole surviving drum in the middle of his camp. His horse was at the last gasp, weak from fatigue and in a lather of perspiration from the heavy day's work. He was quite nonplussed as to how to deal with this situation, yet with his innate sense he asked what would be the best course to adopt to drive out the enemy from the camp, without allowing them to take away the loot they had acquired. He enquired whether there was anyone of sufficient courage to deprive them of their booty: but was met with a blank response. But for the exhaustion of his horse, he would have made no appeal: he himself would have ventured forth on the errand. Had only his chiefs and governors and body-guard commanders shown the same energy and resource on that night the enemy would have given no further trouble.

This was the upshot of the fighting during day-light on Monday, but the pen had written what was to be. When dawn was about to break the enemy with their plunder made their way out of the camp and set off at full speed towards their home, taking with them the horses, camels, and stores of clothing and other articles which they had looted. The looters and main body of the enemy decimated as they had been by us, made for Kiyayaka; if they rejoiced, the rejoicing can surely have only been on account of the property they had gained, for the casualties we had suffered were not a half, nay, even a third of what had befallen them by way of slaughter; our loss was loss of property alone.

When God in His grace caused the next day to dawn, some of our people wished to follow up their tracks without delay, while others held their peace, the Sultan being ignorant of what was their real state of mind.

God had endowed our Sultan with keen intelligence and great perspicacity, and he felt convinced that pursuit would be an unwise course; only God can say what was transpiring in his mind: outwardly however he remained calm and collected; he gave orders to the governors and leaders to collect a large quantity of grass and place it to the east of our camp in front of the road which is between Garkuwa and the town of Kiyayaka. His directions were that every man independently should gather grass until there was a large pile. After they had completed the noon and afternoon prayers he sent a herald with the following proclamation to the people:—

"Hear the proclamation of the Sultan: let every fit man whether mounted or pedestrian go forth from the camp, girding his mind with resolution and cautiousness, and let him assemble where the grass is collected together."

When they heard the proclamation they hastened to the appointed place outside the camp, not excepting the great Imam, the author of this book, with his intimate friend Hajj Umar, chief of the town of Faya; there was not a fit man who failed to respond, except those who were cowardly and weak. After this he led us forth on Thursday evening, and we celebrated the sunset and evening prayers in that place and also the morning prayer in the presence of the Sultan. We continued to leave the camp every evening and return every morning for three consecutive days, in fact, up till the Sunday. Now Sunday was two days before the end of the month Dthu al Ki'da, and at dawn the Sultan ordered the whole force to parade; he mounted and they did the same after which he drew them up in tactical formation turning his course southwards to the region of Kulu and proceeding slowly and with the utmost care and caution until they crossed the river which lies between the land of Kulu and Kanem,

MS. Page 86. We travelled on without cessation until we arrived at the city of Listiri which, we heard, was a town founded by the Kileti (Koyam). At early noon we encamped there and our Sultan ordered the whole of his people to hew down thorn trees and completely to surround the camp with them. They did this in their usual way. It was at this place that the head shield-bearer passed away, Muhammad ibn Barsala. Chiroma Abdullahi ibn Shattima also died on the same day; (may God be merciful to them both). Our noble Sultan with his usual good sense ordered his commanders and governors to set up our quarters around the zariba on the outer rim in a place similar to where the grass had been piled in the case of the town of Garku. The object underlying this order was to avoid the houses crowded together in the town of Listiri. After they had completed the building of the stockade and the setting up of quarters outside it, the Sultan left the camp on Monday evening about the time of evening prayer accompanied by the army according to their usual custom.

At Garku the Imam al Kabir Ahmad ibn Sofia also went out with his friend Hajj 'Umar, the chief of Faya. They spent the night near the Sultan and celebrated the evening prayer in his company and also the night and morning prayers; the chieftains spent the night in the same place outside the zariba, following their previous custom. When day dawned, the Sultan gave the order for departure; they saddled their horses and mounted, travelling northwards in the direction of Kiyayaka. The Sultan had previously arranged their dispositions with prudence and caution and exhorted them to endurance and steadfastness.

MS. Page 87. According to reports, when the Bulala heard of the Sultan's expedition in their direction accompanied by his army, and that they were being attacked from the south, they became bewildered and perplexed and were deprived of the power of thought and reflection on account of the peculiarity of the attack materialising from that direction. What they had reckoned upon was that an eventual attack on our part would come from the west, but the Sultan's strategy entirely checkmated theirs, for on the above assumption they had built a chain of forts between the towns of Garku and Kiyayaka, but between Listiri and Kiyayaka had not constructed a single wooden fort like those between Garku and Kiyayaka. The Sultan continued to advance at the head of his forces towards Kiyayaka until we arrived at a lofty eminence. There the Sultan halted for a short time to enable the army to close up; when he looked round, he saw masses of the enemy to north and south; to the south was visible an expanse of water in a depression in the earth resembling a broad pond; in front of them they saw large forces in the direction of Kiyayaka. These were the forces of Abdul Jalil without doubt; but when our army saw this water, every body wished to drink it. Our Sultan asked his Wazir Idris ibn Harun to advise him regarding the drinking of this water. The Wazir replied " Lord of the Faithful how is it possible to reach the water while the enemy are standing looking on?" he advised him to send forward all the shield-bearers to the water in order to refresh themselves, since their thirst was extreme, owing to the fact that from the time that they had set out from Listiri until they reached Kiyayaka, no water had come their way, right up to the time when we took up our position on the hill. Hence the dire thirst of the men whose shoulders were weighed down with shields. The Sultan ordered his Wazir to lead them forward to the water we have spoken of above. After the Wazir and the shield-bearers had set out towards the water and while the main body were halted on the lofty hill, gazing towards the countless hordes advancing from Kiyayaka and wondering about them, they suddenly caught sight of a tremor passing through the ranks of the enemy, this enemy who were like a swarm of locusts and crawling ants, carrying off the sweeping of winnowed grain from the threshing floors to their dwellings. This tremor was in reality a west to eastward movement. When the enemy arrived in face of our troops, they wheeled southwards seeking a vantage ground for battle and advancing towards us with all celerity.

MS. Page 88.

So much for them: as regards ourselves, our Sultan Idris ibn Ali (whom God ennoble in this world and the next, and whose sons and grandsons be blest until the day of the blowing of the great trumpet) although he perceived the rapid advance of the enemy, neither delayed nor awaited the return of the shield-bearing party of the Wazir who would have brought his army up to the proper complement.

MS. Page 89.

God had suffused his heart with patience and reliance, trust and steadfastness, gratitude and piety, faith and obedience to the noble book and the traditions of His exalted prophet and the writings of the learned doctors and the pure and dutiful leaders; even to epitomize his qualities would take too long and to burden the reader with their perusal would be unfair. Hence our theme is restricted and we have limited ourselves to a description of the main facts; but, had we wished to describe his raids year after year we should have added to the length of this book with all seen and learnt and heard on our passage across the shifting sands of the desert. It is not merely out of pride in our beloved leaders and companions that I say this.

When the Sultan reached the hill called Milmila, the enemy surged forward towards it and the two armies met; our camel corps consisting of Barbars and Koyam did not dismount in spite of the enemy's furious onset in their direction. As for the shield-bearers who had gone to the water with the Wazir, they did

MS. Page 90. not rejoin the main body at this time. Consequently when the attack matured, there was a gap in the ranks and the army was not drawn up in its usual formation. The only cavalry and riflemen and shield-bearers in front of the Sultan were a very small party. At the moment the enemy attacked us fiercely and sent a shock through our entire army, piercing our ranks as if they had been sparks of flame or a swarm of locusts, armed with their cutting weapons and shields, fully accoutred and driven on from behind by their cavalry, spreading death with whatever weapons were in their hands, killing without moderation or cessation.

At that moment the small body who were in front of the Sultan retreated, and swept by him rejoicing to be clear of the battle but our people were involved in a heavy engagement. Our Sultan, Al Hajj Idris ibn Ali Emir Al Muminin (the leader of the Muslims the visitor to the two holy precincts, the descendant of those of noble blood on whom be the honour of God in both worlds and His blessing upon His offspring until all eternity by the grace of our Lord and master Muhammad the Elect and his decendants upon whom be the mercy of God) did not budge from the place where he had stood from the first, but remained immovable like a deep seated mountain, patient and resolute, trusting in God and leaning upon Him, invoking Him and turning humbly towards Him. He remained firm on his grey charger grasping with his blessed hand his drawn sword, naked and sharp. When his horse made a movement to regain his place on account of the retreat of all the people on both sides, he reined him back and made him face the enemy.

MS. Page 91. There he stood unshakable until the Lord his God gave him the spacious delight of complete victory according to what He had written on His Tablets. One of the most wonderful things brought about by Almighty God was His lavishing help and assistance upon the Sultan on this battle field by His grace and generosity and loving kindness. Truly He distinguishes him whom He will with what He will and in His hand is ease and pain. I heard and saw— not I alone, but also my learned friend the master of jurisprudence Hajj Umar, chief of Faya—as the proof of victory and a sign of truth, two mighty winds blowing from the west towards the east so that when they reached the interspace between our Sultan and the enemy, the latter turned and fled as one man in headlong retreat. Then our Sultan and his commanders and governors and bodyguard and chiefs followed as far as prudence dictated, hewing down the enemy with swords and spears, killing them and transfixing them until the sun sank down in the sky. The number of slain is unknown except to God Almighty and even had those of the mightiest intellect among mortal man put forth every endeavour to compute the number, it would have been entirely beyond their power. They could not have correctly estimated the numbers of the slain. When the day became hot the Sultan desisted from the pursuit and went towards their town Kiyayaka and lodged there for the first time at noon. Among our people who **MS. Page 92.** came from Bornu, those who were slain were slain, and those who were wounded wounded, and those who escaped escaped, but as regards the people of Kanem of the Tubu stock and others, we have already related their experiences. God Almighty is the Judge between the people in all their differences and there is no cause for surprise at any of His acts, whether it be the matter of a mote in earth or sky, or whether it be anything greater or less than a mote. But of the famous captains of Bornu, none were slain but two: Mai Duguma Abdullahi and Fukulima Othman ibn Daud. The former was speared on Wednesday during the night engagement and died at Kiyayaka, while the latter was stricken down in the pitched battle, and after being carried to Kiyayaka passed away there (may God have mercy on them and the other slain of our people who died on this and other of the Sultan's expeditions, and may He give them perfect forgiveness by the grace of our Lord Muhammad, the seal of the prophets, and imam of the pure, and by the grace of his pious line, on whom be all praise, for God is a Hearer of prayer). When our Sultan alighted at the abode of Abdul Jalil, he assembled the court poets and others of his people and asked them what was to be done. They replied " We order you to stay at this house." So he took up his abode in Abdul Jalil's courtyard staying there two nights, and drums great and small were beaten in that place for two full days. At this place appeared to them the new moon of the holy month Dthu al Hijja, and on the third day, having set the houses on fire not leaving even one standing, our Sultan Al Hajj Idris gave the order for the drum to be sounded. Setting out at head of his army, he marched east of Kiyayaka till he reached Mih, while his captain the Wazir Idris ibn Harun spent no time there but hastened on in quest of Sultan Abdul Jalil, who, upon being routed at Milmila, had fled towards Kawal or Kawaka or Itnawa. The Wazir pursued him till when he was on the point of overtaking him. The Sultan fled from Itnawa into the deserts, dismayed by the news that the Wazir was tracking him down.

When the Sultan Abdul Jalil had made good his escape and was far away, the Wazir fell on a Tubu settlement there, and making a rich haul of women, children and property. returned with his large store of booty to Al Hajj Idris at Mih remaining there with him until the conclusion of the 'Id Al Azha. After this, the Sultan set out and proceeded without loss of time to the environs of Kiyayaka, encamping to the south. It was here that Tuwama ibn Gafkaru, known as Kori Dunama died.

The Sultan sent Farkama Muhammad ibn Fatima from here to Kalu to remove the inhabitants of that place and settle them in Bornu. At daybreak, the Sultan and his army set out and pitched camp at Garku where a tribe of Bedu sought audience of him and protracted discussions took place. His next move was to issue orders to his three captains, his son Chiroma Biri, Kachella Ali, and Yuroma Yadagha, to remain behind with the main body, while he himself set out on a raid against the Tubu.

They therefore left at once for Sima to await his return from his razzia, while he led his party to a place near Kiyayaka where there was a halt for two o'clock and afternoon devotions. They then rode on their way till after nightfall, stopping for nothing but the sunset prayer which they celebrated on the open road. Having slept through the night, dawn saw them on their way again, this time northwards. They marched on without a break till past noon, and then after the two o'clock and afternoon prayers, took the road again and proceeded on at a brisk pace till the light failed, bivouacking where they were.

MS. Page 95.

The army, of course, were in the dark as to the Sultan's plan of action, but round about midnight, the trumpet sounded the "fall in." The men were soon mounted and on the line of the march, and the dawn prayer was their first halt. Re-mounting, they had not gone far before the standard of the Tubu was displayed clear to their sight. Our soldiers delighted at the encounter, struck up a tattoo on the big drum to rally our forces, and slackening rein, they came galloping in and assembled near the drums.

The enemy, disconcerted by this, broke and fled, pursued by our men, who were occupied in carrying off the women and children until the hottest part of the day. They then turned in the direction of a well in which they knew there to be water in order to freshen up their mounts. On arrival, they found not one well but two dug in the desert sands, and abundant in water; they therefore watered their horses and having offered up the two o'clock prayer as soon as it fell due, turned their steps homewards with their booty, travelling at a very slow walk. A strapping young Tubu not yet quite grown up, who was conversant with the road marched ahead of the troops, to guide them to wells which contained water. The route which he indicated lay through a smiling landscape, a sure sign that we had arrived at a place with wells of water. We came to two wells and watered our horses for the second time. Talba Al Hajj Kadai ibn Jilbu, the deputy Imam Muhammad ibn Ahmad, Al Hajj Umar, Chief of Faya, Muhammad ibn Shattima, Yarima Abdul Lahi ibn Mani and myself offered the prayer of afternoon in a place to the south of the town. After this, the Sultan led the army southwards and encamped at Ililiwa towards dusk. The night was spent there. When the blessed dawn appeared, and the sun rose, the bugler sounded the advance and we travelled south, halting just before noon at Tinu for the afternoon siesta. After the two o'clock prayer we continued southwards and bivouacked in the open shortly before nightfall. At dawn on Wednesday, the Sultan mounted and turned the course of the army towards Sima in which were our sick and the three Khalifas mentioned. This place we reached at noon. After watering our animals, the Sultan took one party, and turning westwards dismounted them there for the night, forming a separate group entirely disconnected from the main body. On that day died Farkama Muhammad ibn Abdullahi—may he rest in peace.

MS. Page 96.

The Sultan spent the night on the western hill, while the three Khalifas slept in the camp. Next day, they remained there a while. After the two o'clock and afternoon prayers had been said a large body of Tubu entered the Sultan's presence in fear and trembling quite unbidden, merely out of respect for him and Sultan Abdul Lahi. Their attitude was marked by subservience and humility and with heads bowed in allegiance they swore fealty, completely renouncing their partisanship towards Abdul Jalil.

No sensible man could help realising now that our Sultan's star was in the ascendant, especially when they added "Abdul Jalil's day is over; from now on, if God so wills, Sultan Muhammad ibn Abdul Lahi, you will find, will rise to great power." This speech on the part of the Tubu was very heartening to our troops, and after this the Sultan and his men mounted and rode out on Thursday evening and encamped. The people of Fitri came to him, as also did Ali ibn Yarda an Arab, with his people and messengers from the tribe of Kuka of Malfe. Many people accompanied the Arabs to Sima bringing food for sale, and this was of great service to the people.

Our Sultan stayed a few days at Sima. The news of this spread far and wide, but Sultan Abdul Jalil had gone far westwards and up to the present has not returned to the east. The next step of Al Hajj Idris, Commander of the Faithful, was to reinforce his Wazir with many leaders such as Kaigama Bukr Yarima Ali, Dalatu N'gizimma, Kachella Ali, Arjinoma Abdul Lahi, Sintalma Kadai, Yarima Muhammad ibn Othman, Albuma Dunama, Buyoma Ahmad ibn Bint Jaldi, Kulima Duna and chiefs of the Koyam and Barbars together with many other military commanders. Their orders were to proceed in force in search of Abdul Jalil. The Sultan in person, rode out as far as the cavalry parade ground to see the expedition off, then returned to his quarters from outside the camp.

They travelled north from Sima and after traversing much ground, struck the tracks of their enemy's army plainly running from west to east. No sooner were they sure of this, than they put forward every effort to track him down, and did not relax the pursuit until man and beast were worn out with fatigue and tormented by thirst; so, realising that it was beyond their power to overtake the quarry, they discussed what was their best objective, and decided that the best course would be to raid Kiriwa, rather than to return empty handed. Accordingly, they passed on to that town and took much booty, also killing the brother of Dunama the infidel, and then returned to Ma'o to await their Sultan. Now our Sultan Al Hajj Idris (whom may God exalt in each of the two worlds and whose children and grandchildren be blessed till the sound of the Trumpet through the grace of our Lord and Master Muhammad the Pure and his race. The glory of God be on them all. Amen) did not remain in Sima after the departure of the many leaders and tribes we have mentioned above, but marched out with what was left of his army towards the west and encamped near Gamira for two days or three; which of the two is known to God. There he entered into a treaty of allegiance with Gamira, for the ruler of the latter gave him cringing submission to the boundless delight of our folk high and low and Muhammad ibn Abdul Lahi's captains and leaders.

After our Sultan went south from Gamira he only remained one day in the district. Awakening on the second day, he left for

Ma'o, where he encamped and rejoined the Wazir, to their mutual delight and congratulation. He only stayed one day however, and having ordered the big drum to be beaten loudly as a signal, mounted at dawn and led his army westwards towards Bornu. At Malahe he encamped and then travelled on steadily till they reached the two Mulis, Muli Ghim and Muli Fuli; thence on to Sulu where Matarama ibn Salma and a man named Masamma Ali died and were interred on the same day: thence to the Kasharda, and after leaving them and passing Ruru, he came to the Sugurti: next to Bulugi and Guguti and the renowned town of Gatiga. There they spent two or three days and after completion of the two o'clock and afternoon prayers passed on to Itnawa and encamped in the evening. The Sultan journeyed on continuously until he reached Ruru in God's month Safar the Prosperous, and Gambaru. There he alighted with the whole of his army but did not enter the city called Birni nor any other of the Bornu town. He remained there some ten days until a great concourse of people were gathered together, male and female. Then he administered an oath of fealty to the leaders and captains and body-guard to remain true to him in attack, defence and deeds of prowess: in shock of combat and in overthrow. All the princesses of the blood royal were present, and the swearing in went on till each of the paramount chiefs and the most senior leaders had bound himself by oath to assist in upholding the supremacy of the Sultan in joy and sadness, bitterness and sweetness, overtly and covertly. Joy and gladness illumined every countenance, both that of the Sultan and those of his captains, and every hand was outstretched in congratulation and good wishes. Afterwards, the meeting broke up and they went in their respective directions. Of the captains, some departed to their dwellings while others stood by the Sultan, waiting for him to rise and enter the great zariba. The captains and leaders met together at Gambaru before dispersing, without asking leave of their Sultan; and, after deliberation, decided on a course of action and laid down an interim of forty days for preparing the preliminaries of the journey. Having agreed on this unanimously, they brought it before their king, Al Hajj Idris. When the latter heard the terms of what they had definitely decided, he gave them the diplomatic reply " Fulfil what you have contracted to fulfil." Thereupon every man returned to his home from Gambaru, and there he remained till the stipulated period should expire. When the appointed day came, however, the full complement was far from complete; but our blessed Sultan was so farsighted and shrewd an administrator, that he realised that it would be foolhardy to set out before the close of the rainy season and passing of autumn, by which time the surface of the ground would everywhere be a carpet of succulent new herbage, depriving a journey of all difficulty. He ordered the chiefs of his kingdom to report to him at the appointed time.

They assembled in the city called Birni. He outlined his plan to them and instructed them to return to their homes to mak the necessary preparations for their journey and to avoid post ponement and delay. Their orders were to collect at Fakara halfway through the month of Jumada'l 'Ula but he did not reveal what he had in mind by saying " My intention is to proceed thither and thither " so that they had no idea of his objective.

Now among the people of Kanem, the Kananiyya tribe who are known as the people of Sulu, led astray by reliance on their numerous soldiers and progeny, had been behaving arrogantly and rebelliously; had indulged in acts of evil, oppression and godlessness; and had obstructed the armies of our Sultan with fierce hatred and hostility. They were in the habit of waylaying them both on the outward and return journey to Kanem, sometimes behaving as foot-pads and sometimes openly attacking them. These depredations had fallen on all four of our expeditions to Kanem and our return journeys. In our fifth expedition, which was to Ikrima we went unmolested, the cause of our immunity from attack being due to the fact that we deviated northwards from their road and thus saved ourselves from their deceitful wiles. The object underlying our Sultan's concealmen of the fact that he was going after these marauders, was a fear lest the news should be noised abroad and give the enemy an opportunity of taking defensive measures. His way was always to walk in the footsteps of the Apostle of God, according to the path which God in His grace and noble open-handedness had traced out for him. A peculair trait among the Kananiyya was that a few would come to the Sultan to beg for what they needed in the way of clothing or household goods and other things. No one who asked him for anything left his presence without marks of his liberality and kindness. Yet nevertheless they displayed the behavior I have described during all our out-goings to Kanem and our incomings, and, in addition, they did not shrink from recourse to treachery; nor did they feel gratitude for kindness and good treatment, nor abandon acts of wickedness day or night. Every member of our nation whether soldier or civilian, who had cause to travel through their country or near it, went in terror of their depredations, except those whom God had spared from their machinations. So matters went on until God led us back to fight them on a Monday. When we reached their town Sulu, they all shut themselves in the Kargba or region surrounded by the waters of Lake Chad, on the banks of which is good pasturing grass. We encamped at Fiyu in the early forenoon and our only reason for spending the night there, was to guard against treacherous thieving.

At dawn we moved on towards Bornu, halting regularly by day and by night, until our arrival at Gambaru as already mentioned. The desire of the Sultan to lead a punitive expedition against them, was not stilled from that day till the concentration at Fakara, what time he hid his plans from his leaders and captains, apprehensive lest the news should filter through to the enemy as we have already stated.

EXPEDITION VI.

On Thursday 15th of Jumada'l 'Ula, the Sultan encamped at Fakara and spent three days there to gather in his forces. When they had reached a big total, he set out (may God advance him and render him victorious and his affairs prosperous) on Friday 18th, and, leading on his men, halted at Dalikna at siesta time and spent the night there. At dawn on Saturday, he left the town of Dalikna and, passing on with his army, stopped at Madawa for the siesta. The army slept right through the night till dawn. Then he gave the signal for departure, on the big drum, and they rode away on Sunday towards noon and halted at Kari Kuruku and spent the night there. After the early prayer on Tuesday, the big drum was sounded and they rode forth at a fast pace encamping at Kuri Karamnu.

On Wednesday they set out and at siesta time halted at Wurni; on Thursday about midday they set out and encamped at Labudu which was left on the Friday and a hasty march made to Kasuda; next day they went on to Buluji and spent the night there, while Sunday was spent at Bari. A halt was made at Ruru at noon on Monday, but the Sultan did not remain there longer than was necessary for the two o'clock and afternoon prayers, after which they rode on fast, halting only for the evening prayer at a pool called Kintak. They continued eastwards in the direction of the Kananiyya country in order to reach there by dawn and fare according as God had decreed for them. They travelled on continuously through the night, without halting for exhaustion or fatigue, until between a quarter and a third of the night was over. In this expedition of ours, since we set out from Fakara on the Friday we have mentioned, inclusive of the subsequent eleven days culminating on the Monday, we were not afflicted with exhaustion similar to that which befell us on this night. So greatly were we taxed, that some of us did not know in which direction to turn when praying unless guided by our camels in that direction; while others were unable to find their quarters although fully accustomed to their position. There were still others who, cut off from the main body, could not find their way back again. Such was the condition of some of our men on that night after the Sultan had encamped. It is surely enough to show that the conditions of that journey were a foretaste of hell (as a matter of fact the word Jihad only receives its name on account of the strife and toil entailed in it). This was why our Sultan Al Hajj Idris (may God exalt his rank and abase his detractors and bless his children and issue for ever and ever) in setting out on this forced march on Monday, particularly avoided all drumming and ordered every soldier to take three days rations neither more nor less. He also laid emphasis on the fact that no fit infantry man should remain behind (Râjil is the singular of Râwâjil and that is a foot soldier*) and that no healthy horse, pack animal or camel should remain with the casualties at the base. He also ordered the various shield-bearers not to follow him but similarly to remain behind at the base. His aim was to concentrate around himself every fit man and beast. He mounted with the forces remaining in his hands, but before setting out appointed his deputy to take charge of the

---

* This is part of text.

sick and baggage. This was Yuroma Yagha. The Sultan set out at the head of his army encamping at Ruru sometime after noon but only stayed there long enough to celebrate the two prayers, that of two o'clock and the afternoon prayer.

Then the force set out and travelled at a rapid pace so that the exhaustion we have referred to above overtook them. We continued on until we reached Siki (a well known place) or thereabouts, and there we spent the night. At dawn the Sultan divided the troops into three portions for the purpose of raiding, fighting, and plunder. His son Kaigama Abdul Jalil, he sent out with his Wazir Idris ibn Harun towards the south against the Kananiyya to proceed as far as Ririkmi and other cities. He sent his son Yarima Idris with the army known as the "Northern Force" which was under the command of Arjinoma and other northern captains, northwards to harass the Kananiyya and penetrate as far as their city Mai and others. They slaughtered a large number of the enemy and took captives many women and children. The Sultan himself had followed the course of the main road with the remaining troops and proceeded as far as Didi and other cities of the Kananiyya.

His troops worked great havoc among the enemy and carried off much property and about a thousand or more of their women and children. The fires of war having died down the Sultan turned his steps towards Ririkmi and there encamped towards evening. His senior captain Kaigama Abdul Jalil and the Wazir Idris ibn Harun had taken up their quarters at Ririkmi before the arrival of the Sultan as they had been detailed to raid it. They had taken a large store of booty. The senior commander Yarima Idris ibn Idris did not return with his army until after nightfall when he arrived with much loot having accounted for large numbers of the enemy.

Sultan Al Hajj Idris ibn Ali was at Ririkmi of good cheer and bright of eye; while discomfiture, rout, slaughter and despoilment fell upon his bellicose enemies who had persisted in hindering the free passage of Muhammadans. The troops were overjoyed and rejoiced at the victory of their Sultan over their rebellious and impious foe. The whole army spent the night at that town without taking any measures of defence; for they felt they had nothing to fear from the enemy, some of whom had been slain, others of whom had fled to a place of refuge and concealment.

Our troops ate their full there of mutton and goats' flesh; their tiredness left them; and they rested and slept the whole night through. When the dawn broke the Sultan gave the signal for departure and mounted, followed by his army, travelling westwards towards Ruru. They went on till the sun was declining and then halted in a place known as Kintak where there was a pond of water. There they stopped for a siesta, and celebrated the two o'clock and afternoon prayers after which they went on to Ruru without any of the captains, commanders, or body-guards remaining behind. The complement was complete even including the pack animals and camel drivers. They carried their booty along with them not forcing the pace but proceeding very slowly. When they reached the place on the frontier where our drum was beaten on our first expedition to Kanem on the occasion when we retraced our steps, our Sultan (the Commander of the Faithful Al Hajj Idris whom may God render victorious and whose children and grandchildren be blessed till the sounding of the Trumpet by the grace of the Lord of mankind, the Bringer of Good Tidings, the Eternal, the Seal of the Prophets, the Imam of the Pure, our Lord and Master Muhammad the Pure, and his descendant on whom be the mercy of God) halted, firmly reining in his horse near some tamarisk trees which I know are known far and wide. The people were dismayed at not rejoining the sick who were with the deputy commander Yuroma, but the Sultan was not minded to rejoin them on that day and dismounted under those trees, the tamarisks we mentioned, at the beginning of the book. Upon seeing this, the army bivouacked without delay, unsaddled both camels and horses, and constructed their quarters for the night as best they were able. They spent the night there cheerful and happy and free from fear of theft or attack together with the rich spoil we had taken.

MS. Page 110. They returned safely without the loss of a single man with the exception of those who were wounded or overcome at the first shock, but our infidel enemy's losses cannot be computed except after long search and investigation. That is because the warriors were killed at the first onset in the field of battle and overthrown, and all those who attempted to withstand our army were at once slain except those who prolonged their life by flight. Our armed patrols were unremitting in searching out fugitives in every place where we encamped, by search and investigation, and they killed our pagan prisoners by order of the Sultan. Not one of them was spared by the guards to remain in anyone's possession. One of the strangest things I have heard about our behaviour was that Kamkama Bamu, one of the Sultan's chief officers, put to death the youths and striplings who were not yet fully adult, in punishment of their evil deeds. Not one survived except him whom God saved. The prisoners were slain there just as their companions had been slain on the field of battle. He who escaped, escaped; and he who died, died. The only survivors in our hands were the women and children.

MS. Page 111. After this, the Kananiyya rapidly became extinct. These were the people who only a short time before were puffed up with pride and insolence and considered themselves second to none. According to what I have heard, they were the most numerous tribe in Kanem, and it has been said that if any of their enemies angered them they used to set out with the whole of their people and attack the country of their adversaries without fear of living man, just as our Sultan does to his enemies. This was what emboldened them to deeds of evil and tyranny until they went to the length of openly opposing the armies of our Sultan by attacking and robbing them. They had no organisation of any sort and were led astray by their overweaning pride and insolence, until spoliation, slaughter, and destruction fell upon them, as we have described, and the country which our Sultan raided became so much scattered dust. These oppressors were exterminated from the face of the earth. This Tuesday came to them a day of deadly poison. May the dawn of the day be hateful to infidels and evildoers. So we have seen in the book of the creation of the world, what time punishment was inflicted on the people of Sodom because of their disobeying their prophet Lot. The Kananiyya took no heed of the fate of bygone scoffers and profited naught by the lessons of this changing life. As the proverbialist has said " He who does not learn in the school of the world's experience will not profit by the exhortations of the preacher, preach he never so long ". But the Kananiyya of Kanem are people senseless and stupid, ignorant and stubborn, lacking in all qualities of intellect and common sense, and entirely devoid of organisation. Our reason for designating them by these three epithets. i.e., Khurq, Humq. and Jahil, which are distinct in form but close in meaning, is because Khurq is a stronger term than Humq, and Humq is stronger than Jahil; for a senseless man (Akhraq) is one who cannot distinguish between what is beneficial and what is noxious and exhortation is entirely wasted on him, while the stupid man (Ahmaq) is one who will accept no service at all whether it be to his advantage or disadvantage and in this he resembles the senseless man. As regards the ignorant (Jahil) his case is simpler than that of the other two for. if he is adjured. he listens, and after listening. turns away from the advice to his own hurt. It is now time to return to the story of Ruru when we went to the great city called Birni. After encamping at Ruru on Thursday we only remained there three days and the whole of our army recovered from their fatigue and rested from their preparations.

MS. Page 112.

At dawn on Sunday the Sultan ordered a tattoo to be sounded on the drums and they set up a mighty drumming, after which the army accoutred itself and saddling the camels, oxen and donkeys. rode away with the Sultan. travelling westwards along the broad highway to Bornu. They forced the pace and encamped at Bari and then proceeded on their way and encamped in front of Buluji; and thence to Furtu and on to the pond called Malfifi. where they encamped and then went on to Mardali where a halt was made. From there the route lay to Ghuwi Kafokwa where also a halt was made. Bands of itinerant merchants from Bornu came in, accompanied by men of Bulma, Kawar. and Ghazbi who had brought caravans from Fezzan. A meeting took place between them and the Sultan in this town. The Sultan bought from them a large stock of horses as God had decreed in His Guarded Tablets, and spent Saturday in the town of Ghuwi Kafokwa.

In the morning, the Sultan did not march owing to his preoccupation with the horses, and observed the Sunday two o'clock prayer. Then after completing his transactions in new horses, he set out westwards and travelled at a fast pace until he reached a

MS. Page 113.

MS. Page 114. gheghir (camp) in the late afternoon. There heavy showers of rain fell. He encamped with the army at this place, but no one obtained food enough to satisfy him, excepting such as had laid in a good store of eatables, owing to the torrential downpour which went on the whole of the night almost unbrokenly.

When God vouchsafed to us the dawn of Monday, the Sultan mounted and hastened on to Ghiskiru where the night was spent, and on Tuesday, reached Zantam where the majority of our army dispersed to their homes with the exception of the Sultan's personal servants and such like.

On Thursday, he set out and by the grace of God crossed the great river and encamped at Gambaru near the river, spending the night there. On the following day, he offered up Friday congregational prayer in the mosque of Gambaru, followed later by the afternoon prayer; then accompanied by what was left of the army, he made his way to the great city Birni, which he entered on Friday evening and remained there some ten days, though I cannot vouch for the exact number. An authentic and reliable piece of news reached us that the Kananiyya of Kanem had set out in large numbers with Al Hajj Hano, the chief of Ruru, in the direction of Bornu to ask pardon of our Sultan for their previous evil deeds and to implore his cooperation. Apparently, they feared additional reprisals in the future and were cowed by what had just befallen them. This news which was quite correct, **MS. Page 115.** reached us before their arrival at Birni, in fact while they were still far away. They travelled across our country till they halted at the river to the north of Gambaru. They sent an envoy to the Sultan and asked leave to cross the river, proceed to Birni, and appear before him. Having obtained full sanction from him, they crossed the river and entered Birni. Al Hajj Hano and the rest of them went to the Sultan's council chamber and were shown into his presence. They behaved humbly and submissively and freely admitted their guilt regarding their past delinquencies in respect to thieving, wickedness, oppression, and deeds of aggression, and begged him for complete pardon and a cessation of raids against them.

They then left the audience chamber to wait outside. They sat in the Sultan's court yard, in company with Idris ibn Harun, the Wazir, and asking for pardon, besought him to spare their lives on paying an indemnity. They swore on the Kura'an that they would offer the Sultan no further opposition in the future. They then departed to their own country having undertaken to deliver a thousand head of cattle or more as a pledge of good faith. Shortly after this, the eventful news reached us that Sultan Abdul Jalil and his army had been routed in an engagement with Sultan Muhammad ibn Abdul Lahi in the north of Kanem on Wednesday in the month of Jumad al Akhira. God help Muhammad ibn Abdul Lahi to an overwhelming victory by routing Abdul Jalil and his champions, after the latter had expressed their contempt for Muhammad and his troops and had insulted them and taunted them with cowardice. Little did they realise that victory is in the **MS. Page 116.** hands of God, not merely the outcome of large numbers and great resources; for God is the object of praise and thanksgiving.

It is told of our Sultan Al Hajj Idris that he attacked Sultan Abdul Jalil at Kiyayaka and that the latter fled to the far desert to escape him. Abdul Jalil and those who followed him and assisted him in his deeds of evil and tyranny, seem in their early days to have been like gazelles pasturing in the desert and browsing on the herbage, who flee in terror to their lairs at the sight of women. Such was the condition of Abdul Jalil and his followers before the battle of Kiyayaka uprooted them; but in their latter days they became like wild cows pasturing in the most inaccessible wilderness who are seen by the eye of no traveller save those whom business or the chase takes to remote deserts.

Our Sultan, seeing this state of affairs, pondered on it, and evolved a plan which would have occurred to no one else but himself on account of its ingenuity. Having thought about the matter he sent for many Beduwin tribes and their leaders, as for example 'Al Yarda and his folk and others, and addressing them in complimentary terms, called them to a conference where flattery and blandishment were not absent. In this way Idris attached all of them to Sultan Muhammad Abdul Lahi, and ordered them to assist him against Abdul Jalil to the limit of their power and perfectly openly without slackness or remissness. They fell in with Idris' orders and became Muhammad's right hand, remaining with him until God gave him victory over his uncle Sultan Abdul Jalil.

EXPEDITION VII.

We now return to the events which occurred on the seventh journey of the Sultan Aj Hajj Idris to Kanem. This great and just king and pious administrator of the lands of Islam and respecter of the rights of all Muhammadans, on setting forth for Kanem on this journey, after the destruction of the rebels, gave orders to his captains, commanders, and body-guard and the remainder of his army to collect rations for the journey without delay. They did so. The Sultan set out from Gambaru in the month of Shawwal and encamped at Zantam; from there he passed on to Ghotuwa, then to Milu, Lada, Burkumwa, Ghawali, Milti, Bari, Gayawa, Malahe, Dagimsil and Hugulgul, in the neighbourhood of Dilaram, then to Ruru and on to Kasuda.

The Sultan stayed at Kasuda three or four days having previously sent Malagalma Dalatu, chief of Miri, to Sultan Muhammad ibn Abdul Lahi to summon him to Sulu in the Kananiyya country with his people the Bulala. Dalatu left Kasuda on Saturday and was followed on Tuesday by the Sultan who travelled eastwards and halted at Siki Dananma to await the Sultan Muhammad Abdul Lahi. The Bulala Sultan arrived with his army headed by our messenger Malagalma Dalatu on Friday night and encamped in front of our Sultan's house. The troops were ordered to parade outside in full strength. Our Sultan and Sultan Muhammad ibn Abdul Lahi sat together in the same council. Many matters were discussed and the boundary was delimited between Bornu and Kanem, whereby we obtained Kagusti and the whole Siru district. This was made public to all and the commanders on both sides who were present at the proclamation heard it without dismay or opposition. Babaliya also was alloted to Bornu, but our Sultan granted them what remained of Kanem through his affection for Sultan Muhammad ibn Abdul Lahi. But for this he would not have given them an inch of territory in Kanem. I lay emphasis on this, because when our Sultan made his expedition to Kanem, and encamped at Ma'o. it was *he* who routed Abdul Jalil in three separate actions; firstly, at the town of Kirsila, then at Tusa or Gamira, and lastly at Aghafi. The Sultan remained there some time to await the arrival of his partisans and was joined by many of the troops of Abdul Jalil. Such captains and commanders as gave him their allegiance, he placed under the command of Sultan Muhammad ibn Abdul Lahi, having previously made them swear on the Kura'an that they would obey him and help him to victory. Having pronounced his friendly intentions towards Sultan Muhammad he gave him sway over the remaining territories of Kanem because of his affection for him. It was this affection alone which led him to alienate his territory.

Everyone of the Bulala whom he swore in at Aghafi heard the speech of our Sultan which we have mentioned above and also the captains and commanders of the Bulala. After the settling of the frontiers of Bornu and Kanem the Sultan returned to Bornu.

Let us now resume the account of the treaty between ourselves and the Bulala entered into at Siki. When the conference took place between our Sultan and Sultan Muhammad ibn Abdul Lahi in front of the Sultan's house at Siki, everyone of the Bulala applauded, and sought pardon and swore by God that they would never again oppose our Sultan neither would they oppose their own Sultan Muhammad or his son. This they swore a second time after having sworn it previously to our Sultan.

Sultan Muhammad ibn Abdul Lahi and his people who had come with him then returned on Friday night, the night of the full moon, after obtaining a complete pardon, with their minds at ease after the terror which they had previously felt. We have heard from those who know the facts, that when the Bulala approached our Sultan's dwelling at Siki, they came into his presence invoking the protection of God, and humbly mentioning His name, and in such terror of their lives that they dismounted from their horses. The only one who felt no fear was their Sultan Muhammad ibn Abdul Lahi in person, for he relied on the affection which our Sultan felt for him. When they had sworn an oath and received a free pardon from our Sultan, they were overjoyed, and praised God for escaping with their lives. On mounting to take their departure, they offered up thanks to God and returned with their Sultan to the place from which they had come.

When Friday dawned, Chiroma Burdima arrived with the remaining commanders and chiefs of the Bulala. They were given audience of our Sultan on Saturday and clapped their hands and sought pardon as their predecessors had done on the previous day.

The Sultan ordered his Wazir Idris ibn Haruna to swear them on the Book of God, and they all took the oath without exception. Our Sultan gave orders that on the following day, a Saturday, every commander and captain was to parade fully equipped, each in a separate position, accompanied by his followers, grooms, and shield-bearers, since he intended to review them one after the other and wished to inspect them without confusion. On the appointed day the whole army in smart array took up their positions one by one in great number without overcrowding, for the Sultan to inspect them. On the Sunday, the Sultan did not inspect the shield-bearers and the Koyam, but did so on the next day. All our commanders and captains rejoiced at our increase of territory and at our eastward journey having come to a conclusion.

On Tuesday, the Sultan ordered the drums to be beaten. After this, the army made its preparations and saddled the camels and horses and set out a long march to reach Ruru. We set out from there on Wednesday and encamped near Dilaram and on Thursday we left there and halted midday near Buluji on Friday, and encamped near Gayawa. We travelled on the Saturday to Bari. The Sultan there gave the order that the troops were not to disperse before reaching Ruwaya. After this we encamped at Milti and from there went on to Didi and Milu and then to Ruwaya. On the next day all mounted after arraying themselves and their horses in armour, cuirasses, shields and their best apparel. When we had proceeded a short distance towards the west we met messengers of the king, the Lord of Stambul, the Sultan of Turkey, who had been sent to our Sultan together with the learned Hajj Yusuf known as " Gate of the Chosen." They were drawn up in order of precedence near the town of Bursalim, and with them were our friends Dirkuma Fatar ibn Ghambu together with many other merchants.

The troops of our Sultan were drawn up on the west in rank after rank, leaving sufficient space between the ranks for the wheeling of a restive horse. Our troops charged towards them and they galloped their horses towards us. This continued for long time until the infantry were tired with long standing. Then the Sultan went westwards and passed through Bursalim and on to Gatawa and then to the river in the neighbourhood of Gambaru. He halted there on Friday. Our army rejoiced and were happy and gave themselves up to relaxation. Their joy was too great to describe.

O my wise friends and companions! Have you ever seen a king equal to our Sultan or like him at the time when the Lord of Stambul, Sultan of Turkey, sent messengers to him from his country, with favourable proposals, indicating his desire to gain his affection and his eagerness for his society and friendship? Alas! every ruler is inferior to these chiefs since they are of the tribe of Kuraish descended from Himyar. The ancestor of our prophet and Lord, Muhammad, was the same as theirs. They are intertwined with him in the strand of the same invisible cord (Luwai-Ghalib) which is sure and certain. Among the marvellous things which we heard from our elders concerning them, a thing more acceptable than the purest water, is that in the possession of the tribe of the Bani Saif was a certain thing wrapped up and hidden away whereon depended their victory in war. This was called Mune and no one among the people of Saif ibn Dthi Yazan had opened it. This remained in their hands unopened until the time of Sultan Dunama ibn Dabale. This Sultan wished to break it open, but his people warned him not to do so, because the victory of his predecessors had depended upon it, and no infidel could withstand them so long as this Mune remained wrapped up and hidden in their possession. They said " This has continued up to the time when God set you up as ruler over the Muslims." He refused to listen to their advice and loosened the woof of their ancient line. It is said that when Dunama opened it, whatever was inside flew away impelling the chief men of the kingdom to greed for dominion and high rank. In the time of Sultan Dunama ibn Dabale, there occurred war between him and the Tubu so that war and strife between them continued for seven years seven months and seven days. So we have heard from narrators but the truth is known to God alone.

Later, much strife and discord arose between Sultan Daud ibn Nikale and the people of Fitri. But we have already mentioned this at the beginning of the book in its proper place, in the account of the country of Kanem. But for the opening of this talisman, known as Mune, in the time of Sultan Dunama, no infidel would have opposed the Bani Saif till the end of time. It was God's will that matters should so happen. It was pre-ordained by the writing on the Guarded Tablets. Thus it was in regard to the opening and setting free of that which was in the possession of the Bani Saif ibn Dthi Yazan until the time of Sultan Dunama called " The Sacred Mune." In consequence of this opening, there disappeared from before the eyes of the beholders, that which God had sent down to the children of Israel, in the days of King Saul as is related in the Kura'an, the ark in which was knowledge of victory.

We have read in the Kitab Al Afrad by ibn Faris that every *Sakina mentioned in the Kura'an brought tranquility except that mentioned in the story of Saul which was like the head of a cat with two wings.

Thus have I also read in the Kamus by the learned Imam, the Seal of the traditionalists and philologists Majd Al Din Al Firuzabadi (whom may God envelope with the cloak of His mercy) in the passage where, after mentioning other interpretations, he goes on to say " It is a thing made of chrysolite, and rubies resembling the head of a cat with two wings." O Muslims, distinguished by justice and equity, know that the race of the Bani Saif ibn Dthi Yazan have been free from the stain of polytheism and the worship of idols from the days of their earliest kings up to to-day. Their conduct is set by the standard of the writings of the Holy Kura'an or by the Sunna or by the law of the doctors of jurisprudence. No one doubts this but he in whose heart is doubt about religion or he who is envious or ignorant or unable to distinguish between truth and falsehood. The nobility of the

---

* The Divine Presence which appeared in the Mercy Seat.

Bani Saif is proverbial at every time and place. They are nobility itself. If their supremacy is disputed, nobility with the tongue of man will say "It is the dust of the earth which is vying with you." May God bless their line and their descendants until the day of resurrection, for God is a hearer of prayer and a fulfiller of wishes. God is our sufficiency and excellent is His deputy. There is no power or strength but in God Almighty, He alone. May God be merciful to our Lord Muhammad and his companions and his wives and children. He granted the completion of the copying of this noble Diwan on Friday, nine days before the end of the month Jumada Al Akhira 1269* of the Hijira of the Lord of the Apostles on whom and on whose race be perfect peace.

[The Kuraish are of the seed of Himyar and their ancestor and the ancestor of the prophet were one—Luwai ibn Ghalib.

O Muslims, hear the word which we have heard from our fathers and from the tribe of Saif, concerning the thing which was veiled and hidden which brought victory in war. It was called Munba. Of the kings of the line of Saif ibn Dthi Yazan no king opened it till the time of Dunama ibn Dabale. He wished to open and expose it. His people said to him "Open it not, for verily this thing was the cause of victory to your ancestors who have gone before: and none of the unbelievers or others gainsaid them; what time this thing remained veiled and covered even till this day."

But the Sultan refused to listen to them, and opened the foundation of the ages. And when he had opened it—so we have heard—there flew out something from inside it, which incited every section of the people after that day to lust for power and rank.

In the days of Sultan Dunama ibn Dabale there were wars between him and the Tubu. These wars lasted seven years and seven months and seven days, so we have heard from those who relate these things, but God knows.

Then in the days of Sultan Daud ibn Nigale there arose great bickering and discord with the people of Fitri. We have mentioned this matter at the beginning of this work on Kanem. Had not this Munba been opened in the days of Sultan Dunama ibn Dabale, no unbeliever would ever have gainsaid the people of the tribe of Saif for all ages for ever, but it happened by the providence of God, the Fore-knowing, who wrote it on the Guarded Tablets.

This thing which was the "Mune" from Saif ibn Dthi Yazan to Dunama ibn Dabale, which flew away, when uncovered and vanished from the eyes of men, was like that which God (exalted be He) as related in the Kura'an sent down to the Beni Israel, the Ark of the Covenant with which was bound up their success in the days of Talut. As God said:—

"Verily God sent to you Talut as a king to fulfil his word that verily there shall come to you the Ark of the Covenant. Therein shall be "Sakina" from your Lord, and the relics which have been left by the family of Aaron. The angel

---

* 2nd of April, 1852.

shall bring it. Verily this shall be a sign unto you, if ye believe."

I have seen in the book Afrad written by ibn Faris that every Sakina brought tranquility except that in the story of Talut which was like the head of a cat with two wings. This I have seen in the Book of God—the Kamus.

The Imam, the learned and God-fearing writer of Hadiths, Majid Ul-Din, the pre-eminent in erudition (may God cover him with His mercy), in the book Kamus Ul Mahib says that "Sakina from your Lord" means that of which the presence is a source of tranquility to you, or something which has the head of a cat made of topaz or ruby and has two wings.

Also in the Commentaries on the Kura'an Al-Kalbiyin says that "Tranquility from your Lord" means the 'Ark of the Covenant'. Kalbiyin says that when the Ark was present it tranquillised their hearts.

Makatilun says that there was a beast with a head like a cat with two wings. If it cried out, that was a sign of victory. It was of green jade and was vocal. It is said that winds roared in it, and it brought victory.

O Muslims, who love truth, take good heed that the people of the seed of Saif are far from practices of polytheism and fetish, and have been so from their earliest days till now. They act not except in accordance with the Kura'an and Sunna, and Law of Islam.

For verily their acts are plain and open and no one will doubt them except he is a religious doubter, a jealous person, or man of crooked heart who does not distinguish between good and ill.

The greatness of the people of Saif is known in every quarter. They are first even though they are put last. Al Ala'u says they are first, even though man put them last. May God pardon them and bless their seed with a great blessing till the day of Judgment. God is the hearer of prayers; God is our boast, and the felicity of His Prophet.

There is no power or strength save in God Most High. The blessing of God be upon our lord and master Muhammad, his relations, and friends, and secure peace.

Allahuma O Lord of Hosts grant to this writer and to all the people who follow the Sunna and the Hadiths, thy heaven. Amin and again Amin.]

NOTES ON THE TEXT.

Daw Rif-Baramusa.—The meaning is that their dominion extended from Nubia to the Niger. The terms are of some interest. **Sec. 3.**

Daw, which may possibly be related to the modern place name Dueim, and mean the country of people called Do or Du, was on the Nile in the region of the first cataract near Ibrim. Both Makrisi and El Nowairi wrote the name Daw, the Nubian historian called it Adwa. In the Kanuri language, hill country was apparently called Do-ma, and the people in turn called Domawa or Adomawa, corrupted by the Arabs into Haudama, if the latter is not a mere variant of the former.

In Bornu, the term Tuwan or Ji-tuwan, was (T being a variant of D) applied to areas to the south of the Kanuri country *e.g.* Tuwa-ti " land of Tuwa " *i.e.* Mandara.

Tu-ab was the Nubian name of the sacred hill at Napata. The meaning of the word " du " or " tu " would seem to be the same as it is in the tribal name Tu-bu " hill-people," and Tu-ba-sti " land of hill people ", and in the name of the sacred hill at Napata (Merawi) Tu-ab, while in Hausa, the ordinary word for a hill is du-si.

Daw was then a Jebel region both in the cataract region and in Northern Kordofan. It seems a reasonable deduction that the name Kordofan is composed as follows:—

    Kor—(Kwar) = people. A prefix added after the rest of the word was in common use.

    Du-afa—equivalent to Tu-ab " people of the Tu or hills,"

    An—Tamashek, plural suffix.

It is suggested that the Tuab were the same class of people, (Kushites, Egyptian Kash) whom the Arabs call Tubba, since the Zaghawi even now speak of the Teda or Tubu as Tobba or Tubba, and that these races became hill (tu) people when the Tuareg Barbars arrived in the Sudan.

Baramusa, on the other hand, as it means the Niger, probably is a mispronunciation of Baram Isa or Buram Isa, written by the geographer Idrisi " Bar-isa." The Buram is a region in the buckle of the Niger still known as such, and Isa, like Yuliba and Kwara is one of the many local names of the Niger.

The Beautiful Egg. The phenomenon described is believed by the Kanuri races to presage defeat. It is possible that in some way it is connected with the fable of the Abyssinian Viceroy of Yaman Abraha's abortive attack on Mecca, recorded in Chapter CV of the Kura'an. The birds which destroyed Abraha's army by throwing small stones on it, are supposed to have resembled swallows. **Sec. 20.**

Mosque of Armi. This is a very interesting statement and it will be observed that the mosque was close to Balagi (now pronounced Balge), which in turn is not far from Gamtilo and Madan, where, as has been noted in the introduction, was the centre of Saifawa power before N'jimi was founded. **Sec. 32.**

The ruler of this Balagi or Balge was termed the Balagema or Falagema (written Falakma), and it was a royal title, *i.e.* usually held by a son or grandson of the Mai.

Armi evidently stands for one of the earliest, if not the earliest, mosques in Kanem, and, presumably, takes its name from the class of people who founded it.

To the west, the Moroccan mercenaries who were armed with " guns " were called Rumawa, of which the singular is Armi, from " ramma " to shoot, meaning sharpshooters. Hence later, the descendants of these people were called Rumawa and are to-day assimilated to the Fulani.

We know from a manuscript found at Tuwat that the early Bornu Mais had a good deal of intercourse with the Western Barbars, and it may be that the Armi in question means a Marabut from the west; but on the other hand, the current Kanuri explanation of Armi is that it is equivalent to the Beni Keyi or Kayi, and Aram in Kanem is used to mean " Arabs " or "Semites." Also in the Southern (Amakitan) Tamashek language, the word aghim (arim) means a " walled city."

The story of the introduction of Islam is pertinent (*see* Mahram No. 45), and it may also be noted that a common variant of Madan is Badan, which in old songs is called Badan Guro.

The most interesting point however is that this Armi mosque near Balagi seems to settle quite finally the question of the " Sahib Yalak," who, according to Idrisi, was tributary to the King of Nubia, and who raided Samina in the country of the Taju about 1150 A.D. Dozy, the editor of Idrisi, correctly reads Yalak as Pilak or Balak; but his conjecture that Aswan was meant is wrong, for the reference is clearly either to this Balagi (the Samina in question being Chibina or Shebina on the Wadi Batha, east of Lake Fitri, then the Dajo capital), or to Balâk (more usually written Barâk), a tribal name for the Barbars of Kanem or Borku. In either case Balak is equivalent to Baram, *i.e.* Barbars.

Sec. 43. *Bâri—Ahel Armi—Ga'uma.* This Bâri is in the south of Kanem and the " a " is long not short as in Bari, the Bornu-Kanem boundary town to the north of Lake Chad. Bari, is thus in the same region as Balagi, Gamtilo, and Madan. The expression " Ahel Armi " is evidently cognate to " Mosque of Armi," (*supra* sec. 32).

The Armi are clearly not the ordinary nomad Arabs of Fitri and Kanem. They were with the Ga'u-ma, *i.e.* ruler of Ga'u or Gaoga (Leo Africanus), near Lake Fitri. These Armi were therefore very probably levantine or North African merchants of some sort. Armi may be the equivalent of Aramaean or Armenian.

Sec. 35. *River which lies between the land of Kulu and Kanem i.e.* the Bahr-al-Ghazal or Buram, which lies between Kanem proper and Abu Gher in Bagarmi.

This region was apparently called Kulu, whence the names Kuluma and Kuluwan (people of Kulu), the burial place of Mai Katuri (circa 950 A.D.). In this region also lay Madan (Malan) the burial place of Mai Fune (circa 850 A.D.) and Tatanu, the burial place of Mai Biyoma or Waiyoma, as well as Biyo or Waiyo, the town from which the name Biyoma comes, and of which Biyoma was ruler towards 1000 A.D. The Kanem N'gala, called N'gala Buta or Buti, was the burial place of Mai Arsu or Archu (circa 900 A.D.) and is also not very far away from Kulu.

It will be apparent then that the earliest Mais who were, according to Idrisi, in some sense feudatory to the Meks of Dongola (King of Nubia) began under Mai Dugu Bremmi by making expeditions, probably for slaves, up the Shari, as far as Yari Arbasan near the Sanaga river, and that they first settled down in the Balagi region—the Kulu region—between the modern Kanem and Bagarmi.

Listiri—Kileti (Koyam). Again an interesting piece of information, since it shows the genesis of the more famous Kulu-n-Bardu (*i.e.* Kulu of the Bardoa), the city of the Koyam, which lay to the north of the Komadugu in Bornu, west of Lake Chad. **Sec. 88.**

It will be seen that the Koyam, *i.e.* the Kayi-am or Kayi tribe, were of the Bardoa who are so frequently mentioned by the mediaeval Arab writers, and who have often been supposed to have been Tubu.

The variant names for this region Kalu and Kulu seem to correspond exactly to the two modern Kanuri words for a 'town' or 'fortified enclosure' Garu and Guru or N'guru. Thus one name for this same region is Badan Guru.

Kulun Bardu (Kulumpardo) then will mean the 'Town of the Bardoa.'

Bulma—Kawar—Ghazbi. *i.e.* Fezzani and Tripolitan merchants from the Kawar oasis who, as a class, are called Wasuri or Buhadi. The horse trade is alluded to in Mahram No. 46. **Sec. 113**

Bulma is situated towards the south of the Kawar oasis. Ghazbi the Kasr-um-Isa (castle of the mother of Jesus) of Idrisi, lies to the north of the present Dirku or Dirki, the capital of the oasis.

It is extremely probable that the Kawarians, who were mixed Tubu and Wasuri, were at one time Christians.

The Mune. The factor regarded as essential to preserve the efficacy of this and similar 'sacra', which were and are still in some cases, jealously guarded, by the Hausa and Jukon chiefs—is "covering." **Sec. 123**

Where the peoples in question became Muhammadans, a copy of the Kura'an itself seems to do duty as the 'hidden sacra' as in the case of the talisman called Dirki (from the name of the capital of the Kawar Oasis Dirki) which was opened and destroyed by the last Hausa Sarki of Kano about 1807.

Concerning him, the Kano Chronicle says:—

"His chiefs said to him, 'Sarkin Kano, why do you refuse to give cattle to Dirki?' The Sarki said, 'I cannot give you forty cattle for Dirki.' They said: 'What prevents you? If any Sarkin Kano does not allow us cattle for Dirki, we fear that he will come to some ill.' Alwali was very angry, and sent young men to beat Dirki with axes until that which was inside the skins came out. They found a beautiful Kura'an inside Dirki. Alwali said: ' Is this Dírki?' They said 'Who does not know Dirki? Behold, here is Dirki. Dirki is nothing but the Kura'an.' In Alwali's time, the Fulani conquered the seven Hausa States."

At Katsina similarly a ' Kudandam ' or round house which had been carefully closed for years was opened by the last Hausa Sarki; while at Wukari there still exists a sacred and carefully guarded forked staff or spear, which is identical in its supposed qualities with the Bornu " Mune " and is called 'Aba Kindo ', which means, or perhaps connotes rather, something occult.

A Zaghawi of Wadai stated that the Zaghawi name for a sacred Kura'an covered with skins like Kano Dirki, was Mâni.

When asked whether Mâni was anything else but the Kura'an, he stated that among the pagan Beli and Zaghawa, Mâni was a ' ram ' which was kept in a cave with other sacred objects, a fact which, if correct, accounts for the curious belief, current even now among Tacruris in the Anglo-Egyptian Sudan, that, in a cave in Dala hill at Kano, there is a ' stone ram ' comparable with those in the Egyptian temples at Luxor and elsewhere.

In addition to this, Mune is the mythical ancestor of several Kanembu tribes or peoples, while at Kano a deity once worshipped at Dala is called Amani in the Chronicle. Amani is, without doubt, the same as the Tamashek word Amanay " God ", which in compound with ' akal ' earth, makes the title Aman-akel or Aman-okal, the clan head or chief. Clearly, Mune or Muni was originally the Egyptian and Nubian God, Amen or Aman.

Sec. 123 *Sultan of Turkey*. These envoys must have been sent either by Salîm II (1566-1574) or by Murâd III (1574-1595). The two passages which relate to them are both corrupt and it was perhaps due to hurry that Barth did not apparently see what was meant, for if he had, he would certainly have noted this Turkish embassy of which we have no other notice.

In one passage the manuscript reads: "Sahib Dubul" and in the other "Sahib abd Dumbul" both of which readings fail to yield a satisfactory meaning, for the envoys had come with the Dirku-ma or ruler of the Kawar Oasis, an important chief, and must clearly have come from some region to the north of Kawar.

There is however no place of any importance now or then in the north with any name very close to Dubul or Dumbul. The messengers were evidently persons of such consequence, that there can be no doubt that the original word was Stanbul, which was not recognised by the copyist and so was copied as Dumbul and Dubul.

A list of Dirkumas is given in the Mahram No. 46.

NAME INDEX (MANUSCRIPT PAGES).

Aaron: 125.
Abdul 'Lahi: 8, 9, 10, 31, 32, 33, 34.
Abu Muhammad Abdul 'Lahi ibn Ali Zeid: 47.
'Ad (people of): 60.
Adam (Sultan): 6, 11.
Afaki: 80.
Aghafi: 24, 25, 27, 28, 29, 31, 32, 36, 71, 72, 76, 78, 119.
Ahel Armi: 43.
Ago: 66, 76, 78, 79.
Albuma Dunama: 97.
Al Hajj Hano: 114, 115.
Al Hajj Idris: 2, 4, 5, 7, 9, 11, 12, 13, 14, 16, 19, 25, 26, 27, 28, 30, 33, 35, 37, 40, 42, 44, 47, 48, 53, 55, 60, 61, 62, 66, 72, 73, 74, 76, 82, 89, 90, 93, 97, 98, 100, 105, 109, 116, 116.
Al Hajj ibn Musa: 46.
Ali called Fado: 34.
'Ali ibn Yarda: 97.
Alma Al-Ahmar: 49.
'Al Yarda: 116.
Al-Kalbiyin: 125.
Amalik: 3.
Amir ul Muminin: 26, 33, 37.
Arjinoma Abdullahi ibn Said: 59, 97, 107.
Arjinoma 'Ali: 22.
Armi: 32.
Asiyama Ali ibn Fuguma Thani: 13.
Asiyana ibn Marghi: 21.
Auno: 64.
Alali: 13.
Alfa: 31.
Abdul Jalil ibn Bi: 14, 15, 16, 35, 57, 58, 66.
Al Ala'u: 125.
Abdul Jalil: 2, 7, 8, 9, 10, 12, 14, 24, 25, 26, 27, 28, 29, 30, 31, 33, 34, 36, 38, 39, 43, 44, 45, 48, 50, 52, 65, 66, 71, 73, 77, 79, 92, 93, 96, 97, 115, 116, 117, 119.

Babaliya: 118.
Bagarmi: 40.
Bahr al Hasis: 47.
Balagi: 32, 70.
Bani Saif: 123, 124, 125.
Baramusa: 3.
Barbars: 89, 97.
Bari: 12, 34, 46, 49, 53, 68, 104, 113, 117, 122.
Bâri: 43, 44.
Bedu: 94.
Beduwin: 116.
Beni Hashim: 3, 4.
Bi: 29, 34, 36.
Birki, Hajj: 12.
Birni: 12, 54, 99, 101, 112, 114, 115.
Biri ibn Dunama: 31.
Biri ibn Sikama: 32.
Bugoma Ahmad ibn Bint Jaldi: 97.
Bornu: 2, 6, 7, 8, 9, 10, 12, 13, 14, 15, 27, 31, 32, 34, 35, 40, 43, 46, 66, 67, 68, 76, 94, 99, 103, 113, 114, 118, 119.
Bulala: 5, 7, 8, 9, 14, 15, 16, 17, 18, 19, 20, 21, 22, 24, 26, 27, 28, 30, 32, 38, 40, 41, 42, 45, 47, 50, 51, 52, 72, 75, 77, 79, 81, 82, 86, 119, 120, 121.
Bulugi: 10, 34, 35, 48, 55, 99, 104, 113, 122.
Bulma: 113.
Burkumwa: 117.
Burum: 14.
Bursalim: 122.
Butti: 48.

Chad: 55, 103.
Chiroma Abdul Jalil: 58.
Chiroma Abdullahi ibn Shatima: 86.
Chiroma Burdima: 121.
Chiroma Biri: 8, 37, 42, 61, 94.

Dabaku: 63.
Dabubu: 53, 69.

Name Index—continued.

Dagalu: 43, 64, 65, 66.
Dagimsil: 117.
Dalatu: 118.
Dalatu N'gizimma: 37, 40, 41, 42, 97.
Dalatu Turga: 44.
Dalli: 58, 64, 78.
Dalikna: 103, 104.
Dalmi: 64.
Daud ibn Nikale: 2, 4, 5, 124, 125.
Dawe: 3.
Diawa: 33.
Dilara: 68.
Dilaram: 117, 122.
Digala: 14.
Didi: 107, 122.
Dili, Hajj ibn: 17.
Diru: 36.
Dirkuma Fatar ibn Ghambu: 122.
Dthu al Hijja: 93.
Dthu 'l' Kacda: 16, 85.
Dunama Ali ibn Gabiya: 22.
Dunama ibn Dabale: 77, 78, 124, 125.
Dunama ibn Muhammad: 7, 8, 10.
Dunama ibn Salma: 55.

Fakara: 101, 103, 105.
Farkuma Mohammed ibn Bint Fatima: 21, 57, 70, 94.
Farkama Muhammad ibn Abdul Lahi: 96.
Farkama (Sultans): 47.
Fatuhu Sham: 4.
Faya: 39, 85, 86, 91, 95.
Fezzan: 113
Fifisi: 28, 29.
Fisla: 32.
Fiyu: 103.
Foga: 64.
Fukulima 'Othman ibn Daud: 92.
Fukuma Ali ibn Garu: 54.
Fukabu of Dilikni: 22.
Fuski ibn Kilili: 16.
Furtu: 13, 14, 113.

Galjadu: 13.
Gamira: 70, 98, 99.
Gamtilo: 36, 40.
Ganjaya: 72, 73.
Garku: 71, 73, 74, 81, 86, 87, 94.
Garkuwa: 85.

Garni Kiyala: 5, 35, 55, 56, 60, 61, 62, 63.
Gambaru: 12, 48, 53, 68, 99, 100, 103, 114, 117, 122.
Gasiku: 29, 30.
Gatiga: 9, 12, 35, 55, 68, 69, 99.
Gate of the Chosen: 122.
Gatawa: 122.
Gacuma: 43.
Gayawa: 13, 49, 68, 117, 122.
Ghalib: 3, 4.
Gbeghir: 114.
Ghawali: 117.
Gheghir: 114.
Ghazbi: 113.
Ghiskiru: 114.
Ghuwi Kafokwa: 113.
Gumani: 70.
Gimara: 42.
Guarded Tablets: 113, 124, 125.
Gurfala: 38.
Guguti: 34, 40, 55, 70.
Gumami: 14.
Gumsu: 36, 40.

Hadiths: 47, 125.
Hajj Umar: 85, 86, 91, 95.
Hajj Yusuf: 122.
Hano, Chief: 39.
Hijaz: 3.
Hijlij: 58.
Himyar: 2, 3, 4, 123, 125.
Hiruma Aigha: 61.
Hiruma Yagha: 37, 55.

ibn Ahmad: 2.
ibn Arsu: 2.
ibn Bikuru: 2.
ibn Biri: 2.
ibn Bubu: 2.
ibn Dthi Yazan: 2, 4, 5, 123.
ibn Duku: 2.
ibn Dunama: 2, 5.
ibn Faris: 124, 125.
ibn Fune: 2.
ibn Huwa: 2.
ibn Ibrahim: 2.
ibn Idris: 2, 7.
ibn Katuri: 2.
ibn Nikale: 2.
ibn Othman: 2.
ibn Rike: 2.

Name Index—continued.

ibn Rusku: 5.
ibn Salma: 2, 5, 11.
ibn Wayama: 2.
ibn Saif: 2, 3, 4.
ibn Sofia: 32, 39, 45, 52, 69.
'Id al Azha: 93.
'Id al-Saghir: 27, 38, 69.
Ifrikiya: 3, 4, 58.
Ikli: 13.
Ikima: 27, 38, 76, 78.
Ikrima: 49, 54, 101.
Ililiwa: 95.
Imam al Kabir Ahmad: 86.
Imam al Saghir: 32, 39.
Irak: 4.
Israel-Children of: 124, 125.
Itnawa: 66, 69, 70, 93, 99.

Jerma ibn Ammat Allah: 71.
Jihad: 1, 105.
Jitku: 48, 49.
Jugulgul: 6.
Jumad al Akhira: 115.
Jumada 'l' ula: 101, 103.
Junoma Muhammad al Saghir: 42.

Kabuwa: 53.
Kadai: 7, 8, 10.
Kagusti: 33, 35, 118.
Kajalma Abdullahi ibn Hawa: 15.
Kaloma Dunama: 35.
Kananiyya: 101, 102, 105, 106, 107, 111, 112, 114.
Kasuda: 14, 70, 104, 117.
Kasimwa: 12.
Kawar: 113.
Kali: 10.
Kawal: 37, 38, 93.
Kanem: 2, 3, 5, 6, 7, 8, 9, 10, 11, 12, 14, 18, 20, 22, 27, 32, 34, 35, 43, 47, 48, 50, 54, 55, 58, 64, 66, 68, 69, 76, 77, 79, 80, 92, 101, 102, 109, 111, 112, 114, 117, 118, 124, 125.
Kamus: 125.
Kaigama Bukr: 37, 42, 49, 97.
Karga Simsim: 43.
Kara: 48.
Kayi: 16.
Kakara: 103.
Kari Kuruku: 104.
Kargha: 103.
Katagarmabe: 55.

Kawaka: 93.
Kamisino: 56.
Kasharda: 80, 99.
Kachella 'Ali: 94, 97.
Kalu: 94.
Kaisira: 80.
Kakama Bamu: 110.
Kagutima Doniyo: 8.
Kaighama ibn' Abdul Lahi: 45.
Kuraish: 2, 4, 123, 125.
Kileti (Koyam) 86.
Kiriwa: 98.
Kikari: 53.
Kitaki: 44.
Kitati: 35.
Kiyayaka: 79, 80, 81, 82, 84, 85, 86, 87, 88, 91, 92, 93, 94, 116.
Kirsila: 18, 19, 119.
Kintak: 104, 108.
Katab al Afrad: 124, 125.
Koyam: 28, 65, 83, 86, 89, 97, 121.
Kori Dunama: 93.
Kuka: 32, 97.
Kuri Karamnu: 104.
Kurkuriwa: 79.
Kura'an: 115, 119, 124.
Kulu: 76, 80, 85.
Kulluma Dunama ibn Bi: 57.
Kulaima Muhammed ibn Kina: 20.
Kufra: 4.
Kuru: 14.

Laba: 56.
Labudu: 104.
Lada: 7, 49, 117.
Lake Chad: 103.
Lafia, Hajj: 12.
Limam ibn Aiyesha: 24.
Limara: 68.
Listiri: 86, 87, 88.
Lot: 11.
Luwai: 3, 4.
Luwai-Ghalib: 123, 125.

Madama: 5.
Madawa: 104.
Madagam: 33.
Madima: 37.
Makatilun: 125.
Majid ul Din: 125.
Mai Duguma Abdullahi: 92
Maath ibn Jabal: 47.

Name Index—continued.

Mandu: 44.
Mardali: 113.
Malfifi: 113.
Malagalma Abdul Lahi: 42.
Malagalma: 118.
Matarama ibn Salma: 99.
Masamma Ali: 99.
Makaran: 79.
Malahe: 14, 99, 117.
Ma'o: 15, 16, 18, 44, 70, 98, 99, 119.
Maidalla Muhammed ibn Fatima: 15, 44, 45, 46.
Manmana: 20.
Malima: 29, 30, 36.
Mai (city): 107.
Malfe: 97.
Milti: 117, 122.
Midday Halt: 29, 30.
Milmila: 89, 93.
Mih: 93.
Mitrama Liyatu: 42.
Mu'alim Hajji: 39.
Munba: 125.
Mune: 123, 124, 125.
Muhammad ibn Abdullahi: 99, 115, 117, 118, 119, 120.
Muli Ghim: 14, 99.
Muli Fuli: 99.
Muhammad ibn Aiyesha: 39.
Muhammad ibn Barsala: 86.
Muhammad ibn Shattima: 95.
Musgid: 32.
Milu: 49, 117, 122.
Majd al Din al Firuzabadi: 125.

N'gafata: 9.
N'gala: 33, 66.
N'gibiwa-Kanjewa: 14.
Nile: 3.
Northern Force: 107.

Rajab (month): 13.
Rajil: 105.
Ramadan: 19, 29.
Rawajil: 105.
Rimbawa: 14.
Rif: 3.
Ririkmi: 35, 70, 107, 108.
Risalah: 47.
Rubku: 49, 53.
Ruru: 14, 55, 67, 70, 99, 104, 106, 108, 112, 114, 117, 122.
Ruwaya: 53, 122.

Safar: 99.
Saghi: 38.
Sana'a: 2.
Saif ibn Dthi Yazan: 123.
Sakina: 124, 125.
Sandu: 26.
Saul (King): 124.
Shattima ibn Tasala: 22.
Shaaban: 13, 19.
Shari'a: 11, 47.
Sheikhs: 3.
Shitati: 45.
Shawwal: 27, 69, 117.
Shami: 27, 28, 29, 36, 37, 44.
Siki: 70, 106, 120.
Siki Dananma: 33.
Siru: 67, 118.
Sintalma Kadai: 97.
Sima: 2, 5, 6, 24, 29, 30, 36, 37, 38, 39, 42, 70, 92, 94, 95, 97, 98.
Siyakama Saka: 21.
Sodom: 111.
Sugurti: 34, 49, 55, 70, 99.
Sunna: 11, 125.
Sulu: 14, 33, 49, 99, 101, 103.
Sunuma ibn Dalma: 22.
Sultan Ibrahim: 2.
Satum: 42.
Sakala: 13.
Stambal: 124.

Tal: 9, 10.
Talut: 125.
Tatala: 9.
Talba al Hazy Kadai ibn Jilbu: 95.
Tatalu: 80.
Tatanu: 66, 67.
Tinu: 95.
Tobol (drum): 13.
Tubu: 38, 40, 43, 59, 60, 61, 77, 78, 80, 92, 93, 94, 95, 96, 124, 125.
Tusa: 20, 21.
Tusa (or Gamira): 119.
Tumagira: 40.
Turkey: 124.
Tuwama ibn Gafkaru: 93.

Wasami: 18, 35, 56, 70.
Wagam: 70.
Walamma: 6.

Wazir Bikoru: 52.
Wazir Idris Harun: 14, 15, 18, 21, 25, 26, 28, 43, 48, 52, 57, 59, 72, 73, 87, 93, 106, 107, 115, 121.
Wunoma Muhammad al Saghir ibn Tuguma: 78.
Wurni: 104.

Yaki: 79.
Yaman: 2, 3, 4, 42.
Yaremi: 49.
Yarima: 34, 57, 107.
Yarima 'Abdullahi ibn Mani: 95.
Yarima 'Ali: 97.
Yarima Idris: 107.

Yarima Muhammad ibn 'Othman: 97.
Yedi: 63, 66.
Yerima Ali ibn Ghuwa: 45.
Yikima: 45.
Yira: 45.
Yisimi: 39.
Yisambu: 35, 56, 62, 66, 78.
Yitukurma: 14, 16, 33, 34, 42.
Yuroma ibn Ahmad: 42.
Yuroma Nasr: 22, 24.
Yuroma Yadagha: 94.
Yuroma Yagha: 36, 42, 57.

Zantam: 12, 69, 114, 117.

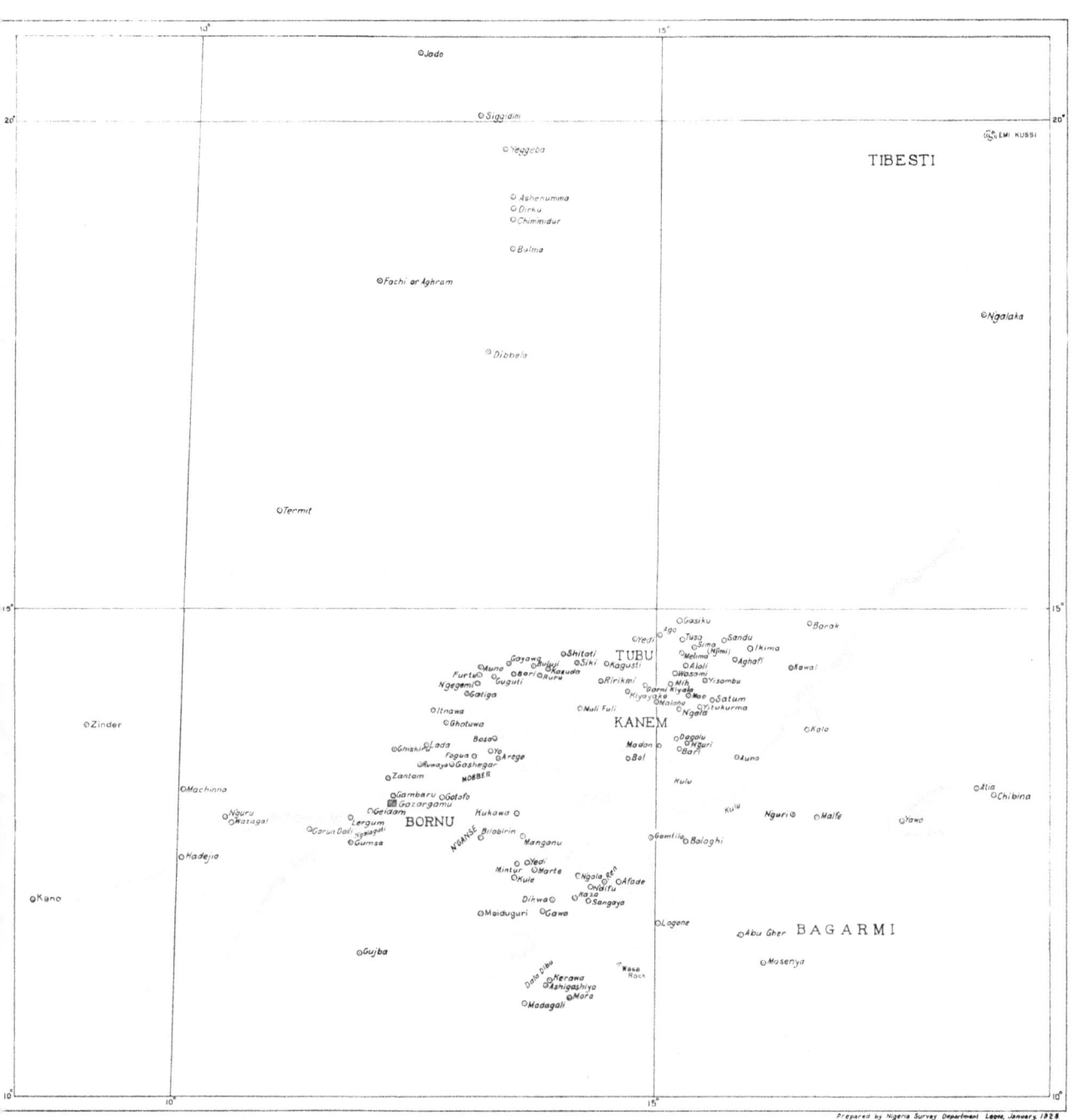

SUDANESE MEMOIRS

VOLUME TWO

Ruins of N'gazargamu (sacked 1808), the old capital of Bornu near modern Geidam.

INTRODUCTION TO TRANSLATIONS OF ARABIC MANUSCRIPTS.

In the subjoined extracts from manucripts local and otherwise relating to the Sudan, especially Nigeria and surrounding countries it is recognised that there is much which is contradictory, much which is inexact; nevertheless these extracts read together, present a picture of the Sudan in past ages, of which the general outline is sufficiently clear to give considerable help both to ethnologists and those who may in future concern themselves with a detailed study of the various peoples and regions mentioned in them.

Whether or no Northern Africa or the Sahara was the original cradle of the human races and early civilization is a question about which hypothesis may supersede hypothesis and the gospel of today may become the heresy of tomorrow. Culturally, however, the Sudan and Sahara have as far back as records, traditions, or legends go, taken their torch from the east and passed it on to the west. This is a fact which is not open to doubt except on the supposition that innumerable peoples now inhabiting half the continent of Africa have, independently of each other, either forgotten or falsified their own traditions and legends and invented others of a significance diametrically opposed to their authentic traditions.

That Egypt, the lower part of the Nile Valley, was from the very earliest times affected both culturally and in ethnic composition by tribes having a greater or less degree of negro blood in them is doubtless historically true, but the fact does not prove that such cultures originated in the negro races themselves.

Naturally, cultures which may have been assimilated by negro tribes are difficult to differentiate from hypothetically indigenous negro cultures, but it seems reasonable to suppose that where an apparently Sudanic negro culture can be equated or compared to one which preceded it in date and from which, according to legend and tradition, it drew its inspiration, there is every reason to respect the legend and tradition.

"This point of view is obviously opposed to that of students who are apt to use the present culture of a community as a means of gauging its place in the scheme of civilization. They tend to ignore tradition, which is a trustworthy witness of the past.

"Any close student of ethnology knows that the theoretical side of the study has made little progress, and this is due in great measure, to the contempt shown by so many students for native tradition.

"The claim on the part of a community of low culture to have been descended from a royal family is marked down as nonsense whereas, it may be, and probably is, true." (W. J. Perry "Children of the Sun" page 129).

It would seem from the earliest historical time that the struggle for existence has been more intense in the uplands of Asia than has ever been the case in Africa, with its climate on the whole inimical to the human race save in the extreme northern and southern portions. Similarly in Asia itself in general, the more virile and fiercer peoples have continuously pressed the less virile races down towards the tropic belt which extends from Southern Arabia to Southern India.

There is therefore no reason to doubt the tradition that at a period which may be placed between 5000—2000 B.C., Asiatic nomad races, called Kushite, were driven first to the south of Arabia, and then across the straits of Bab-el-Mandeb into Africa.

These races appear in the Egyptian records as the inhabitants of Punt in the horn of Africa, and as the " vile Kush " and " dwellers on the sand " in Upper Egypt, and the Egyptian Sudan. They inhabited the Eastern Sudan and Upper Nile Valley as early as 2000 B.C., and must have spread from there into the Sahara, Darfur and Kanem. They were cattle-owning races similar to the Garamantes of Fezzan of whom an early Christian Father wrote " regibus Garamanticis tauri placuerunt."

In the various manuscripts here translated, these early Kushite pastoral peoples are, it is thought, represented by the races called in general by the Kanuri " Fellata " or " Bade " (Bedawin), who are supposed to have inhabited the Fitri region and Kanem at an early epoch, and to have accompanied the Barbar Yamanites (Magumi) in their conquests west of Lake Chad. These " Fellata " tribes have now become negroid and are known as N'gizim, Bade, N'gazar, N'galaga, etc., but, in origin, they were probably akin to the " Ahel Gara " or Teda Gura'an, the Garamantes of Herodotus.

The traditional home of origin of most of them is " Yam " a rather vague term generally meaning either Borku or the country west of the Nile Valley, which, after the Muslim era, became confused with the better known Yaman, *i.e.* Arabia Felix.

The words Yaman and Yamanites are, however, in these manuscripts, more strictly used to denote the newer Hamite Barbar races who though settled in North Africa and Libya from, at any rate, 1400 B.C. or so, and in the Sudan before that era, were dominant in the Upper Nile Valley during the 500 years before and after the opening of the Christian era, and moved into the Central Sahara and Sudan when they were dispersed from the Nile Valley about 500-600 A.D.

To these latter races belonged the Tuwareg Barbars in general, and particularly the peoples called by Ibn Khaldun " Sanhaja of the second race," Kitama, and Zaghawa (Beli).

The Zaghawa inhabited the regions which are now called Kordofan, Darfur and Borku (Wadai), and it was from them that the so-called Yamanite, or Magumi, rulers of Kanem came.

Thus nearly all the ruling stocks of the Chad region claim to be Yamanites, *i.e.* Barbars, though it is probable that in many instances their Hamite blood is derived rather from the early Kushite (Gara) than from the later Barbars (Zaghawa.)

It is however much easier to feel assured that the Kushite and Barbar Hamitic influences in the Sahara and Sudan were distinct in their origin and characteristics than precisely to state all the differences between the two. Though the one in general long preceded the other over most of the Sahara and Sudan, yet the newer or Barbar immigration so completely absorbed the older strain in many instances, that it is difficult to distinguish what belongs to the one and what to the other.

We seem to see indeed quite clearly that the Saharan races whom the Romans called Gaetules, the Garawan, Garamantes of Fezzan, the modern Tubu or Teda. and the Nobatae of the Nile Valley, belonged to the more ancient or Kushite stocks, and that their supposed Persian origin, as stated even in Roman times, as well as by the present day Fulbe (Fulani) to account for their origin, really refers not to the Persians of history but to their predecessors the Elamites and other peoples who inhabited Southern Asia.

But beyond occasional classical references to these peoples, the earliest Ethiopians of classical antiquity, we have little detailed literary evidence about them. On the other hand, from Egyptian times onwards, through the period of Arab ascendancy, we have many references and some ethnographic data concerning firstly the Libyan Barbars of Northern Africa and secondly their cousins the Tehennu or Tamahu of the Nile Valley, who are indistinguishable from the races to whom in Bornu and the central Sudan, the term Yamanites is given.

Speaking broadly, "tracing descent from the king of Baghdad" means a Kushite origin, or refers to tribes originally Kushite who had become servile (imghad) to the conquering Yamanites (Barbars).

Conversely, using modern phraseology, Yamanite means races akin to the modern Tuwareg, or, as they are called in Bornu, Kindin.

The manuscripts, as is natural, deal mainly with the so-called Yamanites, *i.e.* offshoots of the Zaghawa Barbars who had come to Kanem about 800 A.D. from the north and the east; the Kushite races (Gara) being regarded as inferior. It is also quite clear from other manuscripts that to a Kanuri of the 16th century the distinction between Ahel Gara (Kushites) and Ahel Dirki (Tuwareg or Zaghawa) was quite well recognised.

In the present state of our knowledge, therefore, it will be best to let the manuscripts speak for themselves as regards the Kushite stocks, though we may perhaps preface them by a few extracts from Arab works of standing which show that the local Sudanese traditions are not the mere random inventions which are sometimes supposed.

As an instance of tradition surviving in the letter and forgotten in fact and meaning, we have the reference in "The wanderings of the Saifawa" to a sojourn with Abd ul Wahid.

The identity of Abd ul Wahid in question might be a matter of unsolvable conjecture, did we not know from other sources that the Kanem dynasty owed a great deal to the Hafsides of Tunis.

Abdu'l Fida gives the following account of the Hafside dynasty, as printed in Hamaker "Specimen Catalogi" (Leyden 1820). "The first of the dynasty was Abu Hafs Umr ibn Yahya Hanbani of the Masmuda Barbars. He was a companion of Abu

Abdallah Muhammad ibn Tumart. The son of Abu Hafs, named Abdul Wahid, became Governor of Africa in the name of the sons of Abdul Mumin (the Almohads), in the year A.D. 1206-7, and died at the end of the month Dthul Hijja A.D. 1221-22.

"He was succeeded for a time by Abd ul Ala, one of the sons of Abdul Mumin, but on his death, Africa again came under the rule of the Hafsides.

"Abdallah, the son of Abdul Wahid, became ruler in the year A.D. 1226 and made one of his brothers, Abu Zakaria Yahya, local Governor at Fessae, and another brother, Abu Ibrahim Ishak, ruler over the date-producing country called Al Jerid. The people of Fessae, however, drove out Abdallah and made his brother Abu Zakaria their ruler in 1227-8 A.D. The latter occupied Tlemsen, ruled over the Jerid and Al Zab, and died in 1249-50 A.D. leaving four sons, Abu Abdallah Muhammad, Abu Ishak Ibrahim, Abu Hafs Umr, and Abu Bukr, called Abu Yahya, as well as two brothers called Abu Ibrahim Ishak and Muhammad al Lahyan, sons of Abdul Wahid ibn Abu Hafs.

"There succeeded to Abdul Zakaria, his son Abu Abdallah Muhammad. This prince took the title of El Mustanser Billah. Amir ul Muminin.

"In the year 1269-70 he defeated the King of the Franks who had invaded Africa, and wiped out his army. Abdallah's brother, Abu Ishak Ibrahim had, in the meantime, seized the power at Tlemsen and, on the death of El Mustanser, he, in 1276, succeeded him."

As it is well known that these Hafside rulers were in alliance with the rulers of Kanem, the conquests of Dunama Dabalemi (1221-1259) no doubt were, in some measure, due to their support and the prestige that this Mai acquired from being in alliance with them.

It would appear further that up to the period of the civil war this friendship and alliance were maintained, so that the historian, Makrisi (circa 1400 A.D.) was in a position to give in his account of Kanem full details about the ruling family in Kanem down to the year 1397, when Mai Umr Idrisimi finally left N'jimi, the capital.

Relations however between the Saifawa in Kanem and the Barbars of North Africa continued even after the outbreak of the civil war.

A letter dated 10th of Sha'aban 843, that is to say, February 1440, is extant in a translation given by M. Martin in his book "Les Oasis Sahariennes," page 122. This letter is from the Mai of Bornu to the Murabutin of Tuwat. It would appear from it as if some of the Saifawa were eager for support from the Tuwat Oasis.

The letter is as follows:—

"May God aid him. The Sultan Kadai*, son of Jamshish†.

---

* Kadai, a title given to a king who was the eldest son of his father.
† Jamshish is a local word from Arabic "Jamus" a buffalo, and means a "bull," which, like "lion" or "elephant" is, in the Sudan, an honorific term.

May God give him victory. Praise be to God, He alone. May God bless our Lord Muhammad and his family.

"From the exalted and respected Sultan, our master and lord Kadai, the son of our lord and master Jamshish, may God give him victory: to the Murabutin who are descended from Sheikh El Mukhtar and from Sidi 'Amr El Sheikh and to all their brothers and the Darmaksha who live at Tuwat.

"Peace be upon you all. After salutations, we are greatly surprised. Why have you abandoned the custom of your fathers? Why have you ceased to send to our country? Since the treaty between you and the Sultan, our lord Saghrir, you have never come back to us. I swear by God I will do you no hurt nor will I allow any one to hurt you. Come then as you were accustomed to come. Anyone who comes from Tuwat with a letter from you will not be asked to pay anything, for the country is yours as it was your father's. Salutations. Written on the 10th of Sha'aban 843 A.H. (February 1440). Signed the most humble servant of his God—*Suleiman*."

The Kadai who is here mentioned would appear to have been the Kadai who murdered Mai Ibrahim, son of Othman, after the latter had reigned eight years, and himself became Mai about 1450.

During these troublous times, there were often several rival princes who claimed to be Mais and, it is probable, therefore, that Kadai claimed to be ruler sometime before he actually was acknowledged as such or is so shown in the list of Mais.

The Sultan called Saghrir, mentioned in this letter, is an uncertain personality. Probably "little" is the Saghrir, *i.e.* Arabic rendering of the Kanuri word Gaji or Gana, "the little."

One of the immediate predecessors of Kadai was Othman the son of Idris Nigalemi, more usually called Biri, who reigned from 1400-1432. Sultan Othman (Biri) ruled for thirty-three years and probably was the only Mai, at this period, who had the time or opportunity to make an external alliance of this nature.

The Darmaksha who lived at Tuwat are probably the same as the Aulad Daghamsha who had been driven from Kairuan by the Hafsides and settled in the region of Tuwat. Daghamshe is a common woman's name in Kanem.

Concerning the Mais of Kanem during the two centuries preceding the civil war, Makrisi's notice which is almost contemporaneous, that is to say, written about 1400 A.D., is very valuable. He wrote as follows:—

"All the Sudanese derive their origin from Fut the son of Ham. Their tribes number nineteen. Among these are the Zinj who live near the Indian Ocean and inhabit the city called Massowa. They follow the religion of the Majians, and it was they who raised a rebellion under a false prophet (Ali, the son of Muhammad) at Basra, in the time of the Caliph Al Mutamid. Near to them are the Barbars among whom Islam has spread. In their country is the city of Makdishu on the shores of the Indian Ocean. To the south and west of them lie the Damdam, men who go forth with their feet and bodies naked and who, at the same epoch as the Tatars invaded Iraq, made incursions to Nubia and Abyssinia and ravaged the country, after which they went home. The Abyssinians whose country adjoins theirs are most numerous of all the Sudanese and are close to Yaman, living on the coast of the Arabian sea, and professing the Christian religion.

"To the north of the Zinj and Abyssinians live the Beja who are partly Christians and partly Muhammadans and who own the island of Suwakin. Near to them are the Aramaean Nubians who live in the city of Dongola to the west of the Nile. Among these, the majority follow the Christian Faith. Beyond them are the Dagála who are Moslems and among whom are counted the Taju. Beyond their country is Kanem the inhabitants of which are a great people. Islam is predominant among them and their capital is called N'jimi. The first of their kings who became a Moslem was Muhammad (*i.e.* Dunama Dabalemi) son of Jil, son of Abdu'l Lahi, son of Othman, son of Muhammad, son of Ume. They claim that their king is descended from Saif ibn Dthi Yazan and that, between the time of Saif and that of their king, there reigned forty kings. The king of Kanem is a Bedawi in mode of life. When he sits on his throne the people of his kingdom prostrate themselves to him and fall on their faces. The army numbers a hundred thousand including horse and foot and transport.

"Between N'jimi and Talamlam are many tribes of unbelievers. The king of N'jimi (that is to say, the king of Kanem), rules over five lesser kingdoms. Their horses are small in size.

"Kanem is their great kingdom and the blessed Nile passes through it for a considerable distance.

"Between N'jimi and the first of the kings of Tajowin is a distance of ten marches. The peoples of these regions are naked. Among them are the Ikli who have a powerful and just king: then the Afunu whose king is called Mastur and who is very jealous about his dignity.

"After them there is another kingdom which is called Mambu and beyond it a people called Kanguma; then the Kangu, then the Abagarn; then a people greater than these, whose country is called Yedi, and whose king has the title of Rabuma. There follows this another great king who is called Haudamiyu and people who are called N'gazar. These people are numerous and possess oxen and sheep; in their country are elephants. There are also the tribes of Shadi (Chad) and the Mabani and Abahama; then the tribes Atagana and Yafalam and Magari. These are all naked and deride people who wear clothes.

"The Mabani are a big tribe and the greater portion of them are called N'galaga. In their country are great trees and lakes from the overflow of the Nile.

"The king of Kanem made an expedition from N'jimi against these people in the year 650 A.H. (that is to say 1252-3 A.D.), and killed or captured many of the inhabitants. West of these peoples are many tribes extending to Kaukau and the land of the Adarma. And there lies to the west also Dafumu where are mosques of the Moslems. The Sultan of the country is just.

"There are also the people called Abkala (Abogelite) who

are counted among the unbelievers and who are camel-men and clothed in skins. The tribe called Tukama live on the borders of the country of the Taju and grow dates and drink of the water of the Nile. The Taju are a section of the Zaghawa who use stones and slings as missiles and fight against the people of Wathiku.

"Their country is ten marches east of the mountain whence the Nile flows onwards to Egypt. West of the mountain is the land of the veiled Barbars, extending for forty marches along the borders of the Nile to the city of Tadamakkat and from it to Kaukau which is ten marches, and from Kaukau to Ghana, twenty marches.

"Beyond Ghana is the Atlantic Ocean. Behind the Taju is the capital of the Nuba and north of Kanem is the country of Fezzan. Its people are Barbars extending to Zeila which is to the south of Barka. The king of Kanem is the greatest of the kings of the Sudan. West of Kanem lies Kaukau and then Bagana and Tacrur and Mali and Tamim and Janne and N'gazar. These countries extend to the Atlantic Ocean in the region of Ghana in the west.

"Kanem is the centre of power and its people are called Zaghawin. It is bounded on the south by Habash, on the east by Nuba, on the north by the land of Barka, and on the west by Tacrur.

"The king of Kanem, about the year 700 A.H. (1300 A.D.), was Al Hajj Ibrahim, descended from the children of Saif ibn Dthi Yazan. His seat of Government was Kanem, and Kanem is the seat of Government of Bornu.

"There ruled after him his son Al Hajj Idris, then Idris's brother Daud son of Ibrahim, then Umr son of Daud's brother Hajj Idris, then Umr's brother Othman, son of Hajj Idris. Umr ruled a little before A.H. 800 (1397 A.D.). The people of Kanem then revolted and changed their allegiance.

"There remained to these Sultans the Nubas as subjects. They were Moslems waging war on the people of Kanem. Under them were twelve provinces.

"The kings of Ghana also were great kings but they were conquered by the Mulathamin and their dominion grew weak.

"The people called Susu then conquered them; afterwards the people of Mali became powerful and conquered Ghana. We have recounted the history of Mali and its kings in the book Dir Al 'Akud Al Ferid following the work of Mamsha ibn Musa."

Another notice of Kanem contained in Makrisi's work is translated by Quatremère ("Memoirs Sur l'Egypte," vol: ii, page 27), and reads as follows:—

"On the borders of the Nile is the kingdom called Kanem, of which the prince professes the Muhammadan religion. This country is a long way from Mali. The capital is called N'jimi.

"The first seat of this empire on the side which is near to Egypt is called Zeila. Between this town and the town of Kaukau which is on the opposite (western) frontier the distance is three months' march.

"The inhabitants of Kanem cover the head with a veil. The king does not show himself except at the time of the two religious festival, in the morning and after noon; the rest of the year he is not seen and those who talk to him are placed behind a screen.

"The principal food of this people is rice which grows wild in the country. They have also cheese, guinea corn, figs, limes, melons, pumpkins and fresh dates.

"As regards money, they use a kind of cloth which they make and which is called 'Wendy.' Each piece is ten cubits long, but for facility of exchange it is cut up into pieces of a quarter of a cubit or smaller.

"Other substances such as shells of different kinds and pieces of copper or gold are equally used in commerce and their value is estimated in an equivalent amount of cloth.

"In this country the pumpkins are so big that they are used as boats to cross the Nile.

"The kingdom of Kanem which begins between Ifrikia and Barka extends to the south as far as the parallel of Gharb-ul-Ausat.

"The soil is dry, rocky and sterile. The first who introduced Islam into this country was Hady al Othman who claimed to be descended from the Caliph Othman, but after some time the sovereignty passed to the Yazani who are descended from Saif son of Dthi ul Yazan.

"They are of the sect of the Imam Malik. They are particular in enforcing justice and extremely severe as regards religion.

"In the year 640 A.H. (1242 A.D.), they built in the town of Fustat (Cairo), a college for people belonging to the sect of the Imam Malik known as the college of Ibn Rashid. It is in this college that members of this nation reside if they come to Cairo."

The information about Kanem supplied by Makrisi (circa 1400) is confirmed and in some respects increased by ibn Khaldun (1332-1406), who derived his information from Ibn Said who lived earlier (circa 1282 A.D.) and was thus almost a contemporary of Dunama Dabalemi.

Ibn Khaldun on the authority of Ibn Said writes that "they (the Beja) have for neighbours the Nubians who are brethren of the Zinj and Habesh, and have on the west of the Nile a city called Dongola. They are chiefly Christians and border on Egypt, where many of them are sold as slaves.

"Adjoining them are the Zaghawa who are Muhammadans and from whom are sprung the Tajuwa.

"Next comes Al Kanem, a populous kingdom, wherein the true faith is largely disseminated. Its capital city is called N'jimi.

"At one time the people of Kanem held the whole Sahara in subjection, their ascendancy being due to their intimacy with the Sultans of the house of Hafs, when this dynasty flourished in its prime.

"Next to the people of Kanem, on the west, are the people of Kaukau; and after them Baghama and At-Tekrur."

Introduction.

Makrisi and Ibn Khaldun, it will be seen, cover the period 1200-1400.

The chief Arab authorities for these regions previous to the time of Makrisi, are Yakubi, who wrote about 891 A.D., El Bekri 1050 A.D. and Idrisi, who wrote about 1150 A.D.*

An extract from the writings of the first named is given below among the translations. It clearly relates to a time when the Zaghawa were only beginning to penetrate southern Kanem from the north and east.

Idrisi's notices of the Sudan, on the other hand, show that by 1150 A.D. the Zaghawa had become very numerous in the Sudan and, though doubts have been thrown on Idrisi's value as an authority owing to his inaccuracy about distances, the value of his general picture can hardly be disputed, while in matters of detail, it would appear that the extant manuscripts themselves in part, and in part lack of knowledge of the Sudan on the part of editors and translators of his work, are responsible for some misapprehension as to his meaning.

Idrisi under the "third section of his first climate" wrote as follows:—

"The most renowned towns in this section are Kaugha, Kaukau, Tamalma, Zaghawa, Manan, N'jimi, Nuwabia, and Tajuwa.

"Kaugha is situated on the north bank of the Nile, of which its inhabitants drink the water. It is a dependence of Wangara but some of the blacks place it in Kanem.

*   *   *

"From Kaugha to Sama Kanda is ten journeys going east: from Kaugha to Ghana, about a month and a half: from Kaugha to Domcola (Dongola) one month: from Kaugha to Shama less than a month: from Kaugha to the town of Kaukau, *going north*, twenty journeys by camel.

"This road passes through the country of the Baghama (Buram). The Baghama are black Barbars—who speak a Barbar tongue."

Dozy and other scholars seem to suppose that Kaugha means the ancient Kukia, while Kaukau means the later Songhay capital usually written Gao.

The reason of this, doubtless, is the words in italics *i.e.* "going north," whereas, from a study of the text alone, it would appear probable that the reading "fi al-shamal" (in the north) is corrupt and possibly occasioned by the phrase "bi sayir al jamal" (by camel journey) which follows.

No compass direction is given in any of the other cases and it is possible that the words are some marginal note which has crept into the text.

The confusion or uncertainty about names which Idrisi records and admits is between Gao, near Lake Fitri, and Gao on the Niger. The meaning of the Fitri name "Gao" is connected with the Teda-Kanuri word Kagha, which means "south", *i.e.* Idrisi's

---

edition. (Brill Leyder, 1856.)

Kugha or Kaugha is not the equivalent of the place-name Kaukau which represents the ancient Kukia, but of Gao.

The region of the buckle of the Niger is still called the Buram, from the name of the Barbars (Bughama) who lived there even in Idris's day.

Most authorities have assumed that this Kaukau, the ancient Kukia, must have been on the Niger below Gao, but in the descriptions of both El Bekri and Idrisi, there is nothing to point conclusively to such an assumption. So much so that Cooley in his "Negroland of the Arabs," suggested that Kaukau was the same as Karkar or Gargar, which other Arab authors mention in place of Kaukau, and that Kukia (Kaukau) should be placed well to the east of the Niger, between the middle Niger and Air (Asben).

Undoubtedly, in Idrisi's general conception, he was tracing a route from west to east and as Cooley says: "It was a natural consequence of a system which arranged the frontiers of Negroland in an undeviating straight line from west to east, to suppose that a route from Negroland to the desert went northwards."

The exact site of Kaukau (Kukia) is, however, a question which will be easier to solve if we first consider the ethnic factors involved.

The characteristics which differentiated Kukia as early as 600 A.D. from the rest of the western and central Sudan, with the exception of Ghana, was that it was a large commercial base for cross desert traffic.

Its merchants were called Basur-Kayin and these merchants were not Barbars, but North African Semites comparable to the so-called Kano Arab merchants, or the Wasuri of Bornu. They were perhaps originally Syrians or Phoenicians from Surukul or Tur (Tyre), whence the name of "Whitemen" in the Sudan "Tura" or "Turawa."

On the other hand, the ruling element in Kukia was Barbar, in fact the type of Barbar called Zaghawa, the Baghama (Buram) of Idrisi, whose chief in Kanem, according to Yakubi, bore the title "Kâkara"*, a title from which, perhaps, is derived the Fitri title "Ibn Gargar," "son of Gargar." A similar term was apparently in use at the time of Ibn Batuta in the Air region, since he mentions a "Takarkari Sultan" of certain Barbars who are now incorporated in the Ulimmiden, in the region between the Niger and Air. Some manuscripts of Yakubi also read Karkar for Kaukau.

The negro aborigines of Fitri are still called Kuka, and obviously Kuka, Kaukau, Kukawa, Kukia, and Kuka, the name for the baobab tree in Kanuri and Hausa, are all connected.

In Hausa, "Karkara" means inhabited land or tilled settlements, and, in Bornu, the early Mais bore the title "Karkarma," *i.e.* ruler of the "Karkar."

It is conjectured, therefore, that the "Karkara" Sultan was the Sultan of settled peoples, and that Kaukau, Kukawa, or Kukia, referred to the fact that baobab trees were a *sine qua non* of Sudanese towns of that period.

---
*Some MSS. read Kâkur and probably the term is connected with the Kanuri word *kura* 'great' and certain Jukon titles.

Introduction.

The contemporary Barbar races such as the Zaghawa, on the other hand, are called Sama or Shama, and Idrisi's place-name "Sama-Kanda" means some place inhabited by Zaghawa (Sama), ruled over by a Kanda. Kanda was the title of the king in the ancient Kukia, revived later in the title Kanta, borne by the king of Kebbi.

The Kakara then was probably the ruler of a settled area of Shama or Zaghawa Barbars. The title still survives in that of the senior chief in Katsina, Kaura, which is thus seen to be a mere variant of Kanda and Kanta. The Hausa title "Kaura" is to Karkara or Kakara as the Hausa title "Tefida" is to the Tuwareg title "Anastafidet."

The important point is that the ancient Kukia was a negro town occupied by Barbar Zaghawa about 600 A.D. and frequented by Basur-Kayin, i.e. Syrian or Tyrian merchants.

It lay somewhere between the Niger and the Air plateau on one of the big Wâdis (streams) which flow from the west of that plateau towards the Niger, and do, in fact, lose themselves during most of the year in the sand.

If this general hypothesis is accepted, Idrisi's description becomes much more intelligible.

Concerning the position of Kaukau, Idrisi says:—

"Many natives say that this town is situated on the banks of a canal; others say that it is on a river which is an affluent of the Nile; but what is most certain is that before reaching Kaukau, this river follows a long course and then is lost in the sands of the desert, like the Euphrates, which flows through Irak and is lost in the Batâih (Nabataean marsh)."

The reference seems to be to one of the big watercourses from the Sahara which come into the Niger on its left bank between Illo and Say, e.g. the Dendi region where, according to tradition, the Songhay rule originated, and to which the Nigerian Kisara legend traces that hero and his people when they came from the east.

Idris writes: "From Kaukau to Ghana, is a journey of a month and a half:" a statement which if correct, places Kaukau some distance from Gurma and east of the Niger.

He continues: "From the same point (i.e. Kaukau) to Tamalma going east is fourteen days. This village is small and depends on the country of Kawar; it is populous but not walled." In another passage: "The country contiguous to this country Kaukau, on the east, is chiefly Kawar, well known and much frequented."

It is here that the real inaccuracy or underestimation of distance occurs, for Tamalma is clearly in the region of Asben or Damarghu, e.g. Milen, in Asben, or Termit (Tamarmar), near Gamram, which regions, no doubt, at that time were subject to the rulers of Kawar. for it was long before the modern Tuwareg came to Asben and founded a kingdom at Agades. In fact the ruler of Tamalma was possibly in 1150 A.D. the personage who is now called the Sarki of Gobir, and whose ancestors are, by Gobir tradition, said to have come from Bulma in the Kawar Oasis. first to Asben and then to the present Gobir. Similarly the oldest

Daura tradition avers that its earliest Queens were Barbars from the oasis of Kusugu and that they had moved south from Libya and Tripoli.

From Tamalma which was subject to Kawar, the data given with regard to places further east is as follows.

Tamalma to Manan, twelve days: Manan to N'jimi, eight days. N'jimi is said to be on the borders of the Nubian Kingdom and to be three days from the Nile (*i.e.* Bahr ul Ghazal), which lay to the south of it.

Njimi to the town of the Zaghawa, six days: Zaghawa to Manan, eight days.

The town of the Zaghawa is obviously somewhere in Borku *e.g.* N'galaka. N'galaka would in fact be about twelve days from N'jimi which lay about four days north-east of the region of N'guri which in turn is about four days from the eastern shores of Lake Chad.

Manan would therefore seem to have been a name either of " nobles " (Imanan) or of a place in the north of Kanem, perhaps in the region later called Burâk, which might be said to be:—
(*a*) Eight days from N'jimi.
(*b*) Twelve days from Tamalma (Termit).
(*c*) Eight days from N'galaka (Zaghawa.)

This hypothesis concerning Idrisi's meaning renders intelligible a passage which follows these data in Idrisi's work and runs:

"From Zaghawa to Manan is eight days march. It is at Manan that the prince, or chief, of the country resides. Most of his soldiers are naked and armed with bows and arrows. From Manan to Tajuwa is thirteen days march. This is the capital of the Tajowin (Dajo) who are pagans without any religious belief, and whose country borders on Nubia. Another town in this country is Samina (Samia or Samta), which is small. Certain persons who have travelled in Kawar state that the Chief of Balâk, who is a vassal of the king of Nubia (*i.e.* Dongola) attacked Samina, burnt it, captured the inhabitants, and distributed them as slaves in different parts, so that it is now ruined. From Samina to Tajuwa is six days march. From Tajuwa to Nuwabia is eighteen days march."

In this account Samina, no doubt, represents either Samin, a well known ancient site, near Lake Fitri, or the later Shebina in the Wadi Batha, to the east of which was Tajua (Dajo) *i.e.* Southern Wadai.

To the north of this lay the Zaghawa country extending west to N'galaka (Borku). Of these Zagnawa, certain sections had come west and established themselves in Kanem and the Chad region.

They were the Barâk, *i.e.* Barbars, whose chief or Mai (Mek) was subject to the Mek of Dongola in theory.

It is possible, on the other hand, that Manan may denote a Kanembu tribe, *i.e.*, people of Mâni (Amani) the eponymous ancestor of the Kuburi Kanembu.

The name Mâni as an eponymous ancestor of Kanembu tribes has elsewhere been derived from the Merotic Amani, *i.e.* Ammon, but it was also no doubt, in fact, the same as the Tuwareg title for a chief "Amani," plural "Imanan," which is now usually used in the compound "Amanokel" *i.e.* the Amani of the land (akel) or people (kel). The Amani originally was both God and King. A fish idol mentioned by M. Martin was found at Tamentit near Tuwat. The Tuwareg word for a fish is "Aman."

The Manan in Kanem was thus doubtless the residence of the Imanan or rulers of these particular Barbar tribes.

Idrisi in another passage about the sources of the Nile mentions a lake situated in the territory of Kawar which must be meant for Lake Chad.

"The lake is called the lake of Kawar after the name of a negro people who live in the country. From this lake there flows the river of Ghana and that of Habesh. When the Nile (Bahr-ul-Ghazal) leaves the lake (lake Chad) it traverses the country of the Kawarians and that of the Yinu, a negro people who live between Kanem and Nubia." The country of the Yinu is Yam or Yen, *i.e.* Borku and Annadi.

In his "third section of the second climate" Idrisi describes Kawar. After mentioning Kasr Um Isa (*i.e.* Gasbi), he mentions an N'gala forty miles away which is evidently the modern Aghram ar Fashi, even then famous for natron.

From N'gala or Ingal, it is one day to a place called Abzar where there is a lake twelve miles long and three miles broad, and thence to Tamalma is said to be two days journey.

From Ibn Haukal we learn that the trumpeters of the Kandas of Kukia played a tune which represented the words "Zuila Zuila" (*i.e.* Zeila), the capital of Fezzan. The Basur Kayin were the chiefs (Kayi) of the Basur, or Wasuri as these Syrian merchants are called in Bornu.

Kukia must have been on one of the old trade routes from Fezzan to the Niger, which passed either to the west or east of the Asben Oasis, though all that can be said to be demonstrable is that it was in or near the present Ulimmiden country.

From these Basur Kayin came, no doubt, the craftsmen who later were known in the region of Dendi, Borku, and Sokoto (Sagoto) as Zaghoran or Zoghomawa. They were originally Barbars who had learnt crafts from the Basur Kayin.

Similarly, further west, the early Tyrian colonies in the region of southern Morocco had given rise to Turud (now called Toronkawa), *i.e.* peoples of in part Syrian or Phoenician origin, who, fused with the Saharan tribes called Wakore or Sara-kore (Sarakolli), formed the peoples called Fulbe (whites).

The following notes by learned Fulbe of Sokoto supply, in outline, the origin of this race in accordance with their beliefs.

TRANSLATION OF SOKOTO ARABIC DOCUMENT I.

In the name of God the Beneficent and Merciful: and may the peace of God be on the noble Prophet.

"An account of the people of Songhay.

"What we have found from the writings of our learned men is that the origin of the tribes of the people of Songhay is Fulani, for they are from Fatagi, and Fatagi was from the sons of Daito and Daito sprang from the stocks of the Fulani. The country of the Songhay was near to the land of Hausa and was to the west of it, and in the east of the land of Borgu and Melle.

"It is said that the Songhay settled in the district of Gurma and the boundaries of their land were some of the towns of Kabi in the west; for the ancestors of the people of Kabi were the people Songhay: and they possessed the land between Kabi and Melle.

"And their Amir was the Sheikh the Amir Askiya, and one of his sons was Amir of Gurma (his name was Kurbâsi) on the other side of the River Niger. Later, they spread out in the land and settled in the town of Gâo, and Sinder, and Gâiru, and Kirtâshi, and Kanga east of the River Niger.

"This is what we have found written in the books which we have: and according to what we hear, the people of Songhay originated from the land of Melle, and afterwards dispersed and settled near the River Niger to the east and west of it.

TRANSLATION OF SOKOTO ARABIC DOCUMENT II.

"In the name of God the Beneficent and Merciful. May the peace of God be on the noble Prophet.

"Information and evidence in the book Infâq al Maisuri. In the seventh chapter on page nineteen the author says that as to the people of Kabi their distinguishing feature according to their own assertion is that their female ancestor was a woman of Katsina and their male ancestor was a man of the Songhay.

"And he says in the last chapter of the book, that adjoining the land of Songhay on the west was the land of Melle and on the south, Borgu.

"And it is mentioned also in this chapter, after what is said on the second page of the chapter, that the tribes of the Fulani are traced back to four stocks. Daito begat Fatagi and from Fatagi are the tribes of Songhay and others.

"And in the book Tazayîn al Warkât by Sheikh Abdullahi ibn Fodiye (may God have mercy on him) the author says, after describing the return of the army from conquering Alkâlâwa, that they went on an expedition to the banks of the river Niger: he says that Kumbâsi was the name of the chief on the other side of the river in the district of Gurma, and that he was one of the sons of the Amir Askiya al Hajj the Just, Amir of the people of Songhay. And Kirtâsi was the name of one of the districts of the Songhay. All this is related in the explanation of the Arabic poem ' As Sîn '.

"And as to an explanation and meaning of ' Hausa ', there is understood by it a district to the west of Bornu, to the east of the River Niger, to the south of Adar, and to the north of the land of Zak Zak: that is what is meant by the land of Hausa—but it does not include places far from those mentioned.

"An explanation of the word Hausa written with a ح is that it means a species of jinn: and written with a ه

Introduction. 15

means Death and perhaps the people of the tribe were thus named because of their lack of sense, and the multitude of their wrong-doings."

TRANSLATION OF SOKOTO ARABIC DOCUMENT III.

An explanation from the Commander of the Faithful Muhammadu to Mr. Webster.

Your question was: " What is the difference between Sarankuli and Turuzu: are they of one origin or not: what is it that distinguishes them: also, what is the meaning of ' Sar ' and what is the meaning of ' Nkuli '? "

Here is the answer:—

" Sarankuli is the designation of a tribe from Persia who, according to report, arrived at and settled in the lands of the west: that is to say, the lands of Melle, and Banbara and Futâ: this happened long ago: they came from the neighbourhood of the two rivers, the Nile and the Euphrates and settled in this land in the west.

" And as to the tribe Turuzu: the Sudanese blacks of the Sarankuli settled in Banbara, they and certain of the Turuzu. And it is said that the Turuzu sprang from the Jews, or from the Christians, or from the blacks the people of Banbara. The result of this was that the three tribes, the Sarankuli, the Turuzu and the Jews or the Christians settled in the three districts of Melle, Banbara and Fûta.

" This is what we remember: and it is the difference between Turuzu and Sarankuli. Each one of them is in origin a separate tribe: for the Sarankuli are from Persia, and the Turuzu from the Jews or the Christians. This is what we have understood from the book Infâq al Maisuri of the Commander of the Faithful Mohammad Bello (God's peace be on him: may He increase His blessings towards us).

" And the significance of ' Sarankuli ' as one word is as ' Ba'lu Bakka ' and ' Yarda Jardu ', including a town and its Amir."

It will be understood, however, that the origin attributed to the Sarakolli and other Saharan tribes in Persia does not refer to the historical kingdom of Persia but to the peoples of Mesopotamia and Syria, such as the Phoenicians and the Elamites who, according to tradition, spread at a very early epoch from Asia to Africa, and are called Kushites.

It will be observed that in Yakubi's account of the Barbars translated below No. 1 he derives the race from Farik (Ifrikish) son of Baisur, son of Ham, etc.

This name Baisur is, it is suggested, the equivalent of Basur and Wasur, meaning that the races were connected with the Tyrians or Phoenicians of Palestine who came originally from the Persian Gulf. Kayin in Basur Kayin, is equivalent to the Songhay Koyin, sing. Koy (King) and cognate to the Bornu term Beni Kayi, Keyi or Koyi (Koyam), also called Kindin or Kinin, and Imakitan, and the title Kanda or Kanta or Kinta, west of the Niger, or " Kinda " among the Jukons of the Benue region.

The Kayin, Koyin, Kitan, or Kinin (Kindin) are the earliest traceable Barbar ruling caste in the Sudan belt. When they were North Africans or Syrians, they were called Basur or Wasur Koyin.

The Manuscripts translated below are as follows:—
1. Kingdoms of the Barbar and Ifarik. Yakubi 891 A.D.
2. A passage from a native chronicle of Wadai.
3. Bulala Girgam: their well established descent from the Arabs of Yaman as recorded.
4. N'gizam and Bulala.
5. The Bulala secession from the Mais of Kanem.
5a. List of Bulala Mais of Kanem.
5b. Origin of the Bulala Kings of Fitri according to the manuscript of Sarkin Gulfei.
6. The war between the Bulala and Saifawa.
7. The story of the Mai Dunama Dabalemi of N'jimi and his father-in-law the Amir of the Bulala called Mai Bulalama Umr.
8. Sultan Idris and the Bulala.
9. Mai Daud.
10. (Jatku) Yatku and Bulala.
11. Short Bulala Girgam.
12. Bulala (Kayi) Girgam by Mallam Kazalla Darmanmi.
13. The Bulala Wars.
14. Middle Ifrikia.
15. The children of Tubba'ul Awwal.
16. The Kisara Migration.
17. The So.
18. The So Dala N'gumami.
19. Dunama Dabalemi and the Kwana.
20. Kings of the land of Fikka.
21. Book of Blacksmiths.
22. The Bade Tribes.
23. The Bade and N guzum.
24. Garun Doili.
25. Gau Dala Shâliwa.
26. Gujba Girgam.
27. The peoples of Bornu (Gujba manuscript).
28. The legend of the five tribes of Kanem.

Introduction.

29. The story of the seven tribes of Kanem.
30. Translation of a passage from the Tohfut-ul-Albâbi relating to the Sudan.
31. Wanderings of the Saifawa.
32. Mandara Chronicle.
33. The words of Zanua Digeltima Tahir, called Zanua Sidagima, who is ninety-seven years old (1918).
34. The story of N'dif (N'difu).
35. Mai Dugu Bremmi and the connection of the M'bum and Gwana with the Kanuri.
36. Mai Dugu Bremmi and the M'bum.
37. Bagarmi Chronicle.
38. Babaliya Girgam.
39. The story of Masbarma and Mai Muhammad Hajimi.
40. Masfarma.
41. The story of Mai Tsilim Hawami.
42. The story of the coming of Sultan Kwana to fight at N'gazargamu in the time of Sultan Ali Garukurugama.
43. The Zanua of Wukari's Magumi Girgam.
44. The end of the Saifawa dynasty.
45. Mahram of Umme Jilmi circa 1080 A.D.—the introduction of Islam into Bornu.
46. Tura Mahrams.
47. Mahram of the N'galma Duku.
48. Mahram of the Masbarma family.
49. Mahram of Mai Ali Gaji Dunamami, 1471.
50. Mahram of Idris Katagarmabe circa 1504 A.D.
51. Mahram of Mai Ahmad 1793.
52. Old Bornu Towns.
53. The Kayi (Bulala) and Magumi.
54. Girgams of the Kanembu tribes.
55. Translation of Saifawa Girgam in possession of Galadima Kashim Biri.
56. A list of Mais of Bornu down to 1808 A.D. with approximate dates.
57. The Sultanate of Ahir.
58. Chronicle of the Sultanate of Ahir and Notes on the Barbars and Fulani.
59. History of Katsina and Note.
60. The Kano Chronicle.
61. Notes on the History of Daura (Walwyn).

I.—KINGDOMS OF THE BARBAR AND IFARIK.
(YAKUBI 891 A.D.)
Translated from Houtsmar Text (Brill Leyden 1883).

The Barbars and Ifarik are sons of Farik, son of Baisur, son of Ham, son of Noah.

When their brethren (the Egyptians) ruled Masar, they spread from Al Arish to Aswan on the one hand, and from Aiylah to Barka on the other, and passed west.

They took Barka and conquered every tribe in it, and spread west.

Their first king was Luwâta, in the land of Ajdabia among the hills of Barka.

Then the Mazâta ruled in the land of Waddân; they were called after their father. Another section migrated to Tawargha (Turaghen) and ruled there. They are the Hawara.

Others went to Aramik. They were the Badara'a. The section which went to Tripoli was called Mâsâlin, and west of Tripoli were the Wahîla.

Then the path took others to Kairuwan, namely the Balkashana.

Others went north and setted at Tahart, their name being Kitâma an Aji(k)sa.

Others went to Sijilmasa; namely the Nefûsa and Lamaia.

A tribe went to the hills of Hakan. They are called Lamta and also Al Ayâlâb. They live in the desert and have no fixed abode.

A tribe went to Tanjir called Miknâsa, and to Sûs Al Aksa went the Madâsa.

It is said that the Barbars and Ifarik are descended from Barbar, son of 'Aylân, son of Nizar. Others say they are descended from Jithâm and Lakham, and that they lived in Palestine till a king expelled them: that the King of Egypt would not allow them to settle; so that they crossed the Nile and went west and spread abroad.

Others say they came from Yaman, and that a certain king expelled them from Yaman to the furthest west. Every one supports his own theory, but God knows best what is true.

Kingdoms of Habesh and the Sudan.

The sons of Ham, son of Noah, at the time of the division of the sons of Noah, migrated west from the land of Babil, and crosses the Euphrates towards the sunset.

The sons of Kush, son of Ham, separated from the others.

They, the Habesh and Sudanese, crossed the Nile of Masar in two divisions. One division sought Teiman between west and east. They are the Nuba, Beja, Habash and Zenj.

The other division sought the west. They are the Zaghâwa, the Habash, the Gâgô, the Meroîn, the Mirinda (people of Miria), the people of Kaukau, and the people of Ghâna.

Owing to their position on the western bank of the Nile, the

Nuba were neighbours of the Egyptians, who were the sons of Baisur, son of Ham. They conquered Sudan.

Nubia was divided into two kingdoms, one being ruled by a race called Magarra (Makorra), who inhabited both banks, and had their capital at Dongola. They were they who welcomed the Muslims, and paid Bakt. The country is rich in date trees, and vines, and farms. The country extends for about two months travel.

The second kingdom of Nubians is that called 'Alwa which is of greater extent than Makorra; their capital is called Souba, and their land is about three months travel in extent. Here the Nile separates into many branches.

Kingdoms of Beja.

The Beja lived between the Nile and the sea. They have many kingdoms and in each is a separate king. The first from the boundary at Aswan where Moslem rule ends, extends from Teiman between east and west to the boundary of Birkat. They are the people called Ta-Kîsh their capital being Hajara. They have tribes and clans like the Arabs, among them Hadârab, and Hajâab, and 'Ama'ar, and Kûbir, and Manâsa, Rasika, Arbâgba, and Zanafaj. In their country are gold mines and mines of marble and emerald. They salute Moslems, and the Moslems work in the mines in their country.

The second kingdom is that called Bakalîn, where there are many cities. It is of wide extent. In their religion they resemble the Magians and Zoroastrians. They call God, the mighty and exalted, by the name of " Zanjîr the most high ", and call Shaitan " Saha haraka " (pure burning). These Beja pluck out their eyelashes, and the front incisor tooth, and practice circumcision. Rains fall in their country.

The third kingdom is called Bazîn. It borders on 'Alwa in Nubia and also on the Bakalîn of the Beja who are raided and their crops taken by the Bazin. Their food is millet and milk.

The fourth kingdom is called Jarîn, where is a noble chief. His kingdom extends from Badhi'a on the river to the boundary of Birkat in the kingdom of Bakalîn as far as the place called " Leave the fowl." These people extract their front tooth in the upper and lower jaw, as they say they do not want teeth like the teeth of donkeys. They also pull out their eyelashes.

The fifth kingdom is called Kita (Kida), and is the last of the Beja kingdoms. It is a large country and extends from the boundary of the country called Badhi'a to the country called Faikun. They have a boundary hard to cross in difficult thorn country, and they have a field of battle called " Dâr ul Sowâ " where picked youths engage in fight.

The sixth kingdom is that of the Najash, a great and important kingdom, of which the capital is Ka'bar. The Arabs constantly go there to trade, and there are great cities there. On the coast is Dahlak.

All the kings in the land of Habesh are under the King of Kings, and pay him tribute. The Najash professes the Jacobite Christian religion.

The last kingdom of Habesh is the Zenj, who extend to Sind.

As for the people that border on these countries, and extend beyond Zenj, bordering on Sind and Kurk, they are people who are educated and have a civic life.

The Sudanese of the west have divided up the country into many kingdoms.

The first kingdom is that of the Zaghawa who frequent a country called Kanem. Their habitations are merely huts made of corn stalks. They have no kings of cities. Their king is called Kâkara. Among the Zaghawa is a race called Hudin (Fut*), who have a king who is a Zaghawi.

Then there is the kingdom called Malal which is at enmity with the ruler of Kanem. Their king is called Mai Useyi.

Then there is the kingdom of Habesh to which belongs a city called Chibîr†. The king of this city is called Marah.

Gâgô extends to Chibîr but the latter is independent and its king is the king of Chibîr.

Then comes the kingdom of Kaukau, which is the greatest of the kingdoms in the Sudan and most powerful. Every king pays the King of Kaukau tribute.

The name of the capital is Kaukau, and, among the list of the kings who pay tribute and are installed by the King of Kaukau, are the following:—

The kingdom of Marwa (Malle), a large kingdom of which the capital is Janne.

The kingdom of Murduna.
„   „   „ Habir.
„   „   „ Sanhaja.
„   „   „ Tathkarir.
„   „   „ Zayânir.
„   „   „ Arûra
„   „   „ Takârat.

All these are tributary to the kingdom of Kaukau.

Then comes the King of Ghana, a great King. In his territory are mines of gold, and under him a number of kingdoms, among them the kingdom of Augham and the kingdom of Sâma. In all this country there is gold.

Note on the Ancient City of Kaukau.

For many years the exact position of Kaukau, the ancient capital of the Songhay Empire which was founded in the 7th century of our era and preceded the later Songhay capital, Gao, which latter still survives and is on the buckle of the Niger, has been discussed.

---

* *i.e.*, Fit-ri which may be really Fut-ri " place of the Fut, " u " and " i " being almost the same in the Chad Basin.

† *Chibîr.*—This may be either: (1) Chibiri, *i.e.*, Gobir, the Gâgo being Gao in the Upper Niger; or (2) The ' r ' of Chibîr may be a MS error for ' n ' and the place may be Chibîn, *i.e.*, Shebina, near Lake Fitri. In the latter case Gâgo would be Gau in the Fitri Region.

The former explanation is the more probable since one of the capitals of the old kingdom of Kebbi was called Marafa, and Marafa is still one of the most important titles at Sokoto.

Desborough Cooley in his " Negro land of the Arabs " pointed out that the best evidence available shews quite clearly that Kaukau was on a tributary of the Niger which traversed some part of the Sahara.

The traveller Heinrich Barth expressed no definite opinion as to the position of Kaukau, but subsequent writers, particularly French writers, have tended to assume that it was on or very near the Niger somewhere below Gao, while Desplagnes in " Le Plateau Central Nigerien " (Paris Emile Larose 1907) located it in the region of Bentia not far from Sinder.

But assuming, as certainly was the case, that the city rose to fame by reason of the merchants of Barbar, Arab or Jewish extraction who settled there, it is *a priori* probable that it was not situated in parts which were inhabited entirely and densely by negroes, nor in the declivity of the Niger valley which would be unfavourable to camels and other Saharan animal transport.

It must have been on or near one of the principal desert caravan routes, and the fact that the journey from Kaukau to Gao is particularly stated to have lain across deserts occupied by Berdama (Barbars), and that no river route between the two capitals is ever mentioned, seems to point to Kaukau having been located some distance from the Niger valley.

With this is the fact that according to all tradition the Songhay power first arose in the region now called Dendi.

Now most of Dendi was, till recent times, included in the Kingdom of Kebbi, a state which arose at the beginning of the sixteenth century when its local chief revolted from his overlord the Songhay Askia of Gao, and took the title of the ancient kings of Kaukau, Kanda, a title now pronounced "Kanta."

Under these circumstances, it is a fair supposition firstly that the Kantas (Kandas) of Kebbi were in some sense the cultural successors of the Kandas of Kaukau, and secondly that the ancient Kaukau, which lay in the Songhay province of Dendi was situated in the country which later became the state of Kebbi rather than in the riverain portion of Dendi which never came under the authority of the Kantas of Kebbi.

On these premises it seems most probable that the ancient city of Kaukau lay somewhere in or near the district of the present-day Kebbi Emirate called Arewa Yemma, which marches with the district of Beibei now included in the French Territoire du Niger. An enquiry recently addressed to the Emir of Kebbi by the District Officer of Argungu (Mr. P. G. Harris) as to old towns in this region elicited the following reply:—

" *An account of the country called Arewa.*

" Concerning the western part of Arewa (Arewa Yemma) when you asked the Emir of Kebbi, he sent to the district head of Arewa, who found a man called Madu. Madu went to the Alkali and informed him of what he knew: he said, ' A certain man called Mai-Shinkafa of Bwi said that the place called Kaukau was the site of a very ancient city '. There is a well there so ancient that no one knows who made it

Afterwards, in the time of Sarkin Kebbi Sama, a man called Dan Rani went and settled at Kaukau. He saw the old well, but was unable to re-open it. He made a well near to it. He settled there. When he died, Namaiwa lived there, but we do not know all the people who lived there.

"An old town called Ballam was founded by a trader called Uban Gawo. He was the first to live there. In the time of Sarkin Kebbi Toga long ago the trader died at Birnin Ballam. His son Gawo was then made chief and ruled. After his time Fala ruled at Ballam, but migrated to Bwi.

"Kutuluje was also an ancient town. It was founded about 2,000 or 3,000 years ago—and possesses many large Baobab (Kuka) trees. In more recent times the first who settled on this ancient site was Gero. After him came Samma, who then moved to Tago.

"A town called Kotadai is very old, about 4,000 years old. On that site a man called Ra'i Utumana settled and made a well in the time of the Emir of Kebbi, Mainassara. After Rafi's death Nakwargo ruled. On his death the people scattered, and went to a town called Nastira near Beibei. They returned to Kotakai when times were peaceful.

"Damana is another very old town. Older than all the rest except Kaukau. Later, when the capital of Kebbi was at Birnin Kebbi, the Sarkin Fala, called Bunda, settled there, and ruled as chief. After him was Daudu, then Dawaki, then Gabu, then Biga. In the time of the latter the town dispersed before the days of Fari and Nubama and Dauda the man of Zabarma."

The periods of 2,000, 3,000 and 4,000 years mentioned in the above note cannot of course be pressed, but it is at the same time clear that a ruined city called Kaukau which lies north-west of the present Kebbi capital Argungu, and not far from the present town of Beibei is regarded as the oldest city in that part of the country, and as having been founded well over 1,000 years ago.

This "Kufai" (ruin) of Kaukau is actually on a branch of the big wâdi called the Dal ul Mauri, i.e. it is on a wâdi which once was a river, a site which entirely corresponds to the situation of Kaukau as described by El Bekri.

Not long ago, a number of objects (now in the British Museum) which had belonged to one of the Emirs of Kebbi were found at Tumuni, a place which though now in Sokoto Emirate, was before 1805, part of the Kebbi Kingdom.

According to Sir Hercules Read, these objects clearly show North African influence i.e. an influence which must have been responsible for the ancient Kaukau.

It is believed, from the facts recited above, therefore, that the ancient Kaukau was on or near the site now called Kaukau, in the neighbourhood of Beibei to the west of Argungu, and not in the Niger valley as has so often been assumed.

The various legends which connect the people of this Arewa district with Bornu are well known. The Arewa have a universal tradition that they are of the same origin as the old rulers of Kanem commonly called Kanuri; and various stories which present anachronism of various kinds, are current to account for it.

But the simple fact seems to be, as is indeed stated by various other traditions preserved not only in the Arabic works written at Timbuctu, but also in other Arab authorities that the founders of the ancient Kaukau, like the founders of the Kanem Kingdom of the Saifawa, were Zaghawa Barbars called in some mediæval works Bardama, and in others Bardoa.

These were the people who founded Kaukau, and among whom settled the merchant classes from North Africa called in the west Basur Kayin, and in Kanem Wasuri, who first exploited the Sudan and brought it to the notice of the outside world.

The ancient caravan road of which Kaukau was the southern terminus probably lead from Kaukau along the north side of the Gulbin Sokoto, past the modern district of Silame, to the Chibiri region in Gobir, and thence to the Asben Oasis and wells of Asiu—where the caravans divided, some going north-west to Tuwat and Wargla while others went north-east to Ghat and Jerma or Zeila (Murzuk) in Fezzan.

II.—A PASSAGE FROM A NATIVE CHRONICLE OF WADAI.

Know that Wadai is originally part of Ifrikiya, bounded on the north by the great desert: south by the lake of Iru: on the east by the valley of Turja between Wadai and Darfur: while on the west is the lake Shati (Chad).

Its latitude is the distance between these points and the equinoctial line, according to the map fourteen degrees of latitude. In Wadai, the shadow thrown by the sun at mid-day, is about half the length of that thrown at Cairo, since the latitude of Cairo is thirty degrees.

The distance in longitude between Wadai and Mecca is, according to the map, twenty degrees; and the "kibla" of Wadai lies along that line.

The season of a favourable spring is about the time of the heliacal rsing of the star "Nusar".

*The inhabitants of Wadai are in origin a people of Nubia and, in regard to them, the name of each ruling tribe began with "K" as for instance Kaltin and Kindin and Kodok, and other similar names. They are the original stock, but among their subjects are other different peoples, each of these tribes having an "idol" which they worship according to their several customs.

Some take one "idol" others another, disregarding God, They worshipped their Kings, saluting them in a recumbent posture as does he who prays to God.

They also bared their shoulders to them according to the practice in the Hadith of 'Abaya ibn Rufayi' where he says that the Prophet (upon whom be thanksgiving and peace), when he performed the tawâf† first bared one shoulder and pushed the ends of his turban on to his left shoulder, baring the right shoulder; then tied both ends behind leaving both shoulders bare.

The Jababar of Wadai borrowed this observance of the "Sunna" from Mecca and adopted it, and made it obligatory on their slaves and subjects. They also established the custom which As-Samiriyu began of worshipping a calf, therein imitating him. They also made lawful for themselves the goods of their subjects and slaves. They slaughtered and bound and sold and ravished, and the laws of savages and unbelievers became their law.

Even now you may observe the people maintaining these evil practices. They have acquiesced in them till you may see a learned man among us doing evil, thinking it to be right, while he considers the "Sunna" which he has abandoned to be the worst of evil doing.

---

* Mallam Sosal of Wadai states that in origin the Zaghawa and Bideyat (Bele) are one but that those called Zaghawa, who have a Sultan, are those who became town-dwelling, while the Bele have only Sheikhs of each clan and correspond to the Arab Beduîn.

In origin he states the Bele are the same as the Tuwareg (Kindin) though they speak a different language. Kaltin, Kindin, and Kodok are thus all sections of the Bideyat and Zaghawa, the former name Kaltin being probably the same name as the Kalti or Kiletti (Koiyam) of Bornu.

† *i.e.*, Ceremony of walking or running round the holy places of Mecca.

Very we are God's and to Him shall we return.

Such was their condition when the Tunjur came upon them, and conquered them.

The Tunjur—so it said—were of the Beni 'Abâs. Others say they were followers of the Beni 'Abâs, and that the great ancestor of the Wadaians was named Kheir Ullah and nick-named Tunjur because he was a carpenter (najjar), and that he was of non-Arab stock.

When he was at work on his trade, and was asked "What are you doing", he replied "I am a 'Tunjur'"—so he was given the nickname Tunjur, and the name has stuck to his descendants till now.

He was a good upright man, and the people followed him, and he became king in the island of Senaar.

Their kingdom afterwards extended to Darfur and to Wadai. We heard from one of the tribe of Tunjur called Abu Suf that his ancestors who were kings in Wadai were six:—
> one called Al Malik Karâma
> another called Jemal ub Dîn
> another called Durdur
> another called Al-Kâmin

And the Tunjur Sultans who ruled over Wadai were four:—
> The first called Muhammad Tunjur
> His son Yakub al Mu'âkir
> Hamid Abu Wuiba
> Dawurd al Mirîn.

When God was about to take the power from them, he gave them opportunities for wrong doing in the land and as regards their religion, for they were not strict in matters of religion, but mixed up with their faith pagan rites, as has been related above.

In the Tarikh of Othman ibn Fodie (may God be pleased with him) it is said that he who mixes up the practice of Islam and of paganism is a pagan and that he has no claim to the status of a Moslem.

Such was the condition of Wadai when there came among them our Lord, and prince, Abd'ul Karim ibn Jami'u ibn Jaud al Ahmar ibn Ramadan ibn Rakum ibn Hamad Halyus ibn Zain ud Dîn ibn Wadâ'a, *after whom Wadai is called, just as the other name of Wadai, *i.e.* Borku, is derived from the name of one of the clans of the Zaghawa, and their kings before the time of the Tunjur.

Wadâ'a was the son of 'Akir ibn Sanâdi ibn Sofian ibn Muhammad ibn Masmar ibn Sarir ibn Muhammad Kirdama ibn Harkan ibn Abi Dabîs ibn Masbah ibn Sharik Ahmad al Hijâzi ibn Namûs al Yamami ibn Sa'id al Mansur ibn Ahmad al Fadi ibn Abd ul Lahi ibn 'Abâs, the paternal uncle of the Prophet upon whom be peace.

The reason of his coming to Wadai was that his ancestor Sofian left the noble ciity of Mecca and settled on the banks of the Nile in a district of which the inhabitants are now called As-

---

*The Kwalme Arabs similarly derive their origin from one Uwada. Possibly the Arab god "Woda" is responsible for both names.

Sarrariya of the Ja'alin. Sofian settled there and his children were born there. In later days the family of Jami'u the Mukuddam (father of Abd ul Karim) went the pilgrimage, and stayed at Mecca where Abd ul Karim was born.

When he grew up to man's estate, he proved clever, wise and pious; the Sherif of Mecca became afraid for his kingdom and tried to seize him.

So he fled with his son and his brothers Ali and Alwa and A'âmama to Fez; but the news of his being there got known, and the Sherif sent to the Sultan of Morocco to have him caught. So he fled again and came to Wadai.

Or according to another account the family were here before Abd ul Karim. Those who first came were Jami'u and his sons Ali and Alwa. Abd ul Karim was born here. Then when he grew up he was very devout; sought knowledge, went to Bornu in pursuit of learning; and became the pupil of Sheikh Muhammad al Tarmiyu the Bornawi who was killed by the Jabarbara of Bornu of the old dynasty, a crime which caused the loss of their ancient empire.

Abd ul Karim returned from Bornu to Wadai, then went to Mecca the noble, and subsequently came back to Wadai with a large following.

He entered Wadai in the days of the Tunjur Sultan Dawurd al Miriri the Mokaddan, whose capital was at Wâra and Kadam (Ghadam).

The Sultan gave him a good reception, made friends with him, and gave him his daughter 'Ayesha to wife.

She it was who was the mother of the Arabs of Wadai in scattering the Ta'îsha.

'Ayesha stole the goods of her father, his arms and weapons and swords, and gave them to her husband.

The Tunjur were stiff necked, but Abd ul Karim was steadfast in purpose; and the people all came over to his side. He toured over the country and called the people to Islam, and build mosques at Abeshe and at Danbu and Malnik and Madam.

At the time of the 'Id-al- Kabir he built at Wâra a spacious mosque and set people to take charge of it.

When the Sultan of the Tunjur saw that Abd ul Karim was accepted by the people and that they followed him, he was angry and drove him out of Wâra; but his wife 'Ayesha remained there, aiding his cause.

So the people took sides and learned Sheikhs wrote letters.

The first of the kings of the country to follow Abd ul Karim were the king of N'galaka whose name was Tanjak, and the king of the Mimi[*], and the Sheikh of the Muhammid Arabs. These chiefs came to Abd ul Karim's assitance against the Tunjur at Wâra.

As a ruse in the fight Abd ul Karim tied branches of trees on the tails of his camels, and drove them forward so as to create

---

[*] The Mimi are still a tribe of Zaghawa; the people of N'galaka at that time were Zaghawa, but are now Teda Kasherda.

a great cloud of dust, and give the impression that he had a large army.

Towards night the battle grew fierce, and 'Ayesha, who was present, said to her father to frighten him: " O father, save yourself, for here is an army which is too strong for you."

So he mounted his horse called " Son of Al-Kamâri ", and fled to Kadam, which was one of his districts.

It is said that this horse was white with a red mouth and that his dam Al-Kamâri used to pasture near the tomb of the Saint Abu'l Malik, and that there came to her a stallion whence no one knew and was the sire of her first foal—the Sultan Tunjur's horse.

He was of incredible swiftness and it is said that he set off from Kadam and only stopped at Fitri. It is said that the race of Kanem horses called "Arbad Jud Shallâli" (Roan) are descended from this horse.

Then Sidi Abd ul Karim entered Wâra, and the people of this land received him willingly and paid him " Kharaj " as in the early days of Islam the people of Masar and Sham had done to their conquerors. There was no other power but his.

He was the protector of the Moslems and the imposor of the " Kharaj ", which he deposited in their Beit-el-Mal and spent it for the benefit of the Moslems educated and uneducated alike. It is not lawful for a Sultan to give this money to anyone either outright or as a loan, even though it be his deputy. If the Sultan dies, the property is vested in the new Sultan or the Regent. If the Sultan has a son, the son inherits his personal property according to custom, and it is divided among males and females alike.

In Wadai ownership is determined by original occupation or purchase, and inheritance and beneficial enjoyment follow original discovery. He who holds anything as of right, who has either built, or cleared, or improved, has the best right, or failing him, the original possessor.

When the people of Wadai followed our lord Abd ul Karim, he commanded them to be Moslems, and utter the profession of faith twice, observe the times of prayer, give Zakka, fast in Ramadan, and make the pilgrimage. Then he attacked the Tunjur, and besieged them in Kadam for seven years, and finally drove them to Kerna.

After two years more he drove them to Kanem since when they have never returned to fight.

The power of Abd ul Karim was thus established over Kanem and Bagarmi—settled government established, and discord ceased.

Among the hills in the neighbourhood of Wâra was a height called Jebel Thurayya (Pleiades) on the summit of which was a threshing floor. Near this was a rock where the heathen kings of the Tunjur of old used to build a grass house, and made for it seven " Stations " as for instance the station of Thurayya (Pleiades).

When they made a Sultan their chiefs took him up the hill to this place and made him stay in the " Seven stations ", and his followers encamped round him on the hill.

Then they seized the people of the villages at its foot, boys and girls, and sacrificed as many as they thought fit—one each day. They also sacrificed a dark coloured ox, and from the flesh of the ox and that of the children made a pâté from which the Sultan-elect ate, what he left being thrown on the rock.

Then a huge snake came out.

Thus they made food for the Sultan for seven days and they said that any Sultan who did not go through this ceremony would have no real power.

When Abd ul Karim saw this house, he cleared it up and made a town. Then in the rainy season he came there and the people busied themselves with farming.

Now at this time the people of the neighbouring villages were afraid of planting because of the raids of the Tunjur, Abd ul Karim having become their neighbour when waging war on his enemies.

It is said that all the people of Jebel Thurayya came in to him except the Kashmari. Many were the different kinds of worship that house of sacrifice had seen.

Abd ul Karim ruled in this fashion for sixty-six years.

He had a son who came with him from Hijaz, and he had a grandson born here, called Harut or as some wrote it Harut.

When Abd ul Karim (may God have mercy upon him) died, there was a dispute about the succession, and his friend Kalak* Tanjak and his followers called the son who had come with him from Hijaz because he was the elder and put him in the king's palace.

But the people of Wadai made Harut king, because he was their brother, and took him up the rock to the place of pagan worship.

But Kalak Tanjak returned with his people, and turned Harut out of the house and drove him away, and the Wadaians will have nothing to do with his people even now.

But as regards the ancestral custom of making kings on the rock, they have never broken with it altogether, for when Harut's affair was over, Satan suggested to his brother that if he fulfilled the old rites of the rock as practised by the ancient kings, his kingdom would endure.

---

* Kalak Tanjak was a Hadadi (blacksmith) of Zaghawa extraction.

According to Barth, vol. iii, p. 528, the Tunjur founded a large empire which was overwhelmed in less than a hundred years after its foundation. In Darfur Kuru the third predecessor of Sliman, the first Moslem King of Darfur, began the rule of the Furawin.

In Wadai Abd ul Karim, grandson of Woda son of Yame, of the tribe of Ghimr or Gamir, at that time settled in Shendy on the Nile, overthrew the Tunjur in A.H. 1020—A.D. 1611.

III.—BULALA GIRGAM: THEIR WELL ESTABLISHED DESCENT FROM THE ARABS OF YAMAN AS RECORDED.

The first King was Muhammad al Yamani. He came to the Bahr Sau* on his way to the west, and died.

Sultan Salih succeeded, and ruled twelve years and died. Sultan Muhammad al Wan ruled twenty-four years. Sultan Abdul Jalil al Kabir the warrior, who waged many wars ruled Kanem, at Masiu. He fought with Idris Sultan of Bornu, each side prevailing in turn, till Abd ul Jalil heard news of Sultan Ali Dinar, Sultan of Kuka†, who ruled autocratically in his country, and oppressed his people.

When the people of Fitri heard of Abd ul Jalil as ruling in Kanem, they took counsel and sent thirty men to him of the people of Dinni and Gallo and Jîri and Tafalo; and they took corn from Fitri and green grass and fish. The grass was called " Alwa " which is good for horses.

They took all this to Abd ul Jalil who was in Kanem, and they told him about their town and the country and Ali Dinar.

Abd ul Jalil said "How shall we do?" They said " We will return to Fitri, and we will scatter the grass called ' Karkanji ' on the road. In the rains it will spring up. You will follow it until you come to Fitri, and we will thus show you the road." Abd ul Jalil said " Very well ". The people of Fitri returned, and waited six months.

Ali Dinar knew nothing till the time came. Abd ul Jalil came to Fitri to war, and camped at Jebel Meto (east of Dagana); thence to Saraf Kinji (near Bikoro). There he drew up his army of swordsmen and spearmen, and throwers of knives, and rhino-horn spearmen, and his people put on armour, and took shields and quilts for horses.

On a Friday the army went out from Saraf Kinji and came to Bâru.

Ali Dinar al Kîkayi heard of their coming at Gaô and he assembled his army, and they drew up their array.

Abd ul Jalil sent a note to Ali Dinar, and informed him of his coming to war.

Ali Dinar wrote to him and said " Yes, to-morrow morning I will come out."

He came out. They fought till afternoon. The army of Abd ul Jalil was thirsty and hungry. They parted for the day.

Then Abd ul Jalil made a stratagem to conquer Ali Dinar, and said to him " To-morrow we will mount small horses, so do you mount small horses and we will fight." Ali Dinar said " Yes ".

In the morning of Saturday in Jumaa al Awwal, Ali Dinar came out to fight with small horses.

---

* In Bideyat country, East of N'galaka.

† At Ga'o North of Lake Fitri.

Sultan Abd ul Jalil and his people mounted big horses and they fought from morning till afternoon.

Ali Dinar was discomfited, and returned defeated to his house, and found all his people assembled at his house to attack him.

They fought and Ali Dinar was defeated, and 1,500 of his soldiers were killed. But four horsemen conducted Ali Dinar to the south, and gained Dalko. Thence he went to Nyenyi, and then to Jebel Jaya and to Jebel Abu Talfan. All his army scattered, and some went to Seita and some to Shawa and some to Gwin Furgé, and some to Shebîna* and to Dokwochi, and Kunjuru, and Batn al Fil.

Then Abd ul Jalil ruled at Gaô over the Kuka for forty-seven years and died.

His son Muhammad Alwan—nineteen years.

His son Muhammad Rishad—twenty-one years.

His brother Muhammad Adil Saghir—seven years six months.

His son Muhammad Adil al Kabir—nineteen years.

His son Muhammad Beyad—four years four months.

His brother Muhammad Umr—thirty years.

His son Muhammad Jêli al-Saghir—three years.

His brother Muhammad Abd ul Jalil al Kabir—five years.

His son Muhammad N'gâri—fifteen years.

His Son Abdurahman—twenty-five years.

War with the Tubu of the north occurred in Muharram, on the eleventh day. The Tubu had 1,900 camels; and there was a fight at Takaté. The Bulala won because of their enormous numbers. They killed many Tubus and took many camels, and ninety-seven men "warriors". On the Bulala side thirty-five warriors were killed. The Sultan Abd-ar-Rahman was delighted.

After him his son Muhammad Sôwi who was just, ruled forty-nine years.

After him his son Muhammad Abd ul Jalil al Kabir ruled thirty-two years.

His brother Muhammad Abd ul Jalil al-Saghir:

In his time was much sickness and hunger, and the country suffered. He ruled forty-seven years.

His son Muhammad Shawi ruled twenty-nine years. There succeeded his son Idris. There was war between Idris and the Sultan of Bagarmi on account of "Ivory". Idris wrote to Sultan Bagarmi and forbade him to take "Ivory". Sultan Bagarmi wrote to Idris an insulting letter in reply. Idris got his army together, and went out and camped at *Bukhas*, and sent to Sultan Muhammad Ibrahim and said to him "Bring ivory and 5,000 male slaves". Then they made peace and Idris returned. He ruled thirty-seven years.

His son Muhammad Bekuma al Kabir—ruled thirty-nine years.

His brother Jurab al Fîl—ruled forty years: he left two sons.

---

* The Chibina of MS (1) above, if that is the correct reading.

His son Musa succeeded, and there was fighting between him and his brother Jurab al-Saghir. Jurab was defeated and ran to Kanem, and got an army and wrote to his brother Musa saying: " I am coming to attack you ". He went to Fitri and camped at Jîri (near Gaô). Musa heard the news and came out. They met on the 16th of Zul Hijja. Jurab was victorious. Musa and one boy Maina N'gâri ran away, but Musa was killed after ruling twenty-four years.

Sultan Jurab—thirty-eight years.

His son Hassan Bekuma ruled seven years. There was war with Sultan Gudei his brother. Gudei came to Auni (near Meto) and stayed there and collected an army of Kuka and attacked Fitri.

His brother heard he was at N'gusa. The Sultan came out on a Monday the seventh of Zul Ki'da; they fought, horsemen against horsemen, till evening.

Gudei was defeated and retired to Auni. He lost forty horsemen and remained at Auni for a year.

Then he got another army and wrote to Hassan again, and he replied " Come on."

Gudei then attacked Ga'o, and there was a fight on Sunday the ninth of Safar, and the army of Gudei was victorious. Hassan lost seventy-five horsemen. About three hundred others were killed. Hassan was defeated, and Gudei returned to Auni. There was no further fighting, as news of these events came to Sultan Yusuf of Wadai, who sent a messenger to Sultan Gudei and a letter with a seal. Gudei went to Sultan Yusuf and came to Abeshe. The messenger entered before the Sultan and was told to bring in Gudei. The Sultan Gudei came in before Sultan Yusuf, who sent him to Jerma's house. He stayed there for seven years.

Then Hassan Bekuma died and his brother Maina Jîri succeeded. He ruled three years.

Sultan Yusuf attacked him and took him to Abeshe and imprisoned him.

Yusuf sent for Sultan Gudei and made him Sultan of Ga'o. He ruled thirteen years.

He had trouble with the children of Sultan Musa who came from Jurjura their town and attacked Fitri. A battle took place at " Melme ", and Sultan Gudei defeated them. They returned to Jurjura. Sultan Yusuf seized the chief of them, Abu Shekhi, and imprisoned him at Abeshe, where he died.

Then the son of Abu Shekhi, Maina Jîli, came from Abeshe to Fitri, and came to Madogo, and got an army and attacked Sultan Gudei. A battle took place at Dabaltêhe. Sultan Gudei won and killed Maina Jîli.

Gudei remained till the army of Asil and the French attacked him. He was killed at Mulabis. Then Sultan Hassan ruled, and reigned twenty years.

His son Chiroma succeeded in 1922.

IV.—N'GIZÄM AND BULALA.

This is the story of the people called N'gizäm. They were great people in the land of Kanem, and very numerous and strong in war.

Bulala, on the other hand, was the son of the daughter of the Sultan of Bornu, and was called Bulala because of his truculence and misdoing. He would not listen to the words of his parents but committed a murder, and fled and lived among the N'gizam, and finally deprived them of power.

Then the Sultan (of Kanem) sent his soldiers to attack the N'gizam, and subject them to himself, but God did not give him victory.

The Sultan of Kanem was angry and went out himself with his Kaigama Daud*, son of Sultan Ibrahim; but dispute arose between the Sultan and Daud, so that they separated.

Then Kaigama Daud entered among the Bulala, and ruled them, so that to this day they belong to the subjects of the Kaigama, and so are called " People of Saif ".

The N'gizam are related to our lord Aba Othman ibn 'Afan (may God be pleased with him).

The Kayi Bulala are descended from Aba Bilal ibn Hamama (may God be pleased with him), and they are divided into three clans.

The people of Wadai are of three kinds:

The first—the people of the " land of slaves ", the slaves of the Sultan.

The second—the " Tunjur " whom the slaves of our lord Abbas drove away, and sent to their lord Abbas.

The third—the people of Sherif Abd'ul Karim whose disciple was " Jarma "†

Jarma came with his master to Birni N'jimi. The Sultan of the Birni knew of their coming before they arrived. He was told " that a learned man was coming who would take his kingdom ".

So Jarma's master killed the Sultan, and ran to the Bahr-ul-Jamâl, and sought refuge among the Tubu Gur'aan.

Then the Sultan of the Tunjur gave him his daughter to wed, and said " pray God for me ".

But he prayed on his own behalf, and so the Sultan died, but the " Sherifs " rule Wadai till now—the Abassid Sherifs.

* * *

Sultan Daud ibn Ibrahim ibn Sultan Biri ibn Sultatn Dunama.

Sultan Daud ibn Ibrahim reigned for two hundred years in the land of Malkda‡. Their rule gave place to that of the Turks—three hundred and twenty years ago. They were the tribe of Yusuf Pasha of the Beni Abbas.—*PEACE.*

---

* *i.e.*, The man who became Sultan Daud Nigalemi.

† Jarma, *i.e.*, " General "—corresponding to Kaigama in Bornu.

‡ The meaning is that the Mainas (*i.e.*, princes) of the stock of Mai Daud Nigalemi fled to Malkâda (in some Girgams written Malakata) which possibly indicates the Malakha of the ancient world, *i.e.*, the Suez Region, but here means the region generally called Mâkida, the country of the Amakitan, *i.e.*, Northern Kordofan.

V.—THE BULALA SECESSION FROM THE MAIS OF KANEM.

Sultan Bulala of Fitri seized the power of Daud Nigalemi and ruled twenty-five years. After that Sultan Sowi ruled thirty-two years. After him Yari bin Sowi ruled nineteen years. The total of their years was seventy-six years.

After that Ali Gaji Zeinami Kangi Bulalabe seized the power from Yari bin Sowi. Then Maina Bulala bin Yari, and Maina Bikoru bin Yari and Maina Ali bin Yari and Maina Ibrahim bin Yari left. Maina Bulala and Maina Ali joined the Tubu Kasherda (Kaiyarda). Maina Ibrahim became a Tubu Bara-Bara. Maina Bikoru ibn Yari became a Tubu Gwani. These four ran away to the land of Yari with their drums of brass; they sat down in the land of Yari. But Maina Muhammad ibn Yari and Maina Yahya ibn Yari and Maina Gwoni ibn Yari were captured by Ali Gaji Zeinami in the war. Ali Gaji Zeinami kept them at Gazargammu, and Maina Muhammad ibn Yari was made Kai Figidoma.

Maina Yahya was made Kai Malege, and Maina Gwoni ibn Yari was made Kai Chandira. These are scattered in the land (*i.e.* the latter three still belong to Bornu), while the four that joined the Tubu came down* and made the kingdom of Fitri.

Another version of same story.

Sultan Bulala took the power from Daud Nigalemi and kept it one hundred years. Then came Mai Al Gaji Zeinami. Maina Bulala and his brother Maina Bikoru ibn Yari and their drums of brass, went to Yari and stayed there. Then they followed the Tubu. Two of them, Maina Ali ibn Yari and Ibrahim ibn Yari became powerful in Yari and the town of Kunu. Maina Ali, became a Tubu Kasherda. It was Maina Ibrahim ibn Yari Yahya ibn Yari and Maina Gwoni whom Sultan Ali Gaji caught and then let them go. Maina Muhammad became Figodoma Maina Yahya became Kai Malege. Maina Gwoni became Chandira.

The Tarikh of Mai Chandirama.

He is Mai Mommadu Kalirambe, ibn Sultan Shattima, ibn Sultan 'Ali, ibn Sultan Dalla, ibn Sultan Muhammad, ibn Sultan Mâra, ibn Sultan Umr, ibn Sultan Ibrahim, ibn Sultan Maina Gwoni, ibn Sultan Lefia whose country was Fitri, and who seized the power from Daud Nigalemi, and reigned for twenty-five years.

The Sultan Sowi succeeded him and reigned thirty-two years.

Then Sultan Yari ibn Sowi succeeded, and reigned nineteen years.

The total of the years was seventy-six years, during which the power remained in the hands of the children of Lefia not in the hands of the Beni Saif.

---

* *i.e.*, to the town "Kunu" in the Yari (North).

Then Sultan Ali Gaji Zeinami made war on them, and seized the power from Sultan Yari ibn Sowi.

Maina Bulala ibn Yari and Maina Bikoru ibn Yari and Maina Ali ibn Yari and Maina Ibrahim ibn Yari were left.

Maina Bulala and Maina Ali became Tubu and were called Tubu Kasherda.

Maina Ibrahim became Tubbu Bura-Bura. Maina Bikoru became Tubu Gwoni.

These four had a 'drum' and ran to the land of Yari and remained there.

Then Maina Yahya, and Maina Gwoni, and Maina Ali were attacked by Ali Gaji Zeinami and captured, and brought to Bornu and left there.

Then Maina Muhammad ibn Yari asked Sultan Ali for the title of Chief of the Kayi, and he gave it him and called him Figidoma.

Then Maina Yahya asked Sultan Ali for the title of Kayi and he gave him the title of Kayi Malege.

Then Maina Gwoni asked for a title and was given the title of Mai Chandira.

The origin of all of them was Bulala and their country was Fitri. Mai Lefia it was who first settled in Fitri, and lived there.

Note.—These fragments which came from independent sources, shed a good deal of light on the history of the period.

Daud Nigalemi was expelled from N'jimi in 788 A.H.; 1386 A.D. The reigns were therefore:—

Sultan Bulala 788/1386—813/1410.
Sultan Sowi 813/1410—845/1441.
Sultan Yari 845/1441—864/1459.

According to Barth's chronological table, a Mai of Bornu whom he called *Ghaji*, ruled from 861/1456 to 865/1461 and was then killed by Muhammad ibn Abdullah, king of Kanem. This Ghaji is Ali Gaji Kange Bulalabe "Ali the fever of the Bulala" who died (*i.e.* was killed) at Bulala Gawala, wrongly read by Barth in his chronicle as Matakla Ghamar, a place which is non-existent.

It was this Ali Ghaji who was the first and original Ali Ghaji Zeinami, a corruption of which perhaps accounts for Barth's Amata—*i.e.* the 'Z' of Zeinam got mixed with the 'G' of Gaji.

According to the usual account, Mai Ali Gaji Zeinami, though he defeated the Bulala, was mortally wounded and carried home to die. This entirely squares with these accounts, and it seems very probable that Barth's Muhammad ibn Abdallah, is Yari ibn Sowi, for both these two latter names are nicknames.

V (a).—LIST OF BULALA MAIS OF KANEM.

The manuscript is the Girgam of Shattima son of the Bulala Sultan of Kanem Umr son of Kâlah etc., etc.—and ends " The Amir of Kanem was Shattima, and he obtained the Girgam from Komagunama Zanua Arwogama Arworingama."

For convenience of reference the order of the names has been reversed. The list then from bottom to top reads:—

Othman ibn Affan
Hakkiyi.
Umr.
Khuri.
Hadar.
Tadu.
Hari.
Kudu or Kiwada.
Kunna or Kinâ
Gadig or Gadga.
Mai Koma or Mai Gana.
Sadiyi or Sadi.
Lefia.
Gemu or Jimu.
Jurab.
Abu Sakkin.
Baliyi or Baliya.
K'ala.
Haj Halihan or Haj Jil Bêhama.
Asawa or Asawi.
Dahu or Dahi.
Lihu or Lihi.
Hamr or Umr.
Adam.
Bikur.
Tâdu.
Haj Umr.
Adam Kai.
Abdurrahman.
*Ahmad or Hamad.
Sowi or Sawi (Asawi).
Sultan Yari.
†Lefia (Maina Muhammad ibn Yari).
†Dala.
Daward (Khalifa Daudumi).
Lefia.
Dala.
Umr.
Chiroma.
Medu or Maidugu.
Kademi or Kazgin.
Kâlah or Kâle.
Shattima who is 'Mahir-asal-Sheikh.'

} These are all descendants of Khalifa Daudumi; they never ruled Kanem, as they were replaced by *Dala Afunu* a slave of Dunama, *i.e.* of Mai Muhammad son of Edris (1526-1545).

* Ruled about 1387 and called Muhammad Bulala, *i.e.*, Muhammad al Aswad. Deposed by Ali Gaji Kange Bulalabe circa. 1450.

† These two names represent the Bulala clans which became nominally tributary to **Mai Ali Gaji Zeinami (1472-1504).**

V (b).—ORIGIN OF THE BULALA KINGS OF FITRI ACCORDING TO THE MANUSCRIPT OF SARKIN GULFEI.

Muhammad al Kabir al Yamani.
Muhammad.
Muhammad.
Muhammad.
Moama Mahmud.
Muhammad.
Muhammad.
Muhammad al Bulalai in whose time the separation occurred.
Muhammad.
Muhammad Tsilin (Al Aswad) " The prosperous ".
Muhammad.
Muhammad.
Abd ul Kârim.
Abd ul Jalil.
Abd ul Jalil.
Abdalla Fahanam.
Jili (Abd ul Jalil).
Muhammad Chiroma.
Muhammad Wali buried at Seita
Abdalla (Abdullahi).
Muhammad Jurab al Kabir.
Muhammad Abu Sakkin.
Sultan Muhammad Jurab.
Muhammad Kade.

Muhammad al Yamani, may God's blessing and mercy rest on him, was blessed among his people for two hundred years in the time of the prophets of old. Then the prophet Jesus son of Mary was sent. Muhammad al Yamani believed in him, and dwelt with him, till God in His providence took Jesus to the sky, leaving our lord Muhammad al Yamani among his people. His people were all unbelievers and wicked. So our ancestor and lord Muhammad al Yamani prayed and fasted alone and secretly.

Then after the space of exactly six hundred and ten years the prophet Muhammad (upon whom be the blessing of God and peace) was sent . . . . Muhammad al Yamani believed in him, and the rightly directed Caliphs after him, Abu Bakr Sadik, and Umr ibn al Khattab, and Othman ibn Affan, and Ali ibn Abi Talib.

The prophet invested Muhammad al Yamani with kingship, and sent him to the sea, and gave him one of his eight swords.

Muhammad came to the Bahr al Maliya (Red sea) and exhorted the inhabitants to accept Islam, but they did not accept.

The sword then made a sound like thunder before rain, and the people became afraid, and listened because they must. Muhammad al Yamani dwelt amog them one hundred years in accordance with the command of the prophet; then he went to the land of Kordofan and exhorted the inhabitants to embrace Islam, but they would not listen.

The sword again made a noise like thunder, and the people became afraid, and became Moslems perforce.

He dwelt among them one hundred years, and came then to the So called Kotoko and converted them, and lived among them one hundred and fifty years.

Then he was gathered to the mercy of God most high. May God bless our ancestor.

Note—Comparative list of Bulala Mais of Kanem.

The above two lists of Bulala kings (A) and (B) are both faulty but supplement each other. (A) obviously confuses the Ahmad son of Lefia who drove out Daud Nigalemi, with the Ahmad who was father of Mai Sowi about one hundred years later.

The two lists combined and supplemented from other sources enable an approximate list to be made as follows, though the lists from 1600 A.D. onwards are very incomplete, and before 1600 are chiefly valuable for the inferences that can be drawn from them in correction of more common but mistaken accounts of the tribe of Bulala in contrast to its rulers as being indentical with " the Magumi " or " Saifawa ".

Girgam of Kanem Shattima and other sources.	Gulfei manuscript of Bulala.
Othman ibn Affan	Muhammad el Yamani.
Hakkiyi	Muhammad.
Umr ... circa 1221 contemp. of Dunama Dabalemi called also Umr Bulalami ...	Muhammad.
Khuri	Muhammad.
Hadar	Muhammad.
Ta'adu	Maama Muhammad.
Hari	Muhammad.
Kudu or Kiwada	
Kunna or Kin'a	Muhammad.
Gadeg or Gadga	
Mai Koma	
Sadiyi or Sadi	
Lefia Muhammad Bulalama (circa 1386)	Muhammad Bulala " in whose time the separation occured " *i.e.* Sultan Daud was expelled from Kanem.
Dahu or Dahi	
Lehu or Lehi	
Hamr or Umr	
Bikur	
Ta'adu	
Haj Umr	
Adam Kai	Muhammad.
Abdurrahman	
Ahmad or Hamad Lefia (Barth's Muhammad son of Abdalla) ... circa 1456	Muhammad.

Girgam of Kanem Shattima and other sources.	Gulfei manuscript of Bulala.
Sultan Sowi (Tsilim)	.. Ali Tsilimma or Muhammad Tsilin the "Prosperous."
Sultan Yari* (Barth's Omar ibn Abdalla) circa 1461-1472	
Dunama ibn Salma circa 1504	... Muhammad.
Adam ibn Selma	
Kadai ... ... circa 1526	... Abd al Karim (Kade).
Abdul Jalil ... ,, 1546	... Abd ul Jalil.
Abd ul Jalil ... ,. 1564	... Abd ul Jalil.
Abd ul Lahi ... ,, 1571	... Abdalla Fahanani.
Muhammad ... ,, 1575	... Muhammad Chiroma†.
Jalil ibn Abd ul Jalil	
Jil ... ... circa 1600	... Jil.
	... Muhammad Wâli buried at Seita.
	... Abdalla.
	... Muhammad-Jurab al Kabir
Marsho	... Abn Sakkin.
Balgashe	
Musa	
Jurab ibn Balgashi	... Sultan Muhammad Jurab.
Muhammad ibn Jurab ...	... Sultan Muhammad Kadai.
Hassan ibn Abdullahi (present day Mai of Fitri, 1917) ..	

* At this point the Bulala princes split up and, as related below, the Shattima's branch are those descended from Maina Muhammad Lefia ibn Yari, but the only ones who actually were chiefs of Kanem (under the Mais of Gazargamu) were Dala and Daward (Khalifa Daudumi), for after his time they were replaced by Dala Afunu, a slave of Dunama, son of Edris (1526-1545). On the other hand, the six names succeeding the first Lefia in List (A) really represent the Fitri Bulala dynasty—Jimu being a corruption of Jil, and Asawi, at the end, being a mistake owing to the confusion mentioned above.

† Transposed with Jil.

VI.—THE WAR BETWEEN THE BULALA AND SAIFAWA.

After the death of their ancestor the Sultan of Baghdad, the Bulala obtained the power in Baghdad, and after that Saif left Yamen, and came to Baghdad, and attacked the Bulala. He defeated them and became Sultan of Baghdad: he then left Baghdad and came to Badinimguro, and remained there three hundred and thirty-three years, and then came to N'gibi N'gabulo and remained there three hundred and thirty-three years, thence to N'jimi.

The Bulala at that time came to the villages of Kanem. They had come with the Saifawa and had divided Kanem between them. The Bulala domain extended from Borku to Munyio and Ahir, and from Borku to Dirku on the north. They had three hundred and thirty-three markets, and became very powerful: they had many horses whereas the Saifawa had few.

Mai Ali Gaji Zeinami was related to the Bulala Sultan Umr as he had married his daughter. The name of the daughter was Amsa. Ali went to Gazargamu and built it, and then went to Wudi. He remained there twenty years. Umr followed Ali and came to Wudi. They fought and Ali Gaji was wounded by the Bulala. Then the soldiers of Ali Gaji defeated the Bulala who returned to their town first and then went to Manga. At this time Idris son of Ali was small (five years old). Ali Gaji died of his wound. So the kingdom was given to Aisa Kili and all the chief people consented, and swore to obey her. She was seven years in power.

She was the daughter of Dunama Dabalemi whose children were:—

1. Biri Dunamami.
2. Dibu.
3. Dulmutu.
4. Ali Radi Karadinwa.*
5. Labarandi Kashagaragani.
6. Jenana (knife) Dunamami (Jena gani su Jenabewa).
7. Aisa Kili.

Mairam Amsa, wife of Ali and daughter of Umr the Bulala King was afraid for her son and sent him to Manga to her father

When the sons of Dunama heard this, they pursued him and found him. Then the people with him put him in a "gurara" (bag). The pursuers returned. The boy was sent on to Fitri. Mairam Aisa Kili heard the story and wanted to attack Manga. She went to Manga, and sent to Sultan Umr saying " Bring the boy, " bring out all your people to gallop ". They all came out and Idris among them. Idris came under the parasol of his aunt. Aisa saw him and said " Seize the son of my brother ". Idris was twelve years old. Then she resigned and made him Sultan. Then Mairam Aisa said " I have been seven years king without your knowing that I was a woman ". The Sultan of the Bulala sent

---

* Other tribes related to the Saifawa are Labarandi, Tamuz of Kindin, Hindi.

and said "I am coming in twenty-two days, I am coming to fight you." Idris then prepared for war, and advanced to Manga in eight days. The Bulala were surprised, and defeated. Idris became Sultan of Fitri and said to the Bulala Sultan "I have never seen a man's sweat ran down into his beard except in your case". He replied "I never saw a man put into a sack for fear except in your case". Idris then killed Umr.

Then Mai Kunuma*, son of Umr, called Mai Mala Ganami, succeeded and followed Idris because of the death of his father. He came to Lada near Wudi and a battle there lasted for seven days. The Saifawa had swords, and the Bulala had spears.

Mai Idris sent in the night and said "No one is dead on our side, to-morrow you will see us". The Bulala ran away and went to Fitri. Then the Bulala divided between them the land of Fitri and Manga. Some stayed in Manga, some went to Kunu. Those in Manga were under Idris, and those in Kunu* brought one hundred camels to Idris as tribute if they wanted a new king.

The Sultan of Kunu was called Fititima at Gazargamu and afterwards called Figidoma *i.e.* the head of the Kayi.

Wulgam was another Bulala town, and its chief was called Wulgamma.

Other Bulala clans are:—

(1) *Malege*—Malegema—*i.e.* people of Kachella Bilal.
(2) *N'dubugu*—N'dubuguma was the official who tied up prisoners; other officials who did so were:—
   Inside Birni:—
      Zarma.
      Shettima Kanuri.
      Kachella Kaderi.
   Outside Birni:—
      Kagaburi near Gagala (Kagaburima).
      Dikwama.
      Kullima.
      Yoma.
(3) *Kayi*—Kayi Kuabu formerly the chief of the Kayi was Mainin Kinindin.

The chiefs among other Kayi that came to Bornu were six:—
   Kayi:—
      (1) Figidoma.
      (2) Wulgamma.
      (3) Malegema.
      (4) N'dubugoma.
      (5) Kuabu.
      (6) Children of Mata Ganna.

---

* Rabeh fought the French at Kunu. *Kunu* was North-West of Bokoro, the French station in northern Bagarmi.

Other kinds of Kayi are those who followed Figidoma in Gubio:—

        Kai Sulo.
        Kai Dugoti.
        Kai Budugu.
        Kai N'garwa.
        Kai Duguriwa.
        Kai Rigeda.
        Kai Malo.
        Kai Kirganawa.
        Kai Bulowa.
        Kai Kwortowa

VII.—THE STORY OF THE MAI DUNAMA DABALEMI OF N'JIMI AND HIS FATHER-IN-LAW THE AMIR OF THE BULALA CALLED MAI BULALAMA UMR.

The latter had given his daughter to Mai Dunama to wife—but about three months afterwards war broke out between them. They fought till Mai Dunama was wounded. Then the hosts separated, and Mai Dunama when he was returning to Birni N'jimi, died on the road.

The people agreed upon Mai Ali Gaji Zeinami and made him commander. He finally came to N'jimi, and gave alms for seven days on account of the death of his father. Mai Dunama had left seventy wives all enceinte, among them being Ya Juma, the daughter of the Amir of the Bulala Umr.

Mai Ali Gaji Zeinami moved to the town of Gazargamu with his people and his father's wives. He then announced that he would kill any male children to whom these women gave birth, and spare the females. He did so till sixty-nine were duly delivered. He worked his wicked will and only one wife remained, Ya Juma.

She gave birth to a male child in the evening: and afterwards her servant gave birth to a female child in the early morning. A plan was made and these two infants were changed. Ya Juma took the female child of her maid, and gave her the male child, so as to conceal the fact from Mai Ali Gaji Zeinami.

Ya Juma gave her son the name of Mele, the equivalent of the better known Idris ibn Ya Juma. He was reared at Gazargamu with Ya Juma's maid, till he was five years old. Then Mai Ali Gaji Zeinami assembled the learned men of Birni Gazargamu, and sent them apart for contemplation and divination. They sought guidance, and finally all told Ali Gaji Zeinami what they saw, They said "In this city there is a Sultan's son, who will one day become our Sultan."

When Ya Juma heard this she took the boy and gave him to Fezzani Arabs to take him to his grandfather the Amir of the Bulala Umr. Five years passed and then news came that Ali Gaji Zeinami was dead. After his death the Kanuri of Gazargamu chose Aisa Kili N'girmaramma to be their ruler, because there were no male children of any deceased Sultan.

So Aisa Kili was made Sultan at Gazargamu, and she sat on her father's throne for seven years. She attended the Friday prayers with the court officials, and went to war, for a space of seven years.

Then Idris (Aloma) sent a messenger to Birni Gazargamu and said to Aisa Kili "Do you know that I am a son of your father (Dunama), I am in the Bulala country, and I am a son of Ya Juma". Aisa Kili N'girmaramma then sought out Ya Juma and asked her if she had a son called Idris in the land of the Bulala She said "I have no son, only one daughter". Then Aisa Kili N'girmaramma said to the messenger "Do you not hear what Ya Juma says?" The messenger said "Ya Juma, have you not a son in the Birnin Bulala?" She said "Yes, I have a son".

The Sultan said "If he is your son, why did you send him

to the land of the Bulala?" "I sent him", she replied "for fear that Mai Ali Gaji Zeinami would kill him. Therefore I wrote a letter and put it with merchandise and sent him with Fezzani Arabs". Then Aisa Kili N'girmaramma went to the land of the Bulala with her people. The Bulala heard of their coming and prepared for war, but Aisa Kili N'girmaramma said, "We do not come to war; I am looking for my brother, the son of my father." The Bulala said, "We will not give him to you, but if you recognise him, take him from amid the press of galloping horses". The coming of Aisa Kili N'girmaramma to the Bulala country was on a Thursday and she stayed till the following Thursday. On the second Thursday there was a fantasia, and two Bulala horsemen and Idris were faster than the others. They came up to the spot where the people of Birni Gazargamu were, and Idris came right in among the people of Gazargamu.

The two Bulala horsemen however did not come among the people of Gazargamu but stopped. This was the reason of Idris Aloma coming to the people of Gazargamu, and staying the night at the camp of Aisa Kili N'girmaramma.

Aisa Kili then abdicated and gave her throne to Idris Aloma on the morning of a Friday. Idris Aloma then saw his people, listened and understood their talk. They were discontented because they had not known that their Sultan was a woman.

Therefore Idris asked his grandfather the Amir of the Bulala, Sultan Umr, for nine hundred horsemen with coats of mail. He granted Idris' request. Idris then returned to Gazargamu and remained there three months and eleven days. The Bulala then said to King Idris: "We wish to go to our land: you have now come home to Gazargamu in safety." The king said to them: "return to your lodgings, and I will send you the Kaigamma to see about your going."

The Sultan Idris gave the Kaigamma orders personally to go to the lodgings of the Bulala and kill them all, and that only their leader should be spared. Those of the Bulala who survived then went to the land of the Bulala and told the Amir of the Bulala what had happened. The Amir Umr summoned his people and said to them: "After twenty-five days you will be at the gate of Gadir Zauchia and I too will set out and arrive there on a Saturday".

Then a blind man called Dala Dalami went to Birnin Gazargamu, and the news came to Idris Aloma—"Amir Umr says so and so". Idris went out to fight the Bulala on a Wednesday and thus forestalled the Bulala. He camped with his host near the gate of Gadir on a Friday at night; He slept there, and the following morning was Saturday.

His grandfather came up and a battle took place. The Bulala were defeated, and the Amir Umr was captured. Idris asked him "Where is my father?" He replied "Your father is dead: he died of a wound on the day of the battle at Birni N'jimi". Idris said: "Go to the place where my father is, and fight it out between you". He then killed him on that Saturday.

VIII.—SULTAN IDRIS AND THE BULALA.

In the name of God, the Merciful, the Compassionate. This is the account of the wars between Sultan Idris ibn Ali and the Bulala in Kanem.

We have found in the books of our ancestors, that the original cause of war was Idris' mother, Amsa, daughter of Sultan Jil ibn Bikoru. She went to the place of her father named **Langa'a**, a populous city of the Bulala of considerable importance.

A man of the Gura'an, that is to say, a Tubawi, called Dalil Kirjakeyi, robbed the mother of Sultan Idris, Amsa, on the road. He cut off her feet, and took her silver anklets.

This was the occasion of war. Sultan Idris sent soldiers to follow up the tracks of the thieves, which lead to the city of the Bulala, Langa'a. They found the thieves in the city, and wished either to seize or kill them, but the Bulala forcibly prevented them, and their retainers killed seven of the soldiers of Sultan Idris ibn Ali ibn Dunama Dabalemi.

Idris on hearing of this, blew the blast of alarm, for the assembling of all his people, and sent a letter to Kanem informing the inhabitants of what the Bulala had done.

So they girded their loins to fight, seven clans; first the Magumi 'Alâliyu and the people of Fûli, and Shîri, and Gasgi, and Ajihîm, and Sanlutara, and Yakbari, and Tali, and Binda'a, all of them Magumi. Secondly, N'gala Duku. Thirdly, Kajidi. Fourth, Tumagiri. Fifth, Turra. Sixth, Kangu. Seventh, Kinkina.

Each tribe assembled its warriors and came before the Sultan. They said "O Commander of the Faithful, we have come to fight the Bulala". He said, "O my brothers, hear my words today I fear not death, nor will fatigue overcome me, I swear by God, till I leave the land of Kanem."

So Sultan Idris Amsami prepared himself, and they went to the city of Langa'a, and broke the city, and killed the males and burnt their houses. They stayed there three days. Then they moved to another city Gajudi, and Zigede, and fought the inhabitants. The fight went on for forty days fiercely. Then they took the town by assault in the night and burnt the houses.

Idris gained renown among the Bulala women; he said: "I will not desist till we come to Yao in Fitri, if God wills, I am the son of my father Ali, son of Dunama Dabalemi, the famous". They broke the Bulala and followed them, and drove their women and children to another city of their Sultan called Alwa, where was a river of running water.

The Sultan of the Bulala was a great man. All the Bulala assembled at that town, none remained behind, east or west or south or north. They all came and did their utmost, and vaunted their prowess.

Idris' men followed them up and vanquished them with an army of 70,000 men or more, attacking them in the day and defeating them by sheer numbers. The fight went on for seventy days before the Bulala and their Sultan were defeated, and retreated to the bush and north, as far as Dibinati. They camped and gathered their women, and performed magic rites.

Then Idris set out from Alwa, and came to Madogo, and Magirne, where there was much corn and water; he marched for forty days, and sent a blacksmith and informed the army in the night saying " hear my words: general war is over, today the nobles of the Bulala will meet the nobles of the Magumi; we will decide by single combat, and inspire their hearts with terror." The Bulala got up from Dibinati, and went to Jalo, till they came to Bahr al Gura'an.

Idris followed up his victory. The Bulala rallied on the Bahr al Gura'an, and then all scattered in flight. Idris went on to the rock of Gura'an and the rock of Am Gazûz, and to Yao and then returned behind the town and camped on the far side of the Bahr al Gura'an. He then gathered together the plunder, and divided it among all the warriors, and the poor; 1,000 female and 2,000 male slaves. He slew four hundred free persons. They left of them three alive. First Barka Kindileyi, who was the ancestor of the N'gizim. The people of Dibinati had for ancestor N'gizim, a heathen. Secondly, Kayamma Kimâgirima, a poor man, the 'Muezzin', and thirdly, N'jimi Chiram, the blacksmith of the Bulala. They killed all the rest, and moved to Bahr al Gura'an, and came to the city of N'jimi, the city of Idris' ancestor Dunama Dabalemi. Then they moved to Forgwa, and then to Wagam, where Mai Idris' ancestor Dunama Dabalemi was buried; thence to Ririgi (Rigu).

There they divided the land of Kanem among the warrior chiefs.

From Showayi to Kemiyaram belonged to the Dibiri.
From Kemiyaram to Bûra belonged to the Tumagari.
From Bura to Ligidi belonged to the Kajidi.
From Ligidi to Goshi belonged to the Kuburi Beni Luwabu.
From Goshi to Yambadiyam belonged to N'galma Dibu.
From Yambadiyam to Julla belonged to Magumi Furibu.
From Julla to Shîga Kurtii belonged to Sulobu Kinkina.
From Shîga Kurtii to Dabôa belonged to Kuburi.
From Dabôa to Mandara belonged to the Sugurti.
From Mandara to Wudi Fortoa belonged to Tumagari.

He divided the land of Kanem, and then came to Gazargamu, and camped at Al Arkasuwa Guwa, and at Dabôa and Wudi Fortoa and Barwa (near Boso) and Kulwa, and Gashegur, and remained in power thirty-eight years.

Muhammad ibn Idris reigned ten years.
Ibrahim ibn Idris reigned seven years.
Umr ibn Idris reigned eighteen years.
Ali ibn Umr reigned thirty-eight years.
Idris ibn Ali reigned twenty years.
Dunama ibn Ali reigned nineteen years.

Haj ibn Dunama reigned fourteen years.

Dunama ibn Muhammad reigned sixty years.

Ali ibn Haj reigned forty-seven years.

Their power then came to an end, and our tradition states that Gwoni Mpktar stayed many days in Gazargamu and the power then passed to Sheikh Muhammad al Amin the Kuburi.

NOTE IN MS.

The horses of Sultan Idris when he went out to war with the Bulala were 70,000, and when he returned 700.

NOTE ON PLACE NAMES.

Langa'a near Yao north of Fitri.

Alaliya = Babaliya. Alali is now inhabited by Gura'an called Balbaliya.

{ *Shíri* between *Bahr al Ghazal* and *Ma'o*.
  Gashgi
  Ajihim }

Zigede north of Ma'o.

Alwa near Kunjiro, between Madogo and Bulala.

Mugirne near Madogo.

Dibinati north of Madogo, south of Bahr Batha.

Jalo south of Madogo.

Bahr al Gura'an, south-west of Fitri.

Kirmâgirma: The title of the Muezzin of the Bulala.

N'jimi Chiram: The title of the head blacksmith of the Bulala.

Fogwa: near Fitri.

IX.—MAI DAUD.

In the name of God the Merciful the Compassionate.

Mai Daud Nigalemi son of Mai Ibrahim son of Mai Biri son of Mai Dunama.

Know that Mai Daud Nigalemi was the Kaigamma of Mai Dunama the eldest son of Mai Chulumma son of Bikoru.

These two attacked the land of Fitri, the inhabitants of which were Bulala, who are said to be the people of Aba Bilal, but are in fact the tribe of " Kayi Bulala ".

Mai Dunama waged war on them fiercely, and divided them, so that they split up and fled.

Then Mai Dunama returned to his town in the west (N'jimi).

Mai Daud remained with the Bulala in Fitri, and lived there a long time and took away their power. He was in Fitri ruling for seventy-seven years seven months and seven days.

Then came Mai Ali Gaji Zeinami to the land of Fitri and attacked it, and conquered it; thence he proceeded to Gazargamu.

Then Mai Daud Nigâlemi* with his children to the land of Jitwa† and died there.

His son Mai Othman went to Bursulum‡ and died there.

His son Kadai went to Yamdi Kowa (N'galaka§) and died there.

Mai Muhammad ibn Kade went to Jabaru Kirzamma and died there.

Mai Othman (ibn Kade) went to the land of Malakâda (Makâda‖) and ruled the east and west for one hundred years.

Then there came to him the Turks and people of Stambul and waged war on him and deprived him of power. They were the people of Yusuf Pasha.

But there are many of the people of Daud Nigâlemi in the land of Masr, being Yamanites, the people of Saif of the Ansar, the well known tribe of Magumi.

Then it is said that when Mai Daud Nigâlemi went to the east, he had forty sons and twenty daughters.

When he was asked the reason of his coming, he said " we have come for safety ".

Some of his sons returned to the land of Kanem, and are now among the Gura'an of the Tubu Dîbîrî. And some of his daughters married " nomad Arabs " and Usuli (Wasuri) and people of Egypt, and people of Tripoli. Most of them are in the east.

---

* *i.e.*, his descendants—for he was dead.

† Jitwa and Mafala are close together south of Lake Fitri.

‡ North of Lake Fitri.

§ *i.e.*, Borku.

‖ *i.e.*, the kingdom of Sena'ar on the Blue Nile. It would appear that from this name Makâda or Magâda comes the old title of the Mais of Kanem—*i.e.*, " Makâda-be," *i.e.*, of Makâda. The Mais were saluted as " Arjîku Sîku Makâda-be."

We have heard this story from Mu'allim Ali. He heard from a Wasuri called Abdu'l Hamid, whose mother was a Tripoli woman, and his father an Egyptian.

Thus we have heard from our fathers.

In the beginning the Kaigamma was chosen from among the sons of the Sultan; but after this civil war, the office of Kaigamma was given to slaves, and so it has remained till now.

X.—YATKU (JATKU) AND BULALA.

Mu'allim Kiari says that Sultan Bulalâma's town was Kuluwan. The Bulala came from Kuluwan to the country of Alali and dwelt in the country of Alali, for three hundred years with their Sultan.

The Sultan of N'jimi arose and established his capital at Wudi.

The Bulala attacked the Sultan of Kanem in the country between Wudi and N'jimi.

Sultan Ali attacked the Bulala in turn.

Then the Bulala Chief came to Wudi, and the Sultan Ali was wounded at Wudi.

The Bulala followed up the tracks of the Sultan of Bornu and a battle was fought at Lada which lasted seven days.

The Sultan was victorious, and the Bulala fled back, and went to Fitri, where they remained and became "Mainawa" in the land of Kanem.

The Sultan of the Bulala had six sons.

One settled at Kowa—the chiefs of this section are Fugu and Lugali.

One settled at Dubu—their chief is Dubuma.

One settled at Malegaye—their chief is Malegayema.

One settled at Wulgam—their chief is Wulgama.

One settled at Fifido—their chief is Fifidoma.

One settled at Kunu—their chief is Kunuma.

They took one hundred camels and came to the Sultan of Bornu to ask for recognition. They gave him one hundred camels, and were given recognition as chiefs.

The tribe of Jatku (Yatku) came from Yari Jatku.

They are divided into four sections.

One is of the stock of Tumagari Sanda of Daburam and Kara and Yalgadu. Their chiefs were Fugu Kara-ma, and Yalgadu-ma, and Tuwayeama Tumagari Gunsaru. Their title was Lowan.

One of their stocks is Kubri Isaganawa; their title is Lowan.

The chief of the Kubri Gambowa is also Lowan.

The Kubri Gadwaya and Kubri Bigu are followers of the Lowar

The third stock is of the Kangu, and their title was Shatima.

Another branch of the Jatku are the Kaikunu, whose chief was Sultan Kanama.

The people of Kowwa (Kawar) came from Kanana in Sham.

They arose from Kanana (Canaan) and came to Borku Wunu, and remained, and are now twelve tribes.

1. Wunumu.
2. Yawama.
3. Kilele.
4. Washika.
5. Kaluwa.
6. Tih Wusa.
7. Mitale.
8. Warda.
9. Salumsa.
10. Iradu.
11. Kimma.
12. Riwaya.

Peace.

XI.—SHORT BULALA GIRGAM.

The Sultan of the Bulala Jil founded the towns of *Masiu* and *Abkala*.

Jil died and was succeeded by a Sultan Jurab Abu Mango. Sultan Marsho succeeded Jurab and came to Fitri and fought the people of Fitri called Beni Kuka and their Sultan Ali*. He conquered them.

He made Fitri his country and developed it, and dwelt in it with his people the Bulala. Marsho died and was succeeded by his brother Balgashe. Musa ibn Marsho succeeded Balgashe, and civil war then ensued between him and Jurab ibn Balgashe. Jurab killed Musa and became Sultan.

He was succeeded by Hasan ibn Jurab. Then ruled his full brother Sultan Jil ibn Jurab. Then Sultan Muhammad ibn Jurab ruled thirteen years. There followed him Hasan ibn Abdullahi, the present Sultan of Fitri, who has ruled for seventeen years.

---

* *i.e.*, Ali Dinar Garga.
 Masiu was to the East of Yao near Atia. Abkala is now uninhabited bush, but was in the Kreda country north-west of Dagana about two days from Dagana. The Bahr al Ghazal is in the Kreda country.

XII.—BULALA (KAYI) GIRGAM BY MALLAM KIARI KAZALLA DARMANMI.

The Kayi came from the east to N'jimi. The Kayi (Bulala) came to Alali, which is near N'jimi. The Kayi stayed there thirty-three years. The Kayi sought the kingship. They were descended on the mother's side from the same stock as the Saifawa. Their mother was Aisa Bagdarimaram. The tribes of Kanuri with representative chiefs are as follows:—

The Mai	1. Magumi.
(Figidoma)	2. Kayi.
(Liman Karagwaro Ligari Kiari)	3. Mani (Kangu).
(The Shehu)	4. Darman (Kuburi).
(Fugu Hassan)	5. N'gal (N'galaga).
(Liman Abdurraman)	6. Duk (N'galma Duku).
(Ligari Jabur)	7. N'jidi (Kajidi).

The father of the (Kayi) Bulala was *Mai Kairuwan*.

The Mallams say, that the Tuareg are Beni Isra'il, and that the Kayi were not Tubu.

From Borku to Muniyo and Borku to the Nile all the country belonged to the Kayi, and as far as Ahir and Tarabulus. The Kayi were the messengers of the desert.

The Bornu Mai was first at N'jimi but afterwards came to Wudi. Then the Kayi came to Alali and Manga in the north of Kanem. The Mai was at Wudi twenty years. The Bulala came on after him. They fought on the Komadugu Yobe for seven days. Then the Mai came to Lada near Dutsi. Afterwards the Bulala went to Fitri. A Bulala Prince went to Mangari and settled there near N'gegimi.

This was in the time of Mai Mada Gannami Kunuma*. He was the Bulala Chief who fought with Mai Dunama Dabalemi.

---

* Owner of the town of Kunu.

XIII.—THE BULALA WARS.

The Bulala trace their descent back to Othman ibn Afan who was the father of Umr Bulalami, who begat Mutallib Umrmi, father of Abu Umr Gudusu, father of Ali Tsilim, father of Khalifa Daudumi.

Their paternal uncle was Ali N'gisammi. He came to the town of Jâka*. He remained among the Bulala for three hundred and thirty-three years.

Then Umme Jilmi sent his nephew Abdullahi† to fight this tribe of Bulala.

They fought at the town of Kâbila‡ a fierce battle, in which seven hundred and seventy Bulala fell. Ali N'gisammi then submitted to Abdullahi, and peace was established between them.

Then Abdullahi asked for money from the Bulala 7090 rials. They then brought a present and said: "My lord, go to the town of Yamshi§ and stay there; we will then collect the rials and send them to you within seven days, if God wills." Abdullahi then went to the town of Yamshi and stayed there. But after his arrival at Yamshi, the Bulala took counsel, in their town of Kâbila and resolved to hasten and get assistance and refuse to pay. So they refused to pay, and sought out a man called Musa in his town of N'gisam Kowwa‖. He came to their assistance with his armoury of fifty guns. That was the cause of their refusal to pay. So war began again, and a fierce battle took place in which 3,000 men fell of the Bulala and men of Abdullahi. After this battle they all scattered. Abdullahi¶ went to the town of Bikur (Bokoro), and Musa to the town of N'gisam Kowwa, while the Bulala remained in their town Yamshi.

Musa then said "I retire from the contest now, but after two

---

* *Jâka* pronounced Chaka, one day south of the present French station of Bokoro.

† *Abdullahi*, By subtracting the 210 years mentioned below from 775/1373 A.H., the date of Daud's accession, the time when the well known civil war between the Bulala and Saifawa began, the date of these wars works out as about 565 A.H. or 1169 A.D. This date is, according to the chronicles, during the reign of Biri Dunamami who was buried at Gamtilo, and whose successor was Abdullahi Bikur (1177-1193 A.D.).

‡ *Kâbila:* said to be near the Kau Tugudegwa or "rock of four seats," or "rock of Musa," which is in the East of the Annadi country, about five days north of Masrub which is on the Wädi Abu Haras. This rock is called by the Arabs Manzil al'arbaa (four seats) because of four rocks which are at all points of the compass. There are springs and a good supply of water. The modern name of the place is Kâbar and it is on the desert route from Abeshe to Dongola or Kufra. The stages are: Abeshe-Fada-Al Maggârin—thence travellers take water for the desert journey to Kâbar. From thence the Bideyat raided Dongola; and when pursued by the French Dûd Murra, Emir of Wadai, fled there.

§ *Yamshi*—close to Bokoro is meant.

‖ *N'gisam Kowwa . . . Musa.* The Kâbar "rock of Musa" and N'gisam Kowwa seem to mean the same region, *i.e.,* the N'gisam are the same as the modern N'akazzar or N'gazzar of Borku.

¶ It would appear that this was the Mai called Bikur and that his capital was Bokoro or Bikoro (Bikur).

hundred and ten years* the time of war between us will again come, I therefore leave off fighting you and go to my town." So he spoke, and they all gave up war for a space of seventy years†.

Then it came about that Mai Othman Kademi, in the town of Bikur, sent his messenger to the town of Yamshi to the Bulala to summon the Amir of the Bulala named Umr. He came and found Mai Othman Kademi at Dalwara (Dar Wâra). Othman Kademi then seized Amir Umr and killed him and made his nominee, a man of inferior rank called N'gisam, Sultan of the Bulala.

This nominee then returned to the Bulala town Yamshi, but on his arrival, Mai Lefia, Mai Sugu (Ibrahim) Ganna, seized the power from him and slew him and became Amir.

When Mai Dunama Dabalemi heard of what was going on, he so concerned himself with it, that he went to the country of the Bulala. A great battle took place in which 3,070 perished. Then Mai Lefia Sugu Ganna and his henchman Gau Dala Shaliwa Wache Darman Ganna went to the land of Fitri and made a settlement there. Dunama Dabalemi, on the other hand, and his henchman Barka Wadai, came to Kanem to N'jimi and settled. The first man who colonised Wadai was Barka Wadai‡.

---

* *i.e.*, time of Daud Nigalemi, circa 1377 A.D.

† Seventy years from the end of the reign of Dalla Bikur brings us to 1260 A.D., *i.e.*, the end of the reign of Dunama Dabalemi. The interval is probably correct, because it was at the close of the reign of Dunama Dabalemi that, according to Imam Ahmad, the discord arose, because of Dabalemi's impious act in opening the Mune or "talisman."

"Mai Othman Kademi" probably means the son of Dunama who succeeded him, *i.e.*, "Kade Matalami" whose mother evidently came from Matala, east of Abeshe, and who was buried in Borku, at Zui-Zui or Zuar.

The murder of Amir Umr at Dulwâra (*i.e.*, Wâra), the old capital of Wadai, therefore, probably took place a few years before Dunama's death— say about 1250 A.D.—and it was subsequent to this, *i.e.*, between 1250-1260 A.D. that Mai Dunama Dabalemi founded N'jimi.

‡ The meaning of the last few sentences is that the N'gisam or N'gizim, Bedde, Buduma, Kotoko and So races in general are regarded as connected with the Bulala, whereas the more northerly tribes of Wadai belongs more closely to the Saifawa.

XIV.—MIDDLE IFRIKIA.

In the name of God.

The tribes which came to the middle Ifrikia, are found in the Tarikh es Sudan. They came out in the time of the rule of the Ibâdites ('Abidin). At that time there came out the ancestor of the Masâlit, and the Mussaba'at, and the Mîmi, and Masmaji, and the ancestor of the Walad Jama'a* Marârit'.

The Mussaba'at are related to the Kuraish, and so are the Masâlit, but the Masmaji and Mîmi and Walad Jama'a and Marârît are all related to the Abbâsiya.

Know also that the native tribes of Wadai came out in the time of the rule of the Fatimids, and that their names begin with " K ", as Kodayi, Kalenan, Kajanga, Kandango, Kashemere, Kajagse, Kibêt; all these came from Yazîd, son of Muauwiya.

Other tribes who came out in the time of the Abbâsids are:—

Tâma.	Marâsa (Fur).
Birgit.	Suwa (in Darfur).
Gimr.	Mua.
Sinnar.	Barti.
Dajo.	Abdarak.
Bego.	Runga.
Furâgê.	Fur.
Aba Shârib.	Assagôri.
Marfa.	Mura.
Mayu.	Mubi.
Madago.	Minye.

These are the " natives "

We have found in an old account in a Tarikh-es-Sudan the following:—

" The same tribes which came to middle Afrikia, after the end of the Ummayad Empire, and the Abbâsid Empire, and the Alid dynasties, and the Fatimids in Masr, were those which created the Empire of the Emirs of the Seljuks and the Abidin from the remains of the Ummayad power—namely the Beni Abbas.

They ruled over the Sanhaja and Andulus, after the time of the old kings of western Ifrikia, and Egypt.

In that epoch, a great number of people came to the Sudan because of the wars occasioned by these changes in North Africa, among them the Zenanata and other Barbars.

Among these Barbars, a great number came to Fur. Among them were the Bulala, and Babaliya, and Bideyat, and Tunjur, and Makada, and others.

Darfur then fell under the dominion of the Zaghawa, and the Anej and Bideyat. The ancestor of the Tunjur of Wadai came out from among them and came to Wadai, and ruled there.

The rest (of the Barbars) separated. Seven men among them were camel men, of one clan. They migrated to a rock called Shekilla (in Bideyat country), and others to places called Am

---

* Darfur tribes.

Turba, and Gurguri, which was the chief place of Bideyat of old. They settled there, and multiplied into many branches. Originally they were of the same race as the Makâda. (Amakitan).

Among the Bideyat three clans are connected with the Habesh. They are idolaters

When the Bideyat came to their country, they found the inhabitants were Magians and they were forty-six cubits high. Their houses were caves in the rocks called "Karkur" (in Arabic).

But God sent destruction upon them and they perished of thirst and hunger.

The Zaghawa were also there, dwelling in their present habitat, called Kubbi, the Sultan's town, and another place called Karkur Nurein.

The rest of the tribes of Zenanata went west. Among them the ancestor of the Barnu, and of the Bulala and Babaliya.

After that the power of Fur grew weak and it fell under the power of the Beni Hilal.

The Bulala settled in their present habitat (Fitri) after great fighting between them and the Barnu, until the Bagarmi people attacked them also in turn and conquered them.

The Bulala returned to their present country, unable to fight with Wadai, Bagarmi or Barnu.

Barnu had to be content with the country to the west of the Shari. East of the Shari fell to Wadai and other lesser kingdoms which were formerly subject to Fur.

So matters went on till Masr conquered Fur under Zubeir Pasha.

Then came the Mahdi Muhammad Ahmad, and his lieutenants.

Then came the joint rule of England and Masr after a second war. They took the country from the Mahdist power and returned it to its former rulers.

So also Barnu was returned to its original rulers the Kanembu.

Then came Rabeh and conquered Barnu, till the French came and conquered Rabeh.

Then came the English and took over Barnu from the French.

XV.—THE CHILDREN OF TUBA'UL AWWAL.

The story of the children of Tuba'ul Awwal—a true story and new.

After mention of their ancestors, who were forty in number, and believed in the prophet of God (upon whom be blessing and peace) a thousand years before his coming, believed in him without seeing him, they migrated from Wadi Tundil to the land of Sham, and lived there some years.

They returned from Sham to the south, to the country of Yaman and lived there for 500 years.

A quarrel then arose over the kingship among a section of them after the death of Sultan Adam ibn Dunama ibn Dueim ibn Sureid ibn Jubeir al Habashi of the sons of Kabush, of the tribe of Mahmud Sultan of Sham.

It is said that he was their ancestor and the ancestor of all the Barri-Barri (of Bornu) and that they are his children.

Some of the sons of the kings of Tuba'ul Awwal, about 1,775 in all, men and women, big and little, migrated and crossed the big sea, and, after taking counsel, settled by the shore of the sea.

Others left and went on and came to the mother city of Bornu, called Gasar-gamu, and stayed there; in number 722 souls, men and women.

They lived there some time till they grew numerous, when a division occurred, and trouble over the succession.

Then the children of the first Sultan arose, they and their women, about seventy-two men who had crossed the sea, with their wives and little ones, and went to the hills of Bagarmi (Abu Geren).

Thence some of them passed to the hills of Mandara.

About thirty-four men, with their women, took counsel and decided to separate into two parties of sixteen men each. They entered the country of the Babur and the land of Gwombe, and settled there in certain places. (i.e. the Bolewa and Kwararafa).

Then twenty-eight of them crossed the river Gongila (i.e. from Gwombe) and came to the rock of Daniski Fikka, and camped in the midst of the rock of Daniski*, which beforetime, was called Daniski after a hunter of giraffe and elephant.

He had come there on his hunting journeys, he and his family and brethren, and was called Daniski, and it was (said the narrator) his people that the leaders of the migrants Danumashi, and Bulama, and Warfa and Zamo, and Atuman, found at Daniski.

Now they (the migrants) were the children of Adam ibn Ibrahim ibn Dumata ibn Barama Ibn Idris ibn Diyas ibn Muhammad ibn Muhammad ibn Bulama Ibrahim ibn " al Yamani†.

They and their children's children lived at the rock of Daniski, the unbeliever, who had many men and much wealth.

Some of the Yamanites plotted to kill the sons of Daniski

---

* Daniski is connected in the Kanuri mind with Mandara.

† The man who came from Yaman. The kings of Kanem were children of Dugu ibn Ibrahim.

so that after the death of all his sons they should gain the kingdom. The children of Daniski heard of this. Some fled in the night and left their brethren, making for the rocks and hills. They that remained were few.

Within a year the Yamanites were masters of the land and rocks, and killed all who did not submit to them. They cut the throats of the adults, and left the youths and women.

They abode there long without hearing news of their brethren of Bornu, so they went to them and renewed the connection. They kept up the racial tie with their brethren whom they had left at Gasargamu, though they now lived in the land of Gwombe, and Bauchi, and Duku, and Kalam, and Kanan, and Gadam, and Biyri, and Bara and Fali, and Kirfi, and the others who had crossed the river of Wukari. (*i.e.* the Jukons).

Then twenty-one households who lived in Biyri and the rock of Kalam migrated to Lariski, and Fali, and from thence back to the land of Bauchi, to the rock of Gere.

Twelve of these settled in the valley of the river of Fali, and two came to the rock of Kirfi where they found a pagan people in the rock.

These latter had a tyrannical king.

When the Yamanites came, the king ordered his people to kill them, but his Wazir and his son hid them, and told him that they had run away.

At length the king forgot the matter, and in the new year they came out from hiding. The king favoured them so that one of them married the daughter of the King of Kirfi. They begot children and died.

The descendants of these two stocks of Tuba'ul Awwal, who settled at Kirfi, rule the people of Kirfi to this day.

Four other branches settled at the rock of Tiriun, and thence went to Gerawa, where they found pagans.

They ruled them after their leader died, and rule to this day.

The remaining three branches moved on and crossed the river (Benue), and entered a country near a rock beside the water of the river, the name of the place being Wukari.

There they found the chiefs of the pagans, and a Sultan.

The people were cannibals. They heard this in the night and one of their number fled to the rock leaving his brethren among the pagans. He was saved, and his children are the kings of Wukari to this day, though they are not aware of this.

(The narrator) then mentioned the people of Baderi (Bade) who are of the stock of the people of Misau. They belong to the stock of the people of Misau. They belong to the class of Arab nomads, and are a remnant of the people of Saudum (Sodom), and many of them are of the pagans of Hadramant in the east and from Yaman.

They are of the stock of the diggers of the " old wells ", and their country, wherever it is, is called after the name of their wells. They became Moslems after they left their land, and followed the Tuba'ul Awwal from the first, crossing the sea with them.

The Tuba'ul Awwal came to N'gegimi with the Baderi, and they both came on to Gasargamu and settled there.

Then the Tuba'ul Awwal tried to make the Bade their slaves but the Bade refused in anger, and all ran away into the deserts, and spread abroad among the rocks and forests some of them being called Keri-Keri, and others N'gizimawa, and Dambawa.

They are the people of the Kings of Shirra. They shifted about until they came to the islands in the wadis where they now dwell. They came with their brethren and were the original people of Misau.

They took counsel together, and some seceded after a bitter quarrel. Though fighting took place among them, the seceders got away in triumph, but they, the people of Dambam, are the children of the Sarkin Shirra, without doubt.

But the main body ignored them and came to the place where they built Misau. On their arrival they found no inhabitants.

They built houses and settled down, and stayed many years. Then they spread abroad, and some of their leaders migrated to the rock of Shirra, and, finding people there, settled among them. Some of them migrated to Ningi and joined the then inhabitants of Ningi. Then their slaves, the M'butu, fled to the hills of M'butu.

They left them there till they grew numerous, and they do not obey their chiefs even to this day.

The Wali of Misau heard news of his brother of Fikka, who, with his people lived on the hill of Daniski, and sent to see how he was. So his messenger came to the King of Fikka, Muhammad ibn Ibrahim ibn Mai Muhammad ibn Adam, with a present from Wali Misau Muhammad ibn Bukr ibn Aisawa.

The messenger saluted the Mai in the morning, and gave him a female slave, a noble horse, and a bag.

He returned and informed the ruler of Misau how well he had been received.

He again sent a horse to the Wali of Fikka at Daniski to induce him to give him his daughter in marriage.

The Wali of Fikka refused; but his people said: "You ought not to refuse, since he is your brother from the time of our coming out, and has been firmly friendly to us since our coming. Now he seeks our friendship, and we give it."

The Wali then agreed; and friendship was established between them, and tokens of goodwill given, and they consulted together whenever anything of note occurred.

Two men of Misau and one from Fikka went to the land of Hadeijia and found people of a different race on the banks of the river, a wadi which ran between them and the other people, and their settlement

The people were called Auyokawa, from the name of their town Auyo.

The Auyokawa drove them away. They crossed the river in search of another place to settle, and found a sandhill and on it put up grass shelters, they, their women, and youths, and multiplied there, and gave the town the name of Marmar.

They sent to the people of Auyo asking for a girl in marriage, but the Auyokawa refused.

They searched and hunted every inhabited place, but found no one in this region of the earth except the Baderi. Between them and these latter was no friendship or goodwill.

So they consulted, seeking out one place after another, till they heard of a people who lived afar from them, and dwelt in a land called Sosa Baki. There are the forefathers of the original people of Gumel, who afterwards migrated to Dingas. They found no one in those parts except the inhabitants of Wushek and Miria, who were a people.

At that time no one lived in the land of Zinder, except in the hills, here and there.

Daura, however, had people and a tyrannical king. Its inhabitants were the slaves of Nimrudu, son of Kana'an.

The people from Marmar therefore returned to the people of Gumel, and took back a girl they were given by the people of Gumel to Marmar. They did not pass onwards to Katshina or Gobir, for our people had heard about a certain tyrannical king there.

That prevented them journeying to those lands, though they had also heard of a part of Katsina called Katsina Laka na Habe.

It is finished, the history of the people who separated from the people of Bornu, from the beginning until now.

Note.—The document of which the above is a translation, the original of which is said by the Alkah of Fika to be at least 200 years old, was supplemented by a graphic chart of peoples, of which the attached list is a translation. It is prefaced by an introduction which states:

"This is a sketch of the peoples who came from the countries of "Yaman, and crossed the great sea. They are of one stock, "except for the Baderi, who followed the others, but were not "of the same origin, but were bushmen and 'spies'."

In a note on a list of the Kings of Fikka, it is said that from the time of the division or splitting up of the so-called Tuba'ul Awwal in Kanem or Wadai until the end of the nineteenth century A.D. was between 800 and 1,000 years. If this is correct the Bolewa and Kwararafa separated from the Magumi and other Zaghawa of Kanem about 900 A.D.—1,000 A.D.

The sketch of peoples as drawn by the Alkalin Fikka is reproduced overleaf.

| [Kindin] | [Amakitan] | | [Kushites] | [Bolewa] | This is the Sea (Red Sea) Land of Sudan. | |
(Tuwareg)	Zaghawa				[Bolewa]	[Nilotes]
The Tuwareg or	Cities of		Dambawa	Dubum	Biu	So
Am Nimrud of ibn Kana'an	Bornu		Misawa	Wája	Gulani	N'guma
Their slaves are:	Kafila		Shirrawa	Janbi	Bára	Towa
Daura (Hausa)	Gasargamu		Wáfu	Juro	Jéra	Logoni
Maradi (Katsina)	N'gornu		Daurawa	Fági	Kumi	Alifu
Gobir	Birni Kanem		(Bornu)	Dúru	Kubelu	N'difu
Zanfara	(N'jimi)		Jama'ári	Kwam (Gwom)	Dálu	Bagarmi Saghír
Zagzak	Yamani			Jimbam	Diri	N'gala
Kano	Mongonu			Bujudi	Bíyri	Misine
	Maini Soroa			Boro	Kalam	Bagarmi Kabír
	N'guru			Tururam	Malda	N'gau
Zinder	Mashinna			Daniski Fikka	Gadam	Tubori
Washa (Wushek)	Miria			Lariski Bara	Fáli Dimi	Kabbam
Dingas	Kowar				Kwa	Mandara Tsauni
Gumel					Duku	Marghi
	Mixed kinds			Bade of	Tafi	
	of Fellata.			Gorgoram.	Kanan	
				N'gizan,	Kilfíngi	
				etc.	Dabba	

North / East / West / South

XVI.—THE KISARA MIGRATION.

[*Translation of a note written by Mallam Sherif of Argungu, 10th April, 1922.*]

The beginning of my story is that I, Ahmed, son of Muhammad, went travelling, and reached the land of Kiri and the town called Wukari. There I met a man called Mallam Kura* in the house of the "Zanua" of Wukari. This was a long time ago. It is now, perhaps, forty-one or forty-two years ago. It was in the year when a comet appeared in the East, with a long tail.

I asked Mallam Kura about the history of the unbelievers of Wukari, as I saw they were people of no ordinary character, and he replied "I will tell you: they are unbelievers who were driven out of Egypt. I have a book about their origin."

So I made some notes, for he brought me the book and I saw it.

It said that the tribe of Kisara appeared in the Sudan when it fled from Egypt after it had fought the Byzantines (Rum). So Mallam Kura said, and so the book said.

The King of Rum was named Harkilla (Arkel)—and these Kisara when defeated spread abroad in Egypt, and went east and west. Of those who came west, the leader was Tatari.

This man arose in the sixth year of the Hijra of the Prophet (*i.e.* 627 A.D.), since by reason of the descent of the Sura A.L.M. the Byzantines (of Egypt) defeated the Persians† in Egypt in that year. The Persians and their army fled to the land of Fur, now called Darfur.

So said the book, and that they remained a long time in Fur, and that the path of their migrations thence was well known. I however do not know the names of their towns in Fur but they reached Jebel Kwon‡ and Fasher, and settled in Wadai, towards the south of Wadai, and remained there for many years.

Then they came to another place, called Magga (or Magge)§ so the book said, and thence to Balda‖.

---

* Mallam Kura seems to have been, in his day, a famous Mallam. Limam Kona at Zaria knew of him. His grandson is still the "Zanua" at Wukari.

† The race is called "Persian" in origin but Persian means "Kushite" or "Elamite."

‡ Actually in Kordofan not far from El Obeid.

§ Magge or Magga is the Fitri region, "country of the Bulala."

‖ There is a place called Badanijo, south of Mubi, and east of Song, which was, according to Barth, the northernmost seat of the tribe of Fali or Fari. The Bornu people say that, formerly, Dajo tribes ruled near Mubi, and spoke Dajo.

The rock of Balda is not far from Bogo, in the Musgu country, about two days' trek N.E. of Marua. Mr. Webster says that the Fari are closely related to the Batta in race and speech, and are of Fulani type with customs in common. The Jukon of Wukari state that they are the same as the Fali and Bolewa and that they are "Fellata." It appears probable that the M'bum, Dama, and then Fari, represent three consecutive layers of population, the last named with the Batta, belonging to the stratum called Kororofa.

In Fitri also there are legends of an early population of "Fulani". The legends of Bima are said to have been transferred from Balda (Gowers).

Balda is a great mountain, to the west of which is Asob. They remained here many years and thence migrated to the land of Yola (Adamawa).

Then they arose and passed through the Bashima and other similar tribes to Muri, to a region called Bumandá. Then they spread abroad.

Some went to Jebjeb and Gwona (Gwana) and settled. Then some migrated to north of Keffi to a site between Bagaji* and the town of Keffi.

There this section remained many years, and thence went to Zaria† where they established themselves and settled for three hundred years, till their town met an evil fate and broke up in fear of the attacks of the Bornuese of the stock of Tuba'al Awwal.

They then scattered in all directions and into many different places.

Some went, among them their King, to Wukari with two of his brothers, kings' sons, and the chief slave‡.

Others of the kings' sons and their people went west, according to their account.

As for the pagans of the region, they were like the Kuraish (the people of Al-lat and Al Ozza); they were the Kengawa. The Kisara settled at Karshi but did not remain long. These pagan "Kuraish" drove them out, and hence the country was called Karshi.

The name of the town Karshi§, however, was not the name of the people.

---

* The Sarikin Bagaji (N. of Keffi), is called "Sarikin Larabawa". The legend at Keffi has it that hundreds of years ago, a party of " Arabs " settled at Bagaji.

† It appears probable that the stay "at Zaria" and "Karshi" bears some relation to the mysterious kingdom of Guangara (Gangara) which, according to Leo Africanus (1513) lay south of Zamfara. There are traditions in Katsina that at one time there were at Gwozaki 1,000 wells from which a great army drank. The Zaria Chronicles date the Zaria Habe Kings from 1505, which fits in (allowing a certain margin of error) pretty well. Evidently Leo's Gangara was not a "Hausa" country but by influence "Songhay" and this reference to "Zagzag" not "Zaria" trade to the South, and the hostility of Bornu to Gangara, suggest the above explanation. Probably very soon after Leo wrote Muhammad Edrisimi (1526-1545) drove these Gangara kings West.

If this is correct, the Kororofawa would seem to have founded this Gangara Kingdom about 1200 A.D. or so. According to Mallam Sheriff, on the authority of Mallam Kura, their capital was at Kurfena. This capital was probably destroyed as stated by Leo Africanus by Haj Askia Muhammad of Songhay, about 1500 A.D. the chiefs then moving to Gangara.

It would appear again, quoting Mallam Sheriff, that the Zaria Habe Kings who succeeded were Toronke, put in by the Askia, whence the name Bakwa Turunku. It is probable that the Zaria Chronicle is wrong about the date of Queen Amina, who, *vide* the Kano Chronicle, lived about 100 years before this. She was apparently an Amwutsi (Queen Mother) of the Kororofa. On the other hand, the Turunku put in by Askia Muhammad had probably first settled at Kawuri and only later founded Zaria, about 1530, after the destruction of Gangara.

‡ *i.e.*, Doma, Kiama, and Tshendam.

§ Karshi is not far from Sakaba (Sokoto Province). In Nasarawa Province, there are also several villages called "Karshi", all inhabited by "Gwandara" called "Karshi" by Hausas.

Then the Kisara moved on and crossed the river Niger. One chief built the city Wawa, and another built the city of Baku*.

Then the pagan followers of Al-Lat and Al-Ozza (Kengawa) spread among them, and their chief (*i.e.* chief of the Kengawa etc.) built the city of Fissa (near Busa) and his people spread abroad and would not follow any king but their own.

Another of the sons of the Kisara, King of Zaria, was called Attahir. The name was shortened in Atta. He and his people at Attagara went south (*i.e.* to Idah†).

---

* These towns were founded long anterior to Busa. The title of the Kings of Illo, Busa and Kiama, is Ki which seems equivalent to the Bornu ruling Barbar clan title, Kayi, Keyi or Kiyi. Among the Jukon, the spirit of the deified deceased king (Aku) is called Aki, and in Wadai all the names of the ruling clans (originally Barbar) begin with the letter K.

The title of the Kororofa ruling caste, Jukon, is by Captain R. C. Abraham equated to the name of the Barbar or Tuwareg nobles, Imagaren or Imajaren.

The original meaning of Ki seems to have been genitival or possessorial, the "Ki-sara" being "owner of" "king of" the Barbar "sagh" or "sara" (encampment). In Hausa the order of the two words is reversed and Sara-ki = King; while in the Beli-Zaghawa language of Wadai Ki-sar means "father", *i.e.*, "owner of the encampment."

† A Nupe informant states that originally the old Nupe Kings, the Jukon of Wukari and the Igara of Idah (Attagara), were all Bari-Bari (Barbars) of Bornu and that these Bari-Bari came to the region of Karshi (Sokoto) whence

    (*a*) The Nupe Kings went to Lade, Mokwa, and Raba near Jebba.
    (*b*) The Jukon to Bepi and Wukari.
    (*c*) The Atta (Atta-gara) to Idah.

XVII.—THE SO.

A remembrance to avoid forgetfulness of events through lapse of time

Let him who chances on this writing know that the land of Bornu was aforetime in the hands of the So. The So were a Sudanese people. Among their characteristics was that one of them could hunt an elephant and carry it on his head by reason of his strong body and determination.

They lived in the land for many years, and made great progress, and built many towns, among them, Kuturgemi, Martema Gagomi, Ala Alami, Bani Dalami, Mongonu, Amaza'u Memi Ga, Azakira Gemi, Gurzama Wajani, Amzami, Kalwa, Takallam, Mintur, Mazari, Zowimi, Yedi, Zowarge, Burnuski, Salagajimin, Awinarge, Dunguram, Gegeram, Gawogalturma Barbarwa, Burba Alami.

They ruled as we have heard four hundred and fifty-one years. They were related to the people of the Book, the Magians H.M.M. LL. Then came the Sultan of Yaman and conquered them by guile not by the sword, for he saw that they were of great stature, and was afraid that they might prove too much for his people with their spears.

He assembled his people and took counsel with them. They counselled him to learn their secrets in order to gain power over them.

So he met the So and held out the hand of friendship and good cheer, till the opportunity came.

He gained influence with them, and used every ruse of statecraft, till in the end he overcame them, and took the country from them by guile—that is to say Mai Ali who lived at Birni Gazargamu.

The Mai who built the Birni was Mai Ali Dunamami. The Mais had come from the land of Kanem, where they had ruled for four hundred and forty-one years*. It was after that that Sultan Ali came to Bornu.

The first place he came to was Koganaram for seven years, then to Kodalabu (near Mongonu) for three years, then to N'gornu for eighteen years, and so on, till they built their great Birni, Birni Gazargamu and lived in it for three hundred and thirteen years.

Then came the "Mahir al Bornawi" called Gwoni Mukhtar, and drove them to Gashegar and Mongonu, where they met the Sheikh al Amin.

He had come to Kowwar, and called the Sultan Dunama and asked him whether he should pray God to restore his power.

The Sheikh made conditions and offered them to him. The Sultan accepted them. The Shiekh then performed the Sultan's commands, and God accepted his prayers.

---
* 441 Muhammedan years, before the founding of Gazargamu (1484 A.D.) is A.D. 1056, approximately the date of Umme Jilmi. It will be observed that the So are supposed to have come to Bornu shortly before that date.

The Sultan returned to Gazargamu and ejected the Fulani. The Fulani returned, drove out the Sultan in flight, and lived there after their entry for some days.

They then left and went back to their country, the Sultan Dunama being then at Kurna*. Then he left Kurna and went to Degage, where he was terrified to hear of the re-entry of the Fulani into Gazargamu. He sent again to Sheikh Amin. The latter came, and the Sultan went to Kabila, while the Sheikh went to Ngormu.

---

* Between Mongonu and Ngornu, west of Kukawa.

XVIII.—THE SO DALA N'GUMAMI.

This is the story of what happened between the So and Mai Ali Gaji Zeinami.

The town of So Dala N'gumami was called Gagi Dibun, and there he lived with his people. He was a hunter and hunted in the bush.

The Yamanites met the So in the bush, and afterwards went out to pasture from their town, Wudi, in search of a good site for a city. Thus they came to the So country and met So Dala N'gumami, and he them. They looked on each other in wonder.

The Yamanites then invited So Dala N'gumami to come and see them. He did so, and asked the Yamanites " Where is your place of origin? You are men, but we have never seen anything like your ' beasts ' in all our time, you are sons of Adam, though small in stature; but what we marvel at is your beast which has an undivided hoof, and a hairy neck, and no horn but a long and bushy tail. This is a wonderful thing."

They said: " We have come to pasture our flocks and herds in this land."

Then the Yamanites returned to their town, and he to his.

So Dala G'gumami reached his home and told the news to his aged uncle; he said " I have seen a marvel hunting in the bush, which you have never seen in all your days ". His uncle said: " What did you see? " He replied: " I was hunting in the bush, and had found one elephant and killed it, and slung in on my shoulder, when I found people pasturing. They were of a different colour to us, and their beasts were different. I never saw any creature like them. The people are however mortals, sons of Adam, though small and abnormal, but I was astonished at their beasts, the like of which was never seen.

Their beast has no horn, and has a bushy tail; its hoof is undivided so that when it walks it leaves a hole in the ground, so big is it."

The old man told the people the whole story, and said: " Even thus we have found in our histories, that in the north were a people who could come to our country at the end of time, and when they came would inherit this earth."

After this there passed a year and at its close So Dala N'gumami returned to his hunting ground, and the Yamanites struck camp and moved from Wudi to the water course where they pastured, and they met the So as before.

The Sultan called the So and he came.

The Sultan said " O So Dala N'gumami, we have come this year and met in this spot again; God has united us here again."

" Now if people meet a second time in a place, they make friends, and help one another, and make common cause to assist one another. We are all strangers, and your guests. Pray, give us a lodging." He said to them: " Come, follow me ". He followed, and he led them to the place of his farm, where he grew melons and gourds. Now the name for a farm, in the language of the So was N'gazar, and that was the name of this farm, and " Kumu " was the name of the village where it was*.

He gave them a lodging here.

Said the So: " These your people are small, and weak ". So he looked round, and went out, and cut a stockade, and tied up the logs into six bundles. As each bundle was complete, he planted the logs in the ground, leaving a space after the completion of each bundle as a gate.

That is why there were six gates of N'gazargamu, and the Kanuri called it: " N'gazargamu chinna arasku agaisheka firasku ". which means: " N'gazargamu of the six gates, and sixty salutations."

Thus he made a " zariba " round their lodging, and left six gates and said " Do not build a mosque in your town until I return. I purpose to go to Kano to build a mosque for the people there."

But after his departure they were impatient, and did not await his return, and built a mosque.

On his return he said: "Why have you done this, you have little patience? You will come to harm in the fulness of time, but the city of Kano will never decay or be destroyed."

After that the Yamanites and So lived together, but they were not alike.

When their children played together, the Yamanite children could not play with the So, for if they wrestled and fought, the So children killed the Yamanite children.

Thus children's play became a cause of strife. The Yamanites were annoyed at the play, and angry, but were unable to prevent it.

So they took counsel and resolved on war. But the Sultan said " No! Have patience, let us seek a pretext, or reason different to this." They then decided on employing " henna ".

They said: " We all have henna; let us put henna on the hands of our children. Let all our people go to the So, and let them see their hands dyed with henna."

The So saw their hands, and were astonished at the red of henna on the hands of the Yamanites, and said: " We saw your hands were red yesterday, but now they are not, so to-day make our hands like yours were, red and beautiful ".

The Yamanites went and informed their Sultan of this talk about henna. The Sultan said " Gather together henna, and pound it up, and slaughter oxen, and make strips of the skins of the oxen like ropes ". They obeyed the Sultans orders.

The Sultan went to the So, and said " Gather together and come to us that we may bind your hands with henna, like ours were ". They came.

---

* This derivation of Gazar-gamu is probably entirely wrong. It is clear from various vocabularies of the group of languages spoken by the So races, that " Gamu " was the title of a " king " and that Gazar is for " Ingazar " which meant (a) relatives; (b) the tribe Ingazar. Gazar-gamu is therefore either (a) relatives of the king (Gamu); or (b) king of the Ingazar tribe, i.e., these particular So.

Then the people of the Sultan tied up the hands of the So with "henna" and the Sultan said to them "Wait now three days", in order that the thongs might dry on their hands. He told his people to prepare for war against the So. "We will summon them", said he, "and say to them, come and we will unloose the henna thongs."

So the So came to the Sultan, but when they came, he ordered them all to be killed with spears, except So Dala N'gumami, since he was their friend.

So they killed all except So Dala N'gumami. But the So fought with their hands tied up as they were, and killed some of the Yamanites with their blows.

But all the So were killed, save that some fled to the east, and south, and west, and no more remained except So Dala N'gumami alone.

Such is the story of the destruction of the So in the land of Bornu.

XIX.—DUNAMA DABALEMI AND THE KWANA.

Mai Dunama built Birni N'jimi in Kanem, and then went to attack the Sultan of the Kwana. He sat down and described to his people the character of the Kwana.

He said: "They are utter pagans: with holes in their ears; they are not even afraid to eat men and dogs."

After that they went to attack the Kwana and came near to their land.

The Sultan of the Kwana was coming out to meet them, and had encamped with his army in the bush.

Then the spies of Mai Dunama saw him and his army encamped, and eating human flesh and dogs and tying up dogs for food.

They returned to Mai Dunama and were afraid. The army scattered and fled, and returned to N'jimi.

●   ●   ●

XX.—KINGS OF THE LAND OF FIKKA.

In the name of God, the Merciful, the Compassionate. May God bless the noble Prophet and his kindred and companions and bestow peace.

This book is a list of the kings of the land of Fikka from the beginning to the present day.

In the name of God, the Merciful, the Compassionate.

Concerning the origin of the race of the kings of Fikka from the time when they came with the Sultan of Bornu, and then separated on the shores of Lake Chad.

They lived together for some years on the shores of Chad, then discord arose and faction fighting on account of a gazelle.

The people of Fikka then arose, and left the people of Bornu, and came to the land of Dala* and dwelt in it for years. Then they left Dala and came to the land of Kilba and fought with the Kilba.

From Kilba they moved to the Babur country, and thence came to Fikka Geyri. On arriving at Fikka Geyri they saw people and a cave dug like a well, and placed there their books and talked to the people.

They came close and said " This is God's doing, be He exalted, this shall be our home." So they dwelt there in Fikka Geyri for a space of one hundred years and a few more.

The Emir of the Pabir (Babur) attacked them. Then they said " This matter has a cause." The people of Kulami (that is to say the people whose chief was Kulami) said " Get up and march ". they marched to Kulami Kabir, the ancient town, and settled in it, remaining for ninety years.

After that the people of Fikka and the people of Biyri said: " Come and migrate with us ". But the Sultan Kulami ibn Adam al Yamani refused to leave, saying: " I am not tired of this place; go ye: but I will remain behind here ".

So the people of Biyri and the people of Fikka arose and the Sultan of Biyri also arose. He was the " senior ".

The Sultan of Fikka was the junior. The Sultan Gurbali, who was the son of the daughter of the Sultan, was the least among them.

They assembled, and came to the river called Gaji. When they had passed the river in the wet season, Sultan Gurbali said: " I am the son of the daughter of the Amir, my hunting place is here, for I am not with you in your wearisome march."

The Sultan Biyri and the Sultan Fikka joined forces and came to the gate of the town of Jimbam and alighted in the gate of Jimbam, and stayed there a few days. Then the Sultan of Biyri said " I wish to be Sultan and paramount ". The people of Fikka said " If you become a paramount Sultan, your power will be great. But, if you desire paramouncy over us, the people of Fikka, go away and good fortune will remain with us ".

---

*Dala, i.e., Dulo, North of Mora in Mandara. The King of Mandara is called Duloma, the rock is called Dala Diba.

The Sultan Biyri arose in the night, and left the people of Fikka and their army, and came to the place called "Mazwa", and stood round the rock with his host.

They made a sacrifice there, with their chiefs sitting by, and the King of Biyri exhorted them round the rock of Mazwa. They lit a fire. They alighted and took the fire, and then returned to the fire; they took it again and returned; and then again took the fire by companies and looked and saw flesh cut up. They said: "What is this?" Then they returned a third time, and put the fire out. They cut up the flesh, and gave it to a woman who was looking on. Then they sat down, and made a fire, and went and cut up the flesh for the people of the woman who had come down from the rock. She was enceinte. When they cut up that flesh the elders were angry. They cooked the flesh till morning.

The chief people of the place asked and said "Where is Dunamashi and where is Bulama and Afá and Zamo and Atuman ibn Adam, and the woman Zâra who came yesterday night to the sacrifice?" Then they cut up the flesh and gave it to the woman, and took her to her people and handed her to them, so that they took her and sacrificed her, and cut open her womb, and found flesh in the mouth of the foetus which was found in his mother's womb.

Then they left the place, and mounted the rock.

The people of Biyri then left Mazwa because they were bitten by snakes, and scorpions, and leopards, and insects.

This was the reason they left, and then returned to the gate of Jimbam, and found the people of Fikka and their army there.

The people of Fikka asked them: "Where have you been for all these days?" A small boy among them said: "I will tell you the truth. They have committed murder". The people of Fikka said: "Why have you come back after you left us? We do not agree to stay with you."

The people of Biyri got up and went to the wâdi, where they now live, and left the Sultan of Fikka, Dunamashi, in the gate of Jimbam.

Then Sultan Dunamashi died.

Then Sultan Afá succeeded at Jimbam, and remained some days. Then they went to a place Kadibu-al-Kabir. Afâ died at Kadibu.

Then Bulama his brother became King and took his people and left Kadibu and went to Turyul, and died at Turyul.

Then Sultan Zâmo his brother became King. He took his people and left Turyul and went to Shallam (Shillem) and thence to a place called Kufi to hunt, he and his son together. He then entered his house and ruled and hence was called Zâmo.

Then his brother, King Atamun ibn Adam Al Yamani, succeeded. He returned from Kufi. His son Zâmo, took bow and arrows, and shot at his father with them to get his father's throne. Sultan Atamun returned to Fali Ajiji with his people. He said "This is my only son, I have no other, he has no elder brother, and I have no son, or younger brother." Then he asked about a house. He stayed three months.

Then the King Atamun Zámo and his people went out in the morning of the next day at 9 a.m.

The Sultan Atamun Burdama settled at Sabari and died there.

Sultan Idris his son rose (an old and failing man, whose son ruled for him), and left Fali Ajiji and came to Gildafu and lived there. He got up and went to the rock Gamazu and lived there seven years, and he went to Lariski, and from there to the rock of Daniski where he found a people and a cheif Danisku and lived on the rock seven years. He died.

Then his son, Sultan Banua. He reigned thirty years.

Then Sultan Weni succeeded Banua and reigned two years.

Sultan Barma ruled seventeen years.

His son Sultan Gandwa reigned thirty-four years.

Sultan Langu ruled seventeen years.

Sultan Weni, son of Sultan Barma, reigned one year.

Sultan Mabile Mansu, seventeen years.

Sultan Halbu, nineteen years.

Sultan Anbanga reigned eleven years.

Sultan Muhammad Kayi reigned thirty-five years.

Sultan Muhammad Bawakayi reigned ten years. May God pardon him.

Sultan Mele Fusam, son of Muhammad Kayi, ruled twenty-five years and four months.

Sultan Fikka Ibrahima Wamu reigned fifteen years.

Sultan Muhammad Malu reigned six years and three months.

Sultan Adam Bakam, seven years.

Sultan Muhammad Kulli reigned ten years.

Sultan Muhammad Gimsi, five years.

Sultan Suleiman, three years.

Sultan Haji, seven years.

Sultan Langua, six years.

Sultan Othman ruled four years.

Sultan Muhammad Gaze ruled four years.

Sultan Melle Ata ruled four years

Sultan Ibrahim Zara came down from the rock of Daniski. He became a Moslem, and held to the Sharia. He ruled well, and founded the town of Fikka. He ruled at the town of " Lafia Moi ", and that is the original Fikka, fourteen years, and died. May God pardon him.

Sultan Adam Fatuma ruled twenty-one years.

Sultan Idrisa ruled thirteen years, and died.

Sultan Muhammad Fatuma Zâra ruled ten years, three months and twenty days.

Sultan Langua Shishi ruled four years, two months, and fifteen days.

Sultan Muhammad Buwi ruled eleven years.

Sultan Haji ruled eight months and twelve days.

Sultan Muhammad Dâdâ ruled three years, two months, nine days.

Sultan Suleiman, seventeen years, ten months.

His son Idrisu ibn Dawêna reigned twenty years and seven months, fifteen days.

The writer is the Alkali of Fika Yakub, son of Mallam Halilu, son of Abdu Salâm, son of Abd-ul Jalil, in the year of the Hijra 1340/1921.

It is said that since the time of the " division " at Lake Chad, is more than 700 and less than 1000 years.

This is from a true source.

Notes.

Dala in the land of the Babur, *i.e.* Mandara.

Kilba. or Kulba.

Fikka Geyri—near the Gongila river in Gwani. Geyrawa, a People of Bauchi came from there, *i.e.* Gwani. Some of the Geyrawa went to Fâri, Kirfi, and Wukari. Geyrawa and Jukonawa are the same people.

Kulami people of the rock at Kalam in Gombe

Kunde—Biyri—Dutsin Duku.

Gaji between Fikka and Nafada.

Jimbam near the Gongila river.

Mazwa South-east of Fikka.

Kadibu west of Fikka.

Shallam Shillem (near Yola)

Gamazu near Bauchi.

Lariski in Bauchi.

Daniski in Fikka country

XXI.—BOOK OF BLACKSMITHS.

The blacksmiths in origin were slaves. The Prophet captured them in war at Khaibar. He bound the people of Khaibar and took their goods. Their property was divided. All of them then became slaves but they were not divided up.

The people said: "O Prophet, divide up the slaves." He said: "I leave them between Muslims and pagans to be of service, but there is no penalty on killing them, except the killer must fast for two months, and provide sixty poor men with food." Some of the Ulema say that the "diya" for killing a blacksmith is one hunting dog, i.e. forty dirhems. This is the best opinion. Perhaps the blacksmiths were slaves of the Jews. It is said that the origin of the diya of a blacksmith being a dog is that Umr ibn al Khattab was beaten by Abu Luluhu; Umr ibn al Khattab said "a dog has beaten me" and did not say "a man has beaten me". Hence his "diya" was the same as the "diya" of a dog. No blacksmith has any standing of his own, so that he cannot say "I am a blacksmith"; he says "I am so and so, the son of such and such woman".

In reply to a question it was also said that no one gives a blacksmith "Zakka" in Ramadan, nor are they given Sadaka.

He who gives a blacksmith Zakka, does wrong, because it is said "Give no alms to the rich, or to a slave, or to an unbeliever, or a hypocrite, or a wicked person like the blacksmiths, the slaves of the Jews. He who trusts a blacksmith is like him who trusts a goat or jackal".

Slaves and unbelievers and ignorant persons and wrongdoers and Jews and blacksmiths cannot be witnesses; for blacksmiths are the slaves of the Jews.

They are descended from Lakik (slaves) like pagans. The blacksmiths wounded our Lord Muhammad (upon whom be peace).

They are treacherous even to the day of judgment.

Even though a blacksmith give alms it does not avail him on the day of judgment, even though he is a mallam; and since they wounded the Prophet of God, their testimony as witnesses is not received.

Cohabitation with them, legitimately or illegitimately is forbidden, and their women are Magians. If a man takes them either in marriage or adultery, he cannot become pure, even if he washes in nine wells in different quarters of the earth, or yet seven rivers.

The blacksmiths are fourteen kinds—some say, fifteen.

The first are Kangu Beni Lawan.

The second are Kangu Beni Dirimiwa.

The third are Kangu Beni Darawa.

The fourth are Kangu Beni Karusko.

The fifth are Kai Beni Kindirawa or Tsandira*.

---

* Lives in Kaga District Bornu Emirate, where he is head of the village of Tsendiya.

The sixth are Kai Beni Korio.
The seventh are Kai Beni Bultumiwa.
The eighth are Kai Beni Malei*.
The ninth are Kai Beni Bikawa.
The tenth are Kuburi Beni Ukuliwa (Yikilwa).
The eleventh are Kimebu Beni Kanamwa†.
The twelfth are Kachitu Beni Furtuwa (Kajidi).
The thirteenth are Ngizim Beni Kazami‡.
The fourteenth are Tumagiri Beni Aristsowa.
The fifteenth perhaps is Magumi Beni Dala Kura.

They are descended from Abu Luluhu. If you shake hands with a blacksmith, go and wash your hands for their diya is as the diya of a dog, even though a blacksmith is a mallam, just and true. They are not persons to be trusted.

Even though a blacksmith is a free man leave him alone; if anyone forgets these precepts and touches a blacksmith, let him wash his hands. If a man does not wash his hands and prays afterwards, his prayers are of no avail.

This is the law of the blacksmiths, as given by the book of the blacksmiths. it is finished—the book of the origin of the blacksmiths.

God pardon us and our fathers their transgressions and all Muslim men and women, and open the path of knowledge to all.

The writer is Muhammad ibn Aisha, whose father is Garema Kellu. May God pardon you all your sins. Praise God. Lord of the worlds. Finished on a Sunday, at midday. May God give us heaven. Amen! Amen!! Amen!!!

---

* People of Kachella Bilal.
† Head of Bargo, Geidam District, Bornu Emirate.
‡ At Zabulam Fugu Jil. Geidam District.

XXII.—THE BADE TRIBES.

A note on the history of the Bade. The Bade were inhabitants of Badr. Badr was ruled by the Tuba'al Awwal. The latter brought the Bade to Birnin N'jimi, and then to Birnin Wudi.

At that time the Bade inhabited the town of Arege. This town of Arege was four years in existence before Gasrgamu was founded.

The future Sultan of Gasrgamu was at Wudi. A " cheetah " was caught at Wudi, and escaped.

The people of Wudi followed it on horseback, till they came to Gasrgamu, a rich country which exceeded Wudi in plenty and wealth.

So they returned and told their Sultan that they had seen a fair spot.

The Sultan accepted their statement and hence they moved to Gasrgamu.

But the oldest town of all was Gamgar. Its chiefs were:—

Makinta Yat-ku.

Makinta Baro.

Kaloma Arge.

These men were brothers, they came from Wudi to Bornu.

Makinta Baro was born on the march near the town of Baro. Here his descendants remain to this day.

Kaloma lived, first at Bundi, and afterwards at Arege.

All the Bade are one in origin. They followed along the river valley and spread inland to Gwagaram and Dala, and Tagali and Dogana.

XXIII.—THE BADE AND N'GUZUM.

This is the history that Mallam Tijani found concerning the origin of the Bade and N'guzum. They have an identical origin.

The N'guzum are from eight stocks:—

The people of Sunamari.
,, ,, ,, N'gazala.
,, ,, ,, Mugnum.
,, ,, ,, Daja.
,, ,, ,, Galtagum.
,, ,, ,, Dable.
,, ,, ,, N'zami.
,, ,, ,, Alarba (Alorbos).

Their best known town now is Kanuri, which was a town founded by the people of Mugnum.

But N'gizari Kura and N'gizari Gana are towns of the people of N'gazala.

The town of Daja was north of Potiskum. Their chief was Mai Wame. It was a town of the people of Galtagum. The chief of the town was Mai Altakashi.

The tribe of N'gamo lived to the east of Potiskum, their chief was Mai Gazabu, from whom Chiroma Muhammad is descended. So much for the names of their towns, and their chiefs.

As to their history, they were among the number of Yamanites who migrated. From the time of their migration till to-day, they have never agreed with the other Yamanites.

No matter who were the kings of the Yamanites, there was always war between them and these peoples, till they all came to N'jimi. The nobles fought them in frequent wars, till they came to the land of Bornu, to a town called Dadigar.

When they saw the Kanuri standing in a place, they said in the So language, not in Arabic: " Ungo sandi dagata " (see them standing), hence the place was called Dadigar.

When they saw them in another place, they said in the So language not in Arabic: " Ungo sandi dababtana " (see them they are close), hence the place was called Dabiso.

As regards the names of the kings of the Bade, the first was Mai Badema. He was succeeded by Lawan Babuji, who seized the power from Mai Badema. He went blind, and was succeeded by his son, Lawan Haji, who took the power by force.

The names of their towns are Dadigar, Dabiso, Gashima, Tagali, Yam-dugu, Duguna, Linu Kunu, Tawa Masaba, Gangawa, Gadin, Dalla, Gwagaram.

The names of the towns in the old book were Zabatam and Yagule. These two were close to the town called Galamaram, the site being to the north of the present Galamaram, which is close to a town called Mallam Ibramri.

Mallam Ibramri is on a high sandy ridge. Zabatam was south of Mallam Ibramri, and close to Yagule.

XXIV.—GARUN DOILI.

This is the story of the Magumi who came from Yaman to Birni Gasargamu.

Know that Mai Katuri was Sultan of Birni Gasargamu. He sent his son Badema Zabu to war in the east. After he had gone, Mai Katuri died.

The people of the Birni consulted together, and the kingdom was given to Mai Umr Katurimi.

Then Badema Zabu heard of the death of his father while away at the war, and returned and found his brother Mai Umr on the throne of his father.

He then tried to gain the throne, but the result was civil war.

They fought and Mai Umr prevailed over Badema Zabu, and drove his people west, till they came to the river of Gudugal.

Badema Zabu made a stand here, and prevented his brother drinking.

Then Mai Umr again prevailed over his elder brother so that the Bade fled over the river. Mai Umr then returned to Gasargamu, while Badema Zabu and his people went to Gulu Gudugum. He left his family there, and from thence went out into the bush alone because of his chagrin.

His people then went to look for him. They sought him in the bush for three days, and finally found his " crown " and " tasbih " (rosary), " slippers", and " staff " on an ant's nest.

They took this apparel, but this, the place of his tomb, was engulfed by the river.

He (the Bedema) is a Walii of God and his tomb is covered in sand in the midst of the river. The people returned to their town Gulu Gudugum, and took counsel, and chose Mai Gadigu for their king, and, after him, his son Mai Jawa; then Mai Duwaga, Mai Umr, Mai Mele, Mai Dala, his brother Mai Ali, Mai Kubu, Mai Alabeyayi, Mai Duwaga, Mai Bukr, Mai Ibrahim, Mai Mustafa, Mai Othman, Mai Dunama, Mai Baluta, Mai Daudu, Mai Kagu and Mai ibn Baluta, to be their kings in turn.

Then came Mai Alaheyayi ibn Mai Baluta, Mai Musa ibn Baluta, Mai Guluti ibn Mai Musa, Mai Umr ibn Mai Kagu, Mai Dunama ibn Mai Kagu.

Then they split up. Mai Dunama ibn Mai Kagu lived at Garun Doili. Then Mai Dapsoma ibn Mai Umr went to Masaba, north of the river.

Then there ruled his brother Lowan Dunama, then his son Lowan Umr. He is chief of Masaba now, and Lowan Salaiman ibn Mai Dunama is at Garun Doili; he is lord of Garum Doili now, and is a descendant of King Katuri, from whose time until this day (1917) is six hundred years and nine months*.

---

* i.e., 1335 A.D. approximately the date when the Saifawa first began to come west of Lake Chad.

XXV.—GAU DALA SHÂLIWA.

Gau Dala Shâliwa Gaje Darmanmi was in origin a So, he was one of the So Omdahs. His town in the So period was Degwa* near Kirik, and his descendants are called N'gau. Their present representatives have for chief Zanua Gamzakema, who is descended from Gau Dala Shâliwa.

Among the chief So towns which were close to N'gazargamu were Kirik and Gagidibun, and Degwa and Bilabirin and Damasak.

In the west were Kubdi†, Jigalta‡, Dalarge, Gamgalarge§, Yimyim, Zugume, Amerge, Meba, N'giwa, N'gwodedo, Karagu, Kiari, Dungua, Muskuo, Muskonden, Kibande, Muskoa, Dalarge.

The tribe of Kinania were Kindin *i.e.* Tuwareg. They were called Beni Mala Kinda and were the tribe of Mala Kindabu. Their chief towns were Sulo, Ririgu, Mai, and Kirga. They are now all at Kirga. The Beni Mala Kinda had originally no town.

Kirga is now composed of a mixed population of the Mala Kindabu, Takku Buduma, and other Kanembu. They live close to Kitati and Kikawa.

---

* Degwa and Gorogo are near Bilabirin and Gagidibun, in Nganel.
† Near Busugwa in Magumeri District.
‡ In Nganse District.
§ Gamgalarge in Mongonu.

The Gamzakema is chief of the village of Gamzai Gagala near Geidam. His function was to execute criminals sent from N'gazargamu by fastening a pot filled with mud round their necks and throwing them into the River Yobe.

XXVI.—GUJBA GIRGAM.

Maina Gabai came out from Daura and built a town called Bila Fune, and then Dala Buni. He was an N'gazar. He built Nâra Chamu, and Ta'wa, and Kolon N'gorido, and Kêsa Mainawa-'be. He died at Kêsa Mainawa'be.

When he died, Mai Mommadu Kelumi was made chief at Gambarkam. He ruled one hundred years.

Mai Mêle Fusammi then ruled at old Dêya.

Then they went to N'gazar-Gana, and thence to Gabâya, and old Dêya.

At old Dêya Mai Mêle Fusammi ruled fifty years, and died.

Mai Mommadu Silbêma— ruled at Kinza-Kusku fifty years.

Then his younger brother Mai Hassan ruled thirteen years.

Mai Mêle Turama—ruled three years, and died at Turo.

Mai Waudo Kelumi—ruled eight years and died at Daura.

Mai Mêle Kelumi—ruled thirty-three years.

Mai Mommadu Lefia—ruled thirteen years and went to Bilbala and died.

Mai Mommadu Saurima—ruled three years—and went to Kelum, and died.

Mai Ari Damnuma—ruled at Dêya thirteen years, and went to Mazanu and lived there fifteen years, and thence to Gujba for five years. He ruled thirty-three years. He died at Gujba.

Mai Ari Kiamôma—ruled three years. He went to Kukawa and died there.

Mai Musa Melêmi—ruled three and half years. He went to Gabata. He died there.

Mai Annur Lefiami—ruled one and half years near Gujba, and died there.

Mai Mêle Ajimi—ruled twenty-one years at Kadei and died there.

Mai Sumaila Gambômi—nine years at Gujba and died there.

Mai Dunoma Kalami—ruled three years and went to Makubûra and died there.

Mai Arri Chiroma—ruled nine years and resigned.

Mai Arri Musami—resigned after four years rule.

Mai Mêle Musami—five years.

Mai Tujani—resigned—ruled twenty-three years.

Mai Hubar—three years (1923).

The total years are six hundred and ninety-two: till to-day. 6th February, 1923.

Note.—According to this account the Kanuri first come to the Gujba Region in Western Bornu about 1252 A.D., which is about the date when, according to Ibn Said, the King of Kanem (Dunama Dabalemi) penetrated these regions to the West of Lake Chad.

XXVII.—THE PEOPLES OF BORNU (GUJBA MSS).

Of Him we seek help.

We have written this paper concerning the origin of peoples, and the names of tribes.

The first who came to Bornu was a white man—English. He never built a house, but came to see the country, and returned to Aramik at a remote period.

Afterwards came a tribe called M'bum, and then the M'bana, and then the Kuna (Kwana).

Then the Tawarik Kindin Kel Bura, and then the So.

Then the Magumi Saif, then the Kai Bulala.

Then the Fellata, and the Kuburi, then Wadai, then Rabeh.

Then came the English and ruled Bornu.

The old order finished—God is most knowing.

The Magumi Saif ruled three hundred and thirty-three years.

The Fellata remained only forty days at N'gazargamu.

The Kuburi, with the Magumi Saif. The former turned out the latter, and have been ruling one hundred and eighteen years, and there are none left of the tribes of the land of Bornu.

An indication of the Dêya language spoken by the people.

The name of a hen is Gaza.

,, ,, ,, water is Ayli Aman.
,, ,, ,, food is Abin ishaban.
,, ,, ,, spear is Ayli ayam.
,, ,, ,, stomach is Kunu.

The people of Dêya originate from N'galagal, and they are called N'galaga. So a man of Daya told us.

The language of Dêya from ancient times has been called N'galgal. They were descended from Gwoni Ma'azu ibn Jabal, and to them belongs the Kadi Mainin Kanandin.

NOTE.

The manuscript is of considerable interest and, though the early European explorer (probably Barth) is somewhat antedated, the sequence of tribal occupation corresponds to general tradition.

The N'galaga were according to all accounts the earliest comers among the five tribes which constituted the Kanuri nation. It would seem that it was from their proximity that the Arabs of Bornu called their own dialect Galgaliya. From them the ruler of the west, in the old Bornu Empire, was called N'galti-ma (Galadima, *i.e.* owner of the land of the N'gal). The N'galaga appear to be the Kalakin or Galakin of Makrisi, and also to be responsible for the name N'galaka, the old capital of Borku. The Kanembu form of the tribal name N'galaka, the old capital of Borku. The Kanembu form of the tribal name is N'galma.

According to Lowan of Bara (near Gujba) the N'galaga came to the Gujba region at a very early date, replacing the Kwana who retired south, but were subsequently themselves dominated by a member of the N'gasar tribe, who came from Daura, to the north of Gujba.

According to the chronicle of the N'gasar house, they began to rule about 1252 A.D., a date which corresponds exactly with Ibn Said's notice of the expedition of Mai Dunama Dabalemi of Kanem, against Mabana or Mabina. These Mabana or Mabina are clearly the same people who are in 1570-1600 A.D. called by Imam Ahmed " Binawa " and, at the present time " Mabani " or " Mafoni ". According to the present Kadi of Bornu this name means " youths " or " fighting men ", so that the point of Makrisi's remark that most of the " Mabina " were Kalakin (N'galaga) becomes patent.

The N'galaga, who are also called N'galaga Sau, were the predominant people in the regions stretching from the present capital of Bornu (Maiduguri), down towards the Gongila in the 13th century.

XXVIII.—THE LEGEND OF THE FIVE TRIBES OF KANEM.

In the name of God, the Merciful, the Compassionate.

This is an account of the birth and origin of the N'galawiyu, and Kuburi, and Magumi, and Kangu, and Kajidi, five tribes of common stock, but different branches.

They had one mother a woman named Ayesha, the daughter of the Sultan Ahmed, ruler of the town of Baghdad, a great town.

The Sultan's daughter, Ayesha, was beautiful in face and character; there was none like her in her time; and the Sultan gave her to the son of his brother called Maina Ahmed, and married her to him.

She gave birth to a boy called Ngal ibn Ayesha.

Then his father died, leaving N'gal.

After four months, there came the Sultan Abraha, the ruler of Yaman, and married Ayesha. So her father adorned her and sent her to Yaman.

She gave birth to a male child like a lion in appearance named Saif ibn Ayesha.

Then the Sultan Abraha died leaving Ayesha to inherit his property with her son.

They came to her father at Baghdad.

After four months there came the Sultan of Medina, the city of the Prophet, and married Ayesha. So her father adorned her and sent her to Medina.

She gave birth to a male child called Mani ibn Ayesha.

Then the Sultan of Medina died leaving Mani Kangu; and Ayesha arose and took her son and goods and came to the land of her father the King of Baghdad.

Then after four months came the Sultan of Misra and married Ayesha; and her father adorned her and sent her to Misra.

She gave birth to a son named Abdu'r-Rahman ibn Ayesha.

The Sultan of Misra died and left Abdu'r-Rahman. Ayesha once more with her son and property returned to Baghdad.

Thus this woman Ayesha, the daughter of Sultan Ahmed, enjoyed the dower of four Sultans in four different parts of the earth, and great wealth.

Now Ayesha was of small stature, and fair in face, and wealthy.

Hence she remarried, after four months, Kaigama Barka and then bore a son called Jidi Gaji.

Then mother Ayesha, the daughter of Sultan Ahmed of Baghdad the " city of light and revels ", died.

Ayesha was blessed in her descendants. Her children were:—

    First Hafidu, called N'gal:

    Second Saif, whose tribe is Magumi, and whose land is Yaman:

    Third Mani, whose city is Medina and tribe is called Kangu:

    Fourth Abdu'r-Rahman, lord of Misra, whose tribe is Kuburi:

Fifth Jidi Gaji, whose tribe is Kajidi:
All are of common stock, but different branches, which spread abroad in the land.

After the death of Ahmed and Ayesha, the five sons remained orthodox.

N'gal, the eldest, said " O my brothers, let us assemble and appoint one of our number to the throne of the kings, that he may govern the people ".

So they all met, and took counsel, and established a kingdom and agreed upon Saif ibn Ayesha, as a descendant of Tuba'ul Awwal, and made him Amir, and then separated each to his own country.

Then afterward N'gal, the eldest, said to Saif " O son of my mother, the people of this time do not follow you in word and deed. I advise you to cut my throat in your court when all the people are present so that they may see my execution and be afraid of you. But know that one cutting of my throat will not kill me; so give me one good stroke and leave me, then after the people have gone away, call me in a soft voice and I shall arise. This is my advice ".

So Saif did as N'gal told him, and then came to him afterward and raised his voice and said "Get up, O son of my mother, get up." But it was of no avail, for he died at the first blow.

King Saif said to N'gal " O son of my mother, you are now Duku*." So N'gal was called N'galma Duku. But his name was N'gal ibn Ayesha.

So we heard from our father and ancestor Sheikh Ajrami Kukawami (may God pardon him) and all our fathers and brothers.

The writer of this legend is Imam Yakurami ibn al Yamaniyi. Amen.

Probable meaning.

It is clear that these five tribes were the constituent parts of the original Kanem State. It is to them that Makrisi (1400 A.D.) refers in stating that " there follow the King of Njimi, that is the King of Kanem, five kings. The first Moslem King of Kanem was Muhammad (*i.e.* Dunama Dabalemi), son of Jil (*i.e.* Abd-ul-Jalil) son of Abdu'l-ahi (Bikur), son of Othman (Biri) son of Muhammad (Dunama) son of Umme, and the kings of Kanem were nomads in way of life."

Though Makrisi towards the end of the passage gives certain information about Mai Ibrahim and his descendants which was no doubt gleaned by Makrisi himself, it seems clear that the bulk of his notice was copied from Ibn Said and refers to the period before 1282 A.D., *i.e.* about the time of Dunama Dabalemi (1221-1259 A.D.

---

* Among the Kanuri the name Dugu or Duku was originally equivalent to the Tuwareg *tegasi*, *i.e.*, son of a sister or grandson (by a daughter) and so " heir." The N'galtima (Galladima) in the old Bornu kingdom was the Senior Chief almost equal to the Mai or Sultan. This story may be an allusion to that fact; on the other hand Dibu or Diba is a synonym of Duku and the name of the tribe is indifferently N'galma Duku or N'galma Dibu.

The word used in quoting the Saif legend—za'amu (allege)—shows that at least Makrisi, and probably ibn Said, did not believe the story of the descent from the famous Saif-ibn-Dthi-Yazan, and that legend has so many variations locally that it cannot well be accepted. The variation given above viz: that Abraha (the Abyssinian Christian General, who occupied Yaman), marched against Mecca in 570 A.D., and whose sons, Yaqsum and Masruq, were succeeded by the historical Himyarite Saif-ibn-Dthi-Yazan, was the father of the eponymous Saif of Bornu, is however of considerable interest in that it adds another to the numerous other indications that Christianity was at one time prevalent among certain of these Kanem tribes.

The tribe of N'gal, there is little reason to doubt, did not come direct from Mesopotamia. They could not have come from Baghdad, since it did not exist, but they are regarded, quite correctly, as being an early Kanem stock who were later joined by the Magumi and the others.

Concerning them, it would seem, in the first place, that they lay to the west of the country in which the Magumi originally lived since the N'gal-ti-ma (Galladima) was the officer who ruled the land of N'galti, *i.e.* the west, just as the Kaigama ruled the " Kagha " or south, and the Yeri-ma the country of Yim (Yam) or Yeri " the north ".

The earliest certain location of the N'gal-agha and the N'gizam, their cousins, is Lake Fitri, where they were settled as early as 1000 A.D. and were apparently much the same as the Dajo who were of Zaghawi (Tuwareg) stock in part, their capital being Semin or Samina, east of the lake, probably to be identified with Shebina.

In the Girgam or song of the Mais, the Kanuri capitals are given as Yam, Yaman, Badani, Guru Gayawa, N'jimi, Gazargamu, Kafila.

Yam, Yim, Yeri, and Yelan are all Kanuri words for " north ". In the two former the postfix is -am (people) in the two latter -ri and -lan are postfixes meaning " at " or " in ".

It is clear that to some early ancestors of the Kanuri " Ye " or " Yeh " was either a place or people to the north of them.

Now the word N'gal seems to be connected in meaning with, at least, two modern Kanuri words, N'galio or N'gario, which means a throwing knife, and " N'galgaliya " which means like " Barbara " in Arabic, the language of savages.

One infers that to the Magumi, the N'gal spoke a " barbarous language ", and also that they were in primis a people who used " throwing knives " or sticks.

As regards the N'gal language (now extinct) the manuscript from Gujba gives the following words:—

Hen = Gaza (Hausa: Kaza).

Water = Ayli amam.

Food = Abin ishaban.

Spear = Ayli abam.

Belly = Kunu.

All these words bear close analogy to Hausa or Tuwareg (Tamashek) forms, but none whatever to the Teda-Kanuri group.

The German G. A. Krausé is responsible for a statement that the Zaghawi language is " primitive Hausa ": a view borne out by the Zaghawa vocabularies published by Mr. MacMichael in the Anthropological Journal. Barth shewed that the Logone tongues are connected with Hausa; and Colonel Foulkes and the late Mr. Benton shewed that the languages of the N'gas and Bolewa respectively bear Hausa analogies, and, in addition to that, Mr. Carlyle has collected vocabularies of a whole group of Gongila tribes which bear a similar relation to Hausa, and to his list may be added N'gizam and Bade, which are both closely connected with Bolanchi.

There is consequently some reason to think that (a) the language spoken by the N'gal in Fitri, about 1000 A.D. was a language of the Hausa-Tamashek group, (b) that that language was related to the Zaghawa language.

XXIX.—THE STORY OF THE SEVEN TRIBES OF KANEM.

They are Saif ibn Aisa, Bulala ibn Aisa, Darman ibn Aisa, N'gal ibn Aisa, Duku ibn Aisa, Mani ibn Aisa, Jidi ibn Aisa. Their mother was Aisa, daughter of the King of Baghdad. Saif was descended from Abraha. The reason that he was called Saif was that there was war between Abraha King of Yaman, and the King of Baghdad. The latter defeated Abraha; Abraha went to Yaman and got 1,000 elephants, and intended to attack Mecca, but God sent the Abulbil birds. Every bird had three stones, one in its mouth, and one in each claw. Abraha's army were all killed, but he and his slave escaped and returned to Yaman. The birds followed them pelting them with stones.

At this time Saif was in the womb of his mother, and she sent to the King of Baghdad who sent and brought her home with all her goods. Saif was born in Baghdad. At this time the King of Baghdad had made a decree that all male children should be killed.

Saif's mother took him to the bush, and seeing a lioness with her cubs, placed Saif with the cubs, and returned.

The lioness suckled Saif till he became a boy. Then a blacksmith in Baghdad going one day to the bush saw Saif with the lion cubs, and took him home with him, and, when he grew up, taught him the trade of a blacksmith, but he was so strong that he broke the iron. The blacksmith was frightened when Saif glanced at him, so he took pepper and threw it in Saif's eyes. The people called him Saif; " Allah seyo " in Kanuri means " God gave me " which is what Saif's mother said to the lioness. It is thus "Seibo" or " Saifo ".

The blacksmith said " This boy has taken away my position ". When the people in Yaman heard the story, they came and took the boy away to Yaman and made him King of Yaman.

The facial marks of the Kanuri (bêri) are tokens from the marks the boy received from the claws of the lion's cubs in playing with them.

The descendants of Saif are:—

Saif son of Aisa, King of Yaman, the lion of Yaman, died in Yaman.

Ibrahim, son of Saif, died in Yaman.

Dugu, son of Ibrahim, died in Yeri Arbasan.

Fune, son of Dugu, died in Gagi Galanin.

Arjo, son of Fune, died at Galanbuta of the fishes.

Katuri, son of Aro, died at Kulo Yo (farms of Yo).

Boyoma, son of Katuri, died at Kulo Yo.

Bulu. son of Boyoma, died at Zabatam, the Sultan's summer house, the place of dôm palm, and fan palms.

Arigi, like silk to his tribe, son of Bulu, died at Zeila Wuzlan.

Sho, son of Arigi, died in Kutushi, the rocky.

Jil, son of Sho, died in Masar of the Mosques.

Umme, son of Jil, died at Ruwaya of the Mosques.

Dunama, son of Umme, died at Baranbushi of the fishes. (Red Sea).

Dalla, son of Dunama, died at N'gamtilo Jilarge.

Dalla (Abd'alla), son of Bikur (first son), died at Bikuranawa.

Tsilim, son of Bikur, died at Bi N'gizrewa.

Dunama Dibalemi, son of Tsilim, a great warrior, hotter than fire, hotter than the fire of Matabar, died in his house at Zantam.

Kade Arguza died in his town N'garwan.

Dalla, son of Arguza, died at Zantam.

Kade, son of Matala, grandfather of Biyoma, died at Yamduge of the rocks, and " Kurna " trees, at Zui-Zui of the date palms.

Othman, son of Kadai, died at Malakata.

Muhammad, son of Kadai, died at Maiyi Zigidam, the Sultan's Palace, of the dom and fan palms.

Idris, son of Aisa, died at N'guru of the fine " dandal " among the Wulu.

Darin (Hausa " Masanni ") died at Karinwa his town.

Umme, son of Aisa, died at N'galbiwa.

Biri, son of Amina, died in Bagarmi, at Kunguwa.

Kore Laga N'gubun.

Kore Laga N'garewan.

Kore Laga Afunu Dallawan.

Kore Kura died in the sands of N'gileru (near Birni).

Learned in the genealogy of the Jilwa, Jil Kulemi, the lion of Yaman, died in Yaman.

Muhammad, owner of Barambuta, died in his town Barambuta.

Umr, son of Idris, owner of Jimaram, died near N'jimi (baltebe).

Dalla, son of Umr, owner of Dagamo (near Geidam) the place of " kumkum " trees.

Kagu, son of Umr, died at Barambushi the place of fishes. (i.e. Red Sea).

Muhammad, son of Kagul (Hamsa), died at Buniwa (near Gabarawa).

Muhammad Falaga died at Gamgariwa.

Mustafa ibn Idris died at Magi Zigidam the palace where there are dom and fan palms.

Daudu, son of Nigale, died at N'jitiwa.

Osman, son of Daudu died at Burilim at N'jimi Gawala.

Saif Gana died at Badani N'guro Kalewa.

Yusuf, son of Saif, died at Arjino Gawala.

Tsilim, son of Hauwa, grand-daughter of the Bidama, owner of Gaduram, died in N'jimi Gawala.

Dunama, son of Dabale, died at Bursulim N'jimi Gawala.

Biri, owner of Tolamaram, Biri son of Dunama, died at Ukme.

Dalla Bikuru, son of Biri, owner of Gaduran, died at Gaduram Jimi Gawala.

Ali ibn Dunama died at Gazargamu.

Dunama, son of Ali, died at N'giswa.

Muhammad, son of Dunama, died at Marguba.

Duna, son of Amina, died at Wudurge.

Mommadu Fannami-Fanna, grand-daughter of the N'gumama, died at Gazargamu.

Ali Gaji Zeinami, the fever of the Bulala, died at Kanem Gawal.

His sister, Aisa Kili N'girmaramma, Aisa Sultan, Magaram, daughter of Dunama, Maida, died at Mai Kingarwa (near Geidam).

Idris, son of Ali called Alooma, died at Alo of the Dagana Daniski.

Muhammad, son of Idris, died in Kanem.

Brem, son of Gumsa, at Diskam. (between Birni and Geidam) Diskam in N'galagati.

Umar Dusami, son of Fusam, died at Gazargamu.

Biri Talamaramma-Kashim Biri, son of Umr, died at Tolamaram of the Mosques.

Ali ibn Umr died at Gazargamu.

Dunama, son of Ali, died at Gazargamu.

Ali ibn Dunama died at Gazargamu.

Dunama ibn Ali died at Gazargamu.

Ali ibn Dunama died at Gazargamu.

Hajji ibn Fanna died at Gazargamu.

Arri Ajimi died at Gazargamu.

Ahmed ibn Ali died at Gazargamu.

Dunama ibn Ahmed died at Bagarmi.

Ibram died at Kukawa.

N'gilleruma.

Ali died at Minarge.

XXX.—TRANSLATION OF A PASSAGE FROM THE TOHFUT-UL-ALABI RELATING TO THE SUDAN.*

There remain of the hundred years of inhabited country twenty years, of which fourteen are inhabited by Sudanese of different kinds.

Their country starts at the back of the west on the confines of Tanjir, and stretches along the shores of the Sea of Darkness (Atlantic.)

It is said that among their nobles five tribes have become Moslems, the nearest to us being Tambut (Timbuctu).

In the sands of that country is gold, treasure inexpressible. They have much gold, and merchants trade with salt for it, taking the salt on camels from the salt mines.

They start from a town called Sigilmasa, which is the most remote among the towns of the west, and travel in the desert as it were upon the sea, having guides to pilot them by the stars or rocks in the deserts.

They take provisions for six months, and when they reach Ghana they weigh their salt and sell it against a certain unit of weight of gold, and sometimes against double or more of the gold unit, according to the market and the supply.

The people of Ghana are the most civilized people in the Sudan, and the best looking. They have long flowing hair. They are sensible and of good understanding, and make the pilgrimage to Mecca.

But Kanuri (Ganuri) and Kaukau, and Silla and Tukrur, and Ghadamus are brigands. There is no prosperity in those countries. The people have no religion and no sense. The worst of them are the people of Kaukau, with their short necks, flat noses, and red eyes. Their hair is like pepper corns, and their smell is like the smell of burning horn. They shoot arrows poisoned with the venom of a yellow snake. Hit with that venom, within an hour the flesh drops from the bones even in the case of an elephant or other beast.

The cobra and all other kinds of snakes are to them as fish. They eat and care not for the venom of the cobra or any other snake but the yellow one which lives in their towns is preserved and its blood used as poison for arrows.

Their bows are small and short. I saw one of these people in the west with their bows and bow strings which latter are made of the fibre of a tree which grows in their country.

Their arrows are short, in length about a span or two. The tip is a thorn from a tree hard like iron. They bind this thorn into the arrow with fibre, and hunt the roan antelope.

They are evil people in the Sudan, and all the Sudanese do as they do, except Gargar. They care not for aught except war.

---

* The writer states that he saw Sicily in 511 A.H., i.e., he lived circa A.D. 1100-1150 or so.

They have small boards partly pierced and whistle into the holes making an extraordinary noise; then all kinds of snakes, cobras, and mambas, come out to listen, and are caught and eaten.

Some of the people wear snakes like a belt, and some use a long snake as turban and come thus to market, forgetting they are wearing them. They take off their clothes, and the people see the different snakes and thus in fear make presents to their owners to take them away. If they do not give the owner something he throws the snakes into their market stalls.

From the Sudan come different kinds of skins wonderfully tanned. One kind is very thick and soft and preferred in a violet-black colour.

A single skin weighs about twenty " Muna ", a " Muna " being a kantar. The shoes of kings are made from this leather. It does not deteriorate in water, nor lose its softness or pleasant scent.

A skin is sold for ten dinars. The sewing of the shoes rots, but the leather itself does not, nor does it tear. When washed with hot water in a bath, it becomes as new, and grandsons inherit such shoes from their fathers and grandfathers.

The animal from which these good skins are obtained is a big male antelope (oryx) with two horns like spears which are as long as his body and stretch backwards over it. If he wounds any animal with his horns he kills it at once. He has a thick neck.

Shields are made of its skin called Dirk-al-Lamtiya: a name which is connected with the name of this antelope (al amt). The shields are about three cubits long, and light and soft. An arrow cannot pierce them. They are white like paper, and are the best shields; they are beautifully made, they cover the horseman and his horse.

Among the people of the Sudan are the inhabitants of Zeila who are among the best of the Sudanese. They are Moslems. They fast and pray and make pilgrimage to Mecca every year by land.

The country of the Sudan stretches to Zinj and Beja, and is a space of fourteen years travel. The people eat dogs, and tie them up with sheep; they also eat rats.

The remainder of the one hundred years of inhabited earth is a space of six years constituting Habesh, and Hind, and Sin, and Fars, and Turk, and Khazan, and Saghaliba, and Rum, and Faranj, and Al-Ma-Mashâ, and Al-Kadhara, and Tâlashan. They include Arabs and people of Yaman and Irak and Sham and Misr and Andulus, as far as the great Rum, and the other tribes of the unbelievers. Among them the Moslems are as one in a thousand.

According to the chronicler of Sana'a' there is a tribe of Arabs who are represented as being half-men, having half a head, half a body, and one hand and one leg. They are called Obâl and are of the descendants of Aram, son of Shem, and brothers of the 'Ad and Thamud. They have no understanding and live among the 'Ajam in groves on the banks of the Indian Ocean.

The Arabs called them Nasnâsu, and hunt and plunder them.

They speak the Arabic language, and assign to themselves an Arab origin, and called themselves by Arab names.

Al Ashâru writes: "I saw in the Tarikh of Sana'a that a merchant travelled in their country and saw them running on one leg and mounting the trees and running away in fear that the dogs would catch them. He heard one of the singing:—

"'I flee in fear of the King's pleasure
"'Fearing that I may find no avenue of escape.
"'I am feeble of body and far on in years.
"'To-day I am here an utter stranger.'"

Al-'Ashiu mentions them in his verse:—

"See ye not the 'Ad,
"Night and day have obliterated them;
"The Thamud perished after them,
"Since a stronger power entered the fight aginst them.
"Then Jasm and Tasm: their houses have become as the desert.
"Tadis and Yus preserved them alive from the evil that was written
"After them Obâl was wiped out in the desert where there are no wells."*

In Sudan are a people who have no heads.

Al-Shariyu mentions them in his book "Siratu ul muluk" and states that in the desert of the west are a people who are all females, having no males, for the latter cannot live in the country.

It is said that those women enter the water, and are made pregnant by it; that every women gives birth to females only, not males; and that the Tubba' Dth'l Manâr reached their country when trying to reach the Sea of Darkness (Atlantic) which Dthu'l Karnain before him had reached.

God knows best, but this Tubba's son Ifrikish ibn Tubba Dthu'l Manâr was the prince who built the city of Ifrikia, and gave it his own illustrious name.

His father, the Tubba, reached the Wâdi Sabti, a Wâdi in the west, where the sand flows down as water.

No beast can enter but it perishes. When Tubba Dthu'l Manâr saw it, he returned in haste.

When Dthu'l Karnain reached it, he halted till the proper day Sibti (Saturday). Then its sand current ceased and he crossed and came to the Sea of Darkness (Atlantic). So it is said, but God knows best.

The people with no heads have eyes on the shoulders, and their mouths are in their breasts. They are a vast multitude; they breed like cattle and are never jealous, for they have no understanding.

---

* There is a pun here on the words "Abâr" (wells), and "Avâr" for Avalis or Awar, a variant of "Obâl."

XXXI.—WANDERINGS OF THE SAIFAWA.

In the name of God, the Merciful, the Compassionate. The peace of God rest on him after whom is no other Prophet, his relations and friends, and those who follow him.

The learned Sheikh of olden time says that the first Sultan was Saif bin Dthi Yazan. It is related that he went to Kaisira to ask for help against Masrouk, son of Abraha, the owner of the elephant, who killed Aryat and seized the kingdom of Yaman. After Abraha's death, his son Yaksum became king, and then Yaksum's brother Masrouk, son of Abraha.

Saif killed the latter and then ruled over the kingdom of Sana'a in Yaman and the Habesh, and the last of the dynasty was King Bazen.

Saif however was the first of these Sultans, gaining his power by help of soldiers from Bagdad.

The Saifawa ruled over Yaman for one hundred years; then they were at Rugzu for two hundred years: thirdly at Agniva for twenty years: fourthly they ruled Badani for sixty years: fifthly their kingdom was in Sham for seventy years.

Then the sons of Saif migrated to the land of Rum, and became rulers over it: they came to the tribe of Kubri, and lived among them twenty years: and then to the tribe Kangu, over whom they became rulers, and from whom they acquired knowledge.

Then they came to the Habesh, and stayed three years or more; and afterwards to the Dibiri, among whom they dwelt for fifty years.

Their next move was to the Arab tribe of Wahab called Tumakir*, over whom they exercise no rule, but among whom they lived for sixty years.

Then they came to the tribe of Duguti, and lived among them in the land of Babil for fifteen years; thence to the tribe Kachitu (Kajidi) and were united and lived for thirty-three years.

Thence they came to the land called Saman or Samaka, where they stayed five years, and then came to Ibrahim, whose slave was a man called Abagu, and remained for one year.

After this they came to Samta, the town of the Fellaita† Sugur, and pacified and administered that tribe and stayed for five years, after which they arose and lived in Yaman for two hundred years.

From here they journeyed to Medina, where Muhammad the Prophet sent to the sons of Saif his two companions Maath bin Jil and Othman bin 'Afan, as also Abi Bakr Ka'ab and Zeid bin Thabit: and they sent their chief to Muhammad saying "We are Muslims, and are not as those who associate other gods with the God."

The Prophet said to them "Ye are our brothers, Muslims, we will give you a dwelling near us." They said "We ask pardon of God."

---
* *i.e.*, The Teda royal clan of Tumagari.

† [Falasha in Shuwa Arabic *pl.* Falashin means a child of Khadim (slave concubine). The Tripoli people call them Falahsu].

The Prophet of God dwelt twenty years on earth with the children of Saif: then he died.

After this time King Bazen of the children of Saif became a Muslim, and ruled for five years.

After him Ibrahim, son of Saif, ruled fifty years. His son Dugu succeeded him, ruling fifty-three years.

Then they moved to the land of Shami, (N'jimi) and after ruling for ten years more, Dugu was succeeded by his son Fune, who ruled one hundred years.

Then came Arju, son of Fune, sixty years; Katuri, son of Arju, one hundred and five years.

Then they came to the tribe of Tur (Gura'an) sellers of horses with a man called Umr son of Wahid, and dwelt among them in the land of Sham.

Then Boyoma, son of Katuri, became king and ruled for one hundred years.

After him Bulu, son of Boyoma, ruled for seventy years.

Then Argi, son of Bulu, thirty years.

Then Jil Shuwa, son of Arku, seventy years.

Then Umme, son of Jil Shuwa, one hundred years.

Then the Son of Umme, son of Jil, called Dunama, son of Umme, forty years.

Abdu bin Dunama, sixty years.

Abdullahi bin Bikur, fifty years.

Jil bin Bikur, forty-nine years.

Dunama Dabalemi, son of Selma, thirty-three years.

Biri bin Dunama, forty-one years.

Ibrahim bin Biri bin Dunama, forty-four years.

Idris bin Ibrahim, twenty years in peace, in the land of Sham. After that there occurred dissension for twelve years, and the rule shifted to Barnu, and remained there for twelve years.

Then Idris bin Ibrahim drove out the trouble. He was in the land of Kirik Nagu, and ruled for forty years.

Biri, son of Idris, twenty years.

Dunama, son of Biri, thirty-three years.

Ali, son of Dunama, twelve years or forty years.

Muhammad, son of Zeinab, one year.

Dunama bin Muhammad, nineteen years.

Abdallahi bin Dunama, seventy years.

Idris bin Ali, fifty-five years.

Muhammad bin Idris, sixty years.

Ibrahim bin Idris, seven years.

From the time of our Sultan Umr, son of Idris there has been one hundred and sixty years or two hundred years or more of prosperity.

After that Umr, son of Idris, obtained the throne: between these two ten years.

After that Ali, son of Umr, forty-two years.

Idris bin Ali, twenty years.

His brother, Dunama bin Ali, nineteen years.

Haji bin Dunama, fourteen years.

Muhammad bin Hajj fifteen years.

Dunama bin Muhammad thirty months to our Sultan Ali ibn al Hajj.

Dunama Ali, bin Al Hajj Dunama, forty-seven years.

Ahmad bin Ali, seventeen years.

He then went blind, and his son Dunama ibn Ahmad[*], ruled four years and seventy days[†].

---

[*] Dunama ibn Ahmad lived in N'gazargamu for a year and some months, and after that he was killed, testifying to the Faith, in the war of Bagarmi.

[†] The descent of the owner of the manuscript, Mallam Abana from Ali bin Umr, is given as follows:—

Ali bin Umr; Maina Musa bin Ali; Duksamu Kade; Cadi Bukr; Mallam Nuhu; Mallam Ahmad; Mallam Ali; Shattima Al Kinguma; Mallam Abana.

XXXII.—MANDARA CHRONICLE.

This is a record of the ancestors of the Kings of Mandara, and their progress from the east hither, and their relations with the Sudanese of Mandara.

There were three or some say four men, or five of the companions of Himyar who fled from the hatred of the Jews, in fear that they would be persecuted because of their religion. They were followers of Isa*, upon whom be peace, and under the dispensation of the Gospel. They were among the most noble of the Himyarite youths. Dthu Nowas called on them to embrace Judaism, since the Himyarites at that time followed him. They refused and preferred death or slavery. Judaism meant the religion of the Jews.

This was the reason of their leaving Yaman, and the country called Nejran.

From Yaman they came to San'aa of Yaman, and thence to the city of Yathrib: thence to the Hijaz (Mecca) and Jedda, and the land of the Barbar. Then to Sawakin and Khartum and Kurtufan, Nuhut, Jebel Hilla, and Fasher. Then to Masalît, and Wârâ in the land of Wadai, and Bagarmi, where they sought news of this land (Mandara).

They went forward, and left here one of their number—a young man. Then they went on with their provision for the way and reached Bornu, and the region of the city of the Kanuri. They came to the place called Ishgakiwé† of the Sudanese, and found there as Queen a woman called Sugda or, in Arabic, "the clear cut". She was the daughter of the most important King of those countries. Her father ruled the people of that age, and the pagans both on the hills and plains submitted to him and obeyed his orders. He had conquered them, and none of the lesser kings of that land gainsaid him.

There were born to him seventeen children—sixteen sons and one daughter—but he preferred his daughter to all his sons; and made her their mistress and ruler, and put her in his seat in the fulness of his age.

Then he died, and they abode in Ishgakiwe. When the Himyarites reached that land, they stayed in the bush hunting and killing game with arrows.

The Queen heard news of them and sent her messenger to seek them. So the party came to her: their names being Riku, Dunama, and Gaya.

The Queen adorned herself for their coming, and her throne was placed for her to sit.

They were then called, and the people of the country assembled. When the Himyarites came in the first sat in front of the Queen and saluted her with the salutation of the country, as was customary. The second sat beside his brother, and did likewise; but when the third came in, he advanced to the throne, and pulled the Queen down from her seat to the ground. The youth then mounted up and assumed the place of the Queen on

---

* *i.e.*, Jesus.

† Possibly the region now called Ashigashiga near Kerawa.

the throne forthwith, for God had kindled in the breast of the Queen love for him.

The ornaments which the Queen wore on this occasion when meeting her guests, have been the customary ornaments of the Kings of Mandara ever since, nor do they come forth to meet guests till they have put on these ornaments.

So the youth sat in the seat of the Queen, and she asked them questions. They replied, informing her of their change of fortune and its reason, and how they left their country and came to hers.

Their discourse astonished her and her people, and her astonishment at these Arab peoples grew with all she heard and saw.

She said to them: "Can you remain with me in this my land, for verily you will play a great rôle."

They said "Yes" and stayed there as long as God willed, so that the youth who was named Gaya became her husband.

He and his wife had an only son, and called him Afala Akse Kaje.

Whenever the Queen went out to meet her people, her husband accompanied her, but the power remained with the Queen, and her husband was to her as a wazir is to a Sultan. She used him as a Wazir.

When she died, however, the whole power fell into his hands. So Gaya ruled after Sugda died so long as God willed he should reign and live.

Then there rose up one of the Himyarites named Dunama and said to his friend "O brother, may God bless you, whereas you are mighty in your power among these people, I will go humbly to Gawa*." So he went to the bush of this land, to the forest where there are no dwellers nor habitations, but only wild beasts. He dwelt there to hunt game, and settled, and lived some years in the place called Gawa.

Then the other brother Rîku said "O brother, may God prolong your rule and not cut off your days; I will go to the wâdi of the wild beasts." So he became an Amir feudatory to his brothers in the land called Kâbarwa†, or Wadi'l Wahash. Now, after the death of Sugda, when Gaya succeeded her as has been stated, he lived among the people of Mandara, and ruled for some years.

Then he died, remaining still an adherent of the religion of his ancestors. He did not stray from the path, but was a firm follower of the Gospel in all his doings, as also in those things he refrained from doing.

After him, his son mentioned above, Afala Akse Kaje, ruled. He too died at Ishgakiwe.

Then there ruled at Kingira, the Emir Afamakia Kutufa, and at Majwane, the Emir Dagra. In the land of Kerawa, the Emir Zare al Kabir, the Emir Bîra Mashi, the Emir Ajwe Hiku, the Emir Ajwe Fula, the Emir Ajwe Karka, the Emir Kutafe Taha, the Emir Aldawa Wandala, the Emir Aldawa Nade, the Emir Ankre Yawe, the Emir Agaldawa Nazarîze.

---

* On the Yedseram River in Konduga District.

† Kabarwa, *i.e.*, Kambarawa the fief of the Kambarama.

All these Emirs of the royal house were buried at Kerawa.

Then there ruled at Yaguwa the Emir Abarafa, and the Emir Akutafa Katalyawe.

At Iyrira the Emir Aldawa Nazarîzâ.

At Wâzâ the Emir Afalâ Nagaldawa.

At Birni Gasargamu the Emir Akutafa Dafala.

At Tala or Dalawa, as it is called by the Kanuri, lived the Emir Sankare who built the town of Tala, though the capital was at Kerawa.

Sankare ruled widely and long, it is said eighty years. He died at the age of one hundred and thirty-three years, but God knows best.

There is also buried at Tala, in their palace called Hutgâ, the Emir Zarê As-Saghir, the Emir Aldawâ Fusam, and the Emir whose real name was Suleiman, but who was given the honourable name of Dabare. He was very handsome, awe-inspiring, and grave, and the people of his age used to quarrel about the degree of his charm and beauty of person.

Then ruled the Emir Ajwe Kusha.

The number of the Emirs who have been mentioned above in this record down to the time of the coming of Islam, is twenty five.

The Sudanese Emirs who succeeded them as rulers were Moslems, and not one of them reverted to paganism or become an infidel. They worshipped God (be He exalted and praised) and read the Kura'an, and taught their people and children knowledge. Thus God revealed to them Islam and gave secure well-being to those who sought him, in the reign of the Sultan Al Haji Abu Bakr, after he had returned from the house of God in Mecca and from visiting the tomb of the Prophet Muhammad (upon whom be the blessing of God and peace), in the year 1136 of the Hijra. 1723 A.D. He reigned twenty-three years, and then died. May God's pardon rest on him.

To him succeeded the Emir Muhammad Al-Makkiyi, called the Meccan, because he was born at Mecca when his father went the pilgrimage, or so others say, because Makia was the name of his mother, a daughter of the Kanuri of Bornu. He ruled eighteen years.

His son the Emir Balâdi—ruled eighteen years.

His son the Emir Abu Bakr Jamâmi—ruled fifty-four years.

His son Sultan Ilyâsu—thirteen years and ten months.

His son Sultan Abi Bakr, son of Arbana, fifty-two years.

His son Sultan Umr, much praised by the learned, succeeded. The duration of his reign and that of his son called Abi Bakr who was made ruler in the lifetime of his father for four years, was twenty-six years.

The end of the list.

The number of the kings whom we have recorded and arranged in this account is thirty-three.

Ended with praise of God for his bounteous help to the writer of this chronicle called Mustafa ibn Isma'il (may God pardon him), who heard this account from his maternal grandfather Mu'allim Umr ibn Imam Ibrahim, one of the learned of his day in Mandara.

Written in the yeaar 1339, of the Hijra of the Prophet. _(1920 A.D.)

Praise be to God, and thanksgiving and peace upon the noble Prophet of God.

This is the list of the Kings of Mandara who have been mentioned.

In Ishgakiwe—Sugda, and Gaya and Afala Akse Kaje.

In Kingira—Ajamakia.

In Majwane—Emir Dagara.

In Kerawa—Emir Zare al Kabir.
        Bira Amshi.
        Ajwe Hiku.
        Ajwe Fula.
        Ajwe Karka.
        Akutafa Taha.
        Aldawa Andu.
        Aldawa Wandala.
        Ankre Yawe.
        Agaldawa Azare Biri.

In Yaga—Emir Abarafa.
        Akutafa Katul Gawe.

In Ayara—Emir Aldawa Anzarira.

In Waze—Emir Afala Nagaldawe.

In Birni Gazargamu—Emir Akutafa Dafala.

In Tala *i.e.* Dala=Mora—Emir Sankare.
        Zare Saghir.
        Aldawa Fusam.
        Dabre.
        Ajwe Kusha.
        The Emir of Islam. Abi Bakr al Haj Muhammad Makiyyi.
        Bulada.
        Abi Bakr Jamami Ilyâsu.

In Dikwa—Emir Abi Bakr ibn Ilyâsu.

The sum total of these Emirs is thirty-one. Then came Sultan Umr and sat on the throne of his forefathers. May God grant him life, and prolong his power. Finished by the hand of Mustafa ibn Isma'il.

Praise be to God.

XXXIII.—THE WORDS OF ZANUA DIGELTIMA TAHIR CALLED ZANUA SIDAGIMA WHO IS NINETY-SEVEN YEARS OLD (1918).

The origin of the people of Yaman and their migrations.

They set out from Yam, where they had lived for three hundred and thirty-three years and came to Yaman and stayed there three hundred and thirty-three years, and thence to Yamani three hundred and thirty-three years; then to Mecca because of war, but at Mecca they were visited by sickness and famine, and they were defeated: then they prayed.

Their king became sick in the neck, and one of their number (Abraha) went to Mecca. The people of Mecca asked him " Why do you come? " He said: " We come to war." The people of Mecca said: " You will not succeed; this is a holy city, the prophet of God will be born here."

They repented and stayed at Mecca and waited forty years till the Prophet came.

They went to a town called Zuru and remained there three hundred and thirty-three years, thence to Zuru Kowa for three hundred and thirty-three years, thence they moved to N'jimi for three hundred and thirty-three years.

The founder of N'jimi was Mai Brema Melemi.

In the time of Mai Dunama Dibalemi, there was no famine or trouble. He had a friend, a So. The So frequently came to N'jimi and gave Dunama news of Bornu. Then the Mai went with the So to Marirge (near Bilabirin). Mai Dunama died at Marirge, but his body was carried back to be buried at N'jimi.

His son Mai Ari Gaji Zeinami was made Mai. He came to Gazargamu to build it. They had been three hundred years at Gazargamu, when the Mai went to war with Mandara.

The Mai went to Mandara and was defeated and returned to Gazargamu. Then, after that, Gazargamu survived for thirty years.

It was spoilt in the time of Mai Dunama Ahmadumi.

Digeltima Tahir ibn Digeltima Ari Binami b. Idrisi Aisami b. Lefia b. Maina Ari b. Me Brem Gumsumi b. Idris Alooma is the authority for these statements.

Me Brem Gumsumi gave Maina Ari a " girgam ". Maina Ari came to Jigalta (near Bilabirin). Between this date and the taking of Gazargamu by the Fulani was one hundred and eighty-seven years and seven months.

After Gazargamu was taken it was seven years without a Mai in it. Then the Mai became established at Kâbila. Mai Dunama called all the people and said: " God gave us the kingdom, let all go back to their lands: if you do not, you will get nothing."

So Towns.

The first So town in Bornu was Mintur; formerly it was under the Musgu for two hundred years before the So came. The So stayed at Mintur five hundred and ten years before Gazargamu was founded.

XXXIV.—THE STORY OF N'DIF (N'DIFU).

This is what is known of the ancestors of the Sultan of N'difu and of the foundation of his town in ancient days.

His name was Yusuf, and he reigned twenty-four years. He was the son of Sultan Muhammad who reigned thirty years, whose predecessors were:—

Sultan Yusuf, sixty years reign.

Son of Sultan Idris, sixty years reign.

Son of Sultan Abdul Karin, one hundred years reign but lived to be one hundred and fifty.

Son of Sultan Abdu, sixty years.

Son of Sultan Ali.

Son of Sultan Muhammad, son of the giant kings, who fought over the kingdom.

There was a great battle and many were killed, so that the blood flowed down to a lake called Harmagan. After that time a Sultan Ahmar (red), also of the giants, ruled.

In his time came the Arabs who speak "Galgaliya" among them the tribe of Ma'in.

After them came the Sultan Kindin-Kindin, son of the Sultan Kindin-Kindin, son of the Sultan Kara-ga N'du-su-wa, having under him twelve clans.

After their time came Mai Ali who was full brother to Mai Yusuf, who is called Mai Muhammad and who ruled fifteen years.

His son Mai Bakr was full brother to Mai Idris, and ruled three years.

Mai Malik was brother of Mai Abdu'l Karim and reigned three years.

They were sons of Yarima Kankali, who was brother of Mai Abdul Karim, son of Mai Abdu.

Mai Abdur Rahman was son of the uncle of Mai Abdul Karim; Mai Haji was son of Yarima Kankali.

Note:—The exact meaning of this genealogy is not quite clear but it is probably as overleaf.

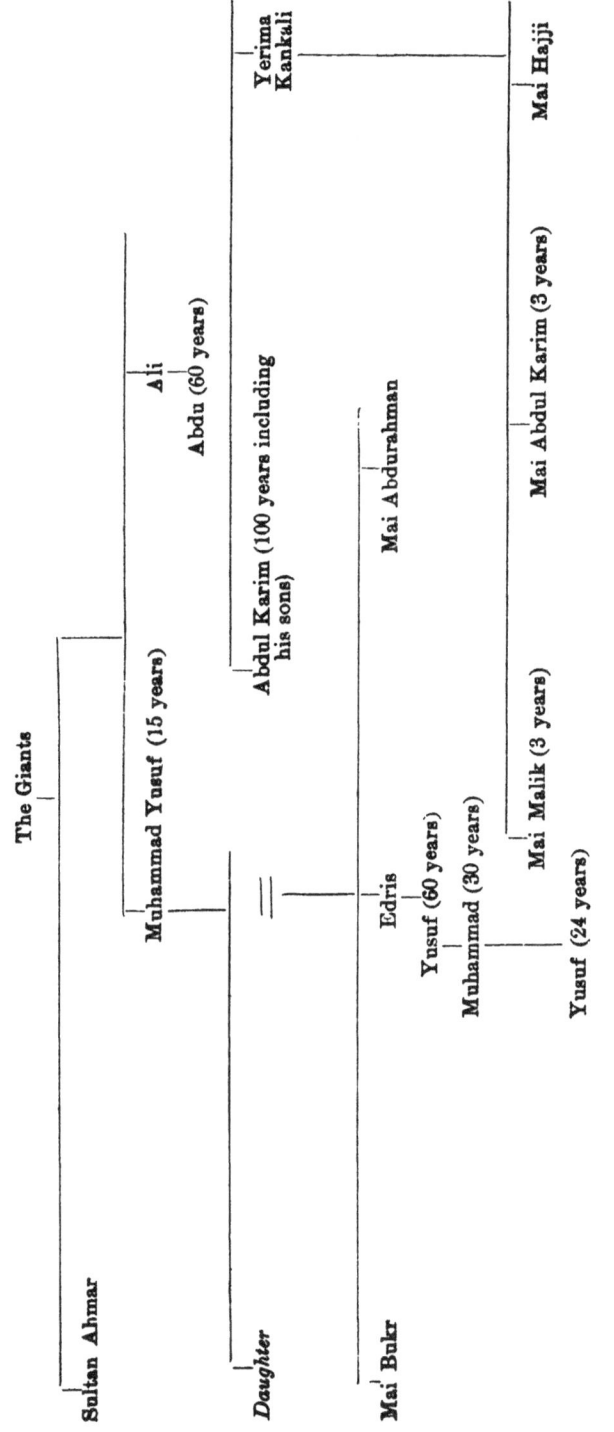

The period up to the time of the two brothers, Muhammad Yusuf and Ali, is thus supposed to be about 300 years back from 1900 A.D., *i.e.* the Moslem Sultans of N'difu date from about 1000 A.H. or 1590 A.D. and were of Kindin or Amakitan (Tuwareg) extraction.

XXXV.—MAI DUGU BREMMI AND THE CONNECTION OF THE M'BUM AND GWÂNA WITH THE KANURI.

In connection with the Gwâna or Kona, it will be of interest to notice the neighbouring kingdom of Mandara in its relation to the M'bum.

The Mandara or Wandala are the ruling caste over a race called Gamargu, a name which is similar to Damargu. "Wan" in Wan-dala means "people", Dala or Dara is a pre-Kanuri word for mountain or hill. Wandala is thus a variant of Koandala "men of the hills," or Gwandara, just as Mandara is for Aman-dara "chief of the hills."

The Wandala have the common legend of a migration from Yaman. It is of special interest by reason of a tradition which they share with the Bulala, that they were once Christians, and the fact that names of places in the Mandara country are specially mentioned in the legends about Yeri Arbasan. This seems to point to the name "So" meaning merely "aborigines," the governing caste being called Dugawa in Kanem, and in the hills Gwandara or Wandala*. Both the former and the latter were originally Ye-ri, people of Ye or Yam, and also Agha-am, or Agham to the Teda, being regarded as the equivalent of the Tamashek "imajaran" nobles.

The story of Mai Dugu Bremmi's adventures in these regions is told thus:—

"Mai Dugu Bremmi set forth to war with Yeri Arbasa, and reached the country of Yeri Arbasa with his army intact, but the people of Yeri Arbasa stopped the path and stopped his progress to the place he wanted so that he and his people could not come on the people of Yeri Arbasa, or fight them.

"So he and his people stayed in a place, and he said to his people, 'What is your advice and plan to defeat their blocking our path. They said, 'Consult the Kaigama (Lord of the South).' So Mai Dugu consulted Kaigama Bukr Gamargu. The Kaigama replied: 'Take counsel with your friend Teskelma† Dalamani.' So the Mai called Teskelma and said to him: 'I asked the Kaigama's opinion and he advised me to consult you.' He replied:

---

* It will be seen that the names Gwan, Kona or Kwana, the name given by the Kanuri to the Kororafa and Jukons is simply the plural of Koa = a male (man) or warrior.

Compare with this the name Gwâni, given to the clan of Bulala who became Teda after their defeat by Mai Ali Gaji Zeinami.

The "n" of Koa-n Kwana is a plural suffix parallel to the Hausa and Tamashek genitival prefix "n."

In Kanem Dugawa or Dogôa were people who were industrials more particularly "blacksmiths," i.e., peoples of Kushite connection who were despised. They were subject to the Zaghawa races and it is either post hoc or propter hoc that the word "tall" (of a human being *only*) is in the Hausa language "dogo" *fem.* "dogwa."

† The word Teske in Teda means stars. He was probably an astrologer like the "Kintaguma" at N'gazargamu.

'Slaves cannot give counsel, nor grapple with anything unpleasant or harassing, only with pleasant things; so it is, that the Kaigama has not borne with ill-fortune and distress, but has referred you to me.' Teskelma said to the Mai, ' Take counsel with your children, your twelve children, of whom you have left four at home and have eight with you; take counsel with the eldest, and do what he advises.' The Sultan said: ' Each one has a plan, and I will take counsel with each separately.'

" So he called his eldest son, Maina Maidalla Kingimi, the former Kaigama (who had been deposed after the army had reached Madagali in favour of Kaigama Bukr Gamargu), and asked his advice. He replied: ' My father, we are eight of us your sons in your army; ask each of us in turn, and take whatever advice suits you; and combine it with your own plan.'

" So he sought counsel with Maina Luntima Fanatami and asked him. He replied ' Ask my brother Chimma Kingimi.'

" When the latter was asked he replied: ' Ask my brother Kanamma Nayama Fanarammi.'

" Mayama when asked in turn suggested his brother Maina Mele Hawami.

" Maina Melle when asked said ' Ask Maina Chiroma Karammi.''

" Maina Chiroma again referred to Titi Sumi Gawalama.

" Titi Sumi referred it to Maina Yusuf Fanatami.

" The Mai took counsel with them all, and said ' Take your counsels to the lodging of Kaigama Bukr Gamargu, and then bring me the result.'

" So they went to the Kaigama's house and took counsel together.

" The Kaigama said to them: ' Your father is sixty years old, and has reigned a long time; do not follow your father's counsels; he is an old man; leave him in the bush, and make your brother Kaigama Maidalla Kingimi king, and I will be your Kaigama till we reach home again.'

" Now Mai Dugu Bremmi had a concubine called Mai Sugur. She went to Teskelma and said to him: ' What is this I hear, this and that?' He said to her ' What?' She said: ' They say that the king's sons all went to the Kaigama's house, and, disregarding their father's counsel, made a plan of their own; and the Kaigama said to them " leave your father who is useless; make your brother Kaigama Maidalla king, and I will be your Kaigama till we reach home." Listen! Are you the king's friend, and the sharer of his secrets? Do not believe the story of a woman who has not borne children to her lord, but the story I have heard to-day does not portend well to the king.'

" Teskelma went to the king and informed him of the plan of his sons with Kaigama Bukr Gamargu, how they planned to depose him, and appoint Maina Maidalla.

" The king then grew angry and determined to fight the men

of Yeri Arbasa*; so he went out with his people towards Yeri Arbasa, but the path was still closed.

"So the king left Yeri Arbasa and took the road to the land of M'bum. When they arrived at M'bum, they saw a wonderful girl, red and fair, so as to gladden those who saw her; she stood at the door of a cave in the rocks.

"The king saw her, and sought her for himself and sent his messenger to her.

"She said to the messenger: 'Tell the king that if he wants me, he must leave his people and come to me alone.'

"So he left his people and came to her alone.

"She said to him 'Follow me.' He followed her, and entered with her into a cave in the rocks. They went on together into the cave, till they came to a level place where there were no rocks nor trees and they saw afar off, the appearance of a river. The maiden said 'Let us go to this river', so they went on.

"The king said to the maid: 'What is your name?'; she said: 'Surely you and your people are thirsty, follow me and I will take you to the river, so that you and your people may drink and encamp close to the river, when I will tell you my name, if you desire me for a wife.'

"But what had the appearance of a river was not a river and the maiden disappeared and he saw her no more.

"The king was dumbfounded at this occurrence, and returned on his tracks till he reached the mouth of the cave, and there saw her at its mouth. Behind her, from above the rock, water was flowing and pouring into a hollow in the rock. The king could not make out where the water came from or where it went to, and said to the maid: 'I have followed your behest, and as far as what we saw is concerned, we have not found water, and I and my people are thirsty still.'

"She said 'Ask my name.' He said 'What is your name?' She replied: 'My name is Maimuna Darari.' He said: 'I want you for my wife.' She said 'What is your name?' He said: 'I am Mai Dugu Bremmi.' She said: 'Do you want me for wife before you have finished my war, attacking Yeri Arbasa? Nay, to-morrow go back to Waraga Dubuwa† and

---

* Yeri Arbasa supposed to be a site not far from the Sanaga river not far from modern Carnotville. Kanuri merchants say that the people of the region still recall their ancient connection with Bornu, and that a chief there still has the title Kaigamma.

† Waraga Dubuwa a region south of Balda in Mandara, said formerly to have been thickly populated. The name is perhaps in reality Waraga Dibu-wa, i.e., Waraga of the Dibu tribe, Dibu being equivalent to N'dif and N'difu.

It may be noted that the Kuka dynasty of Fitri, called Madugu or Madogo came from Wara, the ancient capital of Wadai. There is a Waraga Dibo, East of Abeshe, and West of Badani in Wadai.

Badani, near Abeshe, was one of the early capitals of the Mais of Kanem, and these legends shew that it was perhaps from there that these expeditions of Mai Dugu Bremmi were launched via Fitri and Bagarmi into the Tuburi Region, which thus came under Dajo (Zaghawa) influence. This influence among others developed into the tribal confederation called Gwani or Kôna by the Kanuri, and Kwararafa by the Hausas, the ruling castes of

remain there till you have made me a city there, and built a mosque in it. You came to fight Yeri Arbasa and the people blocked your path, then you and your people took the road to M'bum. But the people of M'bum are under my protection, and it is I who have blocked your path to them by a ruse. After that do you still want me for a wife? Surely you will not take me as a wife?'

"' Why not?' said the king. 'Why should I not marry you?' She said: 'You are Mai Dugu Bremmi, a Sultan of mortals, and I am Maimuna Darari, a Jinnya, so you cannot have me to wife.'

"He said: 'I never thought of your being a Jinnya, I imagined you were a mortal woman; but if you are such, pray, open for us the road that we may return to our country.'

"She said: 'There will be no returning, for you have done wickedly in this affair. How dare you try to wrong this land and attack it, when the people were under my protection? Therefore you will not return to your homes. I told you before you approached me, that I had no desire for you, and only seek to deceive you, and that my only desire is to destroy you and your sons; so will I destroy you for this reason.'

"He said: 'It is my purpose for your sake to make the town of Waraga Dubuwa, and build there a mosque, so that you may become my wife and that I may settle you in a new town; and that I may also live there to be with you.'

"She said: 'Your character and purpose are both bad and you have ruined your people. As for us Jinns, if a mortal sees us, and asks for money or help, he obtains them, but if he is bent on strife, we are to him an occasion of death and ruin. You will perish, you, and your people, because you have attacked people under my protection—the people of M'bum.'

"The story goes that the Jinnya then herself killed Mai Dugu Bremmi and his sons, and her army killed his army.

"After which there was left one man called Madagali, who cried out and said 'I am Madagali' and left her. She said to him: 'You are a dog, you are not a Muslim, I will therefore make you crawl.' Then she asked him and said: 'Where is your country?'

"He said: 'My country is afar, and I only met Mai Dugu on the road: my country is in the south near Dala* south of Dala.' So he left her and went to his country and is a dog to this day, and in that country (Madagali), when a male child is born, he is a dog, while a female is human to this day.

"This is what the Jinnya did to Mai Dugu Bremmi. Mai Dugu had a slave called Barka who had gone sick and been left behind between Madagali and Mitchiga, west of Madagali, and east of Mitchiga. Because of this expedition of Mai Dugu Bremmi and the leaving behind of Barka all the people of this part of the country still cut grass for horses and bring it in every year to Bornu."

which are known respectively as Wandala, Pabir (Babir) and Apa (Wapa) or Jukon.

* *i.e.*, Dala Dibu, the range of hills to the south of which is Madagali.

XXXVI.—MAI DUGU BREMMI AND THE M'BUM.

Mai Dugu Bremmi slept at Yari Arbasan, and lost his followers; they left him behind with his sons and brothers.

His sons became pagans, and their tribe was called M'bum. Some were called Lakkai. The Sugurti who went to the war became the Tuburi Musgu, and the Teda who went with him became pagans also.

XXXVII.—BAGARMI CHRONICLE.

This is what we have heard from the mouth of the son of the Sultan of Bagarmi Manga, whose title was Bawo.

The tribes of Bargami were six: Mugir Manga, Barkate, Galladimâri, Kudu, B'êni, Madugar, and with them a tribe of Fellata called Darké, which lived with them till there came to them a Sultan from Yaman.

This Sultan's people were nine sons of Ibrahim-al-Yamaniyi-al Bagarmiyi. The first of them was B'éni, the second Bitku. These two were full brothers: then Dugu Dargu and Dugu Kega, and Dugu Kuwayero; these three were full brothers: then Tubio Mayi Mêle, Tubio Mayi Châko; these two were full brothers: then Nugu Midwayi, Zuguwayi Kamantu; these two were full brothers.

In all nine men. They came from N'jimi and settled in Bagarmi, with the six tribes of Bagarmi.

After they had been in Bagarmi for six years, B'êni became Sultan and ruled thirty years, and died at the age of ninety.

After him his brother Bitku became Sultan, and reigned twenty years, and died at fifty years of age.

Then Sultan Mâlu ruled for nineteen years.

Abdullahi ruled forty years.

Sultan Dalayi ruled ten years.

Sultan Umr ruled twenty years.

Sultan Abdu Rahman ruled thirty years.

Sultan Othman ruled forty years.

His son Muhammad ruled twenty-six years.

Then his son Abdulkadir Waliyi ruled thirty years. His brother Abdullahi killed him in order to become Sultan.

Abdullahi ruled seven years.

His son Sultan Burku Manda ruled three years.

His son Lowal ruled nine years.

His son Abdulkadir ibn Muhammad came back from the Haj, and settled on the rock Mêto for three years, and gathered people and attacked Sultan Lowal. He killed Lowal and became Sultan and reigned. He went to Mabalenji and sacked it and took much booty. The people gave him Jiza'a and became his slaves, and were converted to Islam.

Sultan Busu heard of him, and was afraid for his life and position, and came to him with his chiefs, and became a Moslem, and became subject to him, and paid him Jiza'a.

Thence the Sultan went to Bunduki to war, and killed many of the people and converted others. They became his subjects and paid Jiza'a.

He attacked the town of Kwiyu, and took it and converted the inhabitants. They became subject and paid Jiza'a.

He took the town of the Sara N'jilim, and slaughtered,

and converted the inhabitants; they became Moslems and paid Jiza'a.

He took Miyen, and did the same.

Then Mâni Fadi.

Then Gidô.

Then Margu.

Then Mayi Goni, which he attacked for three months, and killed many people. He treated them as the others, as also the following towns:—

Mayi Budu.	Bajel.
Madalama.	Wanku.
Muru.	Mujuwé.
Gulai.	Mâkili.
Bâlu Nêri	Gilende.

Anja was a big town. He took half of it, but the other half did not know a war was going on. The fighting went on for four months. The people were converted and paid Jiza'a.

The Sultan returned home. All these towns were on the river. He then came to Mêbi and killed or converted the inhabitants.

Thence he came to Matiaku Tsanguran and Mugulé and Injâyi and Mâjê and Mubruku and Mabarti and converted them all and took Jiza'a.

He returned to the city of Ne Masenya, their first city, the land of the six tribes.

The Sultan Haj Abdulkadir ruled thirty-six years, and waged many holy wars.

His son Sultan Gauranga succeeded, and said "Why does not the Sultan of the Bulala come to us?"

The Sultan Bulala said "I was the greatest King in the reigns of your predecessors; I never visited your kingdom, why should I come now?"

Gauranga sent out his army against the Bulala, among them Faja and Barma and Ki'rama and N'girmani and Khalifa Mêto, and said to them "Go to the town of the Sultan of the Bulala."

They attacked it, and took it, and brought the Sultan Bulala to Gauranga, who executed him.

Thenceforward the Sultan Bulala followed Bagarmi.

Sultan Gauranga died after twenty-two years reign.

His son Burku Manda succeeded and ruled forty-four years. He killed Sultan Bornu Mai Dunama.

Then his son Abdulkadir ruled thirteen years.

His son Muhammad Abu Sakkin ruled twenty-four years.

His son Burku Manda As-Saghir was a powerful king and warlike. He killed many of his chiefs. The people refused to follow him, and he retired, and came to Bornu, and Wadai, where he died. He ruled three years.

His uncle Gauranga succeeded, and he ruled thirty-three years; before Rabeh came he had ruled eight years; seven years he ruled with Rabeh, and after Rabeh, eighteen years.

Peace.

XXXVIII.—BÂBÂLIYA GIRGAM.

Praise be to God, Him alone.
This is the story of Tuba' Himyar who went with his army and warred cunningly. He built Samarkand, and it is said he destroyed it. He was a believer, but his people were *kafirs*. Therefore God blamed them, but not him. He said (may the blessing of God and peace rest on him): " I know not whether Tuba' was a prophet or not." But Tuba' believed in the Prophet (may the blessing of God rest on him and peace) nine hundred years before his birth. The Tuba' in question was the great Abu Karib whose name was Sa'ad to whom the 'Ansar are related. To save them came an injunction from their ancestor " Hasten toward Islam." He was the first who clothed the " Ka'aba ", after he had sought to attack it, and had actually attacked Medina and set about to destroy it.

Yet, when he heard that Mecca was to be the scene of a Prophet named Ahmad's flight, he turned back and sang a song to his lute before his people. The Himyarites kept the song from generation to generation till the time of the Prophet (upon whom be the blessing of God and peace), when they showed it to him.

It is said that the book and the song were in the hands of Abi Ayuba Khalid ibn Zaid. It said:—

"I bear witness to Ahmad that he is a prophet from God,
" The Creator of the air."
" Were I to live till the age when he will live
" I should count the Wazir of love as my cousin."

The reason of Himyar's leaving Yaman.

In consequence of refusal to pay tax, the Himyarites left Yaman and came to the Hijaz, and thence to the lake in Egypt, and followed the track in the desert going west, and left their women in the desert near Jarbûb. Thence they passed west to the land of Aujila, the land of Himîr, and left there the ancestor of the people of Aujila. Then on west to Fezzan, and left there the ancestor of the people Zaidan.

They went on to Tarabolus and left there the ancestor of the Gamdamisiyin and Jabâliyin, thence to Marakish where they stayed, and returned to Tuwat.

They spread abroad to Fez, and then to Ahir, and Damagram, Damargu, Agades, and Sokoto.

From them sprung and to them belonged walled towns.

They are all Kinîn and Tuwârek, and from them sprung Saif the ancestor of the Barnu, and Ahmad the ancestor of the Babalia, and Abdu Jalil, the ancestor of the Bulala.

Such is the genealogy of this great people, in the words of Him, be He exalted.

The greatest people is that of the people of Tuba'.

The End.

XXXIX.—THE STORY OF MASBARMA AND MAI MUHAMMAD HAJIMI.*

They set out together to war against Kano. They set out from N'gazargamu and encamped at Keraya.

Masbarma went to visit his brother the Walii Zigagema who was sick.

The Walii said farewell to his brother Masbarma, and said: "I shall either recover, or if my span is finished, I shall die. If so I want you to perform the last offices and no one else."

Masbarma went with Mai Muhammad Hajimi to attack Kano. They besieged it for seven months, but did not prevail, till the appointed time came. The Walii died, and two Walii wanted to bury him.

But Masbarma left Kano to fulfil his promise, and reached the burial place before they had time to bury the Walii. He performed the rite, while the people of N'gazargamu buried the Walii. Masbarma asked them for news of N'gazargamu and wrote down what they said, and conveyed it to Kano by the power of God.

All this happened between early morning and ten o'clock. The Sultan never arose from his seat at Kano till the news came to him.

---

* Muhammad Hajimi (Barth), 1737-1751. He attacked Kano in the time of Sarki Kumbari, 1731-1743.

XL.—MASFARMA.

The ancestors of the Walii, the very noble Masfar. He was Umr b. Othman b. Biyyar b. Khalaf b. Sânii b. Muhammad b. Mâhir Muhammad b. Saniî b. Takhmir Ar-Rahmâni b. Khalaf b. Malik b. Kadai b. Sânii b. Tiyi b. Watiyi b. Khanzakiyu b. Wahab b. Abakhrani b. Zabariyu b. Al Hasan.

These are the ancestors of Masfar from the son of Othman to Hasan son of Ali.

As to the place of origin of their ancestors, they came from Yaman after the Tuba' al Awwal, and settled in Wadan in the land of Murzuk to the south. Their ancestor Othman left his country Wadan, and came to Birni Gazargamu and asked the Sultan for a place in which to pasture his camels and beasts. The reigning Sultan replied that there were the following towns:— Boso, Birni Kime, Birni Magiyaram, Albu, Wazagal, Lantewa, and Lane.

The Walii Masfarma Umr died at Lane aged ninety-four. His son Ahmed Matalami was put in his place and he died at the age of seventy-three. Then came his son Umr Gulugulama who died at fifty-four. The reason he was called Gulugulama was that Gulugula was the name of his birth place. He was also buried at Gulugula.

After him Masfarma Ahmad Aswami died aged one hundred and one years. After him Masfarma Umr Dabalemi died aged eighty-six years. Masfarma the Imam died aged seventy-seven years. Masfarma Maji Kolomi died at Kukawa aged ninety-three. Masfarma Maji Zahrami died at Kukawa aged ninety-three. Masfarma Bosoma, the present Masfarma is now aged sixty-five (1917); the sum of the years is 891.

Umr ibn Othman the Walii came from Wadan to the towns which have been mentioned above. He lived in each one of them himself with his people. He moved from Boso to Birni Magiyaram, from Birni Magiyaram to Birni Kime, Biri Kime to Albu, Albu to Wazagal, Wazagal to Lantewa, Lantewa to Lane, where he died and is buried.

The number of Walii from Umr ibn Othman to Masfarma Bosoma, the present one, is eleven.

Between Umr the Walii and Hasan ibn Ali were twenty-one Walii, in all thirty-two Walii.

This is what I learnt from the lips of Masfarma Bosoma 25th October, 1917.

XLI.—THE STORY OF MAI TSILIM HAWAMI.

He died in the town called Ren. The three Sultans assembled, Sultan Ren and Sultan Dif and Sultan Afade, and found a horn, and within the horn, a writing, as also two white shirts.

They read the writing and found two sentences as follows:—

"*If I die to the east of the Shari, bury me in the land of "Abagar: if I die to the west of the Shari, bury me at "N'dif (N'difu).*;

Thus the writing.

So the Sultans took the corpse of Mai Tsilim Hawami to N'difu and buried it there.

As regards the manner of Mai Tsilim Hawami's leaving N'gazargamu. He did not stay at any town till he arrived at N'difu. He remained at N'difu three months, and thence moved to Ren. Such was his procedure in visiting N'difu.

The old name of N'difu was Dar Tunus, but after the space of one thousand years it was called N'difu. The story is as follows:—

Sultan Yusuf left his former town of N'difu with his people on account of severe famine, and reached the town called Alarge, one of the towns of Logone. At Logone was a man who wanted to go on the pilgrimage.

This man asked Yusuf his name and where he came from. Yusuf said "From the town of N'difu: for I am the chief of that town, if God vouchsafe to me a safe return."

The Hajj replied, "I have heard of your town of N'difu from the lips of pilgrims, whom I met on the Red Sea. They said to me that when the town N'difu had existed for 5,700 years the Prophet was born, upon whom be blessing and peace."

N'difu is the greatest of towns.

It has four roads. The first leading to Uda* in the west

---

* *i.e.*, Uda-ri = Wuderi, *i.e.*, the Katagum region. It is stated that Alarge was east of N'difu. The Mandara name for the Teda Tumagari is N'dina, which is probably a variant of N'di-fu. The N'guma and Tumagari are both said to have come from Wâraga N'dubu, *i.e.*, Wâraga N'difuwa near Balda.

According to the legend Mai Dugu Bremmi told the Jinniya that he proposed to found a town at Wâraga-Dubu. The Bornu titles N'dinaram and N'dubuguma seem to be connected with the N'dina or N'difu. Balda is often written Malta, a name which may be connected with Malan, the chief centre of Kanem before N'jimi.

The Kuka of Fitri are in origin Am N'dina, hence Ali Dinar = Ali N'dinari, *i.e.*, Ali of the Teda Tumagari.

There is a Mai N'dina at Dakwoski. The N'dina had some connection with the Dajo; the Kuka understood the language of Bagarmi and also the language of the Dajo.

The people of Samina (Abu Simin) spoke the same language as the Kuka; they were ruled by the N'dina first, and then by the Bulala. The Abu Simin were Dajo.

The N'gizim were of the same stock as the Abu Simin of Fitri and the N'yenyi = N'gasam and also N'gujam.

Probably Tumagari = Tama*kara*, *i.e.*, are the same as the Dankir or Dagara of Damargu.

The inference from these names is that when the Barbars came from the East they conquered ruling races who were of Gara or Teda affinity, *i.e.*, Kushites, and became in turn the ruling caste as *e.g.*, in the case of the Tumagari.

the second leading to Masenya, the city of Bagarmi, the road to the east; the third leading to the rock of Wase (Waza), the road to the south; and the fourth leading to Chad, the road to the north.

From N'difu came out six cities; Sangaya, Kaza, N'gala, Ren, Afade and Mintur.

Yedi came out from Mintur, but all came out from N'difu.

XLII.—THE STORY OF THE COMING OF SULTAN KWANA TO FIGHT AT N'GAZARGAMU IN THE TIME OF SULTAN ALI GARUKURUGUMA.

The Sultan of the Kwana sent his present to the Sultan Ali of Bornu. The messengers of the Kwana Sultan saw the walls of N'gazargamu and informed the sultan.

The Sultan Kwana set out from his town, with his army, and came to attack N'gazargamu. Sultan Ali heard of their coming and advanced to attack them. They fought a fierce battle and the Sultan of the Kwana fled in fear of his life. 1,000 Kwana were slain, and 1,000 were wounded, and 1,000 captured, and the rest of the army dispersed.

The Sultan Ali dismounted and sat on his couch, waiting for the end of the slaughter. His people captured the Sultan of the Kwana and plundered his people, and burnt their camp. Then all the Kwana submitted, and asked for mercy. The Sultan Kwana swore fealty.

Sultan Ali left them in their country and returned victorious with much booty.

There was slain in the battle a woman called Gambo Kwanaram.

Three men of the Kwana who were captured had their ears cut off and suspended on their necks, and were thus sent to their country.

They reached their country and told the news. The Sultan of the Kwana said " Shoot them ". They were shot for fear it should be said that the Sultan of the Kwana was afraid.

XLIII.—THE ZANUA OF WUKARI'S MAGUMI GIRGAM.

1. Mai Yusuf Saifumi—Batali Kowwan. (In Burâk west of Borku and east of Kanem.)*
2. Mai Tsilim Hawami—Laza Baltebi. (A stream in the west of Kanem near Bâri.)
3. Mai Tsilim Laga Hawami—Arjino Kulinuwa. (West of Mao.)
4. Mai Muhammadu Wâlimi Kâgalawadi—Misinuwa Kownan. In the Kâga of Bornu (*i.e.* South, Misinu is an acacia tree).
5. Mai Muhammadu Dîma, Lefia lâga—Kagetunuwan. (At another town of small " Kagetu " trees.)
6. Mai Muhammadu Laga—Bursalim.
7. Mai Jil Tubba' al Awalu—Uzudu Makuwan.
8. Mai Saifu Aisami—Bula Yaman.
9. Mai Brem Saifomi ye—Bula Yamanin.
10. Mai Dugu Bremmi—Yari Arbasanin.
11. Mai Fune Dugumi—Muli (Môli) Funiyawan. (Muli place of " veiled people ". The Mulima was master of the horse.)
12. Mai Arsu Funemi—N'galabuta Kukawan. (East of Kanem.)
13. Mai Katuri Arsumi—Kaigam Nanigham Kunawan.
14. Mai Wayama Katurimi—Bikukunwa, Bir Tolwan (*i.e.* Tolmaram).
15. Mai Bulu Wayamami—Maki Chubuduwan.
16. Mai Arki Bulumi Laga—Zeila Kulukunwan (*i.e.* Kulu guwan), " at Zeila of the streams."
17. Mai Arki Bulumi Laga—Zeila Hawazalan.
18. Mai Shu Arkimi—Ayir Kutushi.
19. Mai Shumi—Arwaya Mashiduwan. (North of Damagram: it is said that the " *armi* " are Beni *Keyi*.)
20. Mai Humi Jilmi—N'gururi Kaiyawa bulu Makka. (Kaiyawa is Munfufia near N'jimi.)
21. Mai Dunoma Hamami—Barambushi buniramnin.
22. Mai Bîri Dunamami—Gamtilo Kuluguwan (Gamtilo of the streams).
23. Mai Fafisima—Fafisima.
24. Mai Bikur Birimi—Fafsi Kurnowan.
25. Mai Bikurumi—Gaska Kunidulawan. (A kind of Addua tree.)
26. Mai Dunama Dabalemi Tsilamami—Bula Zantamnin.
27. Mai Kadai—Asfî Zantamnin.
28. Mai Diri Kulinuwa—Bula N'jiminin.

---

* The names of the various Sultans are given and then (after the hyphen) the reputed place of their burial. We may compare with this list the similar list given in " Mai Idris of Bornu "

29. Mai Idrisi Amsami Amsa daughter of Zerma—N'guru Dama (*i.e.* Am Dam).
30. Mai Kadai Matalami—Lada Kadi Matalwan (a stream).
31. Mai Ibram (Gumsumi)—Diskam N'galagatin. (North of N'guri south of Barâk.)
32. Mai Hame Aisami—Tuwa Kukawan.
33. Mai Dunamam Lafiami Lafia, daughter of Manu—Nanigham Kurnawan.
34. Mai Biri-Aisami—in Bagarmi Kanunakun. (Rabeh and the French fought at Kanunakun.)
35. Mai Muhammadu Laga—Kuri N'gulizun.
36. Mai Muhammadu Lagare—N'guna N'gilwan.
37. Mai Jil—Layuwan.
38. Mai Muhammadu—Biri Talowan.
39. Mai Zamarma Umrmi—Zumaramin.
40. Mai Kâka Umrmi—Ngalfiwan.
41. Mai Dakamuma Dâla Umrmi—Dakahami.
42. Mai Muhammadu Laga—Mazma bula Munin.
43. Mai Muhammadu Laga—Aikêdu Muniwan.
44. Mai Muhammadu—Zurukudu Kursimwa.
45. Mai Muhammadu Laga—Matari Gamkururi.
46. Mai Absa Suwa zu Kukunimi— N'galiru.
47. Mai Saidu Suwa Kulinuwa—Duksuwun (Diskuwam).
48. Mai Muhammadu Osman (mi)—Bala Makka.
49. Mai Muhammadu Bremmi Amatâmi—Misra Mashiduwan.
50. Mai Dunama Fusami—Nakukutu.
51. Mai Muhammadu Laga—Bula Mafoni.
52. Mai Daudu Namami—Kutilu Kukunwan. (Kukun is a tree.)
53. Mai Ari Namami—Birni Gazaigama.
54. Mai Idris Ashami—Anim Tuwan. (Tuwan is country behind Dikwa and Mandara=Nji-Tuwa.)
55. Mai Idris Ashami Laga—Katuwarin. (West of Mandara *i.e.* Dura.)
56. Mai Muhammadu Idrisimi—Malme N'gamuramnin. (West of Bagarmi.)
57. Mai Ali Gaji Zeinami—Zantamnin.
58. Mai Dunama Manmi Garu Karuru—Birni Gazargamu.
59. Mai Idris Amsamî Amsa Jumarambe—Alo Kuluguwan.
60. Mai Muhammadu Idrisimi—Daganu Sur Maliya.
61. Mai Brem Gumsumi Gumsu Kagudimi—Birni Gazargamu.
62. Mai Umr Fusami Dusan Kandi Kumaliwa—Gazargamu.
63. Mai Ali Umrmi Dalâka baltebe—Mashru mashiduwan.
64. Mai Idris Alimi—Zeila Tarâkunin.

65. Mai Dala Dunamami N'guru Katele Dalatu Kuluwan—Nguru of Galladima.
66. Mai Dunama Alimi Kanisli Zawabuku—Garmanmanin.
67. Mai Haji Dunamami Birni—Gazargamu.
68. Mai Muhammadu Hajimi—Birnin Gazargamu.
69. Mai Dunama Manmi Kuri Ganna—Birnin Gazargamu.
70. Mai Ali Hajimi—Birnin Gazargamu.

The list of Sultans of Yaman is finished.

Note.—This girgam must date from about the year 1795 or so for Mai Ali Hajimi died in 1793. As usual in these lists the sequence of reigns is, during the period of the civil war, very inexact—and the list really begins at No (7) who is a variant of the more usual Saif ibn dthi Yazan.

The interest of this particular " Girgam " is twofold, firstly because it comes from the Jukon town of Wukari on the Benue, and the Jukon claim a common origin with the Saifawa. Secondly it is probably the oldest copy of this " Girgam " now extant.

The list, which gives the names of the Mais in one or two cases with one or two explanatory words—and then the place of their burial, in Kanuri, their " Kargo " or resting place of their spirits, was sung or chanted by the Babuma or other official singer at the Bornu court at N'gazargamu.

XLIV.—THE END OF THE SAIFAWA DYNASTY.

Sultan Ali b. Sultan Haj ruled forty-four years. After him the son of the Sultan Ahmed ruled fourteen years, and Sultan Muhammad Dunama was then made Mai when Ahmed went blind.

The reason this was done was the news of the coming of the Fellata to Bornu. Dunama ruled six months. Then there came Gwoni Mukhtar, and turned them out of Birni Gazargamu and entered it himself.

After nine months and three days Sultan Dunama returned, and killed Gwoni Mukhtar.

The Emir of Katagum, Mallam Zaki, then came. Sultan Dunama, when he heard the news of his coming, fled to Kurnawa*. Mallam Zaki entered Gazargamu and stayed there forty days.

The Beni Saif then agreed to depose Dunama, and appoint his uncle, Sultan N'gileroma. N'gileroma lived in the Birni of Kabila six years. He was then deposed at the instance of the Wazir Muhammad al Amin, and Sultan Dunama was restored.

The latter ruled seven years more and died as a martyr, in the war against Bagarmi. He was buried at N'gala.

His brother Sultan Ibrahim ibn Sultan Ahmed was then installed. Afterward Sheikh Muhammad al Amin ruled alone for thirty years and his son Sheikh Umr ruled forty-five years. Umr's son Sheikh Bukr ruled three years, and Bukr's brother Ibrahim one year. Sheikh Hashim ruled eight years.

---

* In N'ganse.

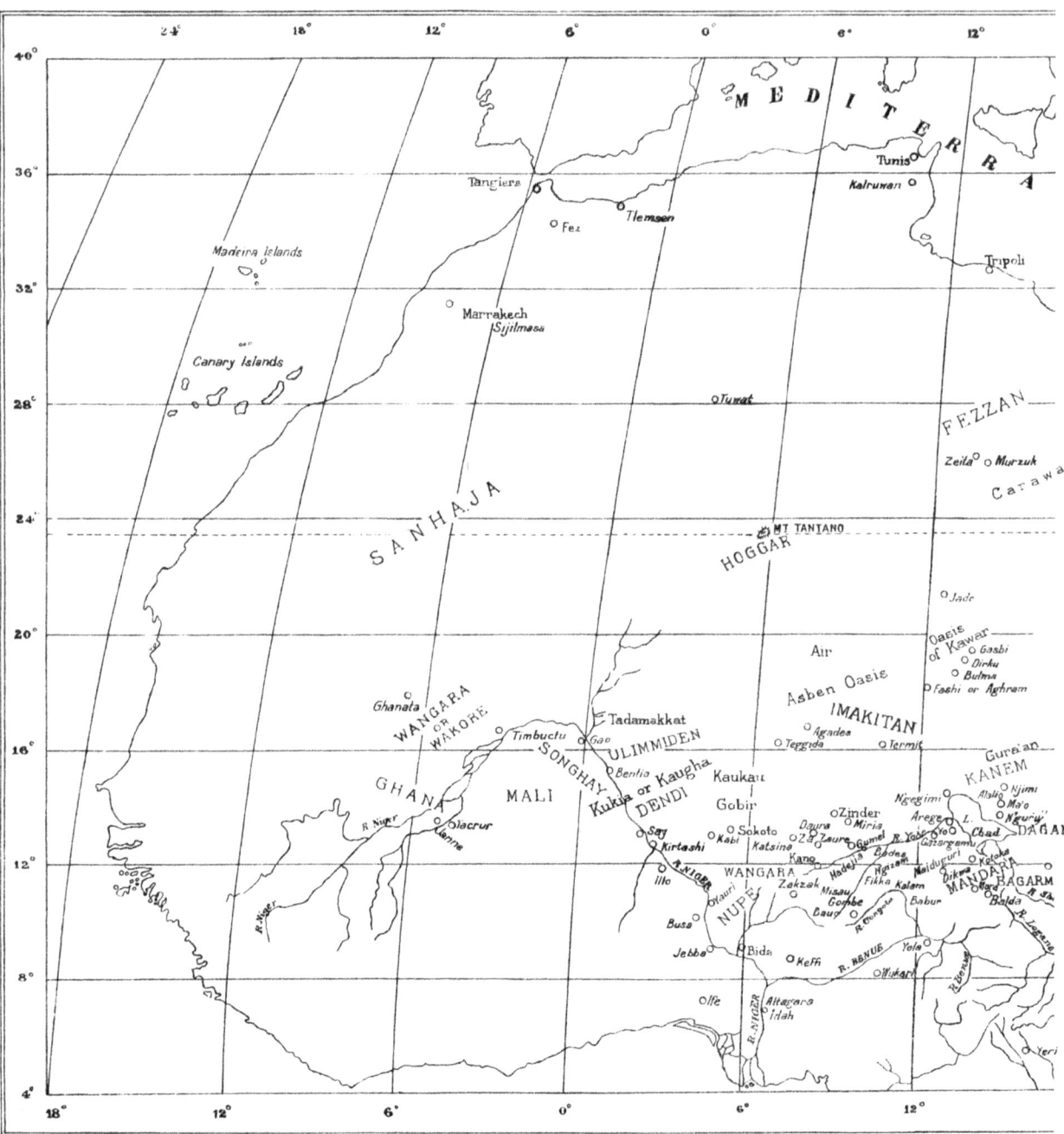

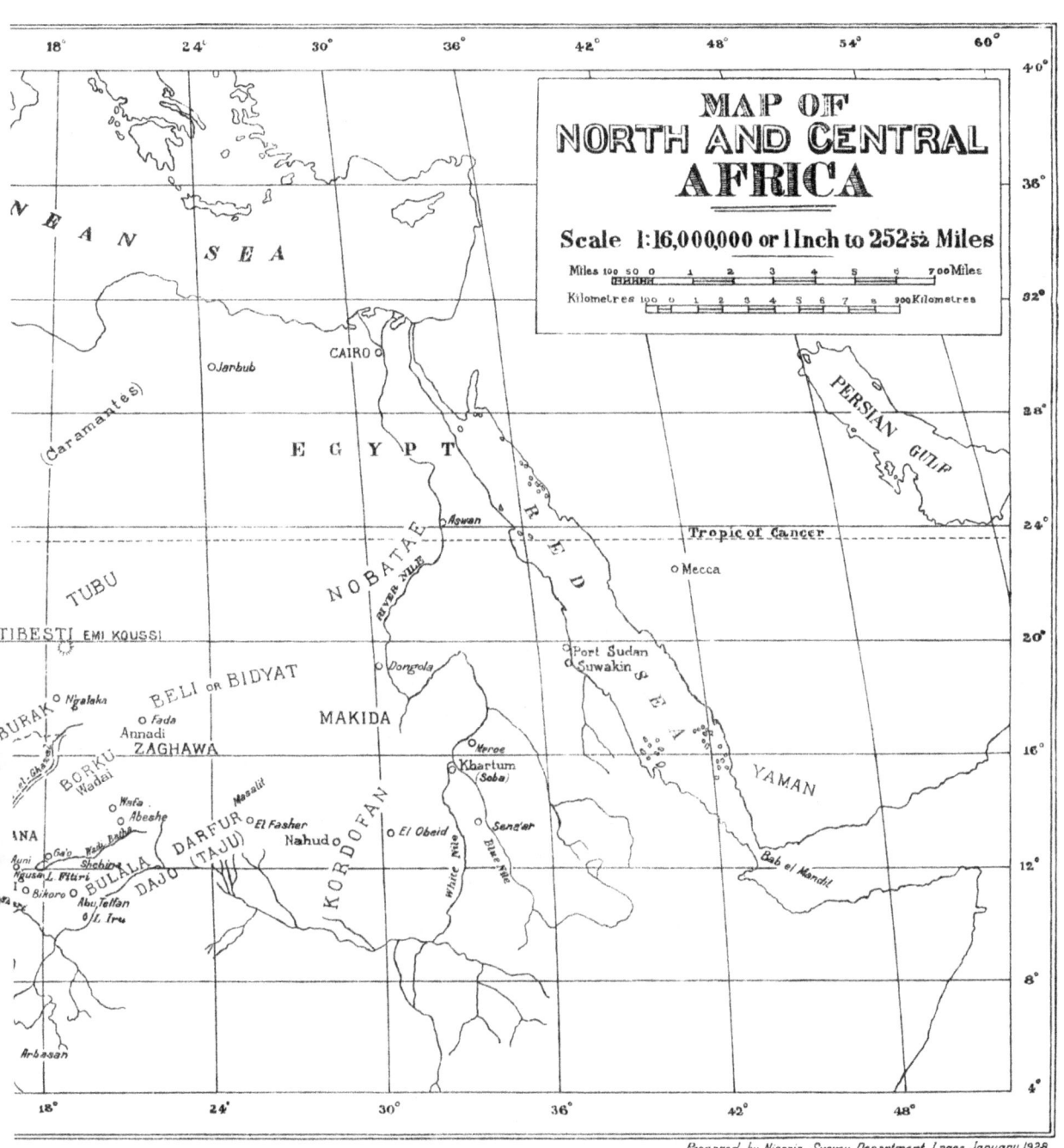

SUDANESE MEMOIRS

VOLUME THREE

Wall of the Mais Summer Palace on the Komadugu at Gambaru.
(Built circa 1570-80).

INTRODUCTION.

The translations of Manuscripts which are included in Vol. II of these Memoirs are mostly concerned with the tribal legends or traditions of the Chad area and countries lying to the east or south-east of it in the Sudan belt. They illustrate, and in some measure explain, references and allusions to certain peoples concerned in the " Kanem Wars " of Imam Ahmed, among them the Kwararafa, with their governing caste the so-called Jukon*, who originally of cognate origin to the Mais of Kanem, occupied at different periods the Chad region, the region of the upper Gongola, and finally the region of the middle Benue, whence from their capitals Bepi and Wukari they extended their influence to the Cross River and even the Atlantic Ocean.

The present Volume includes firstly a number of so-called " Mahrams " *i.e.* letters patent, or grants of privilege, given by various Mais from the earliest times of the Kanem kingdom to certain learned or noble families, which owe their preservation to their contingent material value to the grantees and their descendants. These Mahrams are perhaps the best local data now existing which can be considered in a measure contemporary record, and thus capable of demonstrating that the Girgams and the Arabic histories of Bornu now extant represent, allowing for a certain amount of inaccuracy, historical fact.

Secondly chronological and other Bornu data have been included to aid in focussing the information contained in the Mahrams on the one hand and on the other in the accounts of Asben or Air, Katsina, Kano and Daura which are added.

These latter manuscripts (57-61) contain the main outlines, so far as they exist in Arabic, of the history of the chief Hausa States and of the Southern Tuwareg from whom in part the Hausas derived their language and culture, from about 1000 A.D. to the end of the 19th century. They omit however any general account of the rise, and spread over Hausaland of the Fulani race and power, which, gathering impetus in Gobir under the leadership of the Muslim revivalist Othman Dan Hodio in the year 1796—1804, absorbed into Sokoto Emirate by 1810, the greater part of the three old Hausa kingdoms of Kebbi, Gobir, and Zanfara, made Daura, Katsina, Kano, and Zaria tributary to itself, and even captured and sacked the capital of Bornu N'gazargamu, though unable, owing to the intervention of the Berri-Berri (Barbar) races east of Lake Chad to obtain a permanent political ascendency over Bornu except on its western fringes.

As will be seen from these narratives, the cultural influences acting on Hausaland since 1,000 A.D. were in the main two, an eastern one, Bornu, and a western one, Songhay, and Melle.

---

* Capt. Abraham has recently shewn that this word is probably the equivalent of the Tuwareg word for nobles—" Imoshagh."

Though the western one represented by the Fulani has now been in the ascendant for over 100 years, the basis of Nigerian culture, especially the culture of Eastern Nigeria, is still largely of Berri-Berri (Bornu or Barbar) origin.

The manuscripts contained in this Volume are as follows:—

45. Mahram of Umme Jilmi vixit 1080 A.D. "The introduction of Islam into Bornu."
46. Tura Mahrams.
47. Mahram of the N'galma Duku.
48. A Mahram belonging to the Masbarma family.
49. Mahram of Mai Ali Gaji Dunamami, 1471.
50. Mahram of Idris Katagarmabe circa 1504 A.D.
51. Mahram of Mai Ahmad 1793.
52. Old Bornu Towns.
53. The Kayi (Bulala) and Magumi.
54. Girgams of the Kanembu tribes.
55. Translation of Saifawa Girgam in possession of Galadima Kashim Bîri.
56. A list of Mais of Bornu down to 1808 A.D. with approximate dates.
57. The Sultanate of Ahir.
58. Chronicle of the Sultanate of Ahir and notes on the Kanuri and Tuwareg Barbars, Fulani, and Teda.
59. History of Katsina with notes.
60. The Kano Chronicle, with prefatory note.
61. The History of Daura (Walwyn).

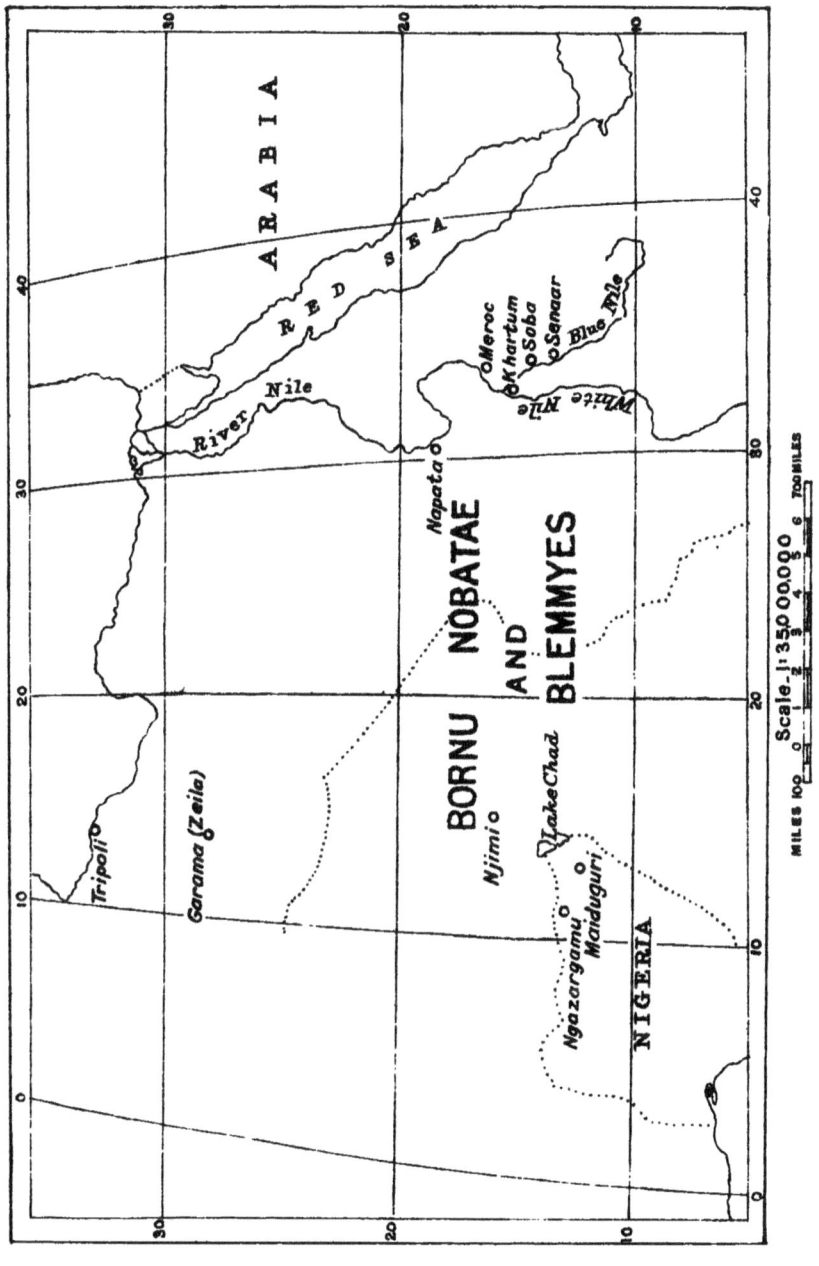

XLV.—MAHRAM OF UMME JILMI (CIRCA 1080 A.D.)
The Introduction of Islam into Bornu.

In the name of God, the Merciful, the Compassionate. May God bless our Lord Muhammad, his relations and friends. Peace from King Umme to my children who will succeed me, be they Amirs or Officers or Chiefs, or Mallams, or others. Peace be upon you. Hear and understand and receive good tidings.

The first country in the Sudan which Islam entered was the land of Bornu. It came through Muhammad ibn Mâni who lived in Bornu for five years in the time of King Bulu, six years in the time of King Arki, four years in the time of King Kadai Hawami, fourteen years in the time of King Umme.

Then he summoned Bornu to Islam by the grace of King Umme.

Islam was spreading for two years before, through Muhammad Mâni, it became general. Then it became established for fifty years in the time of King Muhammad. Then for twenty-six years in the time of King Othman. Then for fifteen years in the time of King Abdullahi. Then for twenty-eight years in the time of King Abdul Jalil. Then for thirty-nine years in the time of King Muhammad ibn Muhammad. Then twenty years in the time of King Othman.

These years were years of Islam, and Muhammad ibn Mâni lived one hundred and twenty years.

King Bulu read with Muhammad Mâni from "*Tabarak alladhi fi yaddahu mulk,*" down to "*min al jinnati waalnâs.*" Bulu gave his teacher fifty camels. King Arki read from "*Yasin*" to "*waalnâs*" and gave him sixty camels. King Kade ibn Arju (Shu ibn Arki) read from "*KH'AS.*" to "*waalnâs,*" and gave him seventy camels. Abd ul Jalil (Jil b. Huwa) read from "*A.L.M.S.*" (Surat al 'Araf) onwards and gave him eighty camels. Mai Umme read secretly from the Surat-al-Bakara to *waalnâs*. Then he read the Risala twice, and gave Mâni one hundred camels, one hundred pieces of gold, one hundred pieces of silver, and one hundred slaves, all because of the reading and instruction he derived from him.

Mai Umme says "Hear and understand that five tribes are *haram* to me; firstly, Mu'alim Muhammad ibn Mâni, from whom I learnt the Kura'an and Risala; secondly, Tura Tuzar; thirdly, Gamayambara; fourthly, Kayi Malakâyi: fifthly Dihiluri; sixthly, Diri Laima; seventhly, Ajama Bulumi."

Mai Umme and Muhammad ibn Mâni spread abroad Islam to last till the day of judgment.

The goods of Muhammad ibn Mâni, the first, are *haram* till the day of judgment, to the Beni Umme or any besides. He who disobeys the command of the King, and transgresses, and sins, may God not give him heaven, but may he fill his belly with the fire of hell.

He who follows my command, may God order his well-being both in this life and the next.

Says the Sultan Umme, the noble—"Their goods and blood from the time of Muhammad Mâni, are in the keeping of the Beni Umme, and all others; I consider them as the flesh of swine, or the flesh of the dog, or the flesh of a monkey or ass."

Says Sultan Umme—"He who eats their goods, may God fill his belly with the fire of hell; there is no hurt in leaving their property to them. He among them who does a wrong let the matter be left to their chief; there is no other way than this. This is the command of the Sultan; change it not nor alter it, and oppress not the children of Muhammad ibn Mâni, for ever.

"I make their land *habus*; let them be ennobled in their faith.

"Change not this injunction, for he who after hearing it changes it, his lot is that of those who innovate; for God will note his action. Spread abroad Islam in Bornu and strive to keep the posterity of Muhammad ibn Mâni *haram*. King Umme says to his children "I make the children of Muhammad ibn Mâni *habus* to you, and I exempt them from the obligation to entertain your men in the dry season or to pay 'diya' and all forms of tribute, to the time of my children's children, and to the day of judgment.

"He who puts forth his hand against them, may God not bless him for he transgresseth my behest."

King Umme spread abroad Islam; on that day he was a victor.

King Umme has ennobled the Beni Mâni with the nobility of the Risala; their goods are *haram* like the flesh of swine, or monkeys or dead things or spilt blood or wine, to the time of his remotest descendants. He says:—

"Tura Tuzan was the pillar of my kingdom; therefore the goods of his children also are *haram* to me and my descendants of the Beni Umme and others, even as swine's flesh, or monkey's flesh or blood spilt in the ground. No hurt shall come to them, but in sparing them there is great reward; therefore spare them in all things till the day of judgment. Hear and understand that which befell on the road to Mecca at the entering in of Islam."

Says the King Umme: "Alter not my word; send them not away nor yet depose them nor constrain them in the affairs of the world, for the sake of God and His prophet and me; forget me not, and do not do otherwise. For he who varies my injunction, God will not guide his character, or station, in this world or the next. He who gives to his fellow the gift of one fount of wisdom is his brother; but he who teaches him twice is his master. Truly our wisdom in the Kura'an and Risala came from Muhammad ibn Mâni. My brethren and sons who will come after me, may God bless you: make not void my behest, for he who voids it, may God not bless him nor grant his need in both worlds, by the grace of God and His Prophet, in whom He is well pleased. Peace be upon my children and he who comes after me. Praise be to the God of the worlds; and may he who changes this have the recompense of changers. May God establish this my behest in both worlds. Understand it, and transgress not, nor act contrary to it, nor curse it nor change it, but cherish it as may God cherish you from all evil and civil strife. Peace be upon you, and my people."

The Mahram of Ahmed ibn Muhammad ibn Walii ibn Farto ibn Bitku ibn Kukuli ibn Farto ibn Othman, etc., etc., Allahuma. May God pardon me and my father and all Moslem men and women living and dead.

Peace be upon us and you.

XLVI.—TURA MAHRAMS.*

KING BIKUR.

In the name of God, the Merciful, the Compassionate.

This document was written that people might know the origin of the Beni Mukhtar among other tribes and their home of origin.

Two youths came from Ahir to Dirku (Kawar) sons of Sultan Sule to look for wives. They found them and carried off two girls on their camels; and fled to their country Ahir.

Then Maina Bagarma, Maina Fatar and Maina Ali heard of it and set off on the tracks of their daughters. They overtook the Kindin youths, and a fight took place on the road. The fathers prevailed and killed Sultan Sule's youths and returned with their daughters to Dirku delighted. Then the Kindin came to attack the people of Dirku. The latter fled by night because they were no match for the Kindin, and came to the land of Sultan Bikur† and entered the Birni by reason of their fear.

Then the Kindin came in to this Birni and asked for the blood of their sons from Sultan Bikur. He gave them three of his subjects who were not of noble family to settle the matter. So the people of Dirku were saved, and the people of Mai Sule returned to their town Ahir. This took place in the year of the Hejira 580.—1184 A. D.

TURA MAHRAM OF DIRKUMA IBRAHIM.

After Bismillah, this document was written in order that people should know the origin of the Beni Mukhtar among other tribes. Their original dwelling was among the Tura Beni Habîbi.

This girgam was written in the time of King Bikur on

---

* These Tura Mahrams indicate how the North African mixed Arab and Teda peoples called Wasuri, or Uzlan came down from Zeila and other centres in Fezzan to Bornu.

† *King Bikur*—i.e., Dalla Bikur ruled 1177-1193 A.D. The Kindin of Ahir were Amakitan, the people of Dirku were Teda; evidently at this date they were not able to fight the Amakitan and hence obliged to ask the protection of the Kanuri Mais who were by inter-marriage allied to the Teda.

account of *Amarma Bint Bure (Zeinam), the daughter of Nana. It was written herein that because of this document King Sule (the Kindin of Ahir) would not commandeer the camels of Bure in war, for that the people of Dirku had fled and sought protection from King Bikur, an event which occurred in the year 588 A.H. (1192 A.D.).

Dirkuma Ibrahim
bin Dirkuma Bukr.
bin Dirkuma Habîbi.
bin Dirkuma Muhammad.
bin Zeilama Muhammad Mustafa.
bin Zeilama Ibrahim.
bin Habibi.
bin Muhammad Barima.
bin Taib.
bin Othman.
bin Muhammad.
bin Umr.
bin Kasim.
bin Muhammad.
bin Tahir.
bin Bakan.
bin Mu'alab.
bin Mutallib.
bin Abdullahi.
bin Muhammad.
bin Muhammad Habîbi.
bin Ali.
bin Abu Talib.

May God favour them all. The Sherifs of Habîbi are the same as the Tura.

TURA MAHRAM—IDRIS BUGALMARAMBE.

In the name of God, the Merciful, the Compassionate.

The bringing of a horse as a present and a token of respect occurred in the time of Sultan Idris ibn Amsa ibn Bugalma†. Again, in the time of Idris Alooma, the Tura were excused from military service in order to avoid evil.

The Sultan Idris Alooma, in the year 1000 of the Hijira (1591 A.D.), made a 'sadaka' of a 1,000 of the following:—camels, oxen, sheep, goats, donkeys, fowls, and all kinds of food.

It was on this day that the obligation of the Tura to go to Dirku and Zeila was abolished. They said we will not bring horses from Egypt because therein are seven perils: the Buduma, the Balgada‡, the Mitimiti§, the Tubu, the Kindin, and Thirst, and Hunger.

---

* Amarma is a title, the name of the site being Tamarmar or Tamalma, a place mentioned by Idrisî, in the vicinity of the present Aghram.

The Tura are sometimes said to be Teda Gura'an, and sometimes to be Arabs. The fact is that Tura simply meant "white," and was used, like Wasuri or Wasuli (Uzlan) is now, to describe a Fezzani.

Probably the Beni Mukhtar and Habibi were tribes of mixed Arab and Teda origin.

It will be noticed that the Dirkumas, *i.e.*, chiefs of Dirku (Kawar), descend from chiefs of Zeila (Murzuk) or Zeila Uzlan, *i.e.*, they were Teda (Garamantes) who had moved South.

In this connexion 'Arab' includes Semites of different kinds who had settled in North Africa: *e.g.*, the Tyrians (Wasuri), Sidonians, and Carthaginians.

† *i.e.*, Idris Katagarmabe, 1504-1527.

(‡)
(§) } Balgada and Mitimiti are the Zaghawa and Bideyat.

King Ahmed* said: "Give me good Bornu horses of pure race, seventy-seven." The Fargama gathered them together at a price of twelve *rotals* apiece.

On each horse was a charge of four *rotals* to the Mulima (master of the horse), and three *rotals* to clothe the attendants of the horses.

Again if the Tura purposed to go to Dirku, the Chiefs Figidoma, Yawama, and Tagama took to Dirku 2,000 *saas* of dukhn as food for the Tura and their horses. They went and returned.

TURA MAHRAM—IDRIS ALOOMA, 1591—GIRGAM OF DIRKUMA MUHAMMAD.

In the name of God, the Merciful, the Compassionate; after mention of God's creation, we have written this document, so that people may know the origin of the Beni Mukhtar among other tribes.

Their original dwelling was among the Tura Beni Habibi. This was written in the days of King Idris, as a protection against hatred and attack.

The King said: "You are not liable for military service, and he who says you are, may God not bless him. I give you *Laluri*."

Dirkuma Muhammad
ibn Dirkuma Muhammad Mustafa.
ibn Muhammad Amarma.
ibn Dirkuma 'Ali.
ibn Dirkuma Ibrahim.
ibn Dirkuma Taib.
ibn Dirkuma Bakr.
ibn Dirkuma Habibi.
ibn Dirkuma Muhammad.
ibn Dirkuma Muhammad.
ibn Dirkuma Ali.
ibn Zeilama Mustafa.
ibn Zeilama Ibrahim.
ibn Habibi.
ibn Muhammad Barima.
ibn Taib.
ibn Othman.
ibn Muhammad.
ibn Umr.
ibn Kasim.
ibn Muhammad.
ibn Tahir.
ibn Bakari.
ibn Mu'alab.
ibn Mutallib.
ibn Abd ul Lahi.
ibn Muhammad.
ibn Muhammad Habibi.
ibn 'Ali.
ibn Abu Talib.

May God favour them.

This document was written in the year of the Hejira 1000 (1591 A.D.), in the days of King Idris.

TURA MAHRAM—HAMSAWA.

In the Name of God, the Merciful, the Compassionate; and after mention of His creation.

This document was written that people may know the origin of the Beni Mukhtar among other tribes, and the origin of the two tribes (*i.e.* Beni Mukhtar and Beni Habibi).

---

* *i.e.*, Dunama Dabalemi.

A man called Adam came to Dirku and desired a girl named Hafsa (Kagul). He married her and joined her tribe. These two by their intention became the tribe of Tura Beni Habibi Hamsawa, *i.e.* Hafsa and the man Adam. Adam belonged to the town of Amarmada, a town of the Tubu of the tribe Dibiri, before he came to Dirku.

Their children entered the tribe of their mother Hafsa, the Tura Beni Habibi (**Hamsawa**).

Muhammad	ibn Muhammad Barima.
ibn Muhammad.	ibn Taib.
ibn Mustafa (1688).	ibn Othman.
ibn Muhammad.	ibn Muhammad.
ibn Ali.	ibn Umr.
ibn Ibrahim.	ibn Kasim.
ibn Taib.	ibn Muhammad.
ibn Bukr.	ibn Tahar.
ibn Kasim.	ibn Hahari.
ibn Ibrahim.	ibn Mu'alab.
ibn Bukr.	ibn Mutallib.
ibn Habibi.	ibn Abdullahi.
ibn Muhammad.	ibn Muhammad.
ibn Ali.	ibn Muhammad Habibi.
ibn Muhammad.	ibn Ali.
ibn Mustafa.	ibn Abu Talib.
ibn Ibrahim.	
ibn Habibi.	

May God favour them all.

TURA MAHRAM—MAI ALI 1688.

In the name of God, the Merciful, the Compassionate; after Bismillah.

This document was written that people may know the origin of the Beni Mukhtar among other tribes, and their original dwelling among the Tura Beni Habibi.

It was written in the days of king 'Ali ibn Hajj, for the sake of our father Hajj Muhammad ibn Dublu who came from Mecca with his mother in scorn of the things of this world. The King said: "I leave them to do as they please." They said to him: "We will go to Mecca to preserve our souls."

The King gave them the town of Laluri.

Dirkuma Muhammad Mustafa	ibn Dirkuma Muhammad.
ibn Ali.	ibn Zelama Mustafa.
ibn Dirkuma Ibrahim.	ibn Zelama Ibrahim.
ibn Dirkuma Taib.	ibn Habibi.
ibn Dirkuma Bukr.	ibn Muhammad Barin.
ibn Dirkuma Kasin.	ibn Taib.
ibn Dirkuma Ibrahim.	ibn Amarma Muhammad.
ibn Dirkuma Bukr.	ibn Othman.
ibn Dirkuma Habibi.	ibn Muhammad.

ibn 'Amir.
ibn Kasin.
ibn Muhammad.
ibn Tahir.
ibn Bahari.
ibn Ma'lub.
ibn Mutallib.
ibn Abd'ullahi.
ibn Muhammad Habibi.
ibn Ali.
ibn Abu Talib.

In the year of the Hejira and time of King Ali Hajj 1100 A.H. (1688 A.D.).

TURA MAHRAM—ALI HAJJ 1752.

In the name of God, the Merciful, the Compassionate. The blessing of God be upon our Lord Muhammad, and his relations.

PEACE.

After mention of God's creation. This document was written that people may know the origin of the Beni Mukhtar from among other people and their original dwelling among the Tura Habibi in the town of Laluri; the owner of this document is Dirkuma Muhammad Aisami.

b. Amarma Ali.
b. Dirkuma Muhammad.
b. Dirkuma Fafami.
b. Kachella Mustafa.
b. Amarma Lefiama.
b. Amarma Kagudimi.
b. Amarma Birnima.
b. Amarma Nigalemi.
b. Dirkuma Ibrahim.
b. Dirkuma Bukr.
b. Dirkuma Habibi.
b. Dirkuma Muhammad.
b. Dirkuma Ali.
b. Uzulma Mustafa.
b. Uzulma Ibrahim.
b. Habibi.
b. Barima.
b. Taib.
b. Othman.
b. Muhammad.
b. Umr.
b. Kasim.
b. Muhammad.
b. Tahir.
b. Bukunga.
b. Ma'lub.
b. Muhammad Habibi.
b. Ali.
b. Abu Talib.

This was written in the year 1166 A.H. (1752 A.D.), in the time of Ali Hajj.

Of Him do we seek help.

In remembrance of Amarma Muhammad Lefiami and his family. Amarma Ali b. Kachella Muhammad. b. Dirkuma Fafami b. Kachella Mustafa. b. Amarma Lefiami b. Dirkuma Ali who owned the town of Laluri.

Then the family of the latter Muhammad b. Mustafa b. Umr b. Sharam b. Amarma Mustafa, the owner of Gawa Dali.

Then the family of the latter Saiyadu b. Talib b. Ibrahim b. Saiyadu b. Othman b. Muallim Umr, the owner of Magabura.

Of Him do we seek help. In dread of forgetting our family and the family of slaves and freedmen, we have written this that there shall be no confusion about our seed the Tura Beni Habibi.

The exalted Dirkuma Muhammad b. Ali b. Fanna had six sons.

1. Muhammad b. Amarma Mustafa.
2. Maina Ali.
3. Dirkuma Ibrahim.
4. Maina Bukr.
5. Saiyadu and the descendants of the son of Bala b. Ali b. Umr b. Ibrahim b. Umr b. Ibrahim b. Umr b. Maina Ali and Kachella Buguma.
6. The descendants of Dirkuma Ibrahim b. Bukr b. Othman b. Muhammad b. Ali b. Idris b. Bukr and Kachella Asirbe.

Maina Bukr has descendants:—

Kachella Umr b. Dirkuma Bukr b. Amarma Ibrahim b. Kachella Abdullahi b. Kasim b. Dirkuma Ali, the owner of Zabatam. Maina Ali b. Dirkuma and Abdu and Abdu Kasim.

Of the seed of Salma, Anno b. Kagu b. Bashe b. Abdul Kasim, b. Maina Ali, was owner of " Bashari ibn Fanna."

TURA—MAHRAM 1752 A.D.

In the Name of God, the Merciful, the Compassionate.

To avoid forgetting:

The Sultan of Bornu 'Ali bin Al Hajj said " Let us enlist the tribe of Tura for war." The Tura said " We are descended from Dirkuma Amarma Guzuma, we will not go to war." So they disputed with the Sultan.

The Tura gathered together and held counsel, and beat the drum, purposing to migrate to their own land Dirku. Maina Kiari came to the Sultan of Bornu and said to him " I bring you news that the tribe of Tura are all about to migrate to the land of Dirku."

The Sultan then called his chiefs before him and said " We will forego our expedition." The Tura then said to the Sultan " We have nothing more to say," and remained.

The Sultan then said " They shall pay no taxes save one horse, and of crops one *saa* of dukhn.

So they concluded the matter by a clear covenant, the leader of the Tura being Dirkuma Muhammad Fafami.

The messengers through whom they approached the Sultan were Fargama, N'gawama Muhammad and Yarima.

The witnesses present to this act were: Talba Kabir Madangilma Bukr, Mallam Yahya bin Talba, and his elder brother Abdul Lahi, Sintelma Kadai, Maina Ahmad bin Sama, Maina Muhammad, Imam Hunaiya, Katib Muhammad Talba.

This event took place in the year 1166 of the Hijira (1752 A.D.)

MAHRAM—MAI AHMAD.

After praise be to God, this was written in the time of King Ahmad, concerning the horses from the North

They said " We cannot do this ". The King said "If you can do this, as a present and sign of respect, give me horses born in your country."

Muhammad ibn Muhammad.
ibn Muhammad. ibn Barim.
ibn Mustafa. ibn Taib.
ibn Muhammad ibn Othman.
ibn Ali. ibn Muhammad.
ibn Ibrahim. ibn Umr.
ibn Bukr. ibn Kasin.
ibn Habibi. ibn Muhammad.
ibn Muhammad. ibn Tahir.
ibn Ali. ibn Barkari.
ibn Ibrahim. ibn Ma'lub.
ibn Bukr. ibn Mutallib.
ibn Habibi. ibn Abd ul Lahi.
ibn Muhammad. ibn Muhammad.
ibn Ali. ibn Muhammad Habibi.
ibn Muhammad Mustafa. ibn Ali.
ibn Ibrahim. ibn Abu Talib.
ibn Habibi.

(King Ahmad).

TURA MAHRAM—1806 A.D.

Of Him do we seek help.

This was written in the time of Sheikh el Amin, for the daughter of the Tura of Marte, named Habiba (Kellu)*. The Tura gave this girl to the Sultan Muhammad N'giliroma who said to them "You are free of taxes."

But Sheikh el Amin said to the Sultan "This is quite impossible, except in the case of the Chiefs of the Tura, and those who are actually descended from our lord Ali ibn Abi Talib, to wit:—

The Sultan of the Tura, b. Bukr.
Dirkuma Muhammad. b. Kasim.
  b. Dirkuma Ali. b. Ibrahim.
  b. Kachella Mustafa. b. Bukr.
  b. Dirkuma Muhammad. b. Ali.
  b. Ali. b. Habibi.
  b. Ibrahim. b. Muhammad.
  b. Taib. b. Muhammad.
  b. Ali. b. Tahir.
  b. Zullama Mustafa. b. Bahari.
  b. Zullama Ibrahim. b. Ma'lub.
  b. Habibi. b. Mutallib.
  b. Barim. b. Abdul Lahi.
  b. Taib. b. Muhammad.
  b. Othman. b. Muhammad Habibi.
  b. Muhammad. b. Ali.
  b. Umr. b. Abi Talib.
  b. Kasim.

---
* Her father was Suleiman. The Tura gave her to the Mai as alms (sadaka).

This was written in the year of the Hejira 1220—1805/6 A.D.
Of Him do we seek help.
The people of Tura inhabited twelve lands.
1. Mecca, three hundred years.
2. Medina, fifty-five years.
3. Stanboul, seventy years.
4. Misra, eighty years.
5. Tarabulus, sixty years.
6. Benghazi, twenty years.
7. Senaar, ten years.
8. Zeila, seventy years.
9. Agades, fifty years.
10. Dirku, two hundred and twenty years.

Their eleventh abode is in the land of Bornu where they have lived for three hundred and fifty years and nine months.

In the land of Dirku their Chiefs were Zulama, Dirkuma and Amarma, three in number.

Of Him do we seek assistance; after mention of God's creation.
This document was written for the information of future generations.

The seed of the King of the Unbelievers Gau Dala Shaliwa and our race were joined together.

The Tura Arwalinwa were descended from Khuza'a ibn Balani.

The Tura Wadâli were descended from his messenger Nasar Zagmi.

The Tura Jilbana were descended from his Chief Dukmi.

The Tura Zuganda were descended from his Chief Anwar

The Tura Amzura were descended from his slave and messenger Nasar Zagmi Baddi.

The Tura are the Beni Hassan. Verily our tribe counts as a blood brother of Hassan the son of our father (Ali) who was killed.

The Tura Beni Ishak (Asek) are of the people of King Gau Dala Shaliwa, by reason of war in which they were captured, and became freedmen and were thus numbered among them. The Tura Beni Ishak were the children of Sa'ad Alheri, their town was Gazbi, and their chiefs were Guzuma, Fugu, Arwalingawamma and Magadam. These were their rulers:—

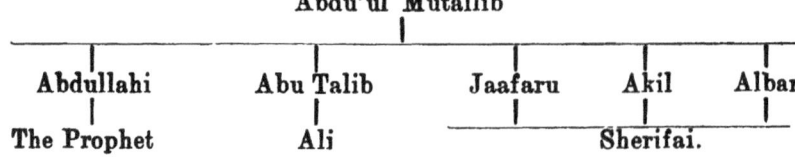

TURA GIRGAM—HABIBI AISAWA.
In the Name of God.

A man called Abdullahi came to the land of Dirku, to seek the girl Aisa Kili for a wife.

He married her and entered the tribe of his wife, and they became the Tura Beni Habibi Aisawa.

This Abdullahi was in origin of the Tubu Balgada. This was the tribe of their father, while their mother's tribe was the Kabila Aisawa.

They were composed of sixteen 'Tobols' (clans) and gave the Sultan every year sixteen horses as a present.

Muhammad
b. Muhammad.
b. Mustafa.
b. Muhammad.
b. Ali.
b. Ibrahim.
b. Taib.
b. Bukr.
b. Kasin.
b. Ibrahim.
b. Bukr.
b. Habibi.
b. Muhammad.
b. Ali.
b. Mustafa.
b. Ibrahim.
b. Habibi.
b. Muhammad Barima.
b. Taib.
b. Othman, etc.

XLVII.—MAHRAM OF THE N'GALMA DUKU.*

In the name of God, the Merciful, the Compassionate. May God bless our Lord Muhammad, his relatives and friends. Peace.

The purpose of this writing is that he who runs may read, be he Amir, or officer, or chief, or Mu'allim, that the learned Imam Abd ul Lahi Dili ibn Bikuru read with the son of the king called Mabradu ibn Salma a hundred and fifty books.†

Therefore the Sultan built the plastered Mosque, and roofed it with clay, after the Mosque of Mecca was covered with cloth.

He established this Fagi as the Imam of the Mosque (may God increase His blessing upon him).

And when the Fagi advanced to pray he saw the two exalted treasures under the unapproachable lotus bud (*i.e.* the Seventh Heaven).

One of the treasures came down to earth in the time of the king Salma ibn Bikuru, and killed the snake. The Sultan had its skin brought before him so that a 'gown' should be woven like it. When the gown was woven, he put it on and went to his council. Then he sought the learned men of his kingdom and asked them: "Do you know an animal which is like this gown?" They were silent, and unable to answer.

Then the Fagi Imam Abd ul Lahi Dili came forward, and asked permission of the king to speak. He was granted permission, and said that the gown was like a snake. The king then produced the snake's skin, and put it in front of him. The courtiers were astonished at the resemblance of the gown to the snake. The Imam Abd ul Lahi Dili said: "This skin has a peculiar property, namely, if a mortal puts it in water and then drinks the water, he will understand the language of beasts."

So the king put the skin in water, and drank it, and heard the conversation of two black birds on the top of a tree.

He then sought out his cavaliers and chiefs, and assembled them in his noble place of assembly. The king Salma ibn Bikuru

---

* The N'galma Duku are allied to the N'galaga, and are one of the chief Kanembu tribes of the present day.
† *i.e.* time of Tsilim (Selma) Bikarmi 1194-1220 A.D.

sought out the Fagi, the Imam Abd ul Lahi Dili ibn Bikuru, and said: "I make you and your descendants *haram* till the day of judgment, I make *haram* the goods of your posterity and their blood; they shall be *haram* to the day of the blowing of the horn. Their property shall be as the flesh of swine or dead things, or blood.

"There shall be for them no military service, or obligation to entertain chiefs, nor shall they be liable to go on a 'jihad' or to be fined, or perform any other customary task; their work is to pray only. Their affairs are in God's keeping. He who wrongs your seed O Abd ul Lahi Dili, and sets at nought my act, may God not bless him in his life and undertakings, but fill his belly and his whole body with fire."

"May he who sets out to wrong them fail, and may he not escape the sure penalty, nor be able to escape it or appeal to us, for we will have nought of it."

This is the sacred injunction of Sultan Salma ibn Makidabe Sultan Salma ibn Bikuru ibn Hau (may God sanctify his body from the fire, and cause him to enjoy the highest joys of paradise without stint).

This act and deed was done on a Sunday, and witnesses to it were:—

Waziri Medi.
Arjinoma Fartu ibn Kadai.
Mustrema Loto.
The Treasurer Arku ibn Suleiman.
Yerima Dunuma ibn Tsilim.
Chiroma Nigale ibn Sa'ad.
Tegoma Mabarlad ibn Tsilim.
Iyrima Dika Dikale.
Kadi Fafisma.
The Treasurer Masfarma.
Faki bin Bakra
Arjinoma Dunuma ibn Meto.
Talba Yunus.

Tâlib al Khatti Masfarma ibn Mâti, and many other witnesses who were present.

This is the sacred injunction of Mâkidabe Sîku Arjîku.

Then afterward came the posterity of Abd ul Lahi Dili ibn Bikuru to our Lord the Commander of the Faithful, Sultan of the Moslems Al Hajj Dunama ibn Dabale. He ratified their privilege, and approved the act of his father.

So too his son Sultan Biri approved the act of his father and grandfather.

So too Sultan Al Haj Ibrahim (Nigale), son of Kagudi, approved the act of his sires:

and Sultan Al Hajj Idris bin Nigale,
and Sultan Al Hajj Biri bin Edris,
and Sultan Al Hajj Dunama bin Biri,
and Sultan Al Hajj Ali bin Dunama,
and Sultan Al Hajj Idris bin Ali,
and Sultan Al Hajj Muhammad bin Idris,

and Sultan Al Hajj Ali ibn Idris,
and Sultan Al Hajj Dunama bin Muhammad,
and Sultan Al Hajj Abd ul Lahi bin Dunama,
and Sultan Al Hajj Idris bin Ali,
and Sultan Al Hajj Muhammad bin Idris,
and Sultan Al Hajj Ibrahim bin Idris,
and Sultan Al Hajj Umar bin Idris,
and Sultan Al Hajj Ali bin Umar.

Then came the descendants of this Fagi Abd ul Lahi Dili and the Sultan ratified their privilege, and approved the act of his sires. So also Sultan Al Hajj Idris bin Ali and Sultan al Hajj Dunama bin Ali, and Sultan Al Hajj Dunama bin Dunama, and Sultan Al Hajj Muhammad bin Dunama, and Sultan Al Hajj Dunama bin Muhammad bin Dunama, and Sultan Al Hajj Ali bin Dunama.

He who changes this after hearing it will be punished with the punishment of innovators. We will have nought of it. May God not bless him in his life and undertakings, nor bless his seed.

Peace upon him who follows the way and is God-fearing.

ABD UL LAHI DILI IBN BIKURU.

XLVIII.—A MAHRAM BELONGING TO THE MASBARMA FAMILY.

Of Him we ask assistance.

The Imam al Kabir ibn Mu'allim Bikur, and his brethren, on whom privileges and protection are conferred as a recompense for their prayers.

(Masbarma Umr son of Othman son of Zubeiru.)*

Their good are *haram*, the goods of Muallim Bikur and the Imam of the Saiyids Baltuta and Dafaruna and Kiywaza and Afanuna.

The King has joined with them other tribes among those who established the Musjid, and endowed the Imam of the Saiyids and his brother.

The King of blessed memory† (may God have mercy upon him) said: "I have made your goods and the goods of your descendants *haram* to the service of God, and his prophet, by reason of the merit of knowledge. Their goods are as swine's flesh and donkey's and monkey's. The chiefs shall not enter their houses, and their portion is far other than that of mere worldings; of that which is the custom they are free, their only duty is to pray, and marry the Sultan's daughter, and settle disputes relating to women, and pray for the Sultan. He who wickedly and wrongfully despoils them of their goods, may God not bless him, and may he not find mercy

---

* The first part of this mahram is dated in the time of Umme Jilmi (1086-1097), the second part was obviously added in the days of Mai Idris Alooma (1571-1603). The sentence in brackets was probably interpolated in Idris' time since his Wazir Idris ibn Harun was a member of the Masbarma family.

† *i.e.*, Umme Jilmi.

or anyone to bury him. King Karkarma*, son of Tigiram and Kadai Dunama, Duna Kadai Gana. . . .

Imam Al Kabir Muhammad ibn Fargama Keyi; Dala ibn Muhammad ibn Khadija; Fatima the daughter of Kabuskema, Bîri Bammama; Shattima Ali ibn Kali, and Tolba al Kabir Kadai ibn Jilbo, and the Royal Scribe, the Imam al Kabir Muhammad ibn Ahmad ibn Sofia. He who alters this after hearing it, incurs the penalty of those who innovate.†

* * *

"This was done in the year of the Hejira of the Prophet, four hundred and seventy-eight (1085 A.D.)."

"The greatest of blessings and peace be upon the Prophet:"

* * *

"There is no god but God: He has no partner. Praise be to God who has made knowledge praiseworthy, and brought us forth from the loins of our father Adam and made us the people of our prophet Muhammad (the blessing of God be upon him and peace), and made him the greatest of Prophets and Apostles.

Let every Amir, or Mu'allim, who chances on this writing know that our Lord, the Commander of the Faithful, vicegerent of God on His earth, is the greatest of His people in this age. Al Hajj Idris ibn Ali, who thrust forward in the path of God, and girded his loins to govern his native land with righteousness, the prince of generosity, and pillar of the Faith, and key of knowledge and support of all who fear from their enemies, the unbelievers, is as honey to all his neighbours and those who are down-trodden by their enemies.

May God fill his belly with wisdom, for he does not flaunt his sovereignty in the faces of the learned, the great and noble.

A witness to this are the Wazir Idris ibn Harun, and the Treasurer Muhammad ibn Kadai.

The saving of your town from the machinations of the Kagustema and chief of the Kaids (Zerma) is right and proper; Ibrahim and Yarima will confirm it."

Note to No. 48—Masbarma.

The attached translation of a local manuscript gives the current tradition about the age (that of 'Ali ibn Dunama) in which Masbarma lived, and also indicates the conception that the Bade (Baderi) and N'gizim peoples belong to a stratum of population (probably best classed as Kushite) anterior to that represented by the ruling Kanem race (Saifawa) and the Tuwareg of the Sahara.

The theory of the manuscript is that the latter group of peoples are originally from Hind (*i.e.* Central Asia), and that when they crossed into Africa they found there the Baderi (Bade) races whose name merely means nomads (Badu).

It may be noted that Stephen of Byzantium speaks of the Daradae (Blemyes of the early Christian era in the Nile Valley), as "gens Indica" and that Daradae as a tribal unit are placed by Ptolemy (140 A.D.) not only in the Eastern Sahara to the west of the Island of Meroe, but in the region of Cape Verde and Cape Blanco in the Western Sahara as well.

---

* *i.e.* Umme Jilmi.
† This list of names of men who lived in Idris Alooma's time is probably interpolated.

For a general account of the Blemyes see Quatremère Memoires sur l'Egypte vol. ii, p. 127.

"*In the name of God. Praise be to God, He alone. The blessing of God be upon the noble Prophet and his relations and friends. Peace.*

"This account is an account of origins, the origin of the Tubba' ul Awwal. It is said that Tubba'ul Awwal was Himyar. It is also said that Himyar 'As'ad was the son of Malik, the Sultan of Yaman.

"The learned Sheikh, the Hakim Muhammad Masbarma, was the son of Ama.* Ama was the son of Othman son of Hakim Bukr, the son of Umr, the son of Muhammad, the son of Abdul Lahi, the son of Humein, the son of Tamim, the son of Humein, the son of Tamim, the son of Bolum Muhammad, the son of Othman the Hakim, a son of one of the Benu Huzeil, muallim Himyar 'As'ad. Masbarma was among the greatest of the learned men of the Benu Huzeil, contemporary with Mallam Adam, the father of Abdulahi Al Bambariu.

"They crossed the Red Sea together in the earliest times and lived in the time of the Sultan of Bornu 'Ali, the son of Dunama, the son of Bîri, the son of Dunama, the son of Umr, the son of Abdulahi. Sultan 'Ali made Masbarma his Hâkim (Wazir) and made him his mouthpiece. They were never separated by night or by day or at any time.

"On a day a certain Arab came to the Sultan 'Ali. He was mounted on a camel. He was a learned man, learned in every science. He was brilliantly clever and eloquent in Arabic. He was called Ahmed the son of Bashir, the son of Muhammad Ghailumi. They asked him to tell them concerning the origin of the Tubba'ul Awwal, that is to say, they asked him concerning the origin of the Sultan of Bornu, Mai Ali, the son of Dunama. He returned no reply for three nights. Then they asked him again, and said "Tell us what is the origin of the Tubba'ul Awwal, for, verily, there is some dispute about it among us."

"The Sheikh Ahmed ibn Bashir then said 'O Hakim Masbarma, son of Othman! What have you to do with the story of Tubba'ul Awwal?' The Hakim Masbarma Al Bornawiyu replied: 'Know O Sheikh, we have a grandfather and some of his companions asked him concerning the truth about the Tubba'ul Awwal and he gave them a book and a paper. It was beautifully written and contained much information. In the book there occurred the name of Umr Himyar, the King of Yaman, as being the first of the Tubba'ul Awwal, but the book said that Himyar As'ad was a son of the king of Hind, and that the beginning of their chieftaincy and their rule was among the people of Hind, and that they nominated a Khalifa after the death of King Himyar As'ad, the son of Mantha, the son of 'Ubail, 'Ubail being of the stock of Ham, the son of Noah (Peace be upon him). He—As'ad—was the brother of Yathrib who founded Medina and was the first Tubba'ul Awwal; there was no Tubba'ul Awwal called Umr Al Himyar who was King of Yaman.'

---

* Ama is said to be equivalent to Othmanmi.

"The Sheikh Ahmed ibn Bashir then said 'I found in an ancient book that Himyar was King of Yaman and the first Tubba'ul Awwal, as witness the passage in the Kuraan which says: ' Are they better or are Tubba'ul Awwal better?' '—as far as the passage which says "And those who precede them", on to the end of the passage. You will find the matter stated thus if God wills. (Be He exalted). The reference is to Himyar, King of Yaman, in very truth; but know, O Hâkim Masbarma, that Himyar As'ad was of the sons of the Kings of Hind, and was of the descendants of Ham. This is what we found in the book called Tanzîl, concerning the beginnings of the kings on the earth. But, O Hâkim Masbarma, know that I have a book, and in it is mention of the Tubba 'ul Awwal, that is to say, Himyar As'ad who was among the sons of the King of Hind? And there was no King of Yaman called Himyar the son of Malîk, whose descendants will rule the Sudan to the end of time. But I found a book called 'Wasail 'Araisi' which mentioned the Kings of Hind what time there died the King of Hind called Sahil ibn Basnasaf. He had ninety-nine children, and the notables of the land chose the youngest of them as king because of his sense and wisdom. He installed him as king. When his brothers saw this, they would not consent to it, so they gathered together and took counsel and called all their brethren together. They sought the King's most learned men, the chief of whom was called Sanana ibn Zuried, then Umr the son of Karibali, and Harith the son of Laim, and Sulaim the son of Harsun, and Bashir the son of Hamdân, and Iskandiyara the son of Baltus, and Isnabus the son of Butrus, and Suwail the son of Benu Razadan, and Zeiâna the son of Kardus. They were of nine tribes. They gave good advice and they prevented the brethren doing what was wrong and the king would not like.

"The brothers took counsel upon the matter in hand but they did not agree to the opinion of the chiefs. Thus they prepared to leave the land of Hind and to wander from land to land.

"The first command of their leader (they being seventy men with forty Mallams) was: 'Let us go out together or let us go out singly in order that we may see the earth and its cities.' Then after three days they went out and left the city of Hind one at a time and they met together in the city of Kandahar. On one day they met together. They migrated and went together to the edge of the sea; then they passed it and settled at Kabila. Thence they moved to Karman then to Sijistan, then to the coasts of Basra, then to the land of Satkha and they alighted at the city of Sabur, then to the town of Sairan, then to the town of Sairaf, then to the land of Balahawaz, then to the land of Iraq (Mesopotamia), then to Baghdad, then to Kufa, then to the land of Anbar, then to the land of Hît, then to Sham, then to Solmain, then to Sowan and 'Ukaz and Damiska (Damascus); then they returned to Tabria, then to the land of Kisaria (Caesarea) then to Jerusalem, then to Askalon, then to Ghazira, then to Madina, then to Tabria, then to Ardun, then to Wadan, then to Tal Habria, then to Yathrib (Medina).

"They said to their leader: 'We hear and follow what you say.'"

"Then the Sheikh, the Hâkim Masbarma Othmanmi, said to the Sheikh: 'Why did they undertake all this wandering?' The Sheikh of the Arabs said to him: 'I found this story in the book Tazain ul Majâlis.' the truth was stated by the perfect and peerless Sheikh in his book *The Marvel of Marvels*. In that book it is said that there is nothing marvellous in the acts of God most high. I saw in the book of the "The Nobleness of the Prophet of God" (may the blessing of God rest on him and peace, the chosen one), a passage which says, O Muhammad Masbarma, the Tubba'ul Awwal are people who came from their country Hind in order that they might explore the world with their huge armies, and when they came certain learned men with knowledge came with them to Mecca. The people of Mecca would have nothing to do with them so that the chief of the people of Hind was angry and resolved to destroy the Ka'aba, and kill many men, and take much property and women. At that time the Sharif of Mecca was Abdul Manaf, the son of Kuse, the son of Kanana.

"When they were preparing to do this, that is to say, to murder the males, and seize their property and their women and children, on the very night they were preparing to do so, there came out from their ears and their noses water which had a foul odour, so that they asked the learned men about the reason for this. In truth their eyes were black and this affliction lay heavy upon them so that they asked the learned men concerning it.

"The learned men said to them: 'We will give you medicine for this sickness by the command of God, for verily this sickness comes from heaven in order that it may stop you.' On that night came one of the learned doctors and said to the Wazir of Hind: 'Know that we will tell your king of the steps we intend taking to cure you, so inform him of this.' He said to the Wazir 'Return to the people for we will pray God most high concerning this plague that he may wipe away the affliction.' So he informed him concerning their intention, and so it came to pass that there was stayed the foul water which came out from their ears. Then they believed in God from that hour, and their king put clothes on the Ka'aba. They were the first who clothed the Ka'aba with garments. They desisted from their intention of plundering the people; they left Mecca and went towards Medina. When they were close to it near its hills, they alighted at its spring. All their learned men of the Benu Huzeil then agreed to stay there.

"News of this reached the King so he made enquiry. The learned men said to him: 'O King have patience and we will inform you fully tomorrow.' In the morning they came and saluted and said: 'O King, we are joyful for in this place will be the city of Medina; into this valley there will come great good fortune; in the fulness of time a prophet will come and live here called Muhammad: he will be born at Mecca but will migrate from thence to Medina. In these hills he will live and here will be his tomb in the place where you are now sitting. He will be reverenced in the east and the west, in the south and the north.

Whoso believes in him will be saved both in this world and the next." When the King heard this he was delighted and built for the learned men, four hundred houses and wrote a paper saying that he resigned himself to God's will and believed in the Prophet.

"It ran as follows: 'In the name of God and praise be to God. From Tubba'ul Awwal As'ad, the Himyarite; O Muhammad, I believe in you, and I belive in your Lord most mighty; we follow your religion and are under your flag and your commands; we follow and obey; this is our boast and this my desire, and if we fail, pardon us and our children and brothers; pray for us in the day of judgment. We the Tubba are among your first followers, Amen.'

"He sealed the paper with an iron seal, and put it in a box of copper, and gave it to the Hâkim, whom he had asked about the future, who gave it to the Hâkim of the Bani Nadir, who was the priest (kahin) in that region. They then returned to their land of Hind. The paper remained shut up in the box in the possession of the Hâkim until he died; and his children inherited it until they died; and his grandsons inherited the box until the age of Aba Ayuba Al Ansariyu (may God be pleased with him), and that was about 1,000 years or more after the events we have described.

"When the Prophet Muhammad left Mecca for Medina together with his companions, and they entered Medina the glorious, the beautiful, the Prophet alighted at the house of Aba Ayuba Al Ansariyu, who handed him the box containing the book of Tubba'ul Awwal. The prophet gave it to the Amir al Muminin, Ali, ibn Abu Talib (may God be pleased with him). When the paper was read in the presence of the Prophet, he (may the blessings of God and peace rest on him) said: 'Greetings to my good brother of olden time, the Tubba'u.'

"When the Prophet Muhammad saw this book of the Tubba'ul Awwal, and the history of his brethren, and prophecy of his coming (may the blessing of God and peace rest on him) written so many years before his entry of Medina, the glorious, he found that the time which had elapsed between the time of the prophecy and his finding the book was 1,000 years or more. That is in truth.

"The sons of Tubba'ul Awwal and his sons' sons in the fulness of time disagreed, O Hakim Masbarma son of Othman, concerning the origin of Tubba'ul Awwal, but the first of them was Tubba 'As'ad of the Kings of Hind. It was Tubba 'Umr the Himyarite, the Yamanite, son of Malík, who got lost and went apart when they left Yaman and came to Medina, the glorious, where his people multiplied till they reached 1,470 souls of the Tubba'ul Awwal al Himyariyu, counting men and women.

"After the death of Umr the Himyarite, the Yamanite, his people migrated to the west and crossed the great sea (Red Sea): they and their learned men of the Benu Adam, the learned Abdul Lahi and his sons and Ibrahim and those who followed them.

"These were the people of Mu'allim the Sheikh Adam al Bambariyu. They were among the chosen learned men of the Himyarite kings of Yaman.

"They crossed the great sea and settled on the African coast for many years. There joined them the people of Baderi (or Bade). When they left this region they all scattered, by reason of the death of their leader Abd ul Rahman ibn Abir ibn Ahmad ibn Huzeil ibn Malik ibn 'Umr the Himyarite, the Yamanite.

"Two of the sons of Abdul Rahman, called Ibrahim and Abdul Lahi, led their fathers' people to the west. Thus the Benu Mu'allim Adam brought their people to the city of N'gazargamu. They settled at three places before they reached N'gazargamu.

"They found on their arrival a great people called Shaushau, of the Benu Shum of the race of 'Ad or, (as some say) Thamud, or remnants of them, whom they slew and drove west and south till they conquered them all by reason of their prayers and invocations. With them the Baderi moved also, so that they and all their people did not cease migrating till they came to the land of Asben. There they remained long, so that intermarriage took place and children resulted. Then they left the land of Asben and came to the city of N'gazargamu, and settled outside in the country near to the city.

"The Bambara people then tried to slay them,* but they fled in the night towards the west and south among the N'gizam. The Bade lived in many different places and countries before they came to this their land about six hundred and fourteen years ago (*i.e.* 731 A.H./1313 A.D).

"Thus is it concerning the people of the Benu Himyar 'Umr al Yamani. They are kings of the Sudan from the Lake of Chad to the borders of the west.

"As for the people of the Benu Adam and Abdul Lahi they are the good men of learning of the Sudan, since the Benu Himyar al Yamani conquered the Sudan long ago.

"To the Benu Himyar al Yamani belong the Bolawa on both their father's and mother's side. Bola is the name of a hill, the name, it is said, of the place where the Bolawa settled when they dispersed after the dispersal of the town of Kwararafa which was a great city. The reason of its dispersal was a great sickness and plague which overtook the inhabitants by reason of their wickedness and wrong-doing.

"Thus they dispersed and scattered in the east. Some lived in the Wadis or moved from hill to hill; others, on the contrary, went to the south-east and are still there; some became muslims, some are pagans, and some are neither the one nor the other, but are Fulani to this day.

"Such is the history of the Tubba'ul Awwal, including the questions of the Hâkim al Barnawiyu, Masbarma Othmanmi.

"The writer is Umr ibn Mu'allim Musa. He wrote this for the Kadi of Fikka Yakub son of the distinguished and learned Khatib al Mustarjam. Amen. Praise be to God. Written in the year 1345 A.H./1926 A.D."

---

* The reference is probably to the campaigns of Muhammad Askia of Songhay and the Kantas of Kebbi against Bornu.

XLIX.—MAHRAM OF MAI ALI GAJI DUNAMAMI 1471 A.D.

In the name of God, the Merciful, the Compassionate.

May God bless our lord Muhammad and his relations and give them peace.

Praise God who made writing as a messenger between near and far, and a means of translation into Arabic and barbarous tongues.

Were it not so, then would all things be confused, and spoilt, even the word of Him (be He exalted), the Loving and the Giver.

This is the covenant of the most puissant Arjiku Siku.

This document was written by order of the Commander of the Faithful, Sultan Ali son of our Amir, the fortunate, pious, and pure of heart, to whom God assigned the task of putting an end to disputes and discord.

He had shown favour to his trusted friend, the learned Chief Kadi and teacher of his people, our lord Ahmed ibn Abdul Kuwata, the distinguished scion of an illustrious race.

He said: "We have given the lands of Marra and Kwolo and Miyo to the service of God and his noble prophet, till the remotest age of our descendants, till the day of the sounding of the horn.

"There shall be no *jiza'a* on these lands; nor obligation of entertaining chiefs by night or day, nor shall there be upon them any call for work for the Sultan nor contribution to the Sultan's treasure or imposts.

"None of the Chiefs, or Captains, or Emirs, shall enter on their lands or houses.

"We have banned their goods, even as swine's flesh; he who takes their goods or land which I have given them, be he of my sons or grandsons or remotest descendants, may God take from him his kingdom, and humble him in the dust before another; may God blast his sons and lineage and may he give his kingdom to the sons and grandsons of a stranger.

"He who oppresses them may God oppress him, and may he receive no kindness at the hands of others; may God fill his belly with the fire of Hell."

"The king has joined with the Kadi his tribe and kindred, the people of Makaramma; whoso divides them, may God divide his house and friends from him in the day of judgment, by the greatness of His prophet, upon whom be the blessing of God and peace."

"Hearken to the story of a good deed. O my children, and posterity, which was done by his forbears, Sambalaima Wacha and Nigale ibn Aiyesha.

"When I was absent, he was patient, and rested not day or night, praying and entreating God to aid us; had it not been for the father of the Faki, the Wali Abdul Kuwata, we should not have obtained the kingdom.

"Learn also that Sultan Ali Gaji once purposed to take and kill him and a counsel was held theron. But when the Sultan's brother heard of it, he said to him ' Do not do what you intend, for if you do, your kingdom will pass to the Beni Daud, and will never come back to you for ever (if God wills) '."

So when the Sultan heard this counsel from his brother, he altered his course. This stands as an admonition to me and to you, for how after that can you take away their land and prestige, after this admonition and proof of their devotion?

"If he to whom God may give this kingdom, does not give to this beneficiary and his children and descendants, land and dwellings, clothes, turbans, and kerchiefs, may God not bless his rule, and may he died despicably.

"For between us and this family there is a covenant and promise; therefore fulfil your promise, for you will be asked concerning it as God says in His exalted Book,—'he who disregards my words and brings to nought my act, and alienates this their land, may God take vengeance on him.

"For God is mighty and avengeth".

"Hear my children and descendants: verily all the land and dwellings that I have given them is little, and it is theirs but for a day; eternity is better and lasts for ever, therefore let the remaining land you have suffice you.

"For what I have given is small in relation to the size of the kingdom, and what remains is vastly greater. Therefore let my descendants and his, follow my injunctions and live in harmony.

"There shall be no 'blood feuds' between them, only pardon, and no killing, only peace and forgiveness, O my children.

"He who fulfils my word, may God prolong his power but as for him who treats them unjustly or takes their goods, he has cast away the tie of Islam. May God not accept his repentance or his prayers.

"He who is charged with this act in my life or after, and yet does wrong to the seed of the Faki, the friend of God, may God cleave asunder his kingdom and fill his belly with the fire of Hell. We have made their goods *haram*, for they belong to God and His noble prophet:

"He who strips them of their goods unjustly, has sinned against God and his Prophet, and cast off the bond of Islam from his neck."

This act was done in the land of Kanem, in the presence of the most puissant Arjiku Siku. Peace.

Sultan Ali Gaji ibn Zeinam ibn Dunama.*
Al Kadi Muhammad ibn Ali.

---

* The Mai who gave this mahram to the Chief Kadi Ahmed ibn Abdul Kuwata of the N'galma Duku, a descendant of the Imam Abdullahi Dili, was Mai Ali Dunamami who founded N'gazargamu.

From the time of the expulsion of the Mais from Kanem, the Beni Daud and Beni Idris had not only been fighting the Bulala, but each other. Ali Gaji Dunamami was of the Beni Idris, i.e., son of Dunama ibn Othman (Biri) ibn Idris.

The date of the mahram is between 1471-1504 A.D.

L.—MAHRAM OF IDRIS KATAGARMABE
(CIRCA 1504 A.D.)

Praise be to God, He alone; and thanksgiving and peace upon the noble Prophet of God.

Our Lord the mighty in action, and unique in his generation and 'isna kunduri' (of happy omen), the Commander of the Faithful and Khalifa, victorious over his enemies, the vigorous, with his two fortunate hands striking his enemies, the prince who guides aright his land, and people, and strives to do the will of God, and enforce the Sunna and prevent innovation, the lamp of darkness, cave of truth, exalted, whose words are good, who holds aloft the flag of the Shari'a, and is victorious, descendant of mighty kings, who brings good fortune, the branch of blessed stock, who directs the youth, and keeps his promise, and is himself bound by the rope of God, illumined by the light of God; who made the pilgrimage to the two sacred cities, the descendant of Saif of the Beni 'Amar and grandson of the Beni 'Amar and of the seed of Tubba' Al Awwal, our great lord Al Hajj Idris, son of our lord Al Hajj 'Ali, (may God pardon him and his fathers) and illuminate their tombs; may God give him a fair ending to his life, and bless his seed and seal his desires with prosperity, and adorn his days, place him in paradise, and give him mighty help.

To him who sees this document among the Amirs, and Officers, and Wazirs, and all the people, peace be upon you, and the blessing of God, Amen! O people, hear and understand and know that our lord Al Hajj Idris, son of Al Hajj Ali, has ennobled the heads of his people, among them Muhammad Su bin Liyatu (that is to say the exalted), the lord of the town of Didima, to the day of blast of the horn, and has made them *haram* to God and His noble prophet, and has exempted them from all the customary dues of the land, from entertaining his officers, and has made their goods *haram* like swine's flesh, and the leg of a monkey, and swine, and dead things, and has made his house as a mosque in Karkarya, in Yehiya, and in Makaran, and as the house of Muhammad Mâni bin Katamma. Thus is the house of Muhammad Su bin Liyatu, it shall be *haram* till the blast of the horn, in love of God and devotion; and by reason of the King's liking for him. The King has placed him in the house of good fortune; may God shade him with the shade of Heaven till the day of the great shade, and may God enrich him with well-being, till his end in Heaven; and may God grant him great help. He who diminishes the fair deed of our lord, in his time, may God not prosper his affairs in this world and the next and may he fill his belly with the fire of Hell.

This is the dedication of Mâkidabe Deli Siku Arjiku.

He who alters this, after hearing it, may his fault be that of those who change.

We call to witness to this, all my people and we call to witness and associate with this act:—

The Imam Kabir Muhammad ibn Sa'id,
The Imam Saghir Muhammad,

Shattima Dagoshema (N'galaga),
Shattima Parkuma,
Dallatu Abdullahi,
Kaigama Mommad bin Sûgu,
Shattima, Tâlibu al Khatti, Kadai,
Farguma Mommadu bin Farguma,
Kajelma Mommadu bin Kajelma,
Ungwama Mommadu bin Ungwama,
Hasema Mommadu bin Hasema,
Arjinoma Bukr bin Gumsu,
N'dubugoma and others—many Moslem witnesses.

They heard this word, and were present at this council. May God show forth the truth, by the grace of our lord Sa'id Muhammad.

This act took place in the time of the Wazir Muhammad and Kaigama Muhammad bin Sûgu. May God give the King, Al Haj Idris, great victory.*

LI.—MAHRAM OF MAI AHMAD, 1793 A.D.

In the name of God, the Merciful, the Compassionate. Praise be to the Lord of the worlds, and prayer and peace upon the prince of envoys and his relations and friends and enmity towards none but evil doers.

This admonition and charter was written to avoid the forgetfulness of passing time, so that upright judges and just rulers and learned servants of the State who follow what is right may know that our lord, blessed and prosperous, just and upright, (may God keep him so till the day of judgment) our lord who shines like phosphorus and is scented like musk, the Amir-ul-Muminin, Ahmad, the praiseworthy, follower of his Lord, the Adored, son of our lord Amir-ul-Muminin, and Sultan of the Moslems, lowly among the lowly, and rock among the rocks, sea among the seas, our lord Sultan Ali who has passed to the mercy of his God, son of the Amir-ul-Muminin, who visited the two sacred and noble cities and ran the course between the two green rocks. Our lord Sultan Hajj Dunama (may God pardon them and their sons after them, with long life and victory) has confirmed the franchise which his father,

---

* This Mahram is undated; but the royal title Mâkidabe Arjiku Siku seems to have dropped in later times, and the Idris in question was evidently not Idris Alooma, judging from the names mentioned. This Idris ibn Ali must therefore be Idris Katagarmabe who re-conquered Kanem and ruled from 1504-1526.

Didima is in Kanem. The mosque in Karkarya is an interesting expression, and is probably to be connected with the title Karkarma (No. 49) and Yakubi's statement that the ruler of Kanem in his day (891 A.D.) was called Kâkara or Kâkura.

Mâkida or Makâda included the region of Kaja and Katuji, Northwest of Nahud in Kordofan, and Kagmar and the Kababish country. From Kagmar it extended through the Jebel country to Kerreri near Khartum.

The aborigines of this country, according to Bornu informants, were called Jange. It is said that the Makâda were a conquering race of Barbars who came from the Blue Nile, from a region called Jabarti, said to be South of Sena'ar. It is held that the name of the region in question is strictly Al Habesh, and that thus Makâda is really the name of a people, still called, so it is said, in the Dongola region, Nikâda or Nigâda.

of pious memory, conferred on Shattima Muhammad, son of the learned and pious Sheikh N'guruma. This he has conferred upon his relatives and successors, so that even to the day of judgment, gratitude and thanks will be due from them by reason of the blessing of their sire's learning; and from Shattima, for the benevolence and generosity of the Sultan in making *haram* his goods and the goods of his three brothers, the sons of Sheikh ibn Maryama, the learned Imam Ibrahim, Mallam Ahmad and ibn Lefia, together with their sons and people and their remotest descendants till the blast of the horn, for God and his noble Prophet.

Our lord has also generously made *haram* the goods of the sons of the daughter of the Sheikh, as in the case of his brothers. They are Mallam Muhammad, Mallam Umr, and Mallam Ahmad, and Mallam Abdu'lahi. They are all full brothers, sons of Fatma.

May God give them full measure of His bounty by the grace of the Prophet and the chosen, and may God exempt their noble bodies from the fire of Jahannama on the day of judgment, even as in this life the goods of the poor who wait on the beneficence of God, and the goods of their children, and descendants, have been made "sacred" as the flesh of swine, and the shoulder of a slaughtered monkey. He has made them free of all common duties towards travellers be they either sons or daughters of the Sultan, and of provision for their entertainment whether by day or night.

He who stretches out his hand to take their goods or the goods of their kindred, may God not bless him, and fill his belly with the fire of Jahannama.

We seek help from God. Let all the Amirs beware lest they hurt them.

This is the word of Sultan Ahmad ibn Sultan Ali, of pious memory.

Witnesses to this are:—
 Al Khâzinu Ali Muhammad,
 Yarima Ahmad,
 Fuguma Muhammad,
 Arjinoma Muhammad,
 Kajalma Umr,
 Hirima Nasr,
 Chiroma Ali Dalatu Abugar,
 Mastrema Ali,
 Yuroma Nasr,
 Ka'id Al Kabir 'Ali (Kaigama),
 Bagarima Dunama,
 Zantama Ali,
 Al Ka'id As-Saghir Muhammad Marghi,
 Kachella Hajib,
 Al Fina al-Kabir Umr ibn al Wazir,
 Gauwama Mustafa,
 Gauwama Lawan,
 Gauwama Ali ibn as-Safîr,
 Gauwama Dunama,

Yakudima Muhammad Yarima,
Dikuma Dunama,
Al Burama Dunama,
Makinta Muhammad,
As-Safîru Muhammad Mandara,
Shattima Muhammad ibn Dabua,
Kachella Mala Balimirimma,
Birima Umr,
Kachella Ali ibn Zantamma,
Teskelma Muhammad Yarima,
Yakimalama Dunama,
Kalelima Ali,
Sulima al Kabir Musa,
Makaramma Muhammad,
Fukulima Bukr,
Kagustema Muhammad,
Shattima Ali ibn Duguma.
Shattima Ahmad ibn Kawi,
and many others who heard and noted.

The scribe of the Council Yakub ibn Shattima Ahmad, in the year 1208* of the Hijira during the Wazirate of Wazir Muhammad ibn Al Wazir Dunama.

---

* 1793 A.D.

LII.—OLD BORNU TOWNS.

The following towns were founded before N'gazargamu:—
- Mangunu (Mongonu).
- Kazarma.
- Mintur.
- Yedi.
- Kule.
- Marte.

The founder of Mangunu was called Mangunu Musa. He was a Kirdi from N'jimi in Kanem, and he came in the time of the So about forty years before the Yamanites came.

The first coming of the Yamanites was to Garu Kime (Wudi), and subsequently to N'gazargamu. They dwelt at Garu Kime. The Mai at that time was Muhammad Hajimi*.

He remained there seven years and seven months and then moved to N'gazargamu.

From the founding of N'gazargamu till its fall was three hundred and thirty-three years and seven months. From the founding of Kabila till its fall was seventeen years and four months.†

Five old towns have survived, they are:—

Kazarma—the people are Kubri of Kanem.
Mintur—the founder was Bulama Mala, the people were Magumi Dabulu of the Yamanites.
Yedi—the founder was Bulamama Muhammad Lefia. The people of Yedi are the same as the people of N'gazargamu.
Kule—the founder was Bulama Manza. The people are Kirdi Beni Manzawa.
Marte—the founder was Martema Muhammad Wayumi. The people are Magumi of the Yamanites.

LIII.—THE KAYI (BULALA) AND MAGUMI.

The Magumi and Kangu came from Sin, thence they came to Yaman.

Mai Dunama Dabalemi's mother was of the Bulala.

Mai Dunama Dabalemi lived at N'jimi.

Mai Lefia, King of the Bulala, lived at Kowa Bagale.

N'jimi and Kowa Bagale were near together.

Trouble came. The Bulala and Magumi fought till many people were killed. They were fighting for one or two years. Then Mai Lefia went east and Mai Dunama went west of N'jimi. Mai

---

* A mistake—the Mai was Ali Dunamami.

† The chronology here given agrees fairly well with other current information. It works out as follows:—
- 881-1476-1477. Ali Dunamami moved from Kanem to Wudi.
- 889-1484. Ali Dunamami founded N'gazargamu.
- 1223-1808. N'gazargamu fell.
- 1240-1824. Defeat of Dunama Lefiami at N'gala and the end of Kabila.

It will be observed that these dates square exactly with Barth's Chronology according to which Ali Dunamami began to reign (in Kanem) in 1470-1471 and reigned till 1504.

The number of years usually assigned to him—twenty-eight, in modern list—thus only refers to the period subsequent to his arrival at Wudi.

Lefia went to Fitri and left Bagale in his son Jil's hands. Mai Dunama went to Wudi.

Mai Dunama then came to N'gazargamu and fought the So and killed the So and dispersed them, and became king.

Then he went out to war; he was seven years and four months at war; then he returned to N'gazargamu.

Then he put tribute on the land; one hundred kings brought one thousand slaves each; then he died. His son Mai Ali Zeinami ruled and built Gazargamu.

Mai Jil, son of Mai Lefia, had a son Mai Anas, a well-known ancestor of the Bulala Kings. Mai Anas was father of Salih, father of Dima Khalifa of Ma'o. After Dima Khalifa's time, Mai Dunama sent his slave Dalla Afuna and made him chief of Ma'o and made him Khalifa.

The Bulala Mais of Kanem are Mai Lefia, Jil, Anas, Salih, Dima Khalifa, Dalla Kura, Dalla Ganna, Dalla Ganna, Fugu Mommodu Satiami, Fugu Mommodu Mariami, Shattima Dalla, Fugu Aisami, Liman Umr, Liman Ibrahim, Mallam Abdalla, Mallam Mommodu, Mallam Mommodu, Salih, Mallam Mommodu.

Mai Yari was ancestor of:—
1. Bulala.
2. Kunu.
3. Yahayia.
4. Gani.

These are the Kayi; they are now called—
1. Yariwa.
2. Bulalawa.
3. Kunuwa (Koniwa).
4. Waniwa.

Old towns in Kanem are:—
Shama, Simsima—now land of Tubus.
Aganiya—North-east of Shami.
Gawala—in Kanem.

Arnuku and Kitati and Gadi are on the east of Gawala. Dara Foiyo on the west, was formerly the land of Dibbiri (Tubu). Dirku north of Agniga on the road north from N'galaka, is in the land of Tubu Tuda.

LIV.—GIRGAMS OF THE KANEMBU TRIBES.

KANGU.

The tribes (1) Kayi, (2) Kangu, (3) Farfari, (4) N'gumma, in the time of Mai Haji Fannami lived together. They lived near a big marsh, Biringam, in Mobber. Mai Haji Fannami lived at Lergum. He went to war with Mandara. His horse was tired and he gave these four tribes his horses to feed. They did so. They brought the horses to him and he then gave them two more to feed and then three more, and then about thirty more.

They said "give us a small piece of land." He gave them Gotofo in Mobber. The Farfari live there and their chief is called Gotofoma.

Kayi Figidoma Musa, Figidoma Ko, and Figidoma Ungwa, were Figidomas in the time of Mai Mommadu Hajimi. He gave to Figidoma Musa, Digumkime. N'giswa was given to Figidoma Ko. Malarge (Marirge) was given to Figidoma Ungwa. Aji Hajimi and Mommadu Arri Fannami and Figidoma had the same grandfather. They were all left *haram*.

The present Lowan Kadai of Gotofo in Mobber claims to be a direct descendant of the Kangu to whom the Mai gave his horses to feed.

MAGUMI (SAIFAWA) TRIBES.

1. Magumi Dugwa.
2. Magumi Arjowa.
3. Magumi Katuriwa.
4. Magumi Bulwa.
5. Magumi Arrigwa.
6. Magumi Jilwa.
7. Magumi Dunamawa (Kaloma).
8. Magumi Tsilimawa.
9. Magumi Arriwa.
10. Magumi Biriwa.
11. Magumi Dallawa.
12. Magumi Mediwa (Medibu).

Maina Kiari Kalomami now living in Mobber was son of Kaloma Arri ibn Dissellam ibn Kaloma Dubu ibn Kaloma Dissellam Kabir ibn Kaloma Dunama ibn Kaloma Dibo ibn Dunama Dabalemi.

At N'gazargamu, twenty chiefs only were allowed to cover their saddles:—

A. Four with a white fleece: Zarma, Iyrima, Kajalma, Yuroma. (Yuroma followed Gumsu the Queen).
B. Four with a black fleece: Kadi Mainin Kinendi, Talba Mainin Kinendi, Imam al Kabir, Imam al Saghir.
C. Four with a big rug falling to the ground: Galladima, Kaigama, Yarima, Mastrema, (followed Magira the Queen mother.)
D. Four with rug falling to leg of horse: Arjinoma, Chiroma, Dallatu, Fuguma.
E. Four with short saddle rug: Kaloma*, Kabuskema†, N'dubogoma‡, N'girbuma.

The boundary of Bornu on the east was Masar, on the west Têko, north Tarablus, south Yeri Arbasan.

The following song relates to the Magumi:—

Kurgulli Yamguroma Yamanguroma (*Lion of Yam and Yaman*).
Kurgulli N'gurodin N'gaiwama. (*And Guro Gaiawa.*)

The Magumi and Bulala know each other's affairs.
The Saifawa fought with a sword, the Bulala with a spear.

---

* Was Chima of Fitri. The Sultan would meet him when he returned from Fitri. Chima means feudal " owner " of the land as distinct from Jirima which means owner or ruler of the tribe (Jiri).

† Kabuskema was Chima of Kanem. He went to Kanem every year and brought 300 horses (algas) back with him.

‡ N'dubogoma was Chima of part of Kanem. The Mai after his accession lived in N'dubogoma's house till forty days had passed.

KUBRI TRIBE.

Tribes of "Darman Aisami."

1. Kurbri Ajawa.
2. Kurbri Bargabu.
3. Kubri N'daraji.
4. Kurbri Manbu.
5. Kurbri Jillum.
6. Kurbri Gwariwa.
7. Kubri Aisa Ganawa
8. Kubri Gambowa.
9. Kubri Kingarwa.
10. Kubri Masobu.
11. Kubri Tamali.
12. Kubri Darmanwa.

Darmanwa are descended from Darman; their ancestor went the Haj and returned. The Sultan gave him the post of Shattima who is head of all the Kuburi tribes except Barkubu and N'daraji.

Ajuwa. Chiefs of the Kuburi are as follows:—

Al Haj Kindema—Shattima Kolo—Shattima Anno Aisami—Shattima Kukuni—Shattima Adre—Shattima Buyoma—Shattima Laminu—Shattima Subu—Shattima Anno Maremmi—Shattima Mustafa—Shattima Tebu—Shattima Kiari—Momodu Kunumi—Shattima Ali—Shattima Momman Fantakaredima—brother of Shattima Falatami—Shattima Sanda—Shattima Kolo (present day).

The Kuburi Barkubu have five sub-tribes as follows:—
1. Amsawa (Shehu's clan).
2. Maduganama.
3. Madukurawa.
4. Kimanwa.
5. Kiriwa.

Kuburi-Amsawa: four sections as follows:—
1. Ninga Kurawa.
2. Ninga Iganwa.
3. Mallam Biriwa.
4. Karewa.

Sheikh Abdurrahman ibn Faiyina b. Ninga b. Muhammad b. al Amin b. Umr b. Abdurrahman b. Bukr Kiari b. Sanda.

The N'Galma Duku are descendants of Duku Aisami.

Duku came with the Yaman people when the Saifawa came to N'jimi.

The N'galma Duku came to Bornu with Ali Gaji Zeinami and came to N'gazargamu. They settled near N'gazargamu, and the new settlement was called Naningham (in N'ganse near N'giswa) hence they were called Naninghamri.

Three tribes of them were:—
1. Kotewa.
2. Marabu.
3. Naningham.

KANGU TRIBE.

Descendants of Mommadu Mâni Aisami. They came to N'jimì with the Saifawa. The Kangu settled at Wandala and Fatargi west of N'jimi near Kitati.

Their Chief, Mallam Ajimi Dagirra (temp. Ali Gaji) settled at N'yau, near Kukawa.

There are four sub-tribes of the Kangu:—
1. Wandala.
2. Adiribu.
3. Zulamari.
4. Limanwa.

This Mâni is the Mâni of the Girgam of the Kangu.

KAJIDI TRIBE.

Descendants of Jidi. (Kajidi or Kashitu). They came to N'jimi and settled at Kitati (Shitati). Then the chief of the Jidi, Muhammad Kagulganna, came to Gumsa with his brother Mainoma Bukr. He had come from Manga in the north of Kanem. He was given the title of Maino.

There are twelve septs of Kajidi. The chief septs are under
1. Fugu Furnabu.
2. Fugu Salabu.
3. Fugu Lulanbe.
4. Fugu N'garwabu.

The chief of the others was Kachella Kali of Nimoku in Kanem, who is the ancestor of Jafar (late Alkali of Bornu).
5. Kachella Kali.
6. Munabu.
7. Kachella N'garibu.
8. Kachella Gegerabu.
9. Kachella Marangwabu.
10. Kachella N'gerabu.
11. Kachella Mammadabu.
12. N'burobu.

Descendants of N'gal also came from Yaman to N'jimi. They settled at Yanga and Sarsambu in Kitati. They were tributary to N'gazargamu. They came to Bornu in the time of Shehu Laminu and settled at Digigir near Kukawa, and also at Dabutaski and Mamargi near Kukawa. They had six septs.
1. Yanguba.   4. Damboa.
2. Sarsamboba. 5. Gelawa.
3. Kalebu.   6. Jilgaltawa.

Their chiefs were Fugu Ali N'galaga, Mommodu Askarami and Abba Ganna Fugumi.

THE KAGWA TRIBE.

They have the same mother as the Kai and count as Bulala. Their town was Kagwa. They came from Kanaan Kagwa. They came with the Yamanites. The Kagwa came to Borku and Wuno (Kanem). Their chief was called by the title Ketala. Their first chief in Bornu was Wunuma Kirgami. He settled in N'galagati. He had the title Wunuma. They have nine septs:—
1. Kagwa Kalewa.   6. Kagwa Tegoma.
2. Kagwa Sadwa.   7. Kagwa Kanwa.
3. Kagwa Kelle.   8. Kagwa Rigwa.
4. Kagwa Washia.   9. Kagwa N'go.
5. Kagwa Yoma.

The Tegoma and Yoma sections were Murabat. Wunuma Kirgami represents the tenth tribe, and head of the others.

BADAWI (NOMAD) TRIBES.

They are nomads like the Shuwa. There are four stocks:
1. Kagwa.
2. Kangu.
3. Dibbiri. } all formerly under Wunuma.
4. Kimebu.

The Kagwa settled at Adia (near N'guru). The Kangu came to Nyo and Awegi. The Kimebu came to Mediram, east of Gashegur. They were originally from N'garna in Kanem whence their chief is called N'garanma.

These four tribes gave Wunuma one hundred cattle when they arrived in Bornu, but in future years they refused to pay. The Mai ordered them to pay, but they said " No, we will give you one hundred camels." The Mai then deposed Wunuma Kirgami and made Wunuma Isa their chief. There are thus two houses. Wunuma Isa, Maina Mommadu, and Wunuma Arri Ajama of Kerjegi represent one house.

THE TUBU TRIBES.

They are called Tubu from their land Tubusti. They are by race Dazza, children of Shaitan; heathen children of Iblis. Their mother was an Arab woman, the sister of a big Sheikh. The girl was in an 'utfa. A man came and got into the 'utfa*. They took her to the bridegroom. They said to the bridegroom " This girl is sent you as *sadaka*." The bridegroom said " I do not like her and she is ugly. Take her back to her father." The father said " Take her to the bush, I said to you do not let her sleep on the *rahad*†; you forgot my order; a Shaitan has spoilt her."

She brought forth in the bush a girl and a boy, twins. She gave the boy the name Bahurde Iblisiyi, and to the girl the name of her grandmother Khadija. She took them both to her father. He said to Bahurde " dazzaiu " in Tubu, " Tunta dazzai'i ", *i.e.* " We are beautiful."

When the Yamanites came to N'jimi, the Tubu came from the east and settled in Tubusti, and then the Dibbiri of Tubusti came to N'gazargamu. They were armed with swords and spears, their talk was like that of the Kanuri. They assembled at the palace. They asked the Sultan for a place to live. He ordered them to be taken to the Kajidi to give them a place. They gave to them Yedi in Kanem.

The Dibbiri came to Kanem and remained there. They said they wanted to be chiefs over the other Tubu. The Mai said you are chiefs, but your title is Fugu. The rest of the Tubu must follow you.

WAR BETWEEN THE DIBBIRI AND WULAD SULEIMAN.

The Wulad Suleiman came to the Dibbiri country from Murzuk. A man of the Dibbiri called Barka Haluf left his people and joined the Wulad Suleiman and acted as a spy.

---

* A kind of howdah.
† Marsh.

His father was N'guri Gowat a chief of the Dibbiri. The latter said to his clan, go and attack Ketala Jazarti and take his camels. They did so. N'guri Gowat then called in the Wulad Suleiman, but Barka Haluf stopped them coming. N'guri Gowat came with his people. Barka Haluf (Allafi ibn Haluf) and N'guri Gowat went to the Wulad Suleiman who were ready to fight.

The Dibbiri attacked the Wulad Suleiman, and the two leaders fought. Haluf helped the Dibbiri and defeated the Wulad Suleiman.

Henceforward the tribes were always at war. The women of the Wulad Suleiman ridiculed their men. The Dibbiri would not leave their country. They went to Gadi and met the Wulad Suleiman and were defeated.

After this, Ketala Gwori Gowat came to Kajel (near Gashegar) in the time of Shehu Umr, but refused to pay *kharaji**. He then moved away back to Kanem, and said he would not fight with the Sarkin Musulmi, but he would with Wulad Suleiman. Ketala Gwori Gowat died and the Wulad Suleiman settled in Kanem.

TUBU DIBBIRI AND DOGORTA.

Ketala Gori was going to attack the Dogorta, eight days away at Age and Fodi, east of Kanem. He surprised them and took all they had and returned to Gadi. The Dogorta followed. Then the chiefs fought. Adam Idrisi was the name of the chief of the Dogorta killed by Ketala Gori.

DIBBIRI AND KURATA†

The Kurata lived at Dagana. The Dibbiri attacked them, but were afraid of them. The Kurata defeated them. Ketala Gori sent round to get allies from all sides and again set out against the Kurata, but they again defeated the Dibbiri.

On the way back the Wulad Suleiman and Dibbiri fell out, and Bultu Bul and Ketala Gwori fought. The spear of Ketala Gwori wounded Bultu Bul in the neck. Ketala Gwori attacked him on his horse and killed him.

JETKU (YAT-KU).

There are four septs:—
1. Jetku Kangu.
2. Jetku Tumagari (chief called Suma).
3. Jetku Kai.
4. Jetku.

Jetku is the name of the town of Yari Jetku. It is part of Kanem, north of Manga, which is north of Mao. The Kai joined the Jetku after Yari Jetku was destroyed. The Jetku used to come in to N'gazargamu.

It was the Tuareg who destroyed Yari Jetku. Every year they attacked it. They came to Bornu and came to Tal on the road to Dirku, north of N'gegemi. The site was called Tal Bul.

---

* Tax.

† The Kurata are in origin Arabs but follow Tubu customs.

The Jetku sent to Mai Arri, and he accepted tribute from them and told them to stay at Tal, midway between Kanem and Bornu, to watch the Kindin (Tuwareg).

About one hundred years later, the Mai sent a slave Agit to remain with them. They then all came to Bornu, and settled at Kilbua north of Fogua. The Tumagari came to Masa, west of Degwa near Gashegar, the town of the Kazalma. The Jetku Kangu came to Tagassa and Gwayi north of Gashegar.

The Jetku Kai came with the Jetku to Bornu. Among the ancestors of the present Lowan of the Jetku are:—

    Lowan Jetku Yeriwa.
    Lowan Kabulowa.
    Lowan Jokoma Tahr.
    Lowan Salah.

The Lowan of the Jetku now lives near Ysufuri.

LV.—TRANSLATION OF SAIFAWA GIRGAM IN THE POSSESSION OF GALADIMA KASHIM BIRI.

1. Me Sebu, son of Aisa, a lion, prince of Yaman. He returned to Yaman.
2. Me Ibrahim, son of Sebu. He lives in Yaman.
3. Me Dugu Bremmi. He is in the land of Yeri Arbasan.
4. Me Fune, son of Dugu. He is at Gani of the N'galaga tribe.
5. Arju, son of Fune. He is at N'gala M'bute, the place of fishes.
6. Me Katuri, son of Arju. He is in Kaigam of many "kurna" trees.
7. Boyoma, son of Katuri. He is in a mound at Yo.
8. Bulu, son of the Biyuma of the race of the rulers of Yam, Yaman, Badani, Guru Gayawa, N'gazargamu and Kafila. At Magi Zabatam of doum and fan palms he rests.
9. He who was as white silk to the Arrikwa, Arki, son of Bulu, he who is as Zeila Uzlan.
10. Shu, son of Arki. He is in the rocky land of Kutushi.
11. Jil, son of Shu. He is in Masar of many mosques.
12. Umme, son of Jil. At Arikwa of many mosques he lies.
13. Dunama, son of Umme. He is at Barabushi of many fishes.
14. Mai-Dalla Biri, son of Dunama. He is at Gamtilo in Jilarge.
15. Dala Bikur who is at Fifisa of many "kurna" trees.
16. Tsilim, son of Bikur. He is at Fifisa N'gizriwa.
17. Me Duna, son of Dabale, the daughter of Tsilim, hotter than fire, the fire of Matabar. Duna at Zantam.
18. Kade Auwajami, in the Land of Zantam he lies.
19. Dala, son of Auwajami. He is at N'guru (N'jimi).
20. Me Ali Gaji, son of Zeinam. He is at Zantam.
21. Me Kade, son of Matala, the daughter of the Biyuma At Yam in the rocky plain of Zui-Zui, of the date palms.
22. Usman, son of Kade. He is at Malakata.
23. Muhammadu, son of Kade. He is at Magi Zabatam of many doum and fan palms.
24. Idirishi, son of Hamsa, at N'guru (N'jimi), of the fine "square" or at Guluru he rests.
25. Me Darin who lay in wait for his enemies; at N'jimi he lies.
26. Me Ume, son of Aisa. At N'galbiwa he lies.
27. Biri, son of Amina. At Kaukau in Bagarmi at Kungwa he is.
28. Another prince who rests by Dalla in Afunu.
29. Another prince. He rests at Guguwa.
30. Another prince. He rests at N'gilewa.
31. Another prince, the greatest of them. In the sands of N'gileru he rests

32. Learned (Jitku) in the history of the Jilwa. Jil, son of Kule, a lion, a prince of Yaman. He returned to Yaman where he died. In Yaman he lies.
33. Muhammadu, prince of Barabata. There he lies.
34. The prince of Jimara. Umr, son of Idrishi. At Jimara, at the nose of the Sun, he died.
35. The prince of Dagamo. Dala son of Umr. At Dagamo of the Kumkum trees he rests.
36. Kagu, son of Umr. He is at N'gala M'buta.
37. Muhammadu, son of N'gaudi. He lies at Buniwa.
38. Muhammadu, son of Falaga. At Gamagaram he lies.
39. Me Muhammadu, Maza, son of Idrishi. He is at Jabaru of many doum and fan palms.
40. Daudu, son of Nikale. He lies at N'jitiwa.
41. Othman Daudumi—at Bursilim N'gawala.
42. Sheikh Gana. He lies at Badani Garu of the N'gal.
43. Yusufu, son of Sefu. He lies at Arjino N'gawala.
44. Tsilim, son of Awwa. Awwa, daughter of the Bidama, Lord of Gaduram. At Birnin N'difu he was killed in war.
45. Me Duna, son of Dibale, Prince of Bursilim. At Bursilim he was killed in war.
46. The prince of Talmaram, Kashim Biri, the son of Dunama. Biri is at Ugme of the Lake.
47. Me Ali, son of Dunama. He lies at N'gazargamu.
48. Dunama, son of Ali. He lies at N'giswan.
49. Muhammadu, son of Dunama. He lies at Marguba.
50. Duna, son of Man. He lies at Guluru.
51. The son of Fanna, daughter of the N'guma tribe. He lies at N'gazargamu.
52. Arri, son of Fanna, son of Umr. Arri of the town of Karuru. Arri lies at Karuru his town.
53. Dala son of Dunama. He is at N'gazargamu.
54. Me Ali Gaji, son of Zeinama. Arri the " smoke " of the Bulala. He lies at Bulala Gawala.
55. Aisa of the great white horse. Aisa the Magaram, daughter of Dunama. Aisa of Mar Kingarwa, where she died.
56. Idrishi, son of Ali, son of Hamsa, whose father was the ruler of Bugal, Wurga, Faraga, Katagar and Jumara, Idrishi of the fair skin and fair town. His wars 1330: his journeys among the rocks 1,000. Mele Gaji at Alau in Uje he rests.
57. Me Muhammadu of Dagnu Daniski, son of Fanna, daughter of the Bugalma, the lion, son of Idrishi. He lies at Dagnu Daniski, in Kanem.
58. Me Burema, son of Gumsu Amina, daughter of Tolba, in whose time to one wet season there were seven autumns, and the he goat and pack-oxen yielded milk. He is at Diskam in N'galagati.
59. A handful of " chaff ": a lump of iron: shade with biting insects: his towns were Dusu, and Ala Talarge: son of Fusam Umr, son of Mele. Umr at N'gazargamu.

60. Arri: the lord of Walan and Walata: four Walans; Walata was the fifth town. His towns were Damjiri and Bambuwi and Abubu-Bungwa and Abua Balango. Ali of the four Dalas. Dalil was the fifth. Dala Me the grandson of Shattima, son of Jilbo. Dala Me, the Me, the grandson of Shattima, son of Jilbo. Dala Me, the grandson of Shattima called "dismount and divide", son of N'gwari. Dala Me, grandson of Shattima, son of Dagumshe. Dala Me, grandson of Shattima, son of Silbe. Dale Me, grandson of Shattima. Ali the "smoke" of Mada, the lion of Mada. Ali begotten like a lion. The lord of Izge and Isbar, the student of Walam. Maririma, the journey to Mecca, was to him as a night ride; the accomplished horseman, the talisman of horsemen, son of Fusam and Umr, son of Mele. Ali erstwhile in the region of Tibesti was buried in Masar.
61. Lord of Talamaram. Kashim Biri, son of Umr. He is in Talamaram of many mosques.
62. Lord of Gambaru, son of Kagul. Lord of Turagen. Kime-Mele son of Ali. He is in the town of Zeila in the land of Turagen.
63. Without a tornado yet there is rain. The red man—dealer of quick death to gain plunder. Son of Askara—Arkwoiya the daughter of the Martema. His town was Adawa the walled town of "kurna" trees. Duna, son of Umr, at Karuru of the N'guma—now in ruin—he lies.
64. Haji, son of Dunama, lord of Limlim and Mugubi. He is at N'gazargamu.
65. Gubo (Ahmed) Lord of the marsh Mugubi, lord of Larga, the black prince with the white turban. On the east his domains were Malamba, on the west, Magabura also Mazagan of the "Kileno", and "kurna" and "play"; the child of Fanna, Muhammadu, son of Haji. Here at N'gazargamu he lies.
66. The son of Lafia "kore". Duna son of Aman. Here he is in N'gazargamu.
67. Son of Dadingelma, son of Lafia, son of Falalima. Ali of Gulmi-Katurge. Ali the bravest of the princes: Gado, son of Dunama, lord of Maramba, son of twelve Alis, all sons of Dunama lord of Maramba. Me Ali, son of Fanna, daughter of the Wurgama, Ali son of Magira N'dinarama. Lion, whose house was in Birni, in the camp he lies.
68. Aman, son of Ali—whose secrecy was as the shade of groundnut plants, son of Gumsu Amina, the daughter of Talba. Gubo, in the camp he lies.
69. Duna, son of Lafia, Duna, son of Aman, lord of Farandu, the river near N'galla, where he lies.
70. East N'gornu Kafila, north Wudi-Gaduram Ngegimi, west Yamia, Silibe N'gileru, and Kesala; son of Gumsu Amina daughter of Talba. Muhammadu N'gileruma, at the Bulungu tree.

71. Bura, son of Lafia. Bura, son of Aman. He lies at the town of Kukawa.
72. Me Ali, son of Dalatu. Ali, son of Bura. Among the "fan palms" of Minargi.

NOTES ON THE GIRGAM.

1 and 2 are probably put in by the Court Chroniclers to support the pedigree to Saif Dthi Yazan.

3. Dugu: equivalent to the Tuwareg "Tegasi" son of sister or aunt. Barth was probably not right in thinking that these Dugawa, i.e., Nos. 3-11 (inclusive), were a different dynasty. Yakubi states that the kings of Kanem in his day (900 A.D.) were Zaghawa, the title of their kings was Kako or Kakura.

Yeri Arbasan lay in the Yangere country or country of the Wa N'koro or N'kotoma, in Longitude 17° E, and Latitude 4° N. This country according to the legends was occupied by negro races called M'bum, at the time Dugu invaded it. The people of that region still preserve the tradition of the invasion, and retain the title "Kaigama" for their war chief, while their king bears the title "Wari." The name Yeri Arbasan was not the original name of the region, but the name given to the people after the invasion.

4. Fune means a "veil" or "litham." The variants Gani, and Gwani, are all found. If the latter is correct, the word is probably the same as is now written Gwani (e.g., the Gwani enclave) and it contains the same root as "Kwana" (Kororafa). In any case Gani is the Zaghawa word for a town.

The N'galaga belonged to the "Habesh" Afunu or "So" races of Kanem. If Barth's reading of Malan as the burial place of this Mai is not a mere mistake, it perhaps stands for Matan or Madan (Madam) which even as late as 1150 A.D. (Idrisi's day) was an important centre, East of Lake Chad, and would probably be inhabited by N'galaga and other Kanembu tribes.

5. Archu or Arju: The name seems connected with (1) Arjunoma, one of the oldest Bornu titles, connected presumably with the name of the town or district called Arjunu, which lay to the East of N'jimi, in Kanem. (2) The title "Arjuku Siku" used of the Mais in old documents. Since the ruling Jukon families are, undoubtedly, like the Bolewa kings of Fika of cognate origin to these Dugawa Mais, it is perhaps permissible to suggest that "chu" or "ju" in "Archu" means "great," as it does in several Jukon titles, e.g., "Abon chu"—great Abon.

It then might be suggested that the first syllable "Ar" conveys the same idea as in such names as Arki, Arigwa, which again seem cognate to the Nubian form "Ark" in Ark-Ammon (Ammon *the begetter*).

N'gala M'bute: N'gala in Kanem—M'bute being the same name as in the case of M'buta in Ningi. The M'bum tribes lived in N'gumati (the Maiduguri-Dikwa region).

The site of the earliest known settlement at Katsina is called M'bute.

6. Kaigam simply means the "South," i.e., Kaga or country inhabited by "Agha" (outsiders to Teda speaking races or Kanuri).

7. Yo, in some manuscripts Yo-shi = Yamshi, i.e., Borku or Tibesti. The Diwan says this king was buried at Tatanuri, which is possibly equivalent to Idrisi's Mount Tantano, i.e., he died among the Barbars of Tantano. There is however a Tatanu in Kanem.

8. Magi Zabatam or Magi Zigidam simply means a place where the King (Magi) made an annual sacrifice of "white oxen and sheep." The string of place names is an interpolation, and denotes the capitals of the Kanuri in order.

9. Argi, in some manuscripts Ark-ama means Ark, the begetter, e.g., as in "Ark-Ammon." Zeila Uzila was near modern Murzuk in Fezzan.

10. Shu = Chu, i.e., "great," cf. Abyssinian title "Shum" and Jukon title "Abon-chu." Kutushi is east of the country now called Damarghu and Damagaram.

11. Jil, possibly a form of Jion or Ajon, the Jukon equivalent of the Egyptian god " Osiris " and the equivalent also of the Kanuri word for tribe " Jiri."

12. Umme, the first Moslem King (Mai). Umme in Zaghawi means " slave "—and probably it is a sobriquet purposely given to avoid mentioning his real name. Arikwa refers to the Kauwar region.

13. Barabushi, *i.e.*, country of the Barabu (Barbars) of the Red Sea. He was drowned on the way to the Haj.

14. Gamtilo in Kanem. The site was visited by Idris Alooma on one of his campaigns to Kanem, described by Imam Ahmed.

17. Zantam, to the north of the Komadugu, in Bornu.

19. N'guru here means N'jimi—lit: a town or Birni.

20. Out of place here—he lived much later.

21. Ye-am (Yam), the people of Ye are also called Yin and Ye-ri. Zui-Zui is possibly the place now called Zuar in Tibesti Borku. Biyu is near the Wadi Batha in Wadai.

22. Malakata—Othman Kademi is said to have been killed by Ali Dunamami. Some manuscripts read Malakatari, and Barth's Diwan evidently read Makida—which is nearest to the present form of the name—*i.e.*, Makâda.

Makâda is the region of Northern Kordofan which became a place of refuge for the Beni Daud at the end of the civil war.

24. Another tradition says he died at Damasak on the Komadugu. Guluru (near Geidam) is not far from Damasak.

25. Me Darin, *i.e.*, Ibrahim Nigale. N'jimi is an error for Diskam.

27. Some manuscripts add " at Udwa " or " Adawa."

28. Dalla in Afunu, *i.e.*, Kano.

32. This is possibly the Bulala Chief called by Barth " Jil Shikomami," (Sukumami) the real founder of the Bulala dynasty of Fitri, or it may mean Ibrahim Nigale.

33. Barabata, means the Barbar country in the East.

36. Kagu " a twin."

37. Some manuscripts read " Ngam-bu-ti-mi "—the N'gam tribe being possibly the same as the N'gau. Both were " So " tribes.

40. Jitiwa is in the Fitri region.

41. The epithet N'gawalan—lit. " of shields " means that he was killed in war, or refers to the Kawal (Gawal) of Kanem.

42. *i.e.*, Abu Bakr Layatu.

43. Probably the Mai whom Barth's manuscript calls Othman, son of Idris.

44. Tsilim Awwami, the general tradition is that he died at N'difu, near Dikwa.

48. Should be " Idris Alimi "—here the " Girgam " is confused.

49. Marguba, *i.e.*, in Kaga (Bornu). This Mai was son of Idris son of Ali

50. This is an interpolation, and 51 and 52 are in wrong sequence.

52. Arri Fannami, *i.e.*, the ancestor of the present Mufioma and regent for seven years for his half brother, Dunama N'gumarama (No. 51). Karuruma was near Mufio.

54. The Mai, called by Barth, Gaji, is not the same man as Ali Dunamami who founded N'gazargamu, though the latter was also called Ali Gaji Zeinami.

55. Regent for Idris Alooma her " brother," and daughter of Dunama Muhammad Idrisimi.

56. Amsa was the daughter of the Sultan of the Bulala of Fitri, and the towns mentioned are in the Fitri region.

57. Dagnu is in the Bulala country, north of Fitri.

58. Diskam: this again is a mistake. It was Ibrahim Nigale, circa 1300, who was drowned at Diskam, and whose reign was the " golden age." Me Burema was buried at N'gazargamu.

60. *i.e.*, Ali Tair, or Ali " the bird " who made the pilgrimage three times.

61. Kashim Biri acted as Mai during the early part of Ali's reign when the latter was away at Mecca and tried to supplant him. On Ali's return, he was seized, blinded and sent into exile at Talmaram.

62. This is the Mai whose tomb is still shewn to travellers at Traghen in Fezzan (alluded to by Duvèyrier incorrectly as Mai Ali).

63. *i.e.*, Karuru near Mufio, the town of Arri Fannami.

66. The name "Aman" is not as Barth supposed a corruption of Muhammad. It is "Amma" or "Ammon." This Mai is "Dunama Ganna."

67. *i.e.*, Ali ibn Hajj Dunama in whose time the Bornu Empire began to decay. He was badly defeated in several expeditions to Mandara.

68. The last Mai who really ruled, *i.e.*, Mai Ahmed.

69. *i.e.*, Muhammad Lefia who was made titular Mai by Sheikh Muhammad al Amin.

70. *i.e.*, N'gileruma who replaced Muhammad Lefia for a time as titular Mai.

71. Mai Ibrahim, murdered at Kukawa on the approach of the Wadai army in Sheikh Umr's time.

72. Declared himself Mai under Wadai auspices about 1846.

LVI.—LIST OF MAIS OF BORNU DOWN TO 1808 A.D. WITH APPROXIMATE DATES.

Arabic Name.	Burial Place.	Approximate Date.	No. in Girgam.	Kanuri Name.
1. Saif	Yaman	Circa 800 A.D.		
2. Ibrahim	,,			
3. Dugu	Yeri Arbasa	*Legendary names.		
4. Fune	Gwani N'galaga			
5. Archu	N'gala Buta			
6. Katûri	Kaigam			
7. Buyuma	Yo (on a hill)			
8. Bulu	Magi Zabatam			
9. Argi	Zeila Uzlan			
10. Shu	Kutushi Kôwan			
11. Jil	Masar			
12. Ume ibn Jil	Ruwaya (Kutushi)	1086-1097	(12)	Umme Jilmi.
13. Dunama	In the Red Sea at Barabashi (Berinice)	1098-1150	(13)	Dunama Ummemi.
14. Mai Dàlâ Bîri	Gamtilo Jilarge (Kanem)	1151-1176	(14)	Biri Dunama.
15. Dala Bikur	Fifisi Kurnawa (Kanem)	1177-1193	(15)	(a) Dala Bikur. (b) Kâle Bikurmi.
16. Abd-ul Jalil	Fifisi N'gazriwa (Kanem)	1194-1220	(16)	Tsilim Bikurmi.
17. Ahmad Dunama	Zantam (West of Gambaru)	1221-1259	(17)	Dunama Dabalemi
18. Kade or Abd el Kadim	Zui-Zui in Yam (i.e. in the land of the Babir= Borku)	1259-1285	(21)	Kade Matalami.
19. Othman ibn Zeinab	Ugme	1288-1306	(46)	Kashim Bîri Dunamami.

* Legendary names.—Among the Igara-Jukon of Idah, a cognate race, nine tombs of Attahs (kings) are always kept in repair, neither more nor less.

LVI.—LIST OF MAIS OF BORNU DOWN TO 1808 A.D. WITH APPROXIMATE DATES.—*Continued*.

	Arabic Name.	Burial Place.	Approximate Date.	No. in Girgam.	Kanuri Name.
20.	Ibrahim Nigale son of Kagudi	Diskam in the country of the N'galaga (Borku)	1307–1326	(25)	(a) Mai Darin. (b) Kali (N'galil) Kalilwama.
21.	Abdallah Kademi	N'jimi	1326–1345	(19)	Dâla Kadêmi
22.	Salma ibn Hawa	N'difu near Dikwa	1346–1349	(44)	Tsilim Hawami.
23.	Kure Ganna	N'gilewa	—	(30)	Kore Laga.
24.	Kure Kurra	Kêsa N'gilêru	—	(31)	Kore Kurisa.
25.	Kure Muhammad	Naningham	—	(38)	Muhammad Falaga.
26.	Idris ibn Hafsa	N'jimi	1353–1376	(24)	Idris Nigalemi.
27.	Daud ibn Fatima	N'jitiwa (Fitri)	1377–1386	(40)	Daud Nigalemi.
28.	Othman ibn Daud	Bursalim Gawala (Fitri)	1387–1390	(41)	Othman Daudumi.
29.	Othman b Idris and Fanna	N'jimi (Simah), according to Blau	1390–1392	Not in Girgam.	
30.	Abu Bakr Liyatu (the illustrious)	Sefiari (Badani N'gizrêwa)	1392	(42)	Sebu Gana.
31.	Omar ibn Idris	Jimara Baltebe	1394–1398	(34)	Mai Umr Idrisimi.
32.	Said	Degage (Arjino Gawala)	1398–1399	(43)	Yusuf Sebumi.
33.	Kade Afunu ibn Idris	Guguwan (Kukawan in Fitri)	1399–1400	(29)	Kore Laga.
34.	Othman (Bîri) ibn Idris	Kungwa in Bagarmi	1400–1432	(27)	Biri Aminami.

No. 29.—This Mai is apparently the second Dalil Kalilwama of the Mufio Girgam, who was buried at N'jimi. It is noticeable that Kalilwa is apparently a variant of N'galaga, and Kâle a variant of Dalil, the name Nigale or Nikale being connected with Kale.

In Barth's list 'Kagudi,' mother of Ibrahim Nigale is of the Kinkina tribe, and Ibrahim's Yarima who murdered him was a 'Kai' (Bulala). Ibrahim therefore and his children seem to have been regarded as having a good deal of N'galaga and Bulala blood. In other accounts this King is apparently called Idris Gadaramma Ladaramma ibn Daud.

No. 31.—*i.e.*, Jimara, about a journey of three hours from the capital.

LVI.—LIST OF MAIS OF BORNU DOWN TO 1808 A.D. WITH APPROXIMATE DATES.—*Continued.*

	Arabic Name.	Burial Place.	Approximate Date.	No, in Girgam.	Kanuri Name.
35.	Othman Kârinma ibn Daud	Dalla in Afunu (Kano)	1432	(28)	Kore Laga.
36.	Dunama ibn Umr	Galambuta (Naningham)	1433–1434	(36)	Kaku (twin) Umrmi.
37.	Dala ibn Umr	Dagamo	1435–1442	(35)	Dagamoma Dâla.
38.	(Ibrahim) Muhammad	Buniwa	1442	(37)	Muhammad Gaudimi.
39.	Kade Awaja ibn Othman	Zantam	1442–1451	(18)	Kade Awajami.
40.	Dunama ibn Biri	Bursalim Gawala	1451–1455	(45)	Duna Bursalima.
41.	Muhammad ibn Matalla	Jabaru	1455	(39)	Mai Muhammad Maza Idrisimi.
42.	Umme ibn Othman (Biri)	N'galbiwa	1456	(26)	Umme Aishami.
43.	Muhammad ibn Kade	Magi Zigidam	1456	(23)	Muhammad Kademi.
44.	Ali Gaji	Bulala Gawalan	1456–1461	(54)	Ali Gaji (Kangi Bulalabe).
45.	Othman Kademi	Makâda	1461–1466	(22)	Othman Kademi.
46.	Umr ibn Abdalla	Yaman	1466	(32)	Jil Kilemi
47.	Muhammad ibn Muhammad	Barabata	1467–1471	(33)	Muhammad Barabatama.
48.	Mai Ali Dunamami (Ali Gaji Zeinami I)	N'gazargamu	1472–1504	(47)	Ali Dunamami.

No. 38.—Barth and Blau have both gone wrong. Blau's text (as quoted Z.D.M.G. 1852 p. 314) means—" Ibrahim never actually mounted the throne, his name was accepted and he was called Mai. His name ' Ibrahim,' however, was only a nickname given, because his mother was called ' Kagudi,' like the mother of the famous ' Ibrahim Nigale ' No. 20.

These identifications of the Girgam names with Barth's list work out fairly correctly, leaving out Aisa N'girmaramma and Kashim Biri Talamaram who are not counted as Mais in the Chronicle, but there are some discrepancies between these lists and those given in ' Mai Idris Alooma ' and it is impossible to be sure in some cases which version is correct.

LVI.—LIST OF MAIS OF BORNU DOWN TO 1808 A.D. WITH APPROXIMATE DATES.—*Continued.*

Arabic Name.	Burial Place.	Approximate Date.	No. in Girgam.	Kanuri Name.
49. Idris ibn Ali	Walam in Shâni (Gongola region)	1504–1527	(48) & (50)	Dunama Alimi Aminami Kotokomabe.
50. Muhammad ibn Idris	Marguba	1527–1545	(49)	Muhammad Dunamami.
51. Ali ibn Idris (Ali Gaji Zeinami II)	Zantam	1545–1546	(20) & (52)	Ali Gaji Zeinami confused with Arri Fannami.
52. Dunama Ngumarama ibn Muhammad	N'gazargamu	1546–1564	(51)	N'gumarama (Muhammad Fannami).
53. Dâla ibn Dunama	N'gazargamu	1564–1570	(53)	Dâla Dunamami.
54. Idris Aisha Alooma	Alau	1570–1602	(56)	Idris Alauma.
55. Muhammad ibn Idris	Daganu Daniski	1602–1618	(57)	Muhammad Idrisimi.
56. Ibrahim ibn Idris	N'gazargamu	1618–1625	(58)	Brêma Gumsumi.
57. Hajj Omar ibn Idris	N'gazargamu	1625–1645	(59)	Umr Fusami Dusami.
58. Ali Tair	Egypt	1645–1682	(60)	Ali Walama
59. Idris Alimi	Turaghen in Fezzan	1682–1701	(62)	Mele Alimi..
60. Dunama ibn Ali	Karuru in Mufio	1701–1720	(63)	Duna Umrmi.
61. Hajj Hamdun	N'gazargamu	1720–1734	(64)	Haji Dunamami.
62. Muhammad ibn Al Hajj	N'gazargamu	1734–1749	(65)	Mommodu Ajimi.
63. Dunama Ganna	N'gazargamu	1749–1752	(66)	Dunama 'Kore.'
64. Ali	In a camp	1752–1791	(67)	Ali Lefiami.
65. Ahmed	In a camp	1791–Feb. 1808	(68)	Mai Ahmed,

LVII.—THE SULTANATE OF AHIR.

In the name of God the Merciful, the Compassionate. May God bless our lord Muhammad and his kin and companions. Perfect peace.

I resign my affairs into the keeping of God, for God watches over His creatures. My purpose cannot be accomplished save by God upon Whom I rely and to Whom I return. This is a book concerning the people of the Kingdom of Ahir and the Kingdom of Bornu.

The Kingdom of Ahir originated from four tribes, the Ita-se-angh, the Jadanar-angh, the Izarar-angh, and the Fede-angh. These tribes came from the land of Aujila and drove out the Sudanese tribes from the land of Ahir. They then settled in Ahir and dwelt there a long time without a Sultan to help them.

Their organization was like the organization of the Arabs of the early days of Islam, who had no rulers but the tribal Sheikhs. Such was the organization of these four tribes, and thus in the early days there were no rulers but the Sheikhs of the tribe.

Then it was found that tribes like themselves raided their families and the weaker communities. For this reason they were compelled to look for a Sultanate.

The five tribes who are called San-dala sought out the first Sultan, and found him in the land of Aghrim Sotafan (city of the blacks or black city), and conveyed him to the land of Tadalida (Tin-tellust) and established him there. Afterwards they saw that Tadalida was not suitable for his residence, since its situation was injurious to the oxen which brought corn to Ahir.

So they moved to Tin Shaman and built a palace for the Sultan: who had no companions save these four tribes who built the residence of the Sultan, and divided up the work of building between the Al-Suwan (Alis-Su-Wan) the Ibal-Karan (Ibal-Koran), the Imiskikin, and the Imissufan, who constituted the ruling class and built their houses in front of the "Musjid al Juma'a" (Friday Mosque) at Agades.

Even to this day there are descendants of the Sultans in these houses.

These five tribes were the "people of binding and loosing" (*i.e* Council) in this polity, nor was there associated in this polity any of the other tribes outside.

Therefore when they and their Sultan were in concord and agreement, the world was at peace, and the land prosperous.

On the other hand, when the Sultan and the people of "binding and loosing" were in disagreement, the world was full of chaos and discord, the land shook, and the country and its produce grew thin. There are but two causes of disagreement—which are well-known.

Political changes on the other hand are not known to the people; nor is aught known to them which is not patent to the eye of the Age in general; similarly past policy and actions are not generally known.

Such is the origin of the Kingdom of Ahir and its history hitherto. He who tries to change it seeks to alter or change its fundamental constitution, and is trying to do the impossible—and will waste his efforts and repent, when repentance is too late.

These five people who installed Ali Su (Alis Su) as Sultan and built for him a palace in their land, made themselves his subjects of their own accord. Their Sultan did not treat them frowardly or forcibly as a conqueror, for it was they who conquered the Sudanese tribes aforetime. They were therefore " people of binding and loosing " (Council) and were only subjects of their Sultan as a loyal and noble estate, even as he ennobled and honoured them above all the other tribes; for the latter had no share in the government of Ahir.

Any tribe which tries to put itself on a level with them or compete with them in their inherited position, wrongs them for it seeks what none of the other tribes have ever sought.

As to the gifts of horses due to them, there is no obligation on them to pay tax, for the 'horse-tax' on the 'caravans' was derived from their custom and their country.

When they installed Alis Su on the throne, Alis Su, who was at that time the chief of the Imoshag, sent to the land of Islam, and said to the Ulema of Islam:—

"The people of the Tawarik who captured the land of Ahir forcibly in war, and took me, and made me Sultan over them, and built me a palace, are accustomed to exact a Jizia of horses from the merchants who pass by their mountains and deserts. I ask God and you, is this Jizia *haram* or *halal*?"

They replied: "As regards the men who guard the road which leads between the mountains, and protect it from horses and robbers and thieves and bandits, and the custom of taking of horses and cloths from the caravans and merchants and giving them to those men who guard the road between Masr and Timbuctu, since it is the world's road on which clothes are exported from Egypt and gold from Timbuctu, these men are the bulwark of your Kingdom, by their means you maintain your authority."

These are the people of the Sultanate of Ahir from its beginning to the present day:

As regards the origin of the San-dala, a woman called Besh, bore three daughters, the first named Fataha, the second named Imalaha, and the third Rahmata.

Fataha gave birth to the Ite-san and Ijadanaran. Imalaha gave birth to the Tafadalat and Tamaghazzarat, and Tamdaghdalat. Rahmata gave birth to Izagharan and Ibarzawan, who are called Imakitan.

The Sherif* gave them the name Imakitan when these tribes

---

* The Sherif means probably the Muslim divine Ali el Jerjerani who died in A.H. 436 (A.D. 1044-5), a fanatic who seems in some degree to have been responsible for the desolation of Fezzan under the hero Abu Zeid el Hilali by the Arab tribes Hillal and Solein at this time, causing the Sanhaja and Hawara of Fezzan, particularly those who had adopted Christianity, to go South and West. Apparently the invasions of Okba and others in the 7th century had driven off the older races of Barbars (Gara) to the South West but since the newer Tuwareg tribes were not then very numerous in Fezzan, had not much affected the South Central Sahara.

pushed forward in his cause, and left Aujila and conquered the people of the Sudan of the land of Ahir, and remained there alone for many years, without a Sultan to help them, their organization being as the organization of the Arabs in the early days, when they had no rulers save their Sheikhs.

Thus were the four tribes—Al-su, Ibal-Karan, Imiskikin and Imissufan.

LVIII.—CHRONICLE OF THE SULTANATE OF AHIR.

In the name of God the Merciful, the Compassionate. May God bless Muhammad. Peace.

I wish to set in order the history of the Sultans of Ahir of the people of Aghir and Taghazzarat for guidance. God is our helper.

The first Kingdom was that of Yunus, son of Tamakkaka, of the Tahinnazayat. Tamakkaka was the sister of Ahinas.

1404-5 A.D. Yunus of the Tahinnazayat was made Sultan in the year 807 A.H. He ruled twenty years.

1424 A.D. There succeeded to him the son of his sister (*i.e.* Tegasi) Ag-assan in the year 827 A.H.

1429 A.D. The power remained in the hands of the family of Tamakkaka sister of Yunus, and changed about from one member to another for the space of six years. Then their younger brother Ali Su (Alis Su) succeeded in the year 883. He ruled twenty years and died.

1447 A.D. His brother Amani succeeded in the year 851 A.H. He ruled four years and was killed while still Sultan. The preceding dynasty lasted fifty years before its fall, after a war of two months or thereabouts. They were people of Tasannaghat (Sanhaja).

The people of Taghazzarat (*i.e.* Kel-Giris) destroyed their supremacy, so it is related, and there was installed as Sultan,

1453 A.D. Ibrahim ibn Hilaz, in the year 857. He ruled sixteen years.

1477 A.D. There succeeded him Muhammad al Kabir in the year 882 A.H. He ruled ten years.

1486 A.D. There succeeded him his brother Ibrahim Muhammad Satafan in the year 892 A.H. He ruled seven years.

To him succeeded the son of his sister Muhammad ibn Abd ul Rahman, surnamed, Taladir Tanta, in the year called "Antais"

1493-4 A.D. 899 A.H. He ruled nine years and was killed.

The power was then given to the children of Fatamalat—

1502 A.D. Muhammad Al Adil and Muhammad Hummadi, in the year 908 A.H.

They ruled ten years. Then there came to them the destruction wrought by Askia, whose invasion was caused by Muhammad

1516 A.D. ibn Shala, in the year 922 A.H. He ruled twenty-five years and died as Sultan.

1542 A.D. There succeeded Muhammad ibn Taliyat in the year 949 A.H. He ruled fifteen years. After he was deposed there ruled

1556 A.D. Muhammad al 'Adil in the year 964 A.H. He ruled thirty-nine years or some say forty—and died as Sultan.

There succeeded his brother Akunfe in 1002 A.H. and ruled a year and six months and died as Sultan. **1593 A.D.**

The next Sultan was the son of Akunfe's sister Yusuf in the year 1005 A.H. He ruled twenty-eight years and died. **1596 A.D.**

His son, At-Tafriju, succeeded in the year 1033 A.H. He ruled thirty-one years. **1623 A.D.**

There succeeded him his brother Muhammad al Mubarak in the year 1064 A.H. He ruled thirty-four years save two months and died as Sultan. **1653 A.D.**

His son Muhammad Akabba succeeded in the month of God Jumada Akhir. He reigned thirty-five years.

There succeeded his brother Sultan Muhammad al Amin in the month of God Jumada the second, and ruled nine months.

He was succeeded by his brother Sultan Al-Wali, who ruled fourteen years.

Then there came Muhammad Al-Mumin, and ruled nine months. Then Muhammad Ag-Gaisha (son of Aiyesha) son of Sultan Muhammad Akabba. He ruled eleven years and nine months.

Then succeeded Muhammad Hummadi ibn Sultan Muhammad al Mubarak and ruled six years.

Then Muhammad Kuma ibn Al 'Adil and ruled five years.

Then Muhammad Hummadi again. He ruled fifteen years and four months. He was deposed in the month Shawwal, at the end of one year plus four days after the completion of the 1100 A.H. (*i.e.* 1101 A.H. and four months). **1690 A.D.**

Sultan Muhammad Kuma ibn Sultan Othman ibn Muhammad ibn Muhammad al Mubarak succeeded in the same month. He ruled for three years and eight months and was deposed in the month of Rajab.

The Sultan Muhammad Ahmad ibn Sultan Muhammad al Barak succeeded again in the month of Rajab in the midst of the year 1176 A.H. He died at the end of the year 1181 A.H. **1762 A.D. and 1767 A.D.**

His successor was Muhammad Al 'Adil in 1225 A.H. **1810 A.D.**

Next was Ahmad Al Dani who reigned five years and four months. He abdicated.

Sultan Al Bakari succeeded in the year 1228 A.H. and ruled one year. **1811 A.D.**

Muhammad Kuma was then installed and ruled five years and one month. He abdicated.

His brother Ibrahim succeeded him and reigned seven years before he was deposed.

Muhammad Kuma was restored and died as Sultan, slain as a martyr for the Faith in 1251 A.H. **1825 A.D.**

After him came Abd ul Kadir but was deposed. Ahmad al Rufa'yi ibn Muhammad Kuma was then installed as Sultan but he was deposed, Muhammad al Bakari succeeded.

Then Ahmad al Rufa'yi was restored. Then Muhammad al Bakari again, and he abdicated.

Ibrahim al Dasuki succeeded (May God give him victory), but was deposed.

The power returned to Muhammad al Bakari known as "Tsofo", and he died still Sultan.

Othman ibn Abd al Kadir ruled four years and abdicated.

1907 A.D. Ibrahim Al Dasuki ibn Ahmad al Rufa'yi ibn Muhammad Kuma succeeded (May God give him victory), in the year 1325 A.H. and he is still Sultan.

May God continue him victorious and prolong his life. Amen.

Note on the Barbars of Bornu and of Ahir (Asben).

The two preceding accounts of the Kingdom of Asben or Ahir are translated from two manuscripts sent by the ruling family of Agades to the present Sultan of Sokoto, and by him given to the Resident, Mr. G. W. Webster, M.B.E.

The second of the two manuscripts is obviously derived from the same source as an Asben Chronicle procured by a Hausa Mallam at Katsina in 1908 and published by the writer in the African Society's Journal. There are, however, discrepancies between this and the Katsina manuscript. It is probable that the manuscripts here translated represent the more reliable information, where they differ as to dates or anything else (not purely a question of interpretation) from the Katsina manuscript.

It will be seen that in relation to the history and ethnology of the Sahara and Sudan, these manuscripts are of considerable importance, and seem to give a conclusive answer to many questions that have been a subject of controversy for years and about which many variant theories have been propounded. The manuscripts are complementary the one to the other.

It will be observed that the general term which is used in Europe to denote these peoples, Tuwareg, is here rendered by the name San-Dala, *i.e.* people of the 'hill' or 'camp'. They are divided into five sections as is the case with other versions of the origin of the 'veiled people', Mulathimim as they are called by the Arabs, all descended from one mother (Besh) through three daughters here called Fataha, Imalaha, and Rahmata.

The names are of course imaginary. There is probably no special significance in the name Rahmata, and Imalaha is a common Barbar woman's name. On the other hand, Fataha denotes that the stocks descended from her became Murabatin or Inislimnan, *i.e.* Muslims, at an early period while the name Besh is doubtless connected with the Tuwareg word 'asheni' (blood) 'agadesh'' (family), etc., and means the universal mother—the Isis or Wesh of Egypt and the Ethiopian Kingdoms of the Upper Nile.

Fataha was responsible for the Itesan and Ijadanaren. The Itesan are regarded as the senior of these tribes. They are the repositories of lore, and perform the office of installing the Sultan. Ibn Khaldun classes them as Sanhaja. But their association with the Ijadanaren, modern Hadanarangh, a branch of the Hoggar or Azgar of the region of Ghat, means that they belonged to the so-called Hawara or Hawaza tribes of Fezzan, who, according to Ibn Khaldun, were descended from an ancestress having a name rather similar to Besh, *i.e.* Tiziki or Tish-ki.

Imalaha's children are the Kel Fade (Tafadalat), the Tamaghazzarat, modern Manghazzatang, another branch of the Azkar or Hoggar, and the Tamdaghadalat (Igadalen).

Finally among the children of Rahmata are the Tuwareg of the eastern Sahara called Izagharan (found under that name in the present Damarghu) who represent the Zaghawa of Ibn Khaldun, and the Ibarzawa who represent the Ifoghas and Kel Ferwan, *i.e.*, the Roman Infuraces, who again are a branch of the Azkar and Hoggar.

All these tribes and their offshoots are San-dala, *i.e.* Tuwareg, but the beginning of the occupation of Ahir by the Tuwareg was when four tribes drawn from these stocks, to wit, the Itesan, the Jadanarangh, the Izagharan, and the Fade-angh, migrated from Aujila (Fezzan) to Asben many decades before 1400 A.D.

The Itesan, as has been explained, were Sanhaja (Sangara) or Hoggar (Ihiggaren) and so were the Jadanarangh (Hadanarangh) while the Fade-angh are, under another name, the Kel-giris or people living in the N'gir, *i.e.* the valley now called Selufiet or Taghazzar (the valley) to the north of Tin-tellust.

Since the Kel-giris and Itesan are closely akin, it is clear that the Itesan, Jadanarangh, and Fade-angh were all Hawara, (Hoggar) of Fezzan, but that, though they were equally Tuwareg, the Izararangh now called Kel Faruwan (Beruwan) were of a different stock to the other three, and regarded as closely connected with the Tuwareg of the Eastern part of the Sahara *i.e.* Zaghawa and Bardoa (Ibarzawan).

The participation of this latter group of tribes in the founding of the Kingdom of Ahir (Asben) explains why the author of " The Sultanate of Ahir " calls his treatise " a book concerning the Kingdom of Ahir and the Kingdom of Bornu ", *i.e.* the Baranu (Bornu) were the Tuwareg of the Eastern Sahara as opposed to the Tuwareg who went west. The fact that some of these stocks lived in, and came from Augila (Fezzan) does not mean either that Fezzan was necessarily the first home of these tribes in Africa, or that all the Baranes stocks lived in that region. The " Chronicle of the Sultans " begins by stating that it concerns the people of the steppes (Aghir) and Taghazzarat (watered valleys in particular Selufiet) of Ahir (Asben) *i.e.* it concerns the home of the Kel-giris (Kel-N'gir, or settled dwellers (Kel) in the N'gir (Aghir) or steppe lands.

The chief section of the Kel-Giris is the Kel-Taghazzaran or Tadamakkaran, the former term referring to their place of residence the latter to their origin; *i.e.* they were the " children of Tamakkaka of the Tahinnazayat " or in other words, were a branch of the same Tadamakkat or Tadamakkaran (Imagharan, Imajaran, or Imoshag) who, as early as 1067 A.D., were located between Tuwat and Gao on the Niger, nine days from Gao and forty from Ghadamis.

The mother stock then of the Sultans of Ahir is simply the group name of the Imagharan, *i.e.* nobles, who are called Tahinnazayat (Tahinnesh-ayat), equivalent to the Egyptian term Tehennu.

From Tahinnesh-ayat (meaning "people who live in skins' *i.e.* tents), a singular patronymic Ahinnas is, it will be seen, invented while Tamakkaka is his sister, and also both the sister and mother of Yunus.

Besides being Tehennu, these people were, it will be observed, Tasannaghat, *i.e.* San-gara or San-haja, equivalent to San-dala, the Arabic *haja* being possibly for 'hajjar" hills, *i.e.* a literal translation of Dala.

Now it has been seen that though the Tuwareg stocks called by the Arabs Sanhaja and Hawara (in reality both terms denoting the same people, the San-gara) reached the Western Deserts and Upper Niger about 1000 A.D. or before, they are regarded as having come, not from the north-west coast of Africa, but from Fezzan and Cyrenaica, *i.e.* Aujila.

Among them is one stock in particular, the Uraghen, now numbered among the Azgar. These are the Aurigha of Ibn Khaldun and counted by him among the Baranes. The term means, in Tamashek, the 'Yellows.' That they once lived in Southern Fezzan is evident from the fact that Southern Fezzan is called by the Kanuri, Turaghen.

Though the Uraghen as such are rather in decay, closely connected with them are:—

(*a*) The Kel Ferwan—whose Amanokel acted as deputy for the Sultan of Agades when the latter was absent.

(*b*) The Keyi Lowi—*not* Kel Owi, who, arriving in Asben about 1740 were not pure nomads; for they lived in villages and it is a *sine qua non* that their chief must marry a black woman, a custom which it seems probable they brought from Fezzan.

The inference from this would appear to be that the Uraghen were the result of intermarriage of Levantine races with the Hagara (Hawara) of Fezzan. From these Levantines came the mercantile proclivities of the former Lauwa (Lewata) and the modern Ke-Lowi and the Wasuri or Buhadi traders of Bornu and Hausaland. In the name of Ke-Lowi we have:—

(*a*) The name of the race (Zaghawi) called in Bornu still Ke, Keyi, or Kayi who according to the historian Yacubi were responsible for the Kingdom of Bornu and Kanem.

(*b*) The root which is responsible for the Greek name for Cyrenaica, *i.e.* Libya, which was derived from the tribal name Lebu, applied by the Egyptians to the tribes to the west of them who had originally come from Syria.

With the exception of the Ke-Lowi therefore it will be seen that all the easterly Tuwareg stocks are included in the term Amakitan, which in fact is equivalent to Ibn Khaldun's tribal name Kitama—a unit which he groups with the "Sanhaja of the second race" who, as well as the Kitama, came according to him from Yaman, and had lived many years in and multiplied in Kordofan and the Blue Nile region.

The home of these races, according to the Bornu tradition and opinion also, was Makida, a name which they give to Northern Kordofan.

As will be seen however from the manuscript "Sultanate of Ahir", the Sultanate and Government of Ahir itself, though supported by the four affiliated Imoshagh (noble) tribes was in the hands of the sedentary or non-noble class of tribes called Imghad, who were the children of the Imoshagh by Sudanese women.

The desire for a Sultan probably came from these *Imghad*. It is clear from other accounts in which it is stated that at the time when the Gobirawa or Gobir Hausas controlled the Asben Oasis there were associated with them the 'Ibal Karan' who were in some way regarded as Mallams, *i.e.* learned, that the Al Su or Al Suwa, the Ibal-Karan, Imiskikin and Imissufan mentioned, were *Imghad* or servile tribes—due to intermarriage of Tuwareg with (a) the Sudanese, (b) the Gara races like the Tebu.

The name of the first of these clans, Alis Su, seems simply to mean "a man" of the "Su" *i.e.* "Chief of the Su," Su being a term for the Saharan tribes possibly adopted from the Arabs. It was a vague term used in such expressions as the "desert of the Su" and is still used by (a) the Kanuri, and (b) the Arabs of the Chad region to denote aboriginal tribes.

The first half of Ibal-Karan probably bears some relation to names like Bul-geda, Bulwa, Balma (or Bulma) etc., in the Chad region, which refer to skin colour.

The compound thus means "White Gara" (Kara), *i.e.* the Ibal-Karan were the children of Tuwareg fathers and Gara mothers. It is possibly the name from which the Greek expression "Leukaithiops" comes.

Imiskikin may be compared with the title of the later Songhay Kings Iskia or Askia which seems to be merely Imiskiki in the singular, and mean the child of a Kiyi (Tuwareg) father, and a Songhay or Zabarma mother, from 'izze' the Songhay word for son.

Lastly, Imissufan is the same name as Massufa, found so often in the mediæval Arab works denoting the "guides" in the desert. This form seems to be a variant of 'Su' or 'Alsu' with Songhay prefixes and suffixes. *i.e.* 'im' (Tuwareg plural), 'is' 'son', 'su' (half breeds), 'ba' or 'fa' (tribal Songhay plural affix); 'n' (the Tamashek plural).

The 'Su' in general were at this epoch the pre-Tuwareg Gara races who had already, to a large extent, fused with the negroes, and were called in the west Wa-Kore, Wangara, Sara-Kore (Sarakolli) and in the east Kardawan, Garawan (Garamantes) etc.

On the other hand it seems clear that the class of Barbar to which the Uragen (Turaghen) belonged were not confined to the regions south of the ancient Carthage and Cyrenaica, but that the meaning of Toro in Futa Toro, the Senegal point of dispersal of the Fulbe (Fulani), is the same as "Tur" in Turaghen, and the Hausa and Kanuri terms for "white" North Africans, which are Turawa and Tura respectively.

In Kanuri the term which is particularly applied to merchants from North Africa is Wa-Suri, a term which, as it is practically equivalent to Turaghen, and Uzlan, a variant Kanuri name for people of Fezzan (presumably from Uzu, the Assyrian name for Tyre) suggests that Tur and Sur in these words mean the same thing *i.e.* that they denote the Semitic " Sur " which we call Tyre, and which the Hausas and presumably the Tuwareg (since the latter half of the word is the Tamashek ' akal ' (land)), called Surukal.

It may be further noted that the name Tur (Toro) or Sur received the Tamashek suffix -ik or -agh, and thus as Surka or Surk denoted, in the Upper Niger Valley, people who were perhaps originally regarded as *Imghad* of the Sandala or Tarkiyin (Tuwarik)—the Sorko or Surko.

According to Barth (Vol. i, p. 357), the so-called Surka section of the Ullimiden were originally *Imghad* of the Kelgiris of Ghir (*i.e.* Ahir), while the Surk or Koron-Koyin (" Chiefs of the Gara or Kara ") mentioned by him (vol. v, p. 468), are manifestly the same people as the Sorko, who, according to Delafosse and other authorities, were with the Ga-bibi (negro agriculturalists) responsible for the foundation of the Songhay Kingdom. On the other hand, El Bekri's Bazur-Koyin were the merchant community of the ancient Kukia (Kaukau) and presumably corresponded to the present day Wasuri further east.

It thus tends to be very probable that the tribal name Yoruba is not as was thought, connected with Yauri on the Niger, opposite Busa, but with Yawaru, the chief town of the Barnagharkoy of Songhay, on the shores of Lake Debo, formerly a centre of these so-called Surk or Surka peoples, some of whom would appear to have migrated first to Moshi (whence comes the Moreba of the Yoruba mythology) and thence to Ife in the present Yorubaland.

This supposition accounts most easily and naturally for the Yoruba belief that they are descended from one Lamarudu, whom fanciful authors have equated to Nimrod or other eastern heroes, but which, it is thought is merely the Tamashek class term *Imghad* to which the Tuwareg " alis " " man " is prefixed as in the name for the chief of these servile tribes—Al Su for Alis-Su.

Authors who have identified peoples of the present day with tribes known to the ancient or mediæval world, have been much led astray by the fact that it has never been sufficiently understood that nearly all the Saharan names for peoples denote a " caste " and not an ethnic unit; that for many centuries the whole Sahara had been divided into two sets of people the ' rulers or nobles ' and the ' ruled or servile ' peoples, in addition to slaves, and that this conception of a natural order of creation has been fundamental not only in the Sahara itself but in all Kingdoms or States which have arisen in the Sudan belt to the south of the Sahara since the earliest times.

The genesis of the Barbar or Tuwareg tongues is lost in the mist of antiquity; but that the invading Tuwareg races took over and absorbed into their different prefixing dialects a considerable amount of the vocabulary of pre-existing Saharan Gara suffixing languages of the type of Tebu and Kanuri and Barbra and perhaps we may add Fulfulde, seems very evident.

It has been seen for instance that Sorko, the name given to supposed ' fishing tribes ' who founded the Songhay Empire, is really a Tuwareg term for their own half castes or servile tribes.

Similarly the name given to their subjects, *i.e.* the Ga-bibi, is derived from ' Bibi ', the ordinary Songhay word for black, and ' Ga ' which represents the Tuwareg prefix pronounced in the desert with the Arabic *ghain* and to the south as a simple g, and means " son of " or " sons of ".

The commonest Hausa form of title to-day for a territorial chief is the form, which was derived from the invading *Imghad* who founded Kano, *i.e.* the form composed of ' Dan ' (son of) and the name of the tribe or place of which he is chief, just as in the Chronicle Ali Su is for Alis Su ' man of the Su ' and so Chief of the Su.

Similarly further west, the Tamashek prefix agh (sounded also ag or ar) was prefixed to tribal appellations to form a title.

It will be seen that the title Ghana of Ghana (the first vowel being short) means merely " chief of the Anna " or people, and Ganata in its modern form Janet—is " the place of residence of the Ghana."

Furthermore, the place name itself became a title in the case of Songhay of which the ruler was called Kanda (*vide* El Bekri), and Kebbi when the ruler was called Kanta*; while in the two chief languages of the present day representing the prefixing and suffixing languages respectively, *viz*: Hausa and Kanuri, this same enclitic, meaning " son of ", has become one of the common terms to express the classificatory idea of ' son '.

In Kanuri the suffix ' gana ' means ' son ' *i.e.* physical paternity. In Hausa the corresponding Kan or Kane means ' younger brother.'

Deductions which may fairly be drawn from these manuscripts seem to point to the possibility that the so-called Semi-Bantu and kindred languages were among the most primitive or earliest forms of speech in North Africa. At some very distant period these tongues were much modified and in part absorbed by agglutinating or suffixing languages, of which the present Brabra, Kanuri and Teda languages are typical (to which Fulfulde also bears some relation) due to Kushite races from the east. At a still later date, possibly, it might be suggested, during the five hundred years before and after the opening of the Christian era, a new group of peoples, the Tuwareg, advanced from the Nile Valley west, and absorbed the older Saharan languages, with the exception of Fulfulde and Teda and Kanuri and spread their languages *i.e.* Barbar Tamashek throughout the Sahara, and a modified form of them, *i.e.* Hausa, into the Sudan. Such a hypothesis would explain many of our Nigerian ethnic problems as for instance why the Bedde, N'gizam, Bolewa, and N'gas speak languages akin to Hausa, as also, according to Barth do the people of Logone. The suggested explanation is that the ancestors of these tribes, known in part to have come from the Fitri region, were originally Ikelan, *i.e.* the eastern equivalent of our local Buzus, the children of Tuwareg fathers by Sudanese women. It is further suggested that the Kwona, Kwararafa, and Jukon, who also came from the Fitri region, belonged originally to the same class of people, while on

---

* *cf.* also the title of the Queens of Meroe Kantakit (Candace) or Kintakit.

the other hand the distinguishing strain in the Fulani (Torobe) is Tyrian, *i.e.* derived from early Phœnician Colonies in north-west Africa.

Note on the Barbars, the Fulani, and the Teda.

As regards the word " Tuwareg " (Tawarik) itself, current explanations of the word are not very convincing, for there is no evidence that the word was invented by the Arabs, though the form Tawarik first occurs in their works as the correctly formed broken plural of Targi.

The ordinary name for the Tuwareg proper, the so-called " nobles," is the root MZGh. That root, however, connotes " males," " masters," " warriors," rather than the tribal or national unit, the proper term for which is in the singular ili, alis, or alil, and in the plural illam or ilella. In the legends, still current in the Chad region, of the Hilalian Arab invasion of Fezzan in the eleventh century and the deeds of the hero Abu Zeid el Hilali, the term used to describe the Tuwareg who opposed Abu Zeid is always Ullam or Illam. The modern tribal name Ullim-miden is thus composed of illam, " members of the tribe," and miden (Tamashek plural=men).

In the eastern half of the Sudan the common word (usually classed as Arabic) for a country or tribal area is Dar. The word is however not really an Arabic word, though adopted and used by the Arabs as such. It is the pre-Arab (*i.e.* Barbar) word for an " encampment," and from this meaning of " camp," *Dar* or *Tar*, with its variant Dala, acquired in many parts of the Sudan and Sahara the meaning of " hill," since camps were frequently on a hill or elevated ground.

In the Chad region the present use of this root DR among both Arabs and Teda-Kanuri is *dor* or *dar*, meaning an encampment; *dirdir* meaning a fence, palisade or wall. Thus in the Ka war Oasis the Tebu title of the chief is Dir-deyi; the capital, so to speak, of the oasis being called Dir-Kiyi(n), though in ordinary conversation the n is dropped and the name is pronounced Dir-ku. The meaning of the name Dir-ku is, in fact, " camp (dir) of the Kiyin or Keyin," *i.e.* the camp of the Zaghawa Tuwareg or Beli who were the first rulers of the kingdom called afterwards Bornu.

The word Kiyin with its variants Kinin and Kindin is the normal word for " Tuwareg " among all the Sudan peoples east of Lake Chad. The masculine singular of this word is Kiyi, making feminine Kita or Kinta, whence the tribal name Amakitan or Maki-dan (Mâkida), and the Barbar word Kinta or Kita, " mother," whence Kita-ki or Kinta-ki(t) (Candace), " my mother."

It will be seen that a " Tuwareg " in this region was called Tar-kivi (Targi), sometimes pronounced Tarauwi, which quite naturally among the Arabs acquired a broken plural Tuwarik. An indication that these early rulers of Kanem were Tuwareg lies in the word Dugu, used as (1) the word for the grandson of a king; (2) the third mythical Mai of Bornu, whose name is given as Mai Dugu.

Dugu, though now in the word Mai-dugu it means any grandson of a Mai, strictly meant the son of the king's daughter, *i.e.* it was a word parallel to the Tamashek têgasi, which latter means "child of a sister" and so "the heir," teg or dug being apparently a feminine form of the Tamashek -ek or -eg = "son". From this it will be seen that the Tamashek word for the "veil" or "covering" which the Imoshek or Imajaren wear, *viz.* Tagilmus, is possibly Tag-el(l)am-us, *i.e.* the covering of the illam or "nobles."

The generic name Sanhaja used of the Tuwareg by the Arabs is an Arab modification of San-gara or San-a-gar, which is the same word as Zenj on the one hand, and Senegal on the other.

The two oldest Sudanese names for the Tuwareg thus seem to be:—

(*i*) Ili, plural, Il-am (or Illam for euphony).

(*ii*) Kiyi or Keyi, plural, Kiyin or Kinin, which has in fact another modern plural in the tribal name Koyam (for Kiyam). The Koyam trace their descent to the Beni Kiyi of early times in Kanem.

Let us suppose that this root word Kiyi (written also Kayi and Keyi) is of the same root as that found in the name of the Kinahhi or Kinahni, called also Χυα or Kina, a people who, according to the Tel-Al-Amarna tablets, came from the region of the Persian Gulf and colonized Phœnicia. The Kina were presumably, a part of the peoples who introduced the "horse" to Babylon and Egypt about 1700 B.C. It would not follow that because these races only arrived in North Africa as colonists towards 1300-1000 B.C. and were then, so far as we know, unveiled, that races homogeneous to them did not at a much earlier period migrate from Iran to the Persian Gulf, Arabian Peninsula, and Horn of Africa, and become the Tehennu who were as early as 2500 B.C. established in the oases near the Nile. It may be noted that the Egyptians called these Iranian nomads Dahi. A supposition that they have some connection with Africa gains very considerable support from the data collected by Professor Ridgeway with regard to the advent of the "horse" in North Africa, as well as from the Tamashek words for horse and ass which may well bear some relation to the Aryan term for the 'horse'—$\alpha\sigma\pi o\varsigma$.

There is also reason to suppose that the early civilizing influences which acted (a) in the extreme west of Africa on the Lixus (Wadi Draa), and (b) in the early civilization of Garama (Jerma), were mainly Syrian, *i.e.* Phoenician, and did not come direct from either Egypt or Europe. That these influences must be classed as Semitic both as regards language and otherwise, and that there is no trace of a veil among the Libyans of the Greek age or on the Egyptian monuments, does not preclude the supposition that races in part homogeneous to them in passing through the Arabian Peninsula and the Horn of Africa did not (a) while retaining to some extent their original language, modify it considerably in the course of years, (b) acquire the use of the "veil."

The theory that in fact the two groups were in origin the same, albeit the ancients believed in two widely secluded but homogeneous races of Ethiopians, might remain pure speculation were it not that (a) a definite Elamite migration from the Persian Gulf to the Horn of Africa is believed by scholars to have taken place about 2000 B.C. or before; (b) the Arabs and Sudan traditions hold as definitely that the Tuareg first came from Syria to Yaman, and thence to Africa and the Sahara.

That El-am (Elamites) is the same word as Il-am is perhaps too easy a supposition to be true, and yet it is difficult to see why El-am should not mean " people of El," i.e. God, as it would do in Barbar languages akin to Kanuri.

It is true that Ibn Khaldun's Barbar origins are somewhat confusing in detail, but in broad outline his account does not materially differ from that suggested above, for (1), he brings the Sanhaja and Kitama (i.e. the Tuwareg or Ilam) from Yaman. He says they multiplied in the " rif of Abyssinnia," and afterwards spread west. They are his " second race of Sanhaja ". Though Ibn Khaldun calls them Gara (San-gara), they were clearly not the same Gara who were in ancient times the subject peoples of Garama (Jerma), the Tebu and Teda races of to-day—the Garawa or Gura'an. (2) Ibn Khaldun's southern Barbars are in general termed by him Beranes, a term which in Bêle, Zaghawi, and other Barbar languages of the Eastern Sudan means " person," or in the plural " people." The present local words for man (i.e. vir) vary. In Teda, a man is angi, plural anya, and in Kanuri, kwa, plural anwa; whereas in Kanuri kam, plural am, means people, and in Teda a person is anu and people amba. The equivalent for man (vir) in Tamashek is masigh, hence Ibn Khaldun talks of the Beranes being children of Masigh.

As regards the Northern Barbars, Libyans, on the other hand, Ibn Khaldun derives them from Madghis (mazigh) el Abtar or el Botr, who like Beranes, was a son of Canaan, son of Ham. Here it may be suggested we have the simple name for the Phoenicians, who were called by the Assyrians Surru, by the Egyptians Dara, and in early Latin Sarra. Botr or Abtar may mean, it is suggested, Aba Tur (Sur) or Abu Tar (Sar) i.e. the Phoenicians, whose country, originally called Usu or Uzul provided the people of Kanem and of Bornu with their name for Fezzan, " Uzlan " in Teda-Kanuri, with its capital " Zeila of the people of Uzu " (Zeila Uzlan) near modern Murzuk. To this day a Tuwareg is still called by the Hausas a Buzu, i.e. possibly Ba-Uzu, while they call Syria " Surukal " (Suru-akal[*]), and a Syrian (in fact, any white man) Ba-Ture, the corresponding words in Bornu being Tura and Wasuri or Wasili.

One Abd Allah ibn Ahmed ibn Suleim wrote a history and description of Nubia for the Fatimid Caliph Al-Aziz ibn Al Mu'izz who ruled 978-996 A.D. Speaking of the Alwa (Khartum) region and its crown prince Simon, presumably a Christian, he[†] wrote: " From this region there are several roads which lead to Suwakin,

---

[*] Akal is in Tamashek " land."

[†] Apud Makrisi. Quatremère. *Memoire sur L'Egypt*—vol. ii.

Basa (Massowa), Dahlak and Islands of the Red Sea. It was this route that some of the Ummayads took, when, having escaped massacre, they fled to Nubia... The Zenafej Beja tribe, which since time immemorial migrated to Nubia, are settled in the province we have mentioned, and have preserved their language and their kind of nomad life, not mixing with the Nubians or living in their towns. They have a chief who holds his authority from the King of Nubia." This is strangely reminiscent of Idris's Sahib Balâk or Barâk who sacked Samina in the Wadi Batha and also was tributary to the King of Nubia.

The same author is further quoted by Makrisi:—

"It is said that the Beja are of Barbar origin . . . . they are nomads, who live in leather tents, ... they count their descent in the female line . . . . each tribe has a chief but they have no king. Inheritance passes to the son of the sister and to the daughter to the exclusion of the son of the deceased. They had formerly a supreme chief, to whom the tribal chiefs were subject, and whose capital was the town of Hajr*, situated at the end of the Beja Peninsula."

It seems fairly evident from this passage, that at one time, a caste or section of the peoples called in general Beja, must have been the rulers of Maris, and this section, whatever the general type of the Beja were, cannot well have been other than the so-called Blemmyes.

The narrative of Aba Allah ibn Ahmed quoted by Makrisi continues:—

"These people mount fawn coloured dromedaries. They have also a large number of camels of Arabian origin . . . Their camels are very fleet . . . . mounted on these animals, which are perfectly schooled, they (Beja) outstrip horses and travel immense distances. They mount when in combat, and when a Beja throws his spear and hits his mark, the camel stops to enable him to recover the weapon; if, on the other hand, the spear falls to the earth, the camel puts down its neck and head to enable its master to pick it up."

It may be noted that among the Tuwareg it is a disgrace not to recover a spear which has been thrown.

"Their shields are made of the hides of oxen, ornamented with their hair. They have also shields which they called ' Aksum shields,' which, as well as those of Dahlak, are made of the skin of ' a wild bull ' or of the skin of ' a marine animal.' "

Probably the two kinds of shields were those of two different races. The former is the Teda-Kanuri shield, the latter probably the " oryx shields " of the Tuwareg called by the Arab writers Lamtenses.

---

* As this Hajr (*i.e.*, mountain) was presumably at the north end of the so-called peninsula, it would appear to denote the region which was ruled by the " Lord of the Mountain," *i.e.*, the extreme northern end of Nubia, called Maris, in which were situated " the town of Bejrash, the capital of " Maris, the fortress of Ibrim, and another place called Dau, which was a " river port and was, so it is said, the native land of the sage Lokman, and " Dthu ul Nun: It has a magnificent *barba* (temple). The Governor of " this province (Maris) is subject to the King of Nubia, and has the title " ' Lord of the Mountain.' "

The Beja of 900 A.D. are described also as using bows and arrows, but it would not follow necessarily that their ruling caste did so; moreover it is curious that the name of their arrow poison " Ghalkah " bears so close a similarity to the name of the people called N'gal or N'gal-agha, who were the Kushite inhabitants of Kanem and Wadai.

The tribal organization of the Beja at the time the Muslims began to work the emerald mines in the Eastern Sudan is thus in part described. " When the Muslims became numerous in the mining region, they intermarried with the Beja, so that a large proportion of the tribe called Hadarab became Muslims, though bad ones.

" These Hadarab are the flower and elite of the nation living in the regions which face the Said, from the furthest frontiers of their country to Alaky, Aidab and that region.

" The Zenafej form another branch of the nation. Though much more numerous than the Hadarab, and in ancient times having had a marked superiority, they are to-day subject. They are vassals of the Hadarab and escort them, defend them and guard their flocks.

" Each chief of the Hadarab owns a certain number of Zenafej, who are considered like slaves, and are inherited."

At this time (813-833 A.D.) the Muslim governors of Aswan were sent from Irak. Reports of Beja incursions reached the Caliph Mumun, who sent against them one Ubaid Ullah bin Jehin. The latter concluded a treaty with the Beja chief called Kenun, who lived in the town of Hajr, *i.e.* was " Lord of the Mountain," in the year 216 A.H. (831 A.D.).

Reading these various passages about the Zenafej together, there seems at least a probability that the Zenafej were formerly a ruling caste and had lost their supremacy, *i.e.* nobility.

The Beja social organization described is the exact counterpart of the Tuwareg social system. The Zenafej superiority, it may be conjectured, was lost owing to war. It may be supposed with *prima facie* probability that it was at the time when the Zenafej were the ruling race that " the Pharaohs of Egypt attacked the country and then made peace, because of their need for the mines . . . . and that the Greeks (Rum) when they were masters of Egypt pursued the same course."

If this was the fact, the remark of the author of the history of Nubia " The Nubians were formerly more powerful than the Beja " would presumably refer to the defeat of the Blemmyes by the Nobatae under Silko and the Romans about 450 A.D. and the rise of the Hadarab to supremacy over the Zenafej might be conjectured to have been the result of Silko's victories.

" The greater part of the Beja," adds the Nubian historian, " recognise a God, the creator, and ask the moon, sun and stars to intercede with him. Others do not believe in a supreme God, but worship the sun and fire. Others worship a tree, an animal, or whatever they like.

"Bedjrasch (the capital of the 'Lord of the Mountain') is a populous and well built town. Further on at the foot of the second cataract (Wadi Halfa) were various churches and monasteries. Near one monastery at Daira was a *barba* (temple), and at Bawsaka was a monastery to a saint called Shenudi.

"The Province of Makorra begins from Yafa which is one day south of Aswan. From Yafa to the capital Bedjrash is less than six marches. It is said that Moses, before his mission, attacked this country and destroyed Yafa. The inhabitants were at that time Sabaeans, and worshipped the stars to which they made statues."

"Before the Christian epoch the Nubians and Makorra had frequent wars; subsequently the people of Nubia and the Makorra embraced the Christian religion.

"At Dermes, near Dongola, was formerly a large temple dedicated to the sun, in which was an idol carved from a single block which had on its breast a figure of the moon".

The Dongola region was the region (Yam) whence came the peoples, like the Barbar Zaghawa, who founded the Kingdom of Kanem with its Mais (Meks) who, in culture, were akin to the modern Tuwareg.

Among the Zaghawa were apparently counted two elements:—
  (a) The original Zaghawa who were Kushities, the Kash of the Nile Valley.
  (b) A later stratum, the modern Bêli, who speak the same language as the former.

It is the Bêli part of the Zaghawa who are accounted "noble" and seem to represent the ancient Blemmyes. The Bêli were accounted "noble" in Kanem and Wadai, so much so that the Emirs of Wadai alone were permitted to marry one Bêli woman, while for the daughters of the Mais of Kanem the proper marriage was a "Terauyi."

The Bêli (loosely called Zaghawa) were in fact "wearers of the veil" *i.e.* MZGh, or Illam.

It can hardly be doubted that the "wearers of the veil" called by the Arabs "Tawarik" are distinct from the other African peoples called Barbar except in similarity of language, and it is not easy to suggest why a people, if originally of Nordic origin, should leave the West African sea-board and then adopt a peculiar and distinctive mode of living.

They would seem always to have been camel-owners. Though their monogamy suggests Aryan origin and possibly the influence of Christianity yet in most respects they are closer akin to Asia than to Europe. The social fabric of the Tuwareg, properly so called, centres round the circumstance that the women will not leave the tribal tents, that rank and official property descends through women, and that thus the only real Tuwareg (MZGh) are persons who are the children of Tuwareg women.

On the other hand, since the Tuwareg men leave home for long periods and their wives do not accompany them, it is the case that on the southern edge of the Sahara the number of communities which are, in part, of Tuwareg descent, and whose language has in greater or lesser degree been influenced by Tamashek, is very great. It would appear that in cases where a noble Tuwareg permanently settles among a non-Tuwareg people, he usually discards the " veil."

So far as the northern coast belt of Africa is concerned, it might be supposed that the infiltration of Tuwareg blood and language there, may have been brought about in a similar way to that which has obtained south of the Sahara, and possibly more so, for in the north the Tuwareg would be meeting a more highly developed and civilized sedentary population than is or was the case to the south of the desert. Whether or no the modern use of the " veil " may be in part ascribed to utilitarian or partly utilatarian motives, there is no doubt that throughout the length and breadth of the Sahara and Sudan such is not the view taken of it. On the contrary it is peculiarly a mark of " rank " and frequently worn by chiefs and others in the Sudan belt for no reason except to maintain dignity. The veil is in the desert and in the countries to the immediate south of it, the mark of a " noble " as opposed to a member of a subject population.

The connotation of thought which the " veil " conveys, may be seen from the fact that the apparent consonantal root of the Tuwareg (Tamashek) word for veil "*tagilmus*" means, in Hausa, not a veil but " sandals ", *i.e.* a " covering " which in some sense denoted rank, and covered a part of the body which, before an equal or inferior at least, it was not the custom to uncover.

The root consonants of tagilmus and takalmi K (G) LM (with the usual metathesis L and R) appear in girma, the word which in Hausa means " greatness or nobility " equivalent to the Tuareg Imagaren and MZGh group of words meaning " noble."

It seems possible that the Hausa " girma " and the Arabic " karim " (noble) both come from an identical root idea. If we apply the LR metathesis rule which is almost universal along latitude 20°. then there may be a connection in idea between these words and the Semitic roots.

(a) $k.l.m.$ = (1) to wound; (2) words; talk.
(b) $k.l.m.$ = (1) to cut; (2) divinatory arrow; (3) pen.
(c) $a.l.m.$ = to mark or slit; (2) to know or excel.
(d) $gh.l.m.$ = to lust.
(e) $k.l.m.$ = to slit a camel's nose.

We are accustomed to the idea of the evil " eye " and the physical means taken by the Tuwareg, among others, to avert it, *e.g.* ornaments and bright horse-trappings, etc., but the dynamic force of the breath or the spoken word is an equal wide-spread cultural belief, which among races like the Tuwareg and Hausa is very potent. It is not the ill-will in a " curse " which is resented so much as the supposed power of the curse in itself to work out its evil purpose.

The *tagilmus* (Tuwareg " veil ") is composed of two parts. The Tomiddagh is a covering to " cover the mouth and nose." The upper part or Imawal covers or " protects " the eyes. The root of the word imawal means to " protect ". But the covering in general is called *tagilmus* and the Tuwareg call themselves Kel Tagilmus.

The Tebu and Kanuri word for the *tagilmus* is " Fune " (pronounced almost like " Fine "), which seems to be connected with the Hausa tafi (n) (palm of the hand), and the Tamashek word for written signs, " Tafinagh—" Tifinagh " being regarded as equivalent to the " spoken word."

Apart from Ibn Khaldun's more general theories about the Barbars, he brings the " veiled Barbars " (Tuwareg) from the " rif " of Abyssinia, stating that they first multiplied in the vast plains of the region between there and the Nile, *i.e.* in the neighbourhood of the Blue Nile. From there, according to him came the Sanhaja, Lemta, Kitama and Zaghawa, etc. The Sudanese Muslim writers carry his story further by stating that the Barbars Tuwareg were originally driven out of Sham (Syria) by the Tubbas and transplanted to Yaman, whence they spread to Africa.

Whatever may be said against the probability of this Arab belief from other points of view, in regard to the " veil," it seems the only " Tuwareg origin " which fits the circumstance that the " veil " was *in primis* a ritual, acquired probably either in S. Asia or in the region of Axum (Abyssinia). It appears to be connected with Oriental ideas and Oriental nomenclature which indicate:—

(1) a covering of the mouth to preserve ceremonial purity or immunity;
(2) hence confers nobility;
(3) it is now a mark of rank in so far as it is not a matter of ordinary decency.

If the veil was perhaps, in some sense, what the Hausa would call " maganin baki," *i.e.* " protection against spoken words," it may be observed that in Hausa " magani " medicine or protection, and " magana ' words, are cognate forms. " Words " repel " words."

The Al-afin in Yorubaland is not allowed to go out of the Afin during the day for fear of influences such as " spoken words " and the Afin is thus as personifying the nation, just what the Kanuri Fune (veil) was to the early kings of Bornu.

In Senegal legends concerning the earliest Barbar Kingdoms of Wagadugu and Ghana, the ancestor of the Kings is called Ya Fune, son of Tamaganke or Magankaya (Kayamaga) son of Yugu Dumbêsi, etc., son of Solomon, son of David.

The original legends of the kings of Ghana apparently reflect the same tradition of a connexion with the region of Abyssinia and Yaman as do those of Kanem and Bornu, in spite of a more recent written Muslim tradition that both drew their royal house from the army of the Caliph Umr ibn Abd ul Aziz, who died about 650 A.D.

In the Kanuri traditions, if we substitute for Yaman in Arabia the regions of the Blue Nile and Kordofan which the Kanuri called Mâkida (Magâda) and accept Ibn Khaldun's account of the origin of the Sanhaja, Kitama and the other veiled races, we arrive at the conclusion that the Sanhaja and Kitama were much the same as the people who were called by the Egyptians Balhemu, and by the Romans Blemmyes, from the name of their so-called leader Blemus.*

But the word Blem-us without its Latin termination is in the Sudan identical with Burum or Buram a name which stands for almost any Barbar people or chief and is the name of several riverain pasture grounds which must, in very ancient times, have been used by the Barbar races, *e.g.* the Bahr-ul-Ghazal in Kanem and part of the Niger Valley near the "buckle," while in the Kawar Oasis we have the old place-name Balma or Bulma which is not derived from Kanuri or Teda inhabitants, but seems to mean exactly the same as Baram or Buram. A connecting link between this Kawar region and the Nile Valley is supplied by the Bêli or Bideyat of Wadai, the El Beliun of Idrisi, who, as Dozy points out, were no doubt Blemmyes.

The root of all these names appears to be "al" or "ar" which makes plural al-am or ar-am, with a determining prefix "b."

Whether there is any direct evidence that the "noble" Blemmyes were "veiled" is doubtful, but their mode of life and general characteristics seem to have been exactly those of the Tuwareg.

It would seem that the Hausa word for "turban" rawani, is the same as the Bornu title (a very early one) "Lawan."

The Lawan was originally the chief constable and executioner of the Mais of Kanem, and the title derived from the Arabic "awn" (armed attendant or guard).

Other interesting Bornu titles in this connection are Graema, *i.e.* Garama, and Jerma (also equivalent to Garama), both titles dating back to a time when Garama (Zeila) in Fezzan was under Bornu rule; and Mayinta or Makinta, originally the head of a Barbar or Tuwareg family, now used as the title of a head of a quarter or small village in Bornu.

Among the Zabarma (Songhay) the word for head covering in general is "Sonde" or "Sunde," *i.e.* the attribute of the Sun or Sonni (the ruling caste). A certain arrangement of it was called Jerma (Garama), while the mouthpiece (Tuwareg veil) is called "fu'i" or "fo'i" (*cf.* Fune in Bornu).

The Sun or Sonni were, according to the Timbuctu authors, of "Libyan Origin" and in the west they were the Sun-gara or Sanagar (Sanhaja being the Arabic transcription) or Aswanik, their subjects being the Wa-n-gara.

The tribal names of the Tuwareg, therefore, (as written by the Arabs), are quite easily explainable on the light of the languages pre-existent to their arrival, *e.g.*:—

    (1) *Sanhaja* is Sun-gara (Sanagar), Sangara, etc.
    (2) *Kitama* (Ketama) is Ki (yi) tama, Makinta.

---

* Compare the passage in Evagrius describing a seizure of the Oasis of Kharga by Blemmyes who told the Patriarch Nestorius that the Mazices (*i.e.* the Imoshagh) were coming to take possession of the Oasis. This was about 450 A.D. and indicates the presence of Tuwareg in the Nile Valley at that date.

(3) *Jidala* or *Gidala* is Kitala or Ketala, the same word as Kitama, with the Tebu suffix -la or -lan as in Yala or Yelan (north), instead of *-ma*.

(4) *Zanziga* or *Guenziga* is Sun-sika the latter being the same as Sikia (Askia) and the Bornu title " Siku " and " Sigi-di-am " (Oasis of Siggidim).

(5) *Lemta* cf. Fulani title Lamido " chief " and Arab name for early Tuwareg of Fezzan, Illam or Ullam.

The Bornu title of nobility Zanwa, corresponding more or less to a knighthood, meant the same as Sun or Sonni further west, so that Zanj or Zinj and similar names used of the people (Barbar) of the horn of Africa had probably the same signification.

Just as the Zan-bar (Zangibar), a combination of syllables which appears in place and other names and words as *e.g.* Sanburo (Hausa proper name), Zanfara (country), Za(n)bar-ma (Zabarma), Zabarra " to charge " (Hausa), were the leaders of the Barbar, so Zan-bar in Hausa, in Songhay Jambar (Jombar), was the figure at the top of the numerals, *i.e.* Zanbar=1,000.

As a name, however, Zanbar is very old in connection with the region in which Ibn Khaldun states that the Sanhaja and other Tuwareg multiplied, for, as early as 600 B.C. in the time of Psammetichus, certain Egyptian mercenaries who were called Asmach (said to mean left-wing), deserted and settled in the Khartum region and were generally known as Sanbaritai. Whether Asmach really meant " left-wing " seems doubtful. It may possibly be the equivalent of Aswanik (Aswan), or Asum-ak, which in later times developed the form Ak-sum (Axum) written by the Romans in North Africa in the form Agisymba.

It appears then possible that the Tuwareg nobility the Masigh, came from the Blue Nile region and the " veil " with them.

Idrisi's El Belium, the modern Beli (Blemmyes), are stated by him to have been originally Rum (Greeks) who became Jacobite Christians in the early days of Islam. It may be possible that so called Asmach were originally Ionian and Carian mercenaries who intermarried with the Asum-ak (Ak-sumiti) women, and thus that it is from them that the Tuwareg derive their straight profiles, though, as sons of Barbar women, they, from the very first, lost the nationality of their fathers.

The key to the original signification of the veil may also possibly be connected with veneration for the acacia tree, particularly the species Acacia seyal, which has a sweet and rather strong scent.

An eastern Tuwareg (Kindin) will not willingly, it is said, look on an acacia tree or come near it, much less handle the gum (gum Arabic) or carry it on his camels. In fact, it is the " totem " of the Kindin in general, and it is said that they closely cover their noses and mouths with the " veil " if they smell an acacia tree. They are said to be afraid of iskoki (spirits) which haunt the acacia, and which are liable to afflict them with leprosy, so they think.

It is also at least noteworthy that the Arabic word for this " veil " is *litham*, the root of which means (1) to kiss, (2) to muffle oneself, and then of a camel " to go lame owing to pebbles on the road."

The root of litham L-TH-M, curiously enough, comes in the dictionary next to the root LTH, which means to "exude gum or resin," which looks as if originally the Litham were a "people" who had to do with "gum and its collection."

The Arabian El-Lath was the feminine of El and the Semitic counterpart of the Babylonian Nana, or Ishtar.

It is suggested, therefore, that possibly the adoption of the "veil" by the Ilam was originally due to awe of the goddess Nana or El-Lath, who was personified in the acacia tree, the acacia being in this way the "Pene Baal," or "face of Baal" (the epithet of Tanit on Carthage votive-tablets). The tree was thus the outward manifestation of the unseen Baal, whence the veil itself was by certain Barbar races called "Pene," (Kanuri *Funi*). Possibly the Egyptian *Funh*, a name apparently applied to Asiatic bandits in general of the type of the Tuwareg, is a cognate name.

It may be added that the Tamashek root *ghar* for acacia occurs in the Tebu kingar, Kanuri karamga (Acacia *seyal*) in the Hausa karu, "gum arabic," and in its Kanuri equivalent kolkol, while the Acacia *verek* is also in Kanuri called kindil.

In the Asben region the "dashi" (Balsamodendron Africanum) is called "sacred" or "blessed," and is not used for firewood. Some Tuwareg state that it is their *kangida* (totem), and it is planted near tombs to confer immortality.

But whatever the origin of the "veil" may be, it is clear that its wearers are comparatively speaking a new race in the Sahara, and that the stocks they submerged or displaced are today partly represented by:—

(a) The Fulani.
(b) The Teda or Tubu.

It is these peoples who *au fond* represent the Ethiopians who, according to the classical writers were to be found both in the extreme east and extreme west of Africa.

Concerning the west, we unfortunately have little direct information except what is contained in native legends and chronicles and some notices which have survived from the Carthaginian era.

These latter are, however, important evidence, not the least important being the fragment which has come down to us about an expedition to West Africa by Hanno the Carthaginian about 500 B.C.

Concerning this much debated voyage of Hanno to the West African coast no one, it may be supposed, would dispute the identification of Soloeis with Cape Ghir, Cerne, with Herne Island, and the Cameroon Mountain with Θεων Ὀχημα.

Regarding the other place names however, much room for discussion remains. It may be said that with exceptions, such as Soloeis and Θεων Οχημα they were names probably supplied to the Carthaginians by their Lixitae interpreters who apparently did not understand the languages of the tribes living south of Cerne and conversely did understand the languages spoken to the north of Cerne. These therefore, were most probably of a homogeneous type, like the modern Barbar dialects,

It is thus most probable that the word "gorilla" was not as has been suggested, the local name of the animals seen by the expedition. As it is improbably that Fulfulde speaking peoples existed as far south as the Cameroon Mountain, the name "gorilla", Fulfulde *gorel*, which is in fact still the existing Fulfulde diminutive for "man" making plural n'goron, was, it would seem, a descriptive term used by the Lixitae to describe the gorillas or baboons or whatever they were, which resembled small-men in their own language*.

An inference from this supposition may well be that the Lixitæ who were "a nomad cattle breeding race" spoke either Fulfulde or a tongue akin to it. If other evidence points in the same direction, that inference would be rendered most probable.

The first question which suggests itself is, what was the meaning of the name Lixos as the name of a river and the people who lived near it, the Lixitæ?

Was Lixos a Carthaginian name or does it represent the peoples' name for the river, bearing in mind that the name afterwards given by the Arabs to this same region was Sus-el-aksa, *i.e.* "the most distant or remote Sus"—the "Ultima Thule" of the Arabs?

In Arabic, apparently, the root Swa (to be bad or wicked) has a connection in thought with the root S.W.D. which means (1) to overcome, (2) to be dark or black.

The Arabs of the middle ages called all the more southerly Barbar tribes of the Sahara by the name "Su" or "Seu" and the name was further applied by the semi-Arab stock which sprang up in parts of the Sudan, like Bornu and Timbuctu to the aboriginal negroes, whom they also called So or Sau.

In the west, the Wangara or Wakore, who became negroid Barbars rather than negroes, were thus called by the Arab writers Susu, a reduplicated form of Su. These Susu overran the Ghana or Ghana-Barbar Kingdom of Ghanata (Walata) about 1200 A.D.

The Mande word for this same type of people is Suwan-inke (the -inke being a Mande suffix or termination). The corresponding Barbar form is Su-wan-ek (Aswanek), the -ek being the Barbar plural affix, meaning "sons of," "children of." This form is also used in the singular "ag" as a prefix.

It would seem, on the one hand, that the name Lixus or Lixos is in some way connected with the Arab name Sus, but on the other, the name Sus itself was not confined to the Lixus region for there was another Sus near Tunis. Sus would thus seem to have been a generic name given to parts of the Sahara lying to the south of the Mediterranean littoral.

It has been mentioned that towards 1200 A.D. we find the word Susu (Sus) applied to semi-Barbar (Wangara) tribes who overran the Ghana Kingdom. These and similar Saharan tribes were known at different periods, and in accordance with local linguistic variation, as Wa-n-gara, Wa-kore, Sa-n-gara (Senegal), Su-wan-ek (Aswanik), Sun-inke, Sun-we (Songhay), Sunni (Sonni),

---

* *cf.* also Korgel *pl.* Korkon (Gorgon) which means, in Fulfulde, a young female slave.

Sa-n-koré, Sa-n-kara, Saran-kolli (Sara-kwolli,) Taru-du, Toron-ke, Toro-be, Tukrur (Tukulur). All these peoples, though politically distinct and differing in language, are, or were, nomad or semi-nomadic people of Barbar origin, living in or near the edge of the desert.

There came into the region now inhabited by these peoples or into the country to the north of them, Sus-el-aksa, during the period of the ascendancy of Tyre, *i.e.* (possibly about the time of Hiram I 970 B.C. onwards) colonies of Phoenicians, who carried their religion with them. Strabo mentions 300 such colonies as being founded at this period.

The Carthaginians came from Tyre, a town built on an island near the mainland of Syria, which was called Sôr, *i.e.* "Sur" (rock) and was known:
- (a) In Assyria as Surru,
- (b) In Egypt as Dara (or Da'ir),
- (c) In early Latin as Sarra,

while from the Amarma letters, it appears that the ancient Assyrian name of the region was Ushu, locally known as Usu or Uzu.

The town of Aoza was founded in North Africa by Ethbaal, King of the Sidonians before Carthage was founded by Elissa (Dido) in 800 B.C. The Phoenicians worshipped deities who had at first been associated essentially with the "earth," "trees," "hills," "rivers," "springs," etc. Each place, hill, river etc., had its El or Baal (Lord), plural Elim or Elonin, while the Babylonian Ishtar (Astarte) represented the female principle in them all.

Variants of the epithet, not name, Baal were Melek, Adon in the masculine, and for the feminine principle, Amma.

Amma or Tanit, as she was called in Africa, was at Carthage called the "face of Baal," *i.e.* the Baal was the generating or fertilizing principle, the "husband"; and Anna, in Carthage Tanit, was the great "mother."

The Tyrians and Sidonians, who became important before the Tyrians, belonged to races called in the Amarma tablets Kinahhi or Kinahni or Canaanites. With this agrees a statement assigned to Hecataeus, who states that, Phoenicia was formerly called Xvâ (Kina).

The inhabitants of Phoenicia, the commercial Phoenicians, were Semites and their language belonged to the north-Semitic group. It has been assumed therefore that the statement in Genesis Chapter X that Sidon, the first born of Canaan, was of the descendants of Ham, is wrong.

Since however the Phoenicians believed that they had come to the Mediterranean from the Persian Gulf, and only after arrival became sea-faring, it is possible that the original Kina (Kinahni) were not Semites.

If that was so, it may be that the Kina were absorbed or displaced about or before 2000 B.C. by Semites, and that the Arab legend of the expulsion of the Hamite Barbars from Sham (Syria) to Yaman and thence to Africa, in the time of the Tubbas of Yamen, is an allusion to this

Such a supposition would also explain why there is seemingly so little difference between the Lebu and Rebu who probably did come from Syria to North Africa during the time of the XIX and XX Egyptian dynasty together with the people of the Sea, who represent Ibn Khaldun's El Botr or El Abtar Barbars, and the other stocks of Barbars whom he terms Beranes and who would, if this conjecture is correct, be the Kina who came south about 1,000 years previously and had worked their way *via* Abyssinia to the Nile Valley.

The word Abtar or Botr and Ibn Khaldun's suggested descent of the Barbars from the Philistines, is in favour of this theory, as well as the fact that he brings the bulk of the Beranes, *i.e.* the veiled races, Sanhaja, Kitama, etc., from the " rif " of Abyssinia.

The cycle of legends concerning the army of Hercules (Arkel), the Milkart, Lord of the town of Tyre, is also in favour.

The indigenous Hausa and Fulani pre-Arab term for Syria is not the Arabic term Sham, but a derivative of the Egyptian (time of Rameses I) and Assyrian words Shasu (Syrian) and Sura or Sharu (Syrian) which through a presumably Tuwareg medium becomes Suru or Suru-kel, which may well be identical with the word common all along the Sudan meaning a " white man " from the North *viz.* Turi or Tura.

The Egyptians called the nomad races to the south of Elephantine Kasu or Kashu (Kash), and the region these races occupied is still called Asuwan (ancient Syene).

The Fulani also in their own accounts of their origin, write that their ancestors first heard prophecies of the coming of Muhammad when they were in the region of the " Jezira Baharein " of the Euphrates and Tigris, *i.e.* they do not call that region by its Arab name of Irak, but by the Egyptian name for the region " Nahuran " or " Naharein."

The inference from these names and their history seems to be that Bedowin were called by the Egyptians and others " Su " or " Shu " (reduplicated in Africa to Susu Shushu*). Lixus may then be the Semitic article " al " with " ek " or " ag " (agha) the Barbar word meaning " leaders " or " sons of " or simply perhaps " people ", and " su " (Susu).

Lixus would then be a general term meaning nomad or Bedawin people, comparable to the place name Axum, south of the ancient Meroe in Abyssinia. The Roman name for some place in the Southern Sahara, Agisyimba, very possibly has a connection with the Tamashek word for the south " agus," " agus-san " being a name for the nomads of the south. In Hausa " gussam " means south.

The earliest Fulani it would seem consisted of the children of Suran-kore (Sarakwolli) or Tura (Toro) fathers, *i.e.* Phoenicians from Surukel (Syria), with Gara or Garawan mothers, the language of the " Gara " (pre-Tuwareg Barbars) being the parent of Fulfulde.

The language of the Lixitae in that case was a language spoken by Gara Barbars, who were of darker colour than the Toro, Tura, or Suran from Sur (Tyre) or Suru-kal.

---
* *cf.* in Hausa the word " shoshowa " = tribal marks.

In Fulfulde we find that "Kera" means a dark skinned woman, while "Daro" means similarly a white skinned woman, and "Saro" means a parent. Fulbe "Surkugo" means "to fasten" and Sara-kulli means "a crossed stick," used as a talisman to guard cattle.

The name of the Wangara ancestress of the Fulani is Bajo Mangu "the great maiden," but sur-bajo is in Fulfulde the common noun meaning girl.

The question arises, why if the Fulani were Turan or Toro (Sur = Tyre) they were called Pullo-Fulbe?

In Tamashek, "afelle" means the north, and "kel-afelle" means northerners or whites. Similarly one of the chief divisions of the Hagar (Ihi-gar-en) or Azgar is the Uraghen, a name which is said to mean "golden" or "yellow" and is equivalent to the more common place name Turaghen, the old Bornu name for the region of Zeila, *i.e.* place inhabited by Turaghen (Turra).

In Tamashek a Pullo is Aful, plural Ifullan. In Hausa he is Ba-Filachi, plural Fillâne. In Kanuri we get a number of tribal names of northerners compounded cf. "Bal" or "Bul" which all refer to skin colour, *i.e.* white.

The most ancient African name for "Fezzan" is Zeila Azela, or Asila, its people being called Wa-suri, which is equivalent to the Tamashek Suru-kel.

It would thus seem probably (a) that the word Pullo refers to skin colour and meant white, (b) that this name is a Barbar word, a name given by Barbars to a "foreign element" which fused with them.

Since the root Tur, Tor, or Taur (Sur) is constant among the Barbars extending over the whole Sudan belt meaning a white northerner from the Mediterranean, it would seem probable that Ful is probably merely an epithet descriptive of the Tor, or people from Tyre or Syria.

At Sokoto, for instance, there is great insistence on the ruling race being Toronké (Torobe) but little on them being Fulbe, which in fact they are not, since they have become negroid.

Even as late as 900 A.D. the dwellers in the town of Zeila in Fezzan, the ancient Jerma or Garama, were mainly merchants from Syria and the country to the east of it, Khorasan, etc. There is therefore every probabilitiy that a large element in the former Garama and Jerma was Syrian or Phoenician, and hence that the original Turaghen (Wasuri or Surukal) were people from Tyre (Sur) and later from Carthage.

It has been seen that judging by the legends about Abu Zeid el Hilali current among the Hilal Arabs of the Chad region, the Arabs of the 10th and 11th centuries called the ancestors of the modern Tuwareg whom they met in Fezzan, Al Illam or Ullam.

They were a "noble caste" and clearly from this name "Illam" came the Tamashek term "ilamidi" (fellow-companion); the tribal name Ullimiden and the Fulfulde term Lamido (King). Illam seems to be compound of Il or Al and -am the Tebu or Gara word for people. If we suppose that Il is El, the Phoenician God, *i.e.* Baal, that would afford a plausible explanation of the name Ill-am used of the Suru-kel or Wa-suri by the older Barbars, *i.e.* by the Garawan or desert Garamantes (Tubu).

If therefore the orgin of the terms Tura, Turaghen Illam and Tuwarek in Fezzan are as above surmised, there is no reason why the same explanation should not apply to the Lixus region planted with 300 Tyrian colonies between 1252 B.C. and 877 B.C.

The inhabitants were, we may assume, Gara races, from the name Kerne (Garanai) given by the Lixitae interpreters to the island of Herne, as also the river name Chretes, which seems cognate to the Gara N'gir, place of Ngi (water), Tamashek N'gireu (stream) Fulfulde garuwol (stream).

The fact that it was Tyre which is said to have planted colonies in the Lixus region, Wadi Draa, and that an altar to Melkart there was still surviving at the beginning of the Christian era, according to Pliny, is particularly significant as affording an explanation for the words Tur, Turra, Ture and Toro, which at different points in the Sudan Belt mean a " white man " or inhabitant of the Mediterranean region.

Thus Futo (not Futa) Toro, the home of the Fulbe as a conquering race, is said to mean the " futo " (*i.e.* rich grazing land in a river valley) of the Toro (*i.e.* white men), the people of the region later being called not Futo Toronke but Toronke, *i.e.* the Toro people, *i.e.* whites.

If we suppose that the first Fulbe, long before the Arab conquest of Africa, were Gara Barbars and fused with Tyrian colonists forming the original Ganar or Canarii whose ruin and dispersion are so graphically described by Idrisi (1150) that will explain the fact that the first recognisable Fulani people (nomads) who lived in the time of El Bekri (1050) in communities apart, near large towns on the Senegal region, like Silla, were called by the curious name of Huneihim or El Faman.

Idrisi lays great emphasis on these Canarii being Jews, while equal emphasis is laid on the half Jewish origin of the Fulbe by their own historian Muhammad Bello of Sokoto.

Both traditions are explainable by the presence of Tyrian colonies in the Lixus region before 500 B.C.

The beliefs of the non-Muslim Fulani have been little investigated, but it would appear that, at one time, they, like the other Barbars, worshipped the sun and moon and also a supreme deity, corresponding to the Egyptian Ammon, while, in other respects, their cult paid great attention to lucky and unlucky days, had great festivals or observances in which " fire " played a part, and in particular they relied on a symbol called by some Fulani Sarankwolli (*i.e.* one of the names of the Wangara of the west), which consisted of cross-sticks to ward off evil from their cattle.

Their cult, in fact it can hardly be called a religion, is more consistent with a mixed Tyrian-Barbar origin than with anything else, and if the tradition about the Lixus region, recorded by the classical writers is correct, there is no need to look further for the origin of the earliest Fulani, though, no doubt, as El Bekri says, the early Arab armies in West Africa contributed largely to their becoming a politically separate people.

It is clear that, from the beginning, the Pullo was distinguished from the Barbar. The mother of the race is said to have been of the Wangara or Taurud (*i.e.* Ta-amghi—a feminine singular form, plural Imghad), tribes servile to the Tuareg, hence in the Fulani traditions, she is called (Bajo) Mangha.

The common saying that the Fulbe are playmates, *i.e.* cousins of the Beri-Beri may be true in a wider sense than that usually ascribed to it. On one side of their tree they, like the Beri Beri of Bornu, may have belonged to the old Saharan population, and arisen as a people from Gara or Anbat colonies in north-west Africa.

An interesting point in this connection is the cattle of the Fulbe, the humped variety like the Indian zebu, which are dissimilar both to (a) the Egyptian cattle with merely a raised spine, (b) the type of cattle found on rock drawings in the Sahara, which would seem in all probability to have been the type common in the ancient Garama in Fezzan.

That the Fulbe got their cattle from the south is improbable if not impossible, so that all the probabilities are (a) that they came from north of the Senegal, (b) that they were imported into Africa by sea.

In Fulfulde, the word for cow is " nagge " with plural " na'i," while the word for sun is "nange." As many Fulani believe that they are descended from cattle, *i.e.* have a totemistic belief about them and hold them sacred, it is probable that " nagge " and " nange " are really the same word, the original meaning being " mother " connected with their ordinary word for mother " inna."

If we suppose, as is probable (a) that the cattle of the Lixitae were " zebu " and ancestors of the present day Fulbe cattle, (b) that the Lixitae cattle were originally imported into Africa by Phoenician colonists, the parallel forms " nagge " cow, and " nange " sun, will have to be referred back to a time before the sun became masculine in the North Semitic languages, *i.e.* to the cosmogony which in Babylonia considered the sun, " Ishtar " or " Nana " as a female.

This Fulfulde name for a cow " nagge," apparently from the same root as the name of the sun " nange," represents quite a different root to the Tamashek " asau " (feminine " tâs ") which in Hausa becomes " sâ " (plural " shanu " feminine, " sania ") " an ox ". Tamashek " ais " plural " iyesan " the horse, and " ished " donkey are cognate roots.

The following words are interesting in connection with the above observations :—

Dirdir=(Kanuri) " zariba " or " encampment."
Derdirao (Fulfulde) brother or sister (classificatory).
Dir (Tebu) "stockade " or " zariba."
Dir-ki (Tebu) " encampment of the Kiyi "=Dirku.
Balani (Kanuri) Saharan sheep.
Dir-deyi (Tebu) " ruler of the Dir " or "encampment."
Targo (Ful.) " to surround," " encircle."
Ataram (Tamashek) West (classical Atarantes), *i.e.* people living west of the Nile in " Dir."

Tin-dir-ma (Tamashek) place-name = " place of the Dir."
Contrast these with Tamashek.

Amazagh; plural, Imazaghen = camp.

Ehe; plural, Ehinnan = tents.

With regard to the " dir " or " tar " and the Fulfulde root " nan " of cattle and the sun, the corresponding forms in Tamashek throw some light on the early ideas current among the African Barbars. Descent was counted through the mother so that Asheni meant " blood " *i.e.* what came from the mother (inna or anna) while heaven, *i.e.* the mother-goddess is Ashinna.

The Fulfulde word for moon " leuru " is cognate to the Tamashek word " ayor."

The sun among the early Fulbe must have been a goddess. The Fulfulde forms nagge, nai, nango (cattle and sun) equate to the Barbar " ashinna " and Fulfulde " inna "—mother. On these analogies Ash-taret called Tanit at Carthage might be supposed to have meant originally the same as the Fulfulde Dir-dirao, *i.e.* " blood " (ashe) of the encampment (dir).

In Fulfulde it is observable that the word corresponding to the Phoenician Baal is Jau. The following words illustrate it:—

Jaudiri; plural, Jaudi (ram).

Jaumo, husband.

Jam—peace, safety.

Jaumirao—the supreme God.

Jaumo—lord

Jauro—(title) chief.

Jungo; plural, jude—hand (forearm).

Jowe—seven.

Julirde—mosque.

Jaudi—wealth.

Jaube—proper name.

On the other hand Fulfulde uses the Barbar godname " Aman " in the form " maun." *cf.*

Maunirao = elder brother.

Maunago = to become big.

Maudo; plural Mauta = chief.

Maude (proper name) = famous.

Manga = great.

Mauni = importance, greatness.

Manore = praise.

Mango = to praise.

Mantirde = fame, praise.

In Tamashek, on the other hand, we have:

Amanai, God.

Aman, fish-god.

Aman-a-kel (akal = land or earth), a chief.

Tamanokalt, chiefdom.

Amanar, the constellation of the " Cross."

Iman, soul.

Amaina, East.

Tamantant, death.

The Jukon principal God is "Amma." The name is also used in compound names such as Ashu-Manu. On the other hand, for ancestors (Tamashek) has the root "mar" or "mal" e.g. "amaren" plural "amarrawan" (an old camel). These may be compared with:—

Malle, place name, (ruling caste).
Mari; plural, malinke, the ruling caste of Malle.
Mar-go (Ful), to possess.
Mar-do, possessor, lord, master.
Marado: slave, (Ful) plural marade.
Imghad; singular Amghi, slave (Tamashek).
Marenga: Moshi name for Songhay.

In Fulfulde:—
Konu, plural konuyi is "war."
Kono'o, plural kunobe is "warrior."
Konnejo, plural kune'in is "raider."
N'gangu is hatred.
Gairo is enemy.

The forms konu, kono'o, etc., seem to denote the earliest enemies of the Fulbe, i.e. the Gannar or Gana (Kona) of Ghanata.

In Fulfulde we have:—
Fudgo: to begin, spring up.
Fu-nage = the East.
Hirgo: to sit.
Hir-nange and Gorgil (country of gor (gar) " men ") mean West.
Wayla, sobire, or rewo = North.
Wargo, fumbina or hore (hudo, " head of grass ") = South.

In contrast to Tamashek in which:—
North = afelle. (Ful-be).
South = agus (cf. Hausa *hagu* " left hand ").
East = amaina. (Aman).
West = ataran. (Atarantes).

It is noticeable that both in Kanuri and Fulfulde, "balte" means 8 o'clock, when the "sun is up," and that the name given to the first-born of the Fulbe (i.e. the son sacrificed to Baal-Amma by the Phoenicians) is Bello.

LIX.—HISTORY OF KATSINA.

Barth (Travels vol. ii, p. 69) gives an outline of the history of Katsina, but in it there are several inaccuracies, and chronological inexactitudes. There exists moreover a good deal of material which was unknown to Barth.

The name Katsinna (Kachinna) is a variant of the place names Masinna (Machinna) and Teshinna (Tashinna)—the latter half of the names being 'inna' the Barbar word for 'mother'—the first syllable being connected with such words as izze (Tamashek " son "), mazza (Hausa " men ") and Fezzan (place name)—and meaning " children of " or " sons of " and perhaps is " Asheni " (Tamashek)—connected with " blood ".

As Barth points out the nearer origin of the Hausa Kings lies in the region stretching from Birnin Gabbas (Biram) near

Hadeija north-east through Machinna and Damergu to Balma (Bulma). At Balma, it is said, the Gobirawa were settled before they came to the Asben region from which they were driven south to their present habitat.

These races who were of Barbar extraction, in part possibly noble (*imoshag*) but mainly mixed (*imghad*), have their nearest modern analogy in the Dagara or Diggera (in Kanuri Dankir), from which the name Daura probably is derived.

According to the legends a Barbar hero (Bayazid) of these invading peoples married the Queen of Daura, and from their sons were descended the kings of the seven Hausa Kingdoms, in which Katsina and Daura represented trade, Daura being considered the senior kingdom, the mother as it were, which was always immune from attack by the others as sacrosanct.

The legendary founder of the Katsina Kingdom was Kumayo, son of Bauwo, son of Bayazid (Bayajiddah). In actual fact it would appear that the invading Kumayo Barbars founded settlements at two places not far from the modern town of Katsina—at Bugaji some 12 miles to the west, and at Durubi Takusheyi near Mani about 18 miles east of Katsina in the Daura direction.

According to the legends the Barbars who settled at these two places used to meet for feasting, wrestling, etc., at Ambuté *i.e.*, the quarter of Katsina town where the new mosque now is, at which place at a later date a stranger from Yandoto (Korau) threw the son of the king, Mashidi, in wrestling, and then murdered his father Sanau.

Bugaji was apparently not very large, though its name indicates that it remained a Barbar settlement—but Durubi Takusheyi contains a number of large tombs which are in fact raised earth mounds similar in type to others which exist in all the regions stretching from the Komadugu Yobe to the " buckle " of the Niger; a type described by El Bekri as having been used for the burial of kings at the ancient Ghana.

At Durubi Takusheyi the several tombs are known by the names of the early legendary kings such as Kumayo, Rumba-Ramba, Sanau, etc., though the generic name given to the race locally is " Durbawa ", whence it would appear that the title of the chief of that district Durubi or Durbi may go back to the earliest times.

Barth dates the beginning of these specific Barbar settlements as at the beginning of the 7th century of the Hejira, *i.e.* about 1200 A.D., but doubtless Barbars had been settled in these regions sometime before that.

In any case the rule of these pagan Diggera Barbars at Katsina, lasted approximately almost till the epoch (1260-1433) when Melle became the chief power in the west and in greater or less degree supplanted the previous dominance of Songhay (Gao and Kukia).

The key to the actual historical facts in this connection is contained in Barth's statement (vol ii p. 76) that " Korau, who came from a place called Yandoto (Yendutu) killed Sanau ".

The Emir of Katsina is called to this day Magajin Korau, (successor of Korau) and the current phrase " yanka Mashidi bakon

Sanau " " he who murdered Mashidi Sanau's son, the guest of Sanau " indicates quite clearly that Korau and his line came into power by some kind of treachery.

But the significant point, which Barth apparently did not know, is that Yandoto (the name of an ancient town) is the title of the ruler of the Chafi—Kwotorkoshi—Kogo region, which lies due north of Zaria (Katsina Laka as it is called), and is universally said to be " the Katsina " which became famous for its Mu'allims and Moslem learning, as distinct from the town now known as Katsina which, until the Fulani conquest in 1807, occupied the place in regard to the desert trade which Kano has occupied since.

It is evident that the region which Leo Africanus (1528 A.D.) calls Guangara (Wangara) which lay in Hausaland south-west of Zanfara and which, he relates, had been lately conquered by the Askia, was no other than this very region of Katsina Laka, from which not only Korau, the supplanter of Sanau, originated, but also the first Kanta of Kebbi at a later date, for Leka from which the first Kanta about 1513 A.D. defied the great Askia was close to Anka now in the district of Zanfara.

Some of the peoples known as Wangara became the people we now know as Mandigoes, but the original Wangara, the subject peoples in the west of the Ghana and Melle Empires were, without doubt, as their name implies, Gara, or Garawan as they are called in Fezzan, *i.e.* the early Saharan races which became subject (*imghad*) to the Sanhaja and other Tuwareg at the close of the first millennium A.D.

When therefore Leo Africanus spoke of the inhabitants of Guangara speaking Hausa, he was not " in error " as Barth (ii, 69) thought, for the meaning is that the inhabitants of Katsina Laka (then called Guangara) spoke Hausa.

What the exact origin of these Guangara people was we cannot be sure, but having regard to the fact that the original Kanta of Kebbi came from this same region, there is a probability that the Kanta who about 1513 threw off his allegiance to Muhammad Askia of Songhay and the Korau who about 200-300 years earlier replaced the Durbawa as ruler of Northern Katsina, belonged to half-Barbar tribes who were subject to the Songhay or Melle Empires which extended through Gao as far as " Hausa," the eastern bank of the Niger.

In the Kano Chronicle it is stated that Amina, a Queen, who is credited with travelling a great deal and building walled cities wherever she halted, was ruling in or near the Zaria region during the first half of the period 1400—1500 A.D. and that she " conquered all the towns as far as Kwararafa and Nupe. Every town paid a tribute to her. The Sarkin Nupe sent forty eunuchs and 10,000 kolas to her. She first brought eunuchs and kolas into Hausaland. In her time the whole of the products of the west were brought to Hausaland. Her conquests extended over thirty-four years."

In Zaria tradition she is credited with being the elder daughter of one Bakwa Turunku, in itself a female name and apparently meaning the " female stranger or guest—belonging to the Toronkawa or Toronke " (*i.e.* Tekrur or people of the Melle-Janne region). According to the Zaria Chronicle Bakwa did not found the present town of Zaria till 1536. Since however he or she lived at the place called Turunku before that date, it is evident that the Toronke came to Zaria before the century 1400-1500.

It seems then that " Queen Amina " means people from the west called Turunku (Toronke), who gave an impetus to city-building with mud walls on a large scale during the century 1400-1500.

In the Kisara legends, however, an Amina, probably the same Amina since she is envisaged as living in the same locality, the daughter of Kisara is supposed to have married the Chief of Nikki, and thus to be ancestress of the Nikki kings. According to the Illo version of that legend, Kisara ruled over the Yorubawa Gurumawa (inhabitants of Gurma) and Kengwa (aboriginies of the Illo region).

At Katsina also the old wall (larger in diameter than the present one) is called the " Ganua Amina " (wall of Amina), being the wall, we may presume, that was first built by Ali Murabus. (1355).

The " cousinship " which, in native phrase is said to exist between Katsina and Kebbi thus means that they had a common origin in Katsina Laka under Melle influence. Furthermore there is no need to question the recorded fact that the Askia conquered Katsina, as Barth does, on account of distance, since the Katsina in question was probably not the modern town of Katsina at all but some town or towns in the Kogo-Kotonkoro region. There is nothing improbable about such an expedition.

As early as 1235-1260, Mari Jatah, the Mansa (King) of Melle, had conquered Ghanata, and according to Makrisi, the dominance of Melle over the older Songhay was established not very long afterwards, till towards 1311 Mansa Musa (Kunkur Musa) developed an " aggressive strength without measure or limit," while towards 1370 the Wangara converted Kano to Islam.

At this time the city of Zaria did not exist; for, according to tradition, the founders of Zagzag, though they are said to have been of the same race as the founders of the other Hausa States settled successively at Rikochi, Wuchicherri and Turunku, eighteen miles south of Zaria, and only finally at the modern Zaria about 1536 A.D.

It is evident therefore that during the century 1200-1300 the Durbawa Kingdom (Katsina) at Durbi Takusheyi as also Zaria were of little account, and the most noteable state or tribal group in Hausaland next to Kano was Katsina Laka otherwise known as Guangara (Wangara).

From here, (Yandoto) probably in the first half of the 13th century, came the so-called Korau and became ruler not only of Katsina Laka but of the more northerly Katsina round M'bute and Durubi Takusheyi.

After an interval of about a century there succeeded to him another Korau who is called Muhammad Korau and is said to have been the first Moslem King.

From the surrounding circumstances we may conclude that this conversion to Islam was due, like that of Kano, rather later, to Wangara influence. Muhammad Korau was succeeded by a king called Ibrahim Sura, the latter word being a Melle title, and he by Ali Murabus who built the wall of the modern town of Katsina, apparently about 100 years before Agades, further north, was built in 1460 A.D.

Towards the end of the next century (1494) there ruled at Katsina the second Ibrahim, Ibrahim Maje. He reigned about the time of the visit to the Sudan of Abdul Magili of Tuwat who had corresponded with the great Es Suyuti. Ibrahim Maje was a contemporary of Haji Muhammad Askia of Songhay, in whose time Magili, after visiting Katsina and Kano, visited Gao.

In a work called Risalat al Maluk attributed to Es Suyuti and extant at Sokoto, Suyuti is said to have written a letter to Muhammad ibn Sottofe, Sultan of Agades, and Sultan Ibrahim of Katsina. Suyuti lived 1446-1505; so that the allusion there is probably to Ibrahim Maje who was the best known of the kings who ruled at Katsina during the zenith of Es Suyuti's fame.

The chronicle given below is derived from three separate lists extant in Katsina of which one is obviously more accurate than the other two, and has in general been followed, the controlling dates being the year 1018 A.H., which is specifically stated to have been the year of the death of Uban Yari, the 1419 A.D. total eclipse* of the sun which is said to have occurred in the time of Karyagiwa, and the known dates of Sheikh El Maghili of Tuwat and Jelal **Es Suyuti.**

---

* For a computation of the years of the total eclipses visible at Katsina I am indebted to the late Sir Robert Ball.

LIST OF KINGS OF KATSINA WITH SUCH MARGINAL NOTES AS ARE GIVEN ABOUT THEM IN THE THREE EXTANT LISTS OF KINGS.

Kumayo.—Was the first king—ruled 140 years.

Rumba Ramba.—Succeeded, conquered the town of Sawata in the Asben country.

Batare tare or Teryau.—Ruled 140 years.

Jernanata—Began war against the Gobirawa—ruled seventy years and died.

Sanau.—Killed by Korau—according to some by the Kaura of Katsina-Gumi*—ruled seventy-seven years.

Korau†.—Ruled sixty years, made war on the Kwararafa—was not of royal blood but by some said to have been a wrestler from Yandoto (Chafi).

Yanka Dari (Ibrahim).—Captured Kwiambana and Kotonkoro; ruled seventy years.

Jida-Yaki.—Ruled forty years; was continually at war with the Gobirawa. Up to the end of his time the kings were pagans.

Muhammad Korau.‡—Made war on the land of Nupe which

Circa 1100-1300

Circa 1320.

NOTES.

* *Circa 1200*—Gumi is on the Gulbin Zamfara near Bukwium.

† *Korau.*—In some lists Yanka Dari and Jida Yaki are placed before Korau, and Sanau is omitted. Probably one consideration was to keep the number of non-Moslem kings at the number seven.

It is also frequently stated that whereas Sanau was "black" Korau was "red."

Kotonkoro should mean "the Kwotto (i.e. Bassa tribes) of the Koro (red men)" i.e. the Bassa of the Kwotorkoshi region who were subject to the Koro i.e., Koro-r-afa. "Apa" Koro = Kwararafa.

Korau may have been as some say a "wrestler", but it is probably true that he was the Kaura (principal chief) of Katsina equivalent to the Madawaki at Kano. He came from Katsina Gumi, the equivalent in those days of Katsina Gusau, or Katsina Laka or Yandoto.

‡ *Circa 1320—Muhammad Korau.*—Ahmed Baba, the Timbuctu historian speaks of Borgu or Barbu (i.e. the present Borgu) as having been a Province of the kings of Melle (1260-1464), though it was never entirely subjected to them. We may thus infer that it had formed part of the Kukia (Songhay) Kingdom, and had offered a more or less successful resistance to the kings of Melle who were the nobles (Mari) of the Aswanik or Wakore (Wangara).

Sonni Ali of Songhay, 1492, died while returning from an expedition against the Fulani and Zoghoran (Zoromawa or Zugurma) who lived in the vicinity of Borgu and Gurma.

Muhammad Korau was thus probably converted by Wangara divines from Melle and Jenne, some of whom had settled in Kano. Ibrahim Sura was probably a Ba-Wangari who had risen to power during Muhammad Korau's reign.

It is curious that about this same time Ali Kolon (1335) should regain the kingdom of Gao and another Kolo or Korau should succeed to the kingdom of Katsina.

It was probably during the 14th century that the Sulibawa tribe of Fulani who in origin are half Fulani and half Wangara, came to Katsina, and settled in the regions of Shinkafi and Bugaji, north of the town.

The Sulibawa were an important element in Katsina long before the Jihad of Othman Dan Hodio, and it is from them that the Fulani Durbis of Mani, and present Emir of Katsina, Haj Muhammad Diko, are descended.

It may be observed that the Habe mosque at Katsina—in part still standing—was apparently built on the model of those of Gao and Jenne in the quarter called Anbara.

was at that time on the Katsina boundary. In his time Islam was introduced. Ibrahim Sura helped him.

1353.	*Ibrahim Sura*.*
1355.	*Ali Murabus†.*—May God pardon him. Amen. He began to build the city of Katsina.
1380.	*Muhammad Toya Rero.*
1419.	*Aliu Karya Giwa.*—Succeeded as a boy. In his time was a total eclipse of the sun. He made war on Yauri.
1431.	*Tsaga Rana.*
1480.	*Ali Jan Hazo.*
1482.	*Muhammad Mai Sa Maza Gudu.*
1484.	*Ali Jan Hazo.*
1486.	*Usuman Tsagarana.*—Son of Jan Hazo‡.

---

* *Circa 1353—Ibrahim Sura.*—Sura is a Wangara title. It is noticeable also that the heir presumptive to the title of Durbi (the most important chief in Habe times) had the title Dan Brahim (Ibrahim), so that very possibly Ibrahim Sura held the office of Durbi.

† *Circa 1355—Ali Murabus.*—The word is really Murabut, *i.e.*, the 'anchorite' or 'religious devotee.' In its plural Murabatin, the word is used to denote the Berber Muslim fanatics who overran Africa 900—1100 A.D. They sacked Andogast 1052, and made the Ghana Empire tributary after 1076 A.D. when they took Ghanata itself.

As Leo Africanus who visited Katsina towards the end of the 15th century speaks of grass-huts but not of a walled town, it is evident that Ali did not complete the wall of Katsina.

On the other hand the names of certain old quarters of Katsina town indicate how great the influence of Melle and Songhay was in Katsina, *e.g.*.

Anbara—the quarter of the old mosque.
Tudun Melle—one of the oldest quarters (market).
Tawatinke—Inke is a Wangara suffix *i.e.*, 'people of Tuwat.'
Gamberawa—*i.e.* people of half-Berber extraction from the west.
Lolokin Kabbawa—Kebbi people.
Kogoyawa—People of Kogo (Yandoto).
Gogo-wa-ri (Gogwari)—people of Gao or Gago.
Kantarawa—people of Kanta.
Ungwa Koni—place of the Koror-afa.
Barazaki—inhabited by Barazakanya. In the ancient Kukiya (Kaukau) on the Niger (*teste* Bekri 1050 A.D.) were a class of traders or artificers called by the Arabs 'Bazurkaniin' or Basur Kayin.

The Barazakanya at Katsina were specialists in leather coats of mail and leather horse trappings, stirrup leathers, etc.

At Katsina were titles, Lambisa, and Dan Sonwe (Songhay). The latter was also a title at Daura, the duty of the holder being to announce the appearance of the moon at the Moslem Festivals.

The leather working for which Agades is famous was introduced by the Songhay. Even in 1850, the majority of the more important merchants at Katsina were Wangara.

‡ *Circa 1486—Usuman Tsagarana.*—It would appear that about the year 1500 the great Kanta of Leka, then a vassal of Haj Muhammad Askia of Gao (Songhay) had been raiding the Amakitan who had recently established themselves as masters of Air, and in particular the new town of Agades, with much success. They very naturally sought help from their kinsmen the Beriberi (Barbars) of Bornu, to wit Mai Ali Ghaji Dunamami who had some years previously been settled in the Yamia and Gure region, before he founded N'gazargamu near Geidam towards 1472 A.D.

Mai Ali, in response to this appeal, advanced through Sosa-baki (the Munio and Damagram region) north of Daura and south of Gobir, on Surame in Kebbi which was evacuated by Kanta.

Maje Ibrahim.—He ordered the people of Katsina to marry **1494.**
and made them pray. He ordered all the inhabitants to make
praying places, and those who did not obey to be imprisoned. In
his time there were many learned men (Mallams). He used the
expression "yunka yunka." When he was about to confer on
a man some honour he would say "yunka yunka pay a thousand
(cowries)." **Circa**
Abd ul Karim. **1520.**
Ashafa.—(Reigned eight days).
Ibrahim Gamdawa (or Gamda). **1523.**
Muhammad Wari.—Son of Abd ul Karim. **1533.**
Suleiman. **1545.**
Usuman Mayi Nawa.—Son of Tsaga Rana. **1557.**
Muhammad Toya Rero. **1576.**
Muhammad Wari Yanka Dari.—Son of Jan Hazo. **1592.**
Uban Yari (Muhammad Dan Wari).—He died on a Monday **1595.**
1018 A.H. A manuscript reads: "In his time Magani mai
anfanin Baki was slain at Kano, as also Sarkin Kano Kutumbi
and his successor Al Haji Sarkin Kano and their Makama. Also
there was war between him and the Zamfarawa" but this pro-
bably refers to a king in the middle of the 17th century since at that
time there was war with Zamfarawa. The date of the death of
Kutumbi and his son, *vide* the Kano Chronicle, was 1648-49. **Circa**
Karya Giwa. **1609.**
Jan Hazo.—Son of Muhammad Wari. **1618.**
Tsagarana Hasan.—Son of Toiyarero succeeded Jan Hazo. **1648.**
Muhammad Kabiya (Wari Maikerayi).—Son of Usuman. **1657.**
Tsagarana Yahaya. **1669.**
Karya Giwa Duban.—Son of Jan Hazo (Karya Giwa Duban). **1688.**
Muhammad Wari.—Sacked Marachi in Zaria country (between **1715.**
Zaria and Birnin Gwari).
Karya Giwa. **1733.**
Agwaragi Maikerayi.—Devastated Gobir and executed Sarkin **1750.**
Gobir Yakubu, hence the Gobirawa got their nickname
"amazeya" (runaways).
Tsagarana Gwozo.—A warrior. When he became king he **1767.**
attacked and took Karashi and passed on and took Anka and also

---

Shortly afterwards Kanta in turn took the initiative and advanced by
the more southern route through the Katsina Laka and Kazaure region to
N'guru (in the west of Bornu) where he defeated the Mai of Bornu, it is
said, in seven battles.

On his way home he had camped at Dan Ashita near the rock of Dugul
not far from Ingawa in Katsina Emirate, when, according to the legends,
leaves of Rimi (silk-cotton) trees, the Rimin Dan Ashita, fell on him and
caused his death. Timbuctu authors ascribe his death to a poisoned arrow,
but in any case it is agreed that (*a*) no Kebbi man will even look at the
silk-cotton trees of Dan Ashita (*b*) Kanta was embalmed by the body being
placed over a smoke fire and carried back to Surame.

Between 1536 and 1556, Askia Daud made an expedition against Busa.
"Busa was completely ruined," writes Es Saidi, "and a great number of
persons perished in the waters nearby," (the rapids).

Gumi. Thence he went to Bini* (Beni) near Madaro and eat it. He returned to Dokau (near Kotonkoro) and died there. His tomb is at Dokau. To him succeeded Bawa Dan Gima son of the "Bakon Sanau" (*i.e.* Korau).

1771. *Bawa Dan Gima.*—He it was who opened the house which the Habe had covered with red leather, which was considered the "seat of power", and which the ancestors of the king had not allowed to be opened for fear war would ensue. When he opened the house, Belbela (aegrets) came out and filled the whole town.

1801-1804. *Maremawa Mahmud.*—Killed by the Fulani Mallam Umaru.

1805-1807. *Magajin Halidu†.*—Driven to Dankama where he fell into a well, Mallam Umaru becoming first Fulani Emir of Katsina.

---

* *Circa 1767—Bini country near Madaro*—Bini country is north of Kotonkoro, and Madaro is west of Kogo and Chafi and south of Gusau. Throughout this region, as well as in Sokoto, Dendi and Borgu, a caste of artificers, metal workers, and leather workers, etc., exists and has since the days of the Songhay Empire, been called Zogoran, Zugu, Zugurma or Zoromawa. They are distinct from the other populations and seem to have come into the country with the so-called 'Kisara' (Zaghawa) migration 600-1000 A.D. It is probable that from them originally came the Nupe metal workers and not improbably those of Benin as well.

† *Circa 1805-1807—Magajin Halidu.*—The successors of Korau reigned from about 1260 A.D. but the (Diggera) Durbawa remained electors to the Kingship, and were repositories of everything connected with magic. The ruling Sarki was, in early times, not allowed to die of old age or ill-health, but was strangled by the official called Karyagiwa. The new King was elected either by some rite with the sacred snake, or by throwing a spear into the ground. If the spear remained upright when the name of the candidate was called, the nomination was confirmed. The new King was then put on a bed and a black-ox was slaughtered above him at the Kan-Giwa (centre of the town) so that he was drenched in its blood. The skin of this ox was then taken to the palace and the deceased Chief put inside it and dragged on the ground to the place of burial. The body was buried in an upright squatting position. After a while the Durbawa, it is said, lost their exclusive right of nomination, which became vested in the three Chiefs —Kaura, Galladima and Durubi.

Contemporary history shows the probability of Katsina having become a fief of the Melle Empire towards the close of the fifteenth century; it was therefore natural that the Askia should attack it, as he did in 1513. At the beginning of the sixteenth century Katsina was disputed between Bornu and Songhay and later between Bornu and Kebbi. At the beginning of the eighteenth century the Kingdom probably reached its greatest extent, including as it then did Maradi and Zamfara and the west as far as Kotonkoro and Yauri. At the end of the eighteenth century, however, Gobir robbed Katsina of Zamfara. On the outbreak of the Fulani Jihad, circ. 1804, the Sarkin Musulmi gave a flag to Na Alhaji, whose ancestors (possibly his father) came from Melle. He had started a school south of Katsina and was married to a daughter of the Hausa Sarkin Katsina. His attempts to subdue the Hausas were ineffectual, and he is said to have died of a poisoned robe given him by his father-in-law, the then Sarkin Katsina. On his death Mallam Umoru, with support from Sokoto, succeeded in establishing Fulani rule over Katsina.

According to Barth the Kings called 'Habe' in a special sense of that word, from Uban Yari down to the last Habe King, Magajin Halidu, who was ousted by the Fulani in 1807,—*i.e.*, the Kings from Uban Yari onwards (169 years)—represent a different dynasty to the preceding Kings. Further he states that a new dynasty began fifty years after the beginning of the reign of the first Muslim King, *i.e.*, with Ibrahim Sura—who would appear to have been probably of Wangara (Melle) extraction.

If Barth's information was correct therefore there were three dynasties:—
1. The Durbawa or Diggera.
2. A dynasty of Wangara origin.
3. The Habe properly so-called.

Members of the two latter seem in most cases to have borne either the surname Tsaga-rana (i.e., eclipser of the sun) or Jan Hazo (red mist of the Harmattan wind), and some the title Karyagiwa i.e., originally the man who broke or throttled the ' Giwa ' (King). Several Kings also have the title Mai Kerayi, i.e., ' carrier of the Kere,' which was a wooden throwing-stick shaped much like a battle-axe and also possibly designed to resemble the humerus and clavicle of a man, i.e the " Royal humerus " which was an emblem of sovereignty.

From about 1450 onwards Katsina was subject to Bornu to some extent and each king when he succeeded sent a tribute (Gaisua) of 100 slaves to N'gazargamu, the Bornu capital. In the time of the Sarkin Kano Muhammad Rimfa (1463-1499) there was a war of eleven years duration between Kano and Katsina, neither side getting the upper hand, but Abd-ul-Lahi, Rimfa's successor (1499-1509) is said to have gained victories over Katsina. Mohamma Shashere 1573-1582 was defeated by Katsina, but Mohamma Zaki 1582-1618, on the other hand, was victorious. Both Sarki Kutumbi of Kano and his son Al Haji (1648-49) were killed in battle by the Katsinawa after which a treaty of peace was made between Kano and Katsina.

This treaty of peace was probably, in some measure, due to a common fear of the Kwararafa, whose capital lay on the Gongola in the region of Kalam, Biyri and Kunde, and who at this time seem to have been very powerful. In 1653, their chief, the Adashu (so written by the Kano Chronicle), in reality the Ada (Attah) Achuwo (great) invaded Kano, and in 1671 the Kwararafa returned and actually took Kano city.

About the same time they besieged the Mai of Bornu, Mai Ali Umarmi (Ali Tair) in his capital at N'gazargamu, but were driven back and apparently severely defeated about 1680.

At this time there was resident in Katsina a famous Mu'allim, called Dan Marina, who was a contemporary with the equally famous Dan Masani, who wrote a history of the Yorubas. Dan Marina composed an ode in Arabic to celebrate the victory of Mai Ali over the Kwararafa which is still extant, and may be translated as follows:—

The Said Muhammad ibn Sabaghi (May God pardon him) in praise of Amir ul Muminin Ali, Sultan of Bornu and in censure of the Kwararafa.

" Ali has triumphed over the heathen, a matchless triumph in the path
" of God.
" No Sultan like him: A Laith among Laiths, ever stout of heart.
" Has he not brought us succour? Verily but for him
" Our hearts had never ceased from dread of the unbelievers.
" Narrow had become to us the earth pressed by the foe,
" Till Ali saved our children and their children yet unborn.
" O people! Say with one accord ' May God grant him recompense for
" our deliverance.
" He drove back to their furthest borders the army of the Jukon,
" And God scattered their host disheartened.
" I heard that Ali, the Amir ul Muminin,
" Went to the land of the heathen and there lay in wait for them.
" O God help him and give him a goodly reward.
" Strengthen us, and give us sustenance.
" Luwefaru worked iniquity in the Sudan, in his over-weening pride,
" Stalking forth with the stride of a tyrant, and setting his promises at
" nought,
" As though he weened that ne'er would a peer subdue him
" He and his people spared not rivers nor cities;
" The Kwararafa followed the track of his doom, and their hour too
" Passed to the grasping palm of the fortunate Prince,

The information provided by these written lists of kings is unfortunately scanty, but what little remains is both interesting and significant, *in primis*, the reference to Sawata in Ahir, and the Gobirawa, and then the expeditions against the Kwararafa, Kwiambana, Kotonkoro, Nupe and Yauri which may be roughly dated as follows:—

War with Sawata in Asben	1100-1200 A.D.
First war against Gobir	1200 A.D.
War against Kwararafa, in the Busa and Karashi region	1220 A.D.
War against Kwiambana and Kotonkoro (Kwararafa)	1260 A.D.
Continual war against Gobir	1300 A.D.
War against Nupe	1320 A.D.
War against Yauri	1419 A.D.

Sawata is a walled town still in being, about two marches north-west of Agades on the track to Ghat. Rumba's expedition must have taken place between 1100–1200, at which time Agades (founded about 1460) was not built. Sawata which is possibly a variant of Samta, was thus in the neighbourhood of Tin Shaman, the old capital of Ahir, which is about twenty miles north-west of Agades and west of the Agades-Ghat road.

The Barbars or Tuwareg are not and never were town dwellers so that the inhabitants of Sawata must have been negro or negroid —a settled population. On the other hand the Katsina people must have been in mode of life, equipment, and nature Barbar or semi-Barbar peoples or they could not have undertaken an expedition of this nature in a desert country.

In 1353 Tegidda (Takadda) three marches west-south-west of Agades in the direction of Gao on the Upper Niger was a flourishing Saharan trade centre. Tin Shaman and Sawata would be about on the line of caravan march between Tegidda and the wells of Asiu whence the roads lead to Ghat and Zeila (Murzuk) respectively.

This expedition to Sawata probably took place at about the time the rule of the Gobirawa in Asben was, as the Asben chronicles say "growing weak," for it was in consequence of this

---

"The pious Haji to the Holy Cities, who in this world and the next has
  "earned the pilgrims highest reward:
"Always fasting and waging war, winning thereby to God's face and
  "safe mercy.
"Give thanks again for what our Mai Ali has wrought;
"For he has ransomed the whole Sudan from strife.
"This is the meed of praise of the servant of God.
"The Sheikh the Said Hamid.
"Upon Ali, King of the two rivers, who stayed war.
"I, Dan Marina, fear no one save the savage, whose law is greed.
"Praise be to God and thanks for his deliverance from the pride of the
  "rebellious.
"And thanksgiving and peace upon the Prophet, the guide to God,
  "our refuge."

End of the Qasida of Ibn Sabaghi in praise of Amir ul Muminin. The blessing of God on the Prophet, after whom is no other.

weakness that the Gobir kings of Asben were conquered by the Barbar Imakitan (Beriberi), and went south to the region of Chibiri.

They were no doubt settled in Chibiri, the present Gobir, when, possibly about 1200, this first Gobir war of Katsina took place. In 1353, Gobir was (*vide* Ibn Batuta) much where it is now and the continual raids between Katsina and Gobir were going on which lasted down to the 19th century.

From about the year 1260 onwards, the old Kukia Kingdom on the Niger had fallen into decay and became more or less subject to the rising power of Melle. The new Songhay—the second Songhay Empire—did not become powerful till about 1460.

It was during the interval 1260-1433 when Melle was supreme, that the kings of Katsina began to lay hands on territory east of the Niger, which had probably before that time been more or less under the protection of Kukia. The region was apparently, if we may believe tradition, ruled by the Kwararafa (so-called followers of Kisara) who had established themselves in the regions stretching from Zaria to Karshi, Busa and Illo in Dendi, who were in origin Zaghawa.*

Attacks of Katsina from about 1220 onwards were possibly responsible for driving the Nupe (who lived north and north-west of the Kaduna) into the country of the "Bini" who lived in the region of the modern Bida.

No sooner was this done however than it would seem that the Melle power under Mansa Musa I (1311-1331), Mansa Suleiman (1335), and the Wazir of Mansa Musa II named Mari Jatah (1373-1387) began to push west, and succeeded in gaining an ascendancy over these same regions, whence part of them—Katsina Laka—was actually called Wangara (Guangara).

The rise of Sonni Ali of Songhay however (1464-1492) and of the Kanta of Kebbi about 1516 again changed the political groupings. Yauri which had no doubt been a fief first of Songhay, then of Melle, then of Songhay again, had to stand by itself and it was attacked by the King of Katsina in 1419-1431 while Busa was sacked by the Askia of Songhay in 1555. From that time onwards, the power of Katsina extended to the Kaduna in the south and the Niger on the west.

To gain a clear idea of these local wars and histories it is however necessary to glance at the general history of the Niger valley.

As early as 680 A.D. (Barth) there had been founded on the Upper Niger, about eight days south of the later Gao, the commercial town of Kukia†, which was a focus of the desert trade. Its rulers are said to have been of the same race as those of Kanem *i.e.* Zaghawa of so-called Libyan stock (Leo Africanus). Like the Bornu kings they afterwards said they came from Yaman.

Their ruler had the title "Kanda" a title afterwards adopted by the rulers of Kebbi in the form Kanta, which is probably the Barbar word Kinta (mother), as in Kintakit (Candace).

---

* The Arab writer Al Hallebi states that "the kingdom of Kaukau "became peopled like the land of the Zaghawa, when the hand of the "Zaghawa extended itself."

† Kukia was most probably in the Dendi region.

At this time the other great power in the west was a kingdom of probably similar origin so far as the ruling race was concerned, *i.e.* the kingdom lying north-west of the " buckle " of the Niger and having as capitals successively, Ghana or Ghanata and Walata or Biru—the title of the ruler however being Ghana.

The Kukia Kingdom is known as the first Songhay Empire. Though before 900 A.D. the town of Gao to the north had eclipsed Kukia in commercial importance, the Kanda ordinarily resided at Kukia till 961 A.D. at least.

But about 1235-1260 A.D. the King of Melle, further west, who had the title Mansa (Mensa) made the Songhay or Kukia Gao Kingdom subject to Melle, and though the Songhay Prince Sonni Ali Kolon, about 1335, was able to assert a certain degree of independence, it was not till the time of Sonni Ali (1464-1492) that the Songhay power really reasserted itself—the second Songhay Empire—and again pushed west down the middle Niger under the Askia (Sikia) who usurped the throne after Sonni Ali's death.

Now the subject population of the kings of Ghana as well as the ruling caste of the Melle Empire which outlived Ghana, was composed very largely, perhaps in the main, of subject peoples of half Barbar extraction called in general Wakore or Wa-n-gara, who corresponded more or less to the older Saharan races. Thus the Susu who laid waste Ghana about 1203 A.D. are said to have been related to the Wakore, while again the Aswanek, Sarakolli, or Sarankwolli would appear to have been in origin a particular type of the Wa-n-gara—the name Wangara being in fact the counterpart in the west of the Garawan or Gura'an further east.

Though the name Wangara is often supposed to be a mere synonym for the later Mandingo peoples, that is not really so. In origin only the Mandingo were a branch of the Wangara. It may be said in fact, apart from the actual ruling dynasties and their immediate entourage, and apart from the later external influence of the Fulani, that the factor which welded the more primitive negro tribes and communities of the western Sudan into states and kingdoms, having a certain degree of civilization, was the half Barbar Wakore or Wangara, who gradually fused with the indigenous populations till they became part of them. Very naturally records, mainly collected by the learned men of Timbuctu, such as Es Saidi who wrote the Tarikh Es Sudan, have concerned themselves more with the ruling families than with the composition of the subject peoples, and naturally also these records are in some degree attuned and adapted to commend themselves to Moslem sentiment, as for instance the descent of the King of Melle is claimed to be from Abu Talib, and a Yamanite origin is ascribed to the Kanda of Kukia.

But if we shed those parts of the recorded history of Kukia and Songhay which are obviously adornments, we find that the accounts of the rise of Songhay which are given by such writers as Ahmed Baba and Es Saidi are very closely parallel to legends which are still current in Hausaland about migrations which can hardly be other than connected with, if they are not quite the same migrations of Barbar peoples which led to the founding of Kukia and Gao.

The legends in question—called the 'Kisara' legends—are to the effect that about 600 A.D. after the Persian invasion of Egypt, a hero Kisara lead his people *via* Kordofan, Darfur, Lake Fitri, Mandara, Yola, and Keffi to the region of Zaria and Karashi. There they split into parties; some going to found the kingdoms of Busa, and Illo on the Niger (the Dendi region whence, according to the western authorities, Songhay originated), while others went south to the regions of Wukari and Panda on the Benue. One chief went to the land of the Gara, which was called from his title of Ata* (father), Attagara, *i.e.* Idah.

Native tradition, supported in some degree by Portugeese records, asserts that before 1200 A.D. there was some kind of a civilization at Edo or Addo which lay about opposite Idah, on the right bank of the Niger, and that the Edos or Addos became the ruling race of the Bini or Benin Kingdom to the south of them. The Edo were replaced about 1200 A.D. by a Yoruba ruler sent from Ife which presumably was pre-existing, for, according to the Oni of Ife, the Edo or Addo had originally gone out from Ife to found their original capital Edo, south of Okeni, from which they came down to Benin.

We arrive then, following these native traditions, at the conclusion that Ife must have been in existence as a religious and sacrosanct centre soon after 1000 A.D. and must have had, even at that date, lines of communication with the races which are now called Yoruba, races which following quite other traditions and evidence, came down to the Oyo and Ife region from the Niger, above Busa.

The Edo civilization, as we have seen, came from Ife; and Ife is bound up with the Yoruba civilization.

On the other hand, Idah, Wukari, and the Kwararafa in general, called Apa, are different in language and in cult, and are not immediately related to the Yoruba group, though they are related to the Nupes who are by the Yorubas called Tapa.

As has been noted above, the original inhabitants of the Bida region, now called Nupe, were called Bini, and the element which, according to themselves, founded the Nupe Kingdom, came from the regions across the Kaduna to the north-west of them· that is to say, the Nupes came from the Zaria-Karashi region in which the Kwararafa Kisara migration are said to have stayed some time (300 years it is said), and thence separated to Idah, Wukari, Busa, etc. Between 1400-1500 however Bida was again colonized by the so-called "Edeji," *i.e.* other "Apas" who came up the Niger from Idah and founded a Nupe Kingdom first at Nupiko at the mouth of the Kaduna, and later at Raba and Mokwa.

If it be held that the Apa peoples, *i.e.* Nupe, Idah, Wukari, etc., had no direct share in the genesis of Ife, the most reasonable hypothesis concerning Ife as "centre of the world" as early as 1000 A.D. is that it was an offshoot or colony of either Ghana or ancient Kukia, *i.e.* that the influence of Ghana, Kukia or both, extended down the Niger through Illo, Busa and Yauri to Oyo and Ife. It

---

* Ada is the southern Tamashek word for father, a meaning it also has in Nupe.

was probably then from Ghanata, Melle or Kukia that the Yoruba masks and statues and other antiquities come, having been conveyed to one or more of these places across the desert from some of the Roman towns which abounded in North Africa *via* Wargelan or Bulma. That the ruler of Moshi was called "Ogan" which certainly came from the title "Ghana" of Ghana or Ghanata, goes to show that this same word "Ogan" used to denote another Ganeth (Ghanata) by which name Benin was also known, came from the same source.

It will be apparent therefore that the "Nupe" which Muhammad Korau attacked about 1320, was the same Nupe or Yufi which Ibn Batuta (in 1350) speaks of as existing on the Niger near large rocks to the south of Gao and Timbuctu, *i.e.* Jebba. The Nupes were, in other words, more or less the same people as the Kwararafa, which Korau I and his successors are said to have attacked a century earlier, in the region of Kwiambana and Kotonkoro. In fact the word Nupe would seem to be the equivalent of Bepe or Bepi, the name of the old Jukon (Apa) capital south of the Benue not far from Wukari. It is said that "Nupe" is really for Anu-ipe which means "city" or "big town."

The subject populations of these regions at that time, 1320 A.D. had probably remained very much the same as those which El Bekri describes as constituting the peoples ruled by the ancient Kukia, but the governing classes would seem, in the main, to have been either (a) descendants of the so-called Kisara, or (b) other semi-Barbar peoples of much the same type.

Kukia or Kaugha, the first Songhay capital was most probably situated on a tributary of the Niger somewhere between Illo and Garu (Sinder). The modern capital of this region (Dendi), is Say, and among its chief towns are Gaya Kirotashi.

The chief districts of Dendi were Kenga and Zagha, with its variant names Zaghai, Sakai, Songhay, or Sonwai. According to M. Delafosse, the earliest Songhays were fishermen (Sorko), and agriculturists (Gabibi) who came up the Niger from the region of Dendi, the former becoming the dominant race.

But at some early period this Dendi country was occupied by Barbars other than the modern tribes of Tuwareg, and these Barbars had some linguistic affinity to the Bornu Barbars, for otherwise the place and other names could not show such remarkable similarity to those of Bornu.

This cannot be accounted for by conquests since 1000 A.D. for there were none, if we except one expedition or raid, for it was nothing more, by Mai Ali Ghaji Dunamami to Surame in Kebbi about 1500.

If then in origin the kingdoms of Bornu and Songhay had a common factor, that factor can hardly have been other than the Zaghawa Barbars who were in fact the early kings of Kanem. Their coming to Dendi (whence Songhay grew) must have been the so-called migration of Kisara, which in Hausaland is held to be responsible for the kingdoms of Illo (in Dendi) and Busa, as well as the Kwararafa Kingdoms, which were so powerful in the middle ages and still claim kinship with the Saifawa of Bornu.

The Wangara or Wakore or Aswanik, on the other hand, were originally the subject Barbar population of the Gana, Ganar, (whence Canarii) Empire which lay north-west of the Upper Niger. They were western Barbars. When the first or so-called Ghana Empire came to an end, submerged first by the Sanhaja Tuwareg (about 1000 A.D.), and later by the Susu (about 1200 A.D.), they founded a new Wangara State called Mali or Melle, having its centre to the south of Bamako on the Niger, beyond the Kenie rapids.

In the Strasburg map published in 1513, the Kingdom of Melle appears under the name of Regnun Musa Melle de Ginoria (Ganar)*.

The ethnic composition of Ghana and the later Melle were thus much the same, differing from that of Songhay which drew its subject population from the Niger Valley, and its rulers from the east (Zaghawa).

It is noticeable, on the other hand, that the word Gago (Gao), the name of the capital of the Songhay Empire is the ordinary title for a chief both on the middle Niger (Jebba region), and among the Nupes and Apa in the Idoma region (Idah). It is possible that this word has some connection with the Kanuri word for 'twin', 'Kagu,' and 'Kagua' which was a name of the sacred grove at Kano, where probably the royal umbelicus was buried. The two rather remarkable bronze statues which are kept on the Nupe island at Jebba are called Gagos; the male having Kambari face marks, the female the body marks of the Nupe and Jukun.

Beginning at the point where the Niger turns south, we have:—

(a) At the turn a low lying grassy region called the "Burum" a name which is the same as the old name for the Bahr-el-Ghazal in Kanem, a similar kind of region.

(b) Gago or Gao similar to and confused by mediaeval authors with Gaoga or Kaugha, the name of the Kingdom of the Bulala at Lake Fitri.

(c) A region called "Bornu Gungu."

(d) A region called Kendaji, *i.e.* people of the Kanda or Kanta, ruler of the old Kukia, probably the Kinta (mother) of the Zaghawa eastern Barbars.

(e) The town now called Sinder (Zinder) formerly called Garu (Bornu word for city or town).

(f) A few miles from Sinder is Neni the island where Muhammad Askia, a native of Songhay, was born.

(g) On the right bank on the northern edge of the Zabarma country comes the old site of "Birni," surrounded by a rocky eminence which in general is called Sare-goru ("declivity of the city") and in particular "Birni" which is purely a Bornu word in origin.

Just south of "Birni" is a village called Kolon-te and a chasm of hills called Kiru-gaji.

---

* Barth, iv, 413.

(h) After passing Say on the left bank comes Kiru-tashi; below it, Gaya, where according to the Illo legends Kisara and his peoples are supposed to have crossed the Niger; then Illo.

Of Sare-goru Barth writes—"no doubt this was formerly a place of considerable importance, and in this respect the name Birni is not less remarkable than that of Sare-goru."

Sare or Sara (the first vowel being short) was the Songhay word for city, whence the Hausas adapted their word for king, in Songhay Sara-koy, in Hausa Sara-ki.

It seems probable that Ki-Sara (Kisara) is composed of these words in reverse order, and that Korishen or Karishen, the famous Kisara town near Kwoto-n-Koro (Kotonkoro) is cognate to the names Kirotashi and Kiro-gaji, and the name of the Songhay Prince who escaped from the Melle in 1335, Ali Kilun. (r. and l. being interchangeable).

The root common to these names is that contained in Hausa " Kolo ", " Koro ", " Kili " and " Kore, etc., a root more or less common to the countries on the edge of the desert, and meaning white, pale-green, or pink.

The explanation of the variant juxtaposition of ' ki ' in Ki-Sara and Sara-ki may be that " ki " in the Zaghawa language (as for instance in Kita-ki, Candace) was a genitival suffix. In Zaghawi Kisar actually means father. The " sar " or " saru ", *i.e.* town was perhaps first the residence of the " Kisar " (father), and when the town, so to speak, outstripped the " father ", its Kings grew to be called after the town, " Sarki ". At Busa the royal title is Ki.

We may compare in this connection the account of the origin of the kingdom of Wagadu (as given in M. Delafosse's *Traditions du Soudan Occidental*).

" The first king of their dynasty was the king of Wagadu, and this is the manner in which this kingdom was set up. It is related that one Digna son of Kiri* Jon son of Tamaganke son of Yugu Dumbesse, son of Job, son of Solomon, son of David, arrived from the east with his companions. He had with him 300 magicians and the chief of these was Karabara Jadane, ancestor of the clan of the Sudoro. They pursued their journey until they arrived at a town called Jenne and stopped there for a long time. Then he removed himself with his tribe from Jenne in order to proceed to Jâga where he married a native woman named Aisa Kulle Sudoro by whom he had two children, one named Ja Fune, ancestor of the Soninke clan known as Jikine. He was the first to establish himself in the province of Jafun. The other, named Jagaba Fune, was the ancestor of the clan known as the Suare. He established himself at Jagaba. Then Digna left Jaga with his tribe and arrived in the province of Kingui. They stopped at a place called Daraga, near Joga. When Digna sent people to draw water from

---

* *Kiri* was a royal title in the Christian Dongola kingdom (*see* Quatremère Notices on Egypt). Possibly ' Kiri Jon ' is really meant for Kiri John, *i.e.*, the fabulous " Prester John."

the well the Jinn of the well prevented them. Digna uttered a cry in the face of the Jinn and the Jinn became blind and had to sit down. The Jinn then uttered a cry in Digna's face and Digna became blind and dumb. Digna then summoned his chief magician who rendered the Jinn dumb and impotent. Finally Digna made a pact with the Jinn and married three of the daughters of the Jinn by whom he had numerous offspring including a serpent called Wagadu Bida. Among the children were Tere-Kine, ancestor of the Sokona, Wagara Guide, ancestor of the Semega, Tugamadi Kabuda, ancestor of the Jabira, and Mamadi, ancestor of the Ture Kankajâbe.

"Digna being old and blind said one day to his eldest son (Tere-Kine) "If you give me some roast meat I will bestow on you the royal talisman." Tere-Kine went off hunting. The chief magician had overheard Digna's request and told Maghan Jâbe the younger son who slew an ox, roasted the flesh and clothed himself in the skin in order to simulate the appearance of his brother Tere-Kine who was a hairy man. His father said "Your voice is the voice of Jabe, but your body is that of Kine." So Digna ate the flesh and bestowed the talisman on Maghan Jabe. When the trick was discovered Digna bestowed the power of rain-making on Tere-Kine.

"Later Jabe went to Kumbi and when he cut down a large tree there, the python, offspring of Digna, suddenly appeared in the well and from the branches of the tree fell a magical drum. 9,999 horsemen suddenly appeared; among them were four chiefs (i) Wagane Sako, ancestor of the Sako, (ii) Jaumi-rao Sokona* ancestor of the Jaguraga, (iii) Maka Dumbe Silla, ancestor of the Silla, (iv) Gumate Fade, ancestor of the Yaressi. Jabe was chosen chief. The python demanded that sacrifice should be offered to him and every year the most beautiful woman in the land was offered. Jabe died and was succeeded by Maghan Tane, Maghan Mamadi, Maghan Kaya in whose reign Wagadu was destroyed through one Mamadi slaying the python. The python had seven heads. The python's last head when severed went to Bure and that is why gold abounds in Bure. After that some of the people of Wagadu went east and some went west."

---

*Fulfulde name for God. cf. p. 75.

LX.—THE KANO CHRONICLE.

Introductory.

The Hausa States, which form a large portion of the country now called Nigeria, have been ruled since the beginning of the nineteenth century by Fulani, who, under their chief Othman Dan Hodio, about the year 1807, ousted the former Hausa rulers on the plea of a religious revival. As it was known that Arabic literature and the Moslem faith had been introduced in the fifteenth century at latest, it was natural to suppose that some records had been kept of the reigns of the Hausa kings (Sarkis). Little, however, had in 1903 come to light except for two manuscripts which Dr. Barth discovered in Bornu dealing with that country, and the Kano Chronicle, of which there are several copies in existence, and which is mentioned by Lady Lugard (Tropical Dependency, p. 236). The copy, however, to which Lady Lugard alludes, is not complete, since only forty-two kings or Sarkis are mentioned. The manuscript which I have attempted to translate below, was found at Sabongari, near Katsina, and goes down to, and breaks off in, the time of Mohammad Belo, the forty-eighth Sarki.

The manuscript itself is of no great age, and must on internal evidence have been written during the latter part of the decade 1883-1893; but it probably represents some earlier record which has now perished. It is said, and no doubt with some truth, that the Fulani, in their fanatical zeal, destroyed many old records and books, on the ground that they were the books of "Kafurai," for their *casus belli* was that the Hausa Sarkis were infidels, and as such deserved to be destroyed with all their works. The records on which the Chronicle must be based were apparently an exception. The authorship is unknown, and it is very difficult to make a guess. On the one hand the general style of the composition is quite unlike the usual "note" struck by the sons of Dan Hodio, Abdulahi and Muhammad Belo, and imitated by other Fulani writers. There is an almost complete absence of bias or partizanship. It is hardly possible that a Fulani mallam of the time of Dan Hodio, or even of the present time, could have related the expulsion of Mohamma Alwali, the last Hausa Sarki, without betraying his race. On the other hand, the style of the Arabic is not at all like that usually found in the compositions of Hausa Mallams of the present day; there are not nearly enough "classical tags", so to speak, in it. A young Arab in the employ of the writer, who, though he can read and write colloquial Tripoli and Ghadamis Arabic, found it difficult to construe the Arabic books which are most commonly found in Hausaland, read and translated the manuscript without difficulty. Kano was always visited by mallams from different parts of the Sahara and Barbary, and they often resided there for long periods. That the author of the work was thoroughly *au fait* with the Kano dialect of Hausa is evident from several phrases used in the book, for instance " ba râyi ba " used in a sense peculiar to Kano of " perforce." The original may perhaps have been written by some stranger from the north who settled in Kano, and collected the stories of former kings handed down by oral tradition.

The Chronicle has been translated as it stands, with the marginal notes of the text, in foot-notes. The names of the Sarkis (given in the margin) are merely for convenience of reference. I have added approximate dates worked out by simply reckoning back from the length of reigns given, assuming the date of the Fulani entry into Kano as September of A.D. 1807 (A.H. 1222), which a careful comparison of various accounts has led me to believe is about the right date.

In themselves the lengths of the various reigns as given in the text would not carry much weight perhaps. There is, however, some confirmation in one or two cases which makes one inclined to believe in their substantial accuracy.

In a work attributed to Shehu Dan Hodio, he quotes Jalàlu-l-Din es Suyuti in a work on the Sudan called Risalat ul Muluk as writing a letter to various kings, among whom were Mohamma Ibn Sotofa, Sarkin Agades, and Sarkin Ibrahim of Katsina. Suyuti died in 1505.

Again, in the same work, Dan Hodio quotes a letter from Ibn Abd ul Karim Magili to " Abi Abdulahi Dan Umoru Mohamma," written in A.H. 897, A.D. 1492, in reply to a letter from " Dan Umoru," who must be Mohamma Rimfa of Kano, asking for an abridged edition of the Mukhtassar of Sidi Khalil.

Sheikh ibn Abdul Karim el Maghili was of the Barbar tribe of Maghili who lived to the west of Tlemsen. He settled in the Oasis of Tuwat in a village called Tamentit about the year 1479. Up to this time the Arab conquerors had apparently adopted a tolerant attitude towards the Jews and Barbar Zenates who had been settled there for many decades. The defeats, however, which Islam had suffered in Europe about this time had aroused the fanaticism of the Moslems, and Maghili preached incendiary sermons, telling the Moslems that their misfortunes were due to " the people of error " that is to say, the Jews. After having become famous as a persecutor of the Jews at Sijilmasa, he did likewise when he came to Tuwat.

Maghili had a disciple called Sidi Abdul Rahman el Talibi, who was the master of Sheikh Muhammad el Sanusi, the great apostle of Sufism.

Maghili was able to reverse the policy of tolerance and in the year 1492 destroyed the Jewish synagogue at Tamentit and massacred most of the Jews. After this massacre, Maghili apparently obtained a considerable following, and marched against a section of the Benî Marîn, whom he accused of being lukewarm Moslems, but his forces were defeated by the Marinite Sultan, Ahmed ibn Yahya ibn Abu Amar el Watasi. He then fled to Tekidda, three days west-south-west of Agades, which had, during that century, become a Barbar Sultanate, and from thence he visited Katsina and Kano and wrote for the Sarikin Kano, Muhammad Rimfa, a treatise on the duties of kings and their legal obligations.

Thence he went west to the Songhay capital, Gao, on the Niger, where he similarly gave advice to the Sultan Al Hajj Muhammad Askia. He was at Gao when he received news that his son had been killed in revenge by the Jews of Tuwat. As he failed to secure help from Askia, Maghili returned to Tuwat, collected a following, and in the year 1503 returned to Tamentit and captured some of the Kasur (forts) in the Oases.

Having avenged the death of his son, he returned to the Zawia (monastery) called Bu Ali where he died in the year 1504.

El Tamentiti, a writer to whom we are indebted for these details of the life of Maghili, states that a certain Jew of Tuwat went and urinated on Maghili's tomb and instantly went blind.

The reckoning based on the length of reigns as given by the text makes Mohamma Rimfa reign A.H. 867-904 (A.D.1463-1499), and fits in with the facts mentioned above (*cf.* Cherbonneau, *Journal Asiatique*, Ser. v, vi, 391).

The Chronicle says that in the time of Yaji (A.D. 1349-1385), Wangarawa came from Melle bringing with them the Moslem religion.

Now the great king of Melle, Mansa Musa, made his pilgrimage to Mecca in 1326, and in 1373 the Wazir Mari Jatah of Melle conquered Tekidda (near Asben), and became master of the Songhay country. It would be extremely probable that about this date the rise of Melle power should make itself felt in the west. There thus seems no reason why the introduction of Islam into Hausaland should not have taken place at the date ascribed to it in the text.

Again the Bornu Chronicles (as abridged by Barth, vol. ii, p. 641) makes Othman Kalinwama take refuge in Kano in A.D. 1432. In Sarki Dauda's time (A.D. 1421-1438) a great Bornu prince called Dagachi (which simply means ruler or king), arrives in Kano and settles with a large following. The circumstances make it very probable that Dagachi is Othman Kalinwama.

The various references in later reigns to Gobir, Zamfara, the Kwararafa, and Nupe are all chronologically correct.

It seems therefore highly probable that, except for the very early kings, the Chronicle is roughly accurate.

The countries which we now call Hausaland are not specifically mentioned by the early Arab writers such as El Bekri (1050 A.D.) or Idrisi (1150 A.D.). On the other hand the southern parts of the Sahara are described as being occupied in their time by Barbar tribes to which various appellations are given such as Lamtuna, Zaghawa, etc. These tribes intermarried with the negroes producing the half-caste or so-called servile Barbar tribes (*imghad*), who gradually penetrated and conquered the tribes to the south of them, and founded kingdoms of Barbar affinity, as, *e.g.* the Hausa Kingdoms.

The traveller Ibn Battuta (who wrote about 1350 A.D.) mentions Yufi (Nupe) and Gubar (Gobir) but almost ignores the rest. It is not till the time of Leo Africanus (1528 A.D.) that Kano and Katsina were important enough to be much known to the outside world.

But between A.D. 900 and A.D. 1513, the date of Leo's visit to the Sudan, certain peoples represented in the text by Bayajidda (Bayazid) arrived at Daura and conquered the indigenous inhabitants of the Hausa States. The native tradition as to who they were varies. The Fulani Sarkin Muslimi Muhammad Bello, says (see *Denham* and *Clapperton*, ii, 399) that they were "slaves of the Sultan of Bornu." The well-known Daura legend, preserved in writing, says they came from Bagdad, and introduced the horse into Hausaland. Bayajidda, the ancestor of the Kings of Hausaland, mentioned in the foot note, p. 98, is represented as having arrived in Daura, slain a snake which inhabited a well, and married the Queen of Daura. He had previously escaped from the treachery of the Sultan of Bornu, who, having tampered successfully with the loyalty of his men, was plotting against his life, when he fled.

Vast ethnographical changes resulted from the rise of the Fatimids in North Africa about A.D. 900 and the revolts and rapine which succeeded, culminating in the devastation of Fezzan by the Hillal and Soleim Arabs about 1050 A.D. must have caused fundamental changes in the habitats of the Saharan races, extending to Asben, Damergu and regions south of them.

The certain fact is that about A.D. 1000, the Hausa States were occupied by Barbar races coming from the east and north. These races or peoples ruled, though at different periods tributary to Songhay and Bornu, until displaced by the Fulani in 1807. It is they who are often called Habe, a word of which the singular is Kado. The name does, as well as any other, to express this people, but it by no means follows that the people of the Hombori region, west of the Niger, called Habe by the Fulani are connected with them, for the Fulani called any conquered negro people "Habe." For this reason it seems better to keep the word Hausa to express the post-A.D. 1000 and pre-A.D. 1807 rulers of Hausaland, provided that it is not used indiscriminately of any peoples who speak the "Hausa" language. In fact, Habe is a far wider word than Hausawa, and practically means any negro race. The primitive peoples of the Hombori and the Dalla stock of Kano may both be conveniently called "Habe."

The name Hausa is the name by which the Barbars of the Sahara, the conquering races, possibly under Egyptian and later Arab influence, knew the Sudanese negroes. It is the same word as Habash, or Ahbasan (Abasenoi) *i.e.* Abyssinians. It is found in the place named Absen (Asben), and in the Teda (Tubu) name for the Kanembu, east of Lake Chad, Aussa.

The only reasonable explanation of the fact that among the Hausas themselves "Hausa" is the name of their language while "habshi" means "to bark" (of a dog), "hauka" "to be mad" and "haushi" means "anger," lies in the supposition that the language of the indigenes was by the Barbar conquerors, supposed to resemble that of beasts, just as Herodotus likened the language of the Ethiopians of Tibesti to the "squeaking of bats."

Hence the indigenous languages were, it may be supposed, called by the Barbar generalized name for the people who spoke them, *i.e.* Habash (Hausa). The inference is that the conquerors themselves originally spoke a form of Tamashek, a language which in grammatical structure and forms of pronouns, etc., is intimately allied to Hausa as it now exists.

It would appear in fact that the invaders who are embraced by the name Bayajidda (*i.e.* Ba-Yazid)

(*a*) So far as Daura, Buram, Kano, and Katsina are concerned, were the *imghad* of Damargu, known as Diggera or Dagara, whence the name Daura.

(*b*) So far as Gobir (Kubar) and its offshoot Zamfara are concerned, were other tribes of Barbar origin, peoples with some pretensions to the status of nobles (*imoshagh*).

Hence, while the other Hausa states were said to be " slaves " of the king of Bornu (*i.e.* the Barbars), Gobir was said to be " free," and its rulers Kiptawa (Egyptians).

It seems probable that these Barbar *imghad* who invaded Hausaland are to be connected with the stocks called Zaghawa, who founded not only the first Songhay Empire at Kukia, east of the Niger, towards 600 A.D. but also not long afterwards founded the kingdom of Kanem, in the Borku and Wadai region.

According to Yakubi 981 A.D. the Zaghawa were originally a Kushite people, *i.e.* they belonged to the older stocks of Saharan races; but the geographer Idrisi circa 1150 A.D., while apparently classing the Zaghawa in general as Kushites, mentions that at Shama (the Asben Oasis) a tribe of Luwata (Libyans) named Sadrata were settled among them and conducted their trade. Ibn Khaldun, at a later date, classes the Zaghawa as "Mulathimin " *i.e.* Tuwareg.

At present it seems impossible clearly to distinguish between the original Kushite Zaghawa and the apparently later accretion which the Sadrata formerly and the present Beli or Bideyat who speak the same language as the Zaghawa represent.

But certainly a political fusion of these stocks had begun to take place before the founding of the Kanem Kingdom towards 800 A.D. for, it is clear that the element which as early as 981 A.D. was in fact the ruling caste in Kanem was classed as Tuwareg and came from the region which the Kanuri call Mâkida or Makâda, *i.e.* the Jebel region of Kordofan to the west of the ancient Meroe.

As the result of these race movements in the region of Kanem, Wadai, Darfur and Kordofan, Zaghawa tribes were pushed west to Balma and then from Kawar to the Asben Oasis.

It is as living at Balma in the Kawar Oasis that we have the first recorded tradition of the Gobirawa. To the present day the Zaghawa of Darfur count Kobir and Daura (Diggera) as among their tribal units.

It may be added that such records as are available of the history and kings of Katsina also present independent evidence of the general accuracy of this Kano Chronicle as regards dates.

The fact that the King of Katsina Muhammad Korau (circa 1320) became a Moslem almost a century before the coming of the Wangara missionaries to Kano towards 1380, is probably to be accounted for by the famous pilgrimage of the Wazir Mari Jatah of Melle to Mecca which took place in the year 1329, while the Moslem revival at Katsina in the time of Ibrahim Maje (1500) roughly synchronises with the reign of Muhammad Rimfa at Kano, as should be the case in view of the known dates of the both Sheikh al Magili and Jelal al Suyuti and the Sultan Muhammad Sottofa of Agades, as recorded in the Asben Chronicle.

THE KANO CHRONICLE.

In the name of God, the merciful, the compassionate. May God bless the noble Prophet.

This is the history of the lords of this country called Kano. Barbushe, once its chief, was of the stock of Dâla,* a black man of great stature and might, a hunter, who slew elephants with his stick and carried them on his head about nine miles. Dâla was of unknown race, but came to this land, and built a house on Dâla hill. There he lived—he and his wives. He had seven children— four boys and three girls—of whom the eldest was Garagéje. This Garagéje was the grandfather of Buzame, who was the father of Barbushe. Barbushe succeeded his forefathers in the knowledge of the lore of Dâla, for he was skilled in the various pagan rites. By his wonders and sorceries and the power he gained over his brethren he became chief and lord over them. Among the lesser chiefs with him were Gunzago, whose house was at the foot of Gorondutse to the east. After him came Gagiwa, father of Rubu, who was so strong that he caught elephants with rope. There were also Gubanasu, Ibrahim, Bardóje, Nisau, Kanfatau, Doje, Janbére, Kamakúra, Sáfataro, Hangógo, and Gartsangi. These were next to Barbushe in rank. Tsanburo lived at Jigiria, and Jandámisa at Magum. The last named was the progenitor of the Rumáwa. From Gogau to Salamta the people traced their descent from Rumá, and were called Rumáwa because they became a great people. Hambaro's house was at Tanagar. Gambarjado, who lived at Fanisau, was the son of Nisau. All these and many more there were—pagans. From Toda to Dan Bakóshi and from Doji to Dankwoi all the people flocked to Barbushe on the two nights of Idi—for he was all-powerful at the sacrifical rites.

Now the name of the place sacred to their god was Kakua†. The god's name was Tchunburburai. It was a tree called Shamuz. The man who remained near this tree day and night was called Mai-Tchunburburai. The tree was surrounded by a wall, and no man could come within it save Barbushe. Whoever else entered, he entered but to die. Barbushe never descended from Dâla except on the two days of Idi. When the days drew near, the people came in from east and west and south and north, men and women alike. Some brought a black dog, some a black fowl, others a black he-goat, when they met together on the day of Jajibere at the foot of Dalla hill at eve. When darkness came, Barbushe went forth from his house with

---

* The name of a rock and also a man.
† Otherwise called Kagua.

his drummers. He cried aloud and said: "Great Father of us all, we have come nigh to thy dwelling in supplication, Tchunburburai," and the people said: "Look on Tchunburburai, ye men of Kano. Look toward Dâla." Then Barbushe descended, and the people went with him to the god. And when they drew near, they sacrificed that which they had brought with them. Barbushe entered the sacred place—he alone—and said "I am the heir of Dâla, like it or no, follow me ye must, perforce." And all the people said: "Dweller on the rock, our lord Amane, we follow thee perforce." Thus they spoke and marched round the sacred place till the dawn, when they arose, naked as they were, and ate. Then would Barbushe come forth and tell them of all that would befall through the coming year, even concerning the stranger who should come to this land, whether good or ill. And he foretold how their dominion should wrested from them, and their tree be cast down and burnt, and how this mosque should be built. "A man shall come," said he, "to this land with an army, and gain the mastery over us." They answered, "Why do you say this? it is an evil saying." Barbushe held his peace. "In sooth," said he, "you will see him in the sacred place of Tchunburburai; if he comes not in your time, assuredly he will come in the time of your children, and will conquer all in this country, and forget you and yours and exalt himself and his people for years to come." Then were they exceeding cast down. They knew well that he did not lie. So they believed him and said: "What can we do to avert this great calamity?" He replied, "There is no cure but resignation." They resigned themselves. But the people were still grieving over this loss of dominion at some distant time, when Bagoda*, a generation later, came with his host to Kano. There is a dispute, however. Some deny this, and say that it was Bagoda's grandson† who first reached Kano, and that he‡ and his son§ died at Sheme. He, at all events, entered Kano territory first. When he came, he found none of Barbushe's men, save Janbere, Hambarau, Gertsangi, Jandamissa, and Kanfatau. These said, "Is this man he of whom Barbushe told us?" Jambere said, "I swear by Tchunburburai if you allow this people within our land, verily they will rule you, till you are of no account." The people refused to hearken to the words of Jambere, and allowed the strangers to enter the country, saying: "Where will Bagoda find strength to conquer us?"

So Bagoda and his host settled in Garazawa and built houses there. After seven months, they moved to Sheme. The district from Jakara to Damargu was called Garazawa; from Jakara to Santolo was called Zadawa; from Santolo to Burku was called Fongui; from Banfai to Wasai was called Zaura. From Wateri

---

* Bagoda. He was son of Bauwo son of Bayajidda, of the stock of Ham the son of Noah. It was by reason of his high lineage, that Bauwo conquered all Hausaland—he and his six sons. The first of them was Kazura: then came Bagoda, Ubandoma, Gamgama, Kumaio, and Kasanki. When Bauwo died, Kazura became Emir of Daura. Bagoda went to Kano, Ubandoma to Kobir, Gamgama to Zakzak, Kumaio to Kashina, and Kasanki to Kur or Nero. This is a reliable account in a book of the names of the Emirs of Kano.
† Gijinmasu.   ‡ Bagoda.   § Warisi.

to the rock of Karia was called Dundunzuru; from Santolo to Shike, Shiriya; from Damargu to Kazaure, Sheme; from Burku to Kara, Gaude; from Kara to Amnagu, Gija; from Karmashe to Ringim, Tokawa. Now the chiefs whom Bagoda found holding sway over this land acknowledged no supreme lord save Tchunburburai and the grove of Jakara. Jakara was called "Kurmin Bakkin Rua," because its water was black, and it was surrounded by the grove.*

The pagans stood in awe of the terrors of their god and this grove, which stretched from Gorondumasa to Dausara. The branches and limbs of its trees were still—save, if trouble were coming on this land, it would shriek thrice, and smoke would issue forth in Tchunburburai, which was in the midst of the water. Then they would bring a black dog and sacrifice it at the foot of Tchunburburai. They sacrificed a black he-goat in the grove. If the shrieks and smoke continued, the trouble would indeed reach them, but if they ceased, then the trouble was stayed. The name of the grove was Matsama and the name of Tchunburburai was Randaya.

The greatest of the chiefs of the country was Mazauda, the grandfather of Sarkin Makafi. Gijigiji was the blacksmith: Bugazau was the brewer: Hanburki doctored every sickness: Danbuntunia, the watchman of the town at night, was the progenitor of the Kurmawa. Tsoron Maje was "Sarkin Samri," and Jandodo was "Sarkin Makada Gundua da Kuru." Beside these there was Maguji, who begot the Maguzawa, and was the miner and smelter among them. Again there was Asanni the forefather of minstrels and chief of the dancers. Bakonyaki was the archer. Awar, grandfather of the Awrawa, worked salt of Awar. He was Sarkin Rua of this whole country. In all there were eleven of these pagan chiefs, and each was head of a large clan. They were the original stock of Kano.

I.—BAGODA, SON OF BAUWO.

A.H. 389-455.   A.D. 999-1063.

Then came Bagoda with his host, and was the first Sarki of this land. His name was Daud. His mother's name was Kaunasu. He began by occupying Adirani for two years. Thence he moved to Barka, and built a city called Talutawa, where he reigned two years.

The names of the pagan chiefs whom Bagoda met were Jankare, Biju, Buduri (who had many children—about a hundred) and Ribo. Bagoda overcame them and killed their leader Jankare. Then he came to Sheme, and found Gabusani, Bauni, Gazauri, Dubgege, Fasataro, and Bakin Bunu there. He conquered them all, and built a city, and reigned as Sheme sixty-six years.

---

* The "Ghailata" means trees.

II.—WARISI, SON OF BAGODA.
A.H. 455-488. A.D. 1063-1095.

The second Sarki was Warisi son of Bagoda. His mother's name was Saju. Those who were near him were Galadima Mele, Barwa Jimra, Buram (so called because he was the Sarki's son), Maidawaki Abdulahi, Sarkin Gija Karmayi, Maidalla Zakar, Makuwu, Magaaiki Gawarkura, Makama Gargi, Jarumai Goshin Wuta, Jarmai Bakushi, Bardai Duna, and Dawaki Surfan. These were the most important chiefs, but there were many more. Gawarkura said, " O Sarki of this land, if you wish to govern it, east and west and south and north, keep close to Garazawa, since it is the key of the country, and has not a strong god. When you come here, beguile the chiefs with gifts, and so rule them and their god." The Sarki replied, " No, I have not the strength; I am too old." Warisi ruled Kano thirty-three years.

III.—GIJIMASU, SON OF WARISI.
A.H. 488-528. A.D. 1095-1134.

Gijimasu, son of Warisi, was the third Sarki. His mother's name was Yanas. When he came to power he left Sheme and went to Garazawa. Some, however, say that it was his son Tsaraki who came to this place and built a city. The latter is the better version. It was here he ruled. Mazuda said, " This Sarki has come here in order to destroy our god and our grove of sacrifice." The people said, " He has not power to destroy our god, in our time at least." So Gijimasu and his people built a house in Garazawa. He beguiled the elders with gifts, till by his gifts he obtained dominion over them. They said, " What a good man this is! how well he treats us!" Mazuda said, " I want to give my daughter to his son in marriage." But Bugazau prevented him carrying out his plan. The Sarki consulted the people about building a city. The people agreed: " Come " they said, " let us build, for we have the power and the strength." So they began to build the city. They began the wall from Raria. The Sarki slaughtered a hundred cattle on the first day of the work.

They continued the work to the gate of Mazugi, and from there to the water gate and on to the gate of Adama, and the gate of Gudan; then past the gates of Waika, Kansakali and Kawungari, as far as the gate of Tuji. There were eight gates. Sarkin Rano built a city called Zamnagaba. He began building from Rímin Kira, and carried the wall through Wawan Toro, Tafasa, Kusarua and Kadába to the gate of Bai. He ruled all the country as far as the lands of Sarkin Gano, Sarkin Dab, Sarkin Debbi, Sarkin Ringim and Dan Bakonyaki. Santolo alone stood out against him, for its people were many and pagans. No one was able to rule over them. The Sarkis of Gano, Dab and Debbi came to Hausaland nine years before Bagoda. But Buram, Isa, Baba, Kududufi, Akassan, and others of the Kano chiefs, men of the princely clan,* came with Bagoda. Gijimasu ruled forty years—then he died.

---
* For this reason all their descendants were called after these, their forefathers, and the names have remained as " titles " of princes to this day. Such titles are Dan Buram, Dan Isa, Dan Baba, Dan Akassan, Dan Kududufi and others like Dan Dermai and Dan Goriba.

IV.—NAWATA AND GAWATA.

A.H. 528-530.   A.D. 1134-1136.

The rule of the twins Nawata and Gawata, children of Gijimasu, was the fourth reign. Their mother was Munsada. Together they ruled the city of Kano for seven months; then one of them died; the other was left. The remaining one ruled one year and five months, and then he died. Altogether they ruled two years.

V.—YUSA OR TSARAKI, SON OF GIJIMASU.

A.H. 530-590.   A.D. 1136-1194.

The fifth Sarki was Yusa, called Tsaraki. He was the son of Gijimasu. He it was who completed the walls of Kano, as is well known. He raided Karaie, and camped at Badari five months till the inhabitants submitted to him. From Gurmai to Farinrua the people paid him tribute. Then he returned to his country. His mighty men of war were Tuje, Fasau, Iyagari, and Kamfaragi. All these had no fear in war. In Yusa's reign shields (*Garkwa*) were first used. He reigned sixty years. The name of his mother was Yankuma or Yankuna. He died.

VI.—NAGUJI, SON OF TSARAKI.

A.H. 590-645.   A.D. 1194-1247.

The sixth Sarki was Naguji. His mother's name was Yankuma or Muntáras. He was generous, but a man of violent passions. From Kura Tsangaya he ravaged the country, and forced the people, willing or unwilling, to follow him. He camped at Basema two years for the purpose of attacking Santulo, but he was worsted in the war and returned to Kano. He found the pagans there on the verge of revolt; so he cajoled them with talk, and executed their leader, Samagi the son of Mazadu, Dorini, son of Bugazau, Burtsar Ganguta, son of Tsoron Maje, and Buzuzu, son of Jandodo. When they were dead the rest of the people said, "We are willing to follow you, O Sarki, because we must." The Sarki said to them, "If you are willing to follow me show me the secrets of this god of yours." But they replied, "We will not show you the secrets of our God." So the Sarki punished them. Naguji was the first Sarki who collected a land tax of one-eighth of the crop from all husbandmen. He ruled all the land of Kano save Santulo which stood out against him. He ruled fifty-five years.

VII.—GUGUA, SON OF GIJIMASU.

A.H. 645-689.   A.D. 1247-1290.

Gugua was the seventh Sarki. His mother's name was Munsada. He was a man of much tact and subtlety. He had a face remarkable for its expression. He was liberal, eloquent, wise, and magnanimous. All these qualities he turned to account in ruling the pagans and in discovering the mysteries of their god. They hated him. When he knew that they hated him he said to his men, "How shall I plan to get the better of these pagans and destroy their god." Ture and Galadima Bangare and Berde Kilmo said, "There can be no plan between them and us, nothing but war; we will conquer them and their god." When the pagans heard of this they said in secret, "When the ears hear, then is the body saved." The chief pagans assembled at dead of night, forty in number, at the foot of the sacred tree. Allah alone knows what took place there. They came forth when the sun rose and went to the Sarki. They said, "O Sarki, when the night of Idi comes we will tell you the mysteries of our god." He agreed, for he was glad at heart, and gave them gifts abundantly. That night an apparition appeared to the Sarki in his sleep—a man with a red snake in his hand. He struck the Sarki with the snake and said to him, "Of two things choose one. Either thou mayest know the mysteries, in which case thou wilt die, or thou mayest not know the mysteries, in which case thou wilt not die." The Sarki said, "No! No! No!".

Now when the Sarki rose from his sleep he told his men what he had seen in the vision. They said to him, "What do you see in it?" He said, "What do *you* see?" They said, "We see war!" The Sarki said nothing, he spoke not a word, but suddenly he was struck blind. He remained blind for many years. He ruled Kano forty-four years. Twenty-two yars he saw, and twenty-two he was blind. Then the power passed from him.

VIII.—SHEKKARAU, SON OF TSARAKI.

A.H. 689-706.   A.D. 1290-1307.

The eighth Sarki was Shekkarau. His mother's name was Auta. When he became Sarki his men said to him, "Sarkin Kano, what do you see in the talk of the people of this city?" He said, "I see nothing between us except things we can settle without fighting." They replied, "If you try to make peace with the people they will say that you are afraid. If they come to you and make smooth talk, turn away from them; then you would not be acting wrongly. If matters do not fall out thus we will fight them, and if we prevail over them we will cut the throats of all their chief men and destroy their god." These counsels prevailed. All the pagans came to the Sarki with many presents and said, "Sarki, and Lord over us, we come to you to say to you one word: do not take notice of what we have done, we pray you, but put away the slanderous counsel of your advisers. If the domains of a ruler are wide, he should be patient; if they are not so, he will not obtain possession of the whole country by impatience." The Sarki said to them, "Your talk is true," and left them their customs and power. They said, "Were it not for fear of what may result we would have told the Sarki the secrets of our god." The chief of them, Samagi, said, "If we show him the secrets of our god we shall lose all our power, and we and our generation will be forgotten." So the dispute continued till the Sarki died. Shekkarau was Sarki seventeen years.

IX.—TSAMIA, SON OF SHEKKARAU.
A.H. 706-743.   A.D. 1307-1343.

The ninth Sarki was Tsamia, called Barandamasu. His mother's name was Salmata. In his time the cult of Tchibiri was first practised. When he came to the throne he assembled the pagans and said to them, " Love transmits love, and hate transmits hate; there is nothing between us except bows and spears and swords and shields; there is no deceit and no deceiver except he who is afraid." Tsamia excelled all men in courage, dignity, impetuosity in war, vindictiveness and strength. He had nine men who were equal to a thousand. The greatest was Madawaki Bajeri, and after him Burdi-Kunkuru, Dan-kududufi-Tanko, Dan Burran Bakaki, Jarumai Garaji, Makama Gumki, Danunus Baurire, Sarkin Damargu Gabdodo and Jekafada Masabi. When these men came to the battle field with their Sarki they feared nothing, but were ever victorious. Now when the pagans of Kano heard the words of their Sarki fear seized their hearts. They assembled at the place of their god and prayed to be shown who would gain the mastery, they or the Sarki. It was foretold them that they would be overcome. They knew that their god would not lie. Their chief said, " I see no means of deliverance from the Sarki except we pay him money." His men said, " We agree." So they were made to pay jizia. They collected two hundred slaves within seven days and took them to the Sarki. The Sarki said, " I do not want your slaves." So they returned home. Now on a certain Saturday the Sarki sent a messenger called Marukarshi to them saying to him: " Tell them that on Thursday I am coming to Kagwa,* if Allah so wills, that I may enter, and see what is inside. I will destroy the wall and burn the tree." So the messenger went and told them. When they heard the word of the Sarki, they assembled on the Thursday at the place of their god, pagans of town and country alike—a crowd as had never been seen before. Of drums and cymbals there were a thousand and four hundred and more than four hundred captains of spearmen. They marched round the place of their god from evening until the morning. When the morning broke Sarkin Kano came forth from his house, and went to the place of the god. In front of him were seventy men, each with a shield made of elephant's hide. When the Sarki came near to the place of the god he prevented the pagans entering. As the fight waxed hot, the Sarki cried, " Where is Bajeri? " Bajeri heard the words of the Sarki, and took a spear and rushed into the battle, cutting his way until he reached the wall of the sacred place. He entered, and seeing a man with his back against the tree holding a red snake, attacked him. The man leapt up and made a great shout; fire breathed from his mouth until smoke filled the whole place round about; he rushed out: and, in his attempt to flee, made for the water-gate, followed by the Sarki, and plunged into the water. The Sarki and his followers stayed hunting for the man

---

* The place of their sacrifices.

in the water, but he escaped and went to Dankwoi where they left him. Hence it is that if any warrior drinks the water of Dankwoi he does not prevail in battle. The Sarki returned to the tree, and destroyed the wall together with all else connected with " Tchibiri " which was beneath the tree. All the pagans had in the meantime fled, except Makare Dan Samagi and Dunguzu Dan Dorini. The Sarki said to them, " Why do you not run away?" They said, " Where were we to run to ?" " Praise be to God," said the Sarki. " Tell me the secret of your god." They told him. When he had heard, the Sarki said to Danguzu, " I make you Sarkin Tchibiri." He said to Makare, " I make you Sarkin Garazawa." He said to Gamazo, " I make you Sarkin Kurmi." In the time of this Sarki long horns were first used in Kano. The tune that they played was " Stand firm, Kano is your city." He reigned thirty-seven years.

X.—OSUMANU ZAMNAGAWA, SON OF SHEKKARAU.

A.H. 743-750.   A.D. 1343-1349.

The tenth Sarki was Zamnagawa, called Osumanu. The name of his mother was Kumyerku. He was called Zamna-gawa because he killed Tsamia. He shut the doors of the palace and remained in his house for seven days. After that day he went out. It is not known how Tsamia was made away with; whether Zamnagawa ate him or buried him, no one knows. In the time of Zamnagawa, there was no war in the land, east and west, north and south. All was peace. The Maguzawa left the city and went to live in the country at Fongui. The Rumawa came in a body to the Sarki. They said to him, " You are our Sarki, you have made a Sarkin Gazarzawa and a chief of the Kurmawa, make us a chief also." The Sarki said, " I hear." So they went back to their homes. The Sarki then took counsel with his men and said, " I want to give my son the chieftainship of the Rumawa." And all his men said, " We agree." So he gave his son the chieftainship of the Rumawa, whose town had become great and populous. Zamnagawa ruled seven years.

XI.—YAJI, SON OF TSAMIA.

A.H. 750-787.   A.D. 1349-1385.

The eleventh Sarki was Yaji, called Ali. His mother was Maganarku. He was called Yaji because he had a bad temper when he was a boy, and the name stuck to him. He drove the Serikin Rano from Zamma Gaba, went to Rano, and reigned at Bunu two years. Then he removed to Kur together with the Ajawa and Worjawa and Aurawa. He stayed there. In Yaji's time the Wangarawa came from Melle, bringing the Muhammadan religion. The name of their leader was Abdurahaman Zaite. Others were Yakubu, Mandawali, Famori, Bilkasim, Kanaji, Dukere, Sheshe, Kebe, Murtuku, Liman Jibjin Yallabu, the father of Serikin Pawa, Gurdumus, Auta, Laual, Liman Madatai and others—about forty in all. When they came they commanded the

Sarki to observe the times of prayer. He complied, and made Gurdamus his Liman, and Laual his Muezzin. Auta cut the throats of whatever flesh was eaten. Mandawali was Liman of all the Wangarawa and of the chief men of Kano. Zaite was their Alkali. The Sarki commanded every town in Kano country to observe the times of prayer. So they all did so. A mosque was built beneath the sacred tree facing east, and prayers were made at the five appointed times in it. The Sarkin Garazawa was opposed to prayer, and when the Moslems after praying had gone home, he would come with his men and defile the whole mosque and cover it with filth. Danbugi was told off to patrol round the mosque with well-armed men from evening until morning. He kept up a constant halloo. For all that the pagans tried to win him and his men over. Some of his men followed the pagans and went away, but he and the rest refused. The defilement continued till Sheshe said to Famori, " There is no cure for this but prayer." The people assented. They gathered together on a Tuesday in the mosque at the evening hour of prayer and prayed against the pagans until sunrise. They only came away when the sun was well up. Allah received graciously the prayers addressed to him. The chief of the pagans was struck blind that day, and afterwards all the pagans who were present at the defilment—they and all their women. After this they were all afraid. Yaji turned the chief of the pagans out of his office and said to him, " Be thou Sarki among the blind." In the days of Yaji, it is said, Sarkin Debbi, Sarkin Dab and Sarkin Gano brought horses to Kano, but this story is not worthy of credence. Yaji said to the Wangarawa, " I want you to make prayer so that I may conquer the men of Santulo, for if I conquer Santulo every town in the country will follow me, since Santulo is the key of the south." They said, " We will pray for you—but we will not pray except beside the moat of Santulo itself." So the Sarki set forth together with the Wangarawa and they went to Santulo. He had with him a hundred and eleven men. Fifty of them were in front of the Wangarawa and sixty in front of himself. The chief among his men were Jarumai Gobarra Dagga Samma, Jakafada Kulli, Ragumar Giwa, Makama Butache, Maidawaki Koamna, Berdi Sheggi, Sarki Zaura Gamati, Dan Buram Gantururu, Dan Maköo Dagazo, Galadima Tuntu and Sarkin Surdi Maguri. Others were Gauji, Garoji, Tankarau, Kargagi, Karfasha, Kutunku Toro, Kampachi, Gorongiwa the Galadima,* Zaki, Bamboli and others—altogether sixty.

Now when he came to Santulo, the Sarki camped near Duji. Duji was the name of a man. In the dead of night the Wangarawa went to Santulo together with Yaji and marched round the city and prayed till daybreak. When the day broke they returned to their camp. When the sun was up they returned to Santulo eager for battle. The men of Santulo came out of the town and met them in the open. Fighting went on from morning until night. Neither side prevailed. The Kanawa retired to Duji; the men

---

* From this all Galadimas are called Gorongiwa.

of Santulo returned to their homes. The Sarkin Kano was very sore at heart. Famori said ," Do not be grieved! if Allah so wills we will defeat them." The Sarki was pleased with his talk. Kosa, the Sarki's slave, said, " My Lord, I will tell you the secrets of the enemy; there are eight men inside the city and no one can pass the moat unless he kills them." Famori said, " Do you know their names? " He said, " I know them." So Famori said, " What are their names? " And Kosa replied, " The name of the greatest is Hambari, and after him Gwoshin Bauna, Kafiwuta, Gurgurra Karifi, Gandar Giwa, Hamburkin Toka, Zan Kaddakere and Gumbar Wakke. Gwoji said, " If I see Hambari I will kill him, if Allah so wills." At sunrise the Sarki returned to the attack on Santulo with black looks. He took a spear in his hand. Gwoji* was in front of him, Zaite was on his right hand, Famori on his left, and behind him was Sheshe. Behind them were the rest of the Wangarawa and Kanawa. When they came near to Santulo all the pagans came out to battle. Gwoji saw Hambari, and girding up his loins dashed in to the fray. The pagans rushed at Gwoji, but he withstood them, and when they gave way, lunged at Hambari with his spear. Hambari caught him by the throat and dragged him from his horse; but in vain, for Gwoji drew his knife, and ran him through, and so he died. Then Gwoji mounted his horse and entered Santulo, and all the Kanawa followed him and stormed the town. The Sarki commanded all the inhabitants to be killed except women and little children. Gwoji entered the place of their god, with Kosa and Guragu, and found a bell, and two horns, a battle-axe and leg-irons. Gwoji took the bell and the two horns. Kosa took the battle-axe, and Guragu the leg-irons. Yaji stayed seven days in the town and destroyed the place of sacrifice, and after dismantling its wall and tree, returned to Kano. He said to Gwoji, " Choose whatever you want." Gwoji said, " I only want to become Madawakin Kano " The Sarki said, " I give you the office."

Gasatoro, who was turned out of the post of Madawaki, built a house at Gawo, and for that reason was known as Madawakin Gawo, to distinguish the two. The next year the Sarki went to war with Warji and stayed there some time. At this time all the pagan tribes were subject to him, from Bivri to Fanda. The Kwararafa alone refused to follow him, so he went to their country. When he came to their town, they were afraid to fight and all fled up the hill at Ata-gara. The Sarki camped there also for seven months. No one came down from the rock. At last the pagans paid him a hundred slaves. Because of this the song in praise of Yaji was made, which runs: " Yaji, conqueror of the rocky heights, scatterer of hosts, lord of the town." It is said that he died here at Kwararafa. Perhaps he died at Kano. He ruled thirty-seven years.

---

* Hence the Madawakin Kano is sung as Gwoji Maikwugi, Kosa as Kosa Maibarandami, and Guragu as Guragu of the Meri. Afterwards Kosa was given the title of Dawaki, and Guragu that of Dan Maji—thus it is related.

XII.—BUGAYA, SON OF TSAMIA.

A.H. 787-792.   A.D. 1385-1390.

The twelfth Sarki was Bugaya, called Mohammed. He had the same father and mother as Yaji. The name of his mother was Maganarku. The reason he was called Bugaya was as follows:— After Zamnagawa killed Tsamia, he made overtures to his widow, Maganarku, but she said, "I am with child." So Zamnagawa gave her drugs, without her knowledge, to procure an abortion. In spite of this, however, she gave birth to a living child, and gave him the name of Bugaya. It was this Sarki who ordered the Maguzawa to leave the rock of Fongui and scatter themselves through the country. He then gave all power into the hands of the Galadima, and sought repose. The country was now peaceful, and regular tribute was paid to the Sarki. No one knew anything of his character even to the day of his death. He reigned five years. When he died the Liman Madatai was ordered to pray over his body and Lowal to wash it and Turbana, Jigawa and Kusuba to help him. They washed the body and put it in a shroud, and took it out to burial. The Liman prayed over the body. Bugaya was the first Sarkin Kano who was buried at Madatai.

XIII.—KANAJEJI, SON OF YAJI.

A.H. 792-812.   A.D. 1390-1410.

The thirteenth Sarki was Kanajeji. His father's name was Yaji. His mother's name Annaka. He was a Sarki who engaged in many wars. He hardly lived in Kano at all, but scoured the country round and conquered the towns. He lived for some time near the rock of Gija. He sent to the Kwararafa and asked why they did not pay him tribute. They gave him two hundred slaves. Then he returned to Kano and kept sending the Kwararafa horses while they continued to send him slaves. Kanajeji was the first Hausa Sarki to introduce "Lifidi" and iron helmets and coats of mail for battle. They were introduced because in the war at Umbatu the losses had been so heavy. He visited Kano and returned to Umbatu the next year, but he had no success in the war. He returned a second time to Kano, and again went out the following year. He again failed, but said, "I will not return home, if Allah wills, until I conquer the enemy." He remained at Betu two years. The inhabitants, unable to till their fields, were at length starved out, and had to give in to him. They gave him a thousand male, and a thousand female slaves, their own children. They also gave him another two thousand slaves. Then peace was made. The Sarkin Kano said: "No one shall again conquer Umbatu as I have conquered it, though he may gain spoil." In the following year the Sarki made war on Zukzuk and sat down in Turunku. The men of Zukzuk came out and defeated the Kano host, saying, "What is Kano! Kano is 'bush.'" The Sarkin Kano went back to Kano in a rage and said: "What shall I do to conquer these men of Zukzuk?" The Sarkin Tchibiri said: "Re-establish the god that your father and grandfather destroyed." The Sarki said: "True, but tell me what I am to do with it." The Sarkin Tchibiri said: "Cut a branch from this tree." The Sarki cut a branch. When it was cut, the Sarki found a red snake in the branch. He killed the snake, and made two *huffi* with its skin. He then made four *dundufu* and eight *kuntakuru* from the branch. These objects he took to Dankwoi and threw them into the water and went home. After waiting forty days he came back to the water, and removed the objects to the house of Sarkin Tchibiri. Sarkin Tchibiri sewed the rest of the snake's skin round the drums and said to Kanajeji, "Whatever you wish for in this world, do as our forefathers did of old." Kanajeji said: "Show me, and I will do even as they did." The Sarkin Tchibiri took off his robe and put it on the *huffi* of snake's skin and walked round the tree forty times, singing the song of Barbushe. Kanajeji did as Sarkin Tchibiri did, and walked round the tree forty times. The next year he set out to war with Zukzuk. He encamped at Gadaz. The Sarkin Zukzuk came out and they fought; the men of Kano killed the Sarkin Zukzuk. The Zukzuk men fled, scattered in ones and twos, and the chiefs of Zukzuk were killed. The Sarkin Kano entered Zukzuk and lived there close to the Shika eight months. The people gave him a vast amount of tribute. Because of this feat the song of Kanajeji was sung, which runs: "Son of Kano, hurler of the *kere*, Kanajeji, drinker of the water of Shika, preventer of washing in the Kubanni, Lord of the town, Lord of the land." Kanajeji returned to Kano. Among his great men of war were Berdi Gutu, Jarumai Sabbo, Maidawaki Babaki, Makama Toro, Dan Burram Jatau, Jakafada Idiri, Jambori Sarkin Zaura Bugau, Lifidi Buzuzu and Dan Akassan Goderi. He reigned twenty years.

XIV.—UMARU, SON OF KANAJEJI.

A.H. 812-824.   A.D. 1410-1421.

The fourteenth Sarki was Umaru. His mother's name was Yatara. He was a mallam earnest in prayer. He was a pupil of Dan Gurdamus Ibrahimu and a friend of Abubakra. When he became Sarkin Kano his friend upbraided and left him and went to Bornu, where he remained eleven years. On his return to Kano finding Umaru still Sarkin Kano, he said to him: "O Umaru, you still like the fickle dame who has played you false, with whom better reflection refuses to be troubled. In time you will be disgusted, and get over your liking for her. Then regret will be futile even if you do regret." He preached to him about the next world and its pains and punishments. He reviled this world and everything in it. Umaru said, "I accept your admonition." He called together all the Kanawa, and said to them: "This high estate is a trap for the erring: I wash my hands of it." Then he resigned, and went away with his friend. He spent the rest of his life in regret for his actions while he had been Sarki. Hence he was called "Dan Terko." He ruled twelve years. In his time there was no war and no robbery. The affairs of Kano were put into the hands of the Galadima. For this reason it was said of the Galadima Dana that he was the "Trusted guardian of the city, the dust-heap of disputes."

XV.—DAUDA, SON OF KANAJEJI

A.H. 824-841.   A.D. 1421-1438.

The fifteenth Sarki was Dauda Bakon Damisa. His mother was Auta. In his time Dagachi, a great prince, came from South Bornu with many men and mallams. He brought with him horse-drums and trumpets and flags and guns. When he came he sat down at Bomfai. The Sarkin Kano went to see him. When he saw that he was indeed a great prince, he returned home and took counsel with his men and said, "Where is this man to stay?" The Galadima Babba said, "If you let him settle elsewhere than in Kano town, he will soon be master of that part of the country." The Sarkin said, "Where can he stay here with his army—Kano is full of men—unless we increase the size of our town?" The Galadima was sent to see Dagachi and returned with him, and built a house for him and his men at Dorai. The Sarki said to his men, "What shall I give him to please him, and to make his heart glad?" The Galadima Babba said, "Give him whatever you wish, you are Sarki, you own everything." The Sarki said nothing. At that time he was about to start for war with Zaria, so he said to Dagachi, "When I go to war I will put all the affairs of Kano into your hands, city and country alike." So the Sarkin Kano went to war and left Dagachi in the town. Dagachi ruled the town for five months and became very wealthy. Then the Sarki returned. At this time Zaria, under Queen Amina, conquered all the towns as far as Kwararafa and Nupe. Every town paid tribute to her. The Sarkin Nupe sent forty eunuchs and ten thousand kolas to her. She first had eunuchs and kolas in Hausaland. In her time the whole of the products of the west were brought to Hausaland. Her conquest extended over thirty-four years. I will leave now the story of Amina and return to Sarkin Kano. Dauda Bakon Damisa ruled seventeen years.

XVI.—ABDULAHI BURJA, SON OF KANAJEJI.

A.H. 841-856.   A.D. 1438-1452.

The sixteenth Sarki was Abdulahi Burja. His mother's name was Tekidda. There was no one like him for generosity. He was the first in Hausaland to give Bornu "tsare or gaisua." He opened roads from Bornu to Gwanja. He was the first to own camels in Hausaland. Sarkin Bornu left his country at this time and went to attack Asben, but as he could not find any water for his army he returned home. The next year every town in the west paid him "tsare." The Sarkin Kano went out to Kudu and encamped there one year and six months. The Galadima Daudu went to wage war in the south. In Burja's time Karmashi conquered the Migawa. The Sarki went to Dussi. The Galadima Daudu said to him, "Return to Kano I will do for you whatever you want done, and defeat your enemies." So the Sarkin Kano returned home. When he arrived in Kano, he found that Dagachi had assumed great power in the town, and collected wealth without end, and had built houses from his house as far as Salamta. It was Dagachi who made the market of Karabka. All this time the Galadima Daudu was in the south making war on the pagans every day, conquering them and taking them as slaves. Every month he sent a thousand slaves to Sarkin Kano. All the people of Kano flocked to him. There was no one left in Kano except the Sarki and very old men. Every day the Sarki sent to the Galadima horses, clothes and horse trappings.

The Galadima was sung as follows:—
    Gatherer of the axes of the south:
    Gatherer of the youth of the south:
    Drum of Wealth, Galadima:
    Drum of Land, Galadima.

He stayed seven years in the south. Slaves became very numerous in Kano. The Sarki sent to him to tell him to come back, so he returned. When he was returning, he stopped every three miles, and built a town. He left at each a thousand slaves, five hundred males, and five hundred females. He thus founded twenty-one towns, before he came to Kano. On arriving there he gave the Sarki three thousand slaves and said to him, "I have founded twenty-one towns, and in each I have left a thousand slaves, all yours." The Sarki asked him, "What are the names of the towns you have built?" The Galadima said, "Their names are Ibdabu." The Sarki said, "I make you ruler of all these towns and their domains." Because of this the Galadima was called "Daudu, the strength of the city." The next year the Sarki sent to Dussi to ask for a wife. He was the first Sarki who married a daughter of Sarkin Dussi, Sarkin Shirra and Sarkin Rano, and also a daughter of the Galadima. He ruled fifteen years.

XVII.—DAKAUTA, SON OF ABDULAHI BURJA.
A.H. 856. A.D. 1452

The seventeenth Sarki was Dakauta. He was dumb. The people said, "If he becomes Sarki he will be able to speak." When he had been made Sarki, and after one night did not speak, they turned him out again.

XVIII.—ATUMA, SON OF DAKAUTA.

The eighteenth Sarki was Atuma, son of Dakauta. He was king for seven days only. He was turned out of the office of Sarki, for fear of trouble with the Galadima Daudu.

XIX.—YAKUBU, SON OF ABDULAHI BURJA.
A.H. 856-867. A.D. 1452-1463.

The nineteenth Sarki was Yakubu, son of Tasafi. He was a good Sarki. In his time Agalfati came to Kano; he was Sarkin Gaia, and son of Sarkin Machina. Gaia came with his three brothers who became Sarkin Hadeijia, Sarkin Dal and Sarkin

Gaiam. The Sarkin Hadeijia became Sarkin Gabbas, and was given Hadeijia. The Sarkin Gaia came to Kano and was given Gaia. The Sarkin Dal came to Kano and was given Dal. Sarkin Gaiam went to Zaria and was given Gaiam. In Yakubu's time the Fulani came to Hausaland from Melle, bringing with them books on Divinity and Etymology. Formerly our doctors had, in addition to the Koran, only the books of the Law and the Traditions. The Fulani passed by and went to Bornu leaving a few men in Hausaland, together with some slaves and people who were tired of journeying. At this time too the Asbenawa came to Gobir, and salt became common in Hausaland. In the following year merchants from Gwanja began coming to Katsina; Beriberi came in large numbers, and a colony of Arabs arrived. Some of the Arabs settled in Kano and some in Katsina. There was no war in Hausaland in Yakubu's time. He sent ten horses to the Sarkin Nupe in order to buy eunuchs. The Sarkin Nupe gave him twelve eunuchs. Yakubu ruled Kano eleven years.

XX.—MOHAMMA RIMFA, SON OF YAKUBU.

A.H. 867-904.   A.D. 1463-1499.

The twentieth Sarki was Mohamma, son of Yakubu, commonly called Rimfa. His mother's name was Fasima Berana. He was a good man, just and learned. He can have no equal in might, from the time of the founding of Kano,, until it shall end. In his time the Sherifs came to Kano. They were Abdu Rahaman and his people. There is a story that the Prophet appeared to Abdu Rahaman in a dream and said to him, " Get up and go west and establish Islam." Abdu Rahaman got up and took a handful of the soil of Medina, and put it in a cloth, and brought it to Hausaland.

Whenever he came to a town, he took a handful of the soil of the country and put it beside that of Medina. If they did not correspond he passed that town. So he journeyed until he came to Kano. And when he compared the soil of Kano with Medina soil they resembled one another and became as one soil. So he said, " This is the country that I saw in my dream." And he took up his abode at Panisau. Then he sent in to the Sarkin Kano. The Sarkin Kano Rimfa went out together with his men, and escorted Abdu Rahaman back to the city together with his men, of whom the chief were Hanatari, Gemindodo, Gadangami, Fokai and others, ten in all. Abdu Rahaman lived in Kano and established Islam. He brought with him many books. He ordered Rimfa to build a mosque for Friday, and to cut down the sacred tree and build a minaret on the site. And when he had established the Faith of Islam, and learned men had grown numerous in Kano, and all the country round had accepted the Faith, Abdu Karimi returned to Massar, leaving Sidi Fari as his deputy to carry on his work.

Rimfa was the author of twelve innovations in Kano. He built the Dakin Rimfa. The next year he extended the walls towards the Kofan Mata from the Kofan Dagachi and continued the work to Kofan Gertawasa and Kofan Kawayi, and from the Kofan Naïssa to the Kofan Kansakali. The next year he entered his house. He established the Kurmi Market. He was the first Sarki who used " Dawakin Zaggi " in the war with Katsina. He was the first Sarki who practised " Kame." He appointed Durman to go round the dwellings of the Indabawa and take every first-born virgin for him. He was the first Sarki to have a thousand wives. He began the custom of " Kulle." He began the " Tara-ta-Kano." He was the first to have " Kakaki " and " Figinni," and ostrich-feather sandals. It was in his reign that the Sallam Idi was first celebrated in Kano at Shadakoko. He began the custom of giving to eunuchs the offices of state, among them, Dan Kusuba, Dan Jigawa Dan Tarbana, Sarkin Gabbas, Sarkin Tudu, Sarkin Rua, Maaji, Sarkin Bai, Sarkin Kofa. There were four eunuchs left without a title. He said to them, " I make you chiefs of the Treasury." The name of one was Turaki, another was Aljira; the names of the other two were Al-Soro and Kashe Kusa.

The Galadima Dabuli built a house at Goda, and the Madawaki Badosa built a house at Hori. Chiroma Bugaya built a house at Dabazaro. Surely there was no Sarki more powerful than Rimfa! He was sung as " The Arab Sarki, of wide sway." In his time occurred the first war with Katsina. It lasted eleven years, without either side winning. He ruled thirty-seven years.

XXI.—ABDULAHI, SON OF MOHAMMA RIMFA
A.H. 904-914. A.D. 1499-1509.

The twenty-first Sarki was Abdulahi. His mother's name was Auwa. Her influence was very strong among the rulers of the day, She built the house at Doseyi, hence its name, " Giddan Madaki Auwa." In his time Ahmedu, who was afterwards Liman of Kano, arrived. Abdulahi conquered Katsina. He advanced as far as Katsina itself and encamped on the river near Tsagero. He remained four months at Tsagero and then went to Zukzuk and made war there. After conquering the men of Zaria he went on to Kadaura and to Kalam and made war on the inhabitants, after which he returned to Kano. On his arrival home he found that Dagachi was preparing to revolt, and that the Madaki Auwa alone had prevented serious trouble, as her influence was very great in Kano. This was the reason that Sarkin Bornu came to attack Kano, and camped at Gunduawa. The Sarkin Kano went out to meet him together with his mallams and humbled himself before him. The Sarkin Bornu went back to his country. As soon as he was gone, Abdulahi beguiled Dagachi into submission and then turned him out of his office and gave his own slave the title. He ruled Kano ten years.

XXII.—MOHAMMA KISOKI, SON OF ABDULAHI.
A.H. 914-972. A.D. 1509-1565.

The twenty-second Sarki was Mohamma Kisoki. He was the son of Abdulahi and Lamis, who built a house at Bani-Buki and established a market there, and was the mother of Dabkare Dan

Iya. Kisoki put him in the "Kano nine," and for that purpose expelled Berde. Kisoki was an energetic Sarki, warlike and masterful. He ruled over all Hausaland, east and west, and south and north. He waged war on Birnin N'guru because of Agaidam. When he entered the town, Sarkin Kano took his seat beneath the "kuka" tree, at the Kofan Fada, and assembling the inhabitants of the town at the Kofan Bai, reduced them to terrified submission. He gave orders that no men were to be made prisoners. but that only clothes and horses were to be taken. Then he left N'guru and lived for a month in the bush. The Sarkin Bornu sent to him and said: "What do you mean by making war?" Kisoki replied: "I do not know, but the cause of war is the ordinance of Allah." The Sarkin Bornu said nothing more. The men of Kano returned to Kano. In the next year the Sarkin Bornu came to attack Kano, but could not take the town and returned home. Then Kisoki said to one of his men, Dunki, "Mount the wall, and sing a song in praise of the Sarki and his men of war." Dunki went. The song that he sung was this: "Kisoki, physic of Bornu, and the Chiratawa." He sung it again and again, and after that he praised all those who were present at the fight; as Galadima Bawa, Mai-Dawakin Maisanda, Mai-Dawakin Gawo Magani, Dan Kudu Dufi Koamna, Makama Abdulahi, Makama Atuman, Dan Yerima Gajeren Damisa, Dan Buram Sagagi, Umoru Dan Maji, Dan Makoiyo Jigu, Dan Goriba Jar Garma, Dan Darmenkorau and Gaji Dan Bauni and many others, about forty in all. Dunki sang their praises for forty days on the top of the wall. After these he celebrated anyone else he thought worthy, as Madaki Koremma, Dagachi, Alkali Musa Gero, Sarkin Kasua, Liman Kano, Sarkin Bai, Dan Maji, Sarkin Yara, the eunuchs and San Turaki. The Madaki Auwa, because she was grandmothter of Abdulahi, was also celebrated, in a song beginning: "Mother! Kano is your country. Mother! Kano is your town. Old lady with the swaggering gait, old lady of royal blood, guarded by men-at-arms." Others there were too—thirty-four in all. In Kisoki's time Shehu Tunus, who brought *Eshifa* to Hausa, came to Kano. Dan-Goron-Duma also came, and Shehu Abdu Salam, who brought with him the books *Madawwanna, Jami'us-saghir* and *Samarkandi*. In the next year Tubi came from Zukzuk to learn from Shehu Tunus and became his chief disciple in Kano. Shehu Tunus told Kisoki to build a Friday Mosque for the Rumawa. Kisoki built it. A certain mallam named Shehu Karaski, and Magumi and Kabi came from Bornu. They were brothers. Kisoki took a liking to Shehu Karaski and asked him to become Alkali. He refused, and suggested his brother Magumi. Magumi agreed, and built a portico at the Kofan Fada. In Kisoki's time, Zaite, Tamma, Buduru, and Koda came to Kano. Kisoki ruled the town with his mother Iya Lamis and his grandmother Madaki Auwa, and Guli, the brother of Madaki Auwa. Guli was much respected by the Sarki; he came to have power over the whole country. This is the reason every counsellor is called Na-Guli. Kisoki ruled Kano fifty-eight years.

XXIII.—YAKUFU, SON OF KISOKI.
A.H. 972-973. A.D. 1565.

The twenty-third Sarkin was Yakufu. His mother's name was Tunus. He was Sarkin Kano four months and twenty days. Guli deposed him. The Galadima Kano Sara Katunia and Guli carried on civil war. There was forty days' fighting in Kano before the Galadima overcame and killed Guli and determined to re-establish Yakufu on the throne. Yakufu refused, and returned among the learned men to study. So he went and lived in the country which bears the name of Yakufawa. He was the father of Mohamma Shashere, Dauda Abasama, Sarkin Taura, Buduru, Sarkin Majia, Sarkin Gilima, Sarkin Kazura and Sarkin Gwunaka.

XXIV.—DAUDA ABASAMA, SON OF YAKUFU.
A.H. 973. A.D. 1565.

The twenty-forth Sarki was Dauda Abasama. His mother's name was Zuhara. He ruled one month and twenty days before he was turned out. His brothers, Kazura Majia, and his sister, Buduru, so called because she was unmarried, Gilima, Taura and Gwunka, the youngest, joined him in his exile at a place called Karmashe. Dauda settle there and a house was built for him. The brothers each chose a place to live.

XXV.—ABUBAKR KADO, SON OF RIMFA.
A.H. 973-980. A.D. 1565-1573.

The twenty-fifth Sarki was Abubakr Kado, son of Rimfa and full brother of Abdulahi. His mother's name was Auwa. In his time the men of Katsina worsted the men of Kano until they came to the very gates of Kano.

They encamped at Salamta. The men of Kano went out to fight, but they were beaten and scattered, and had to take refuge in the town. Devastation went on, and the country was denuded of people. The only place where anybody was found was in walled towns or rocks, as Karayi, Gwan-gwam, Maska, Tariwa, or any other rocky place. Abubakr Kado did nothing but religious offices. He disdained the duties of Sarki. He and all his chiefs spent their time in prayer. In his time eunuchs and mallams became very numerous. Kano was filled with people. Mallam Sherif, Tamma, Gesu and Wuri came to Hausa from Lagoni. Some people say they came from Bagarmi.

Tamma was the greatest of them. When they first came they lived in Katsina land. For this reason the place where they lived is called Tamma. Afterwards they moved to Kano and settled at Godia. The town was called Godia after a certain woman, a harlot. She and the Sarki reigned jointly over the town. The Sarkin Godia said to Tamma, " Settle at Godia." So Tamma settled at Godia and married Godia. Abubakr was the first Sarki who read the book called *Eshifa* at the house of Dan Goronduma Kursiya.

He was the Sarki who made the princes learn the Koran. This he did because of his own sons. They read the koran well, and the reading was in the middle of Shaäban. Every morning after sunrise the princes assembled. The Sarki came out after early morning prayer. He had seven sons, each of which read a seventh of the Koran. He gave his sons great wealth. The eldest of them was Abdulahi, otherwise called Dan Kado Kisoki; Chiroma Yan Sarki was another; then Dauda Tsaga, Dan Ashia (Ashia was the Sarki's sister), Dari, and Tella. The Sarki built Goron Pugachi for the reading of the Koran. He began reading *Jam 'as-saghir*. He ruled Kano seven years and six months and then was deposed.

XXVI.—MOHAMMA SHASHERE, SON OF YAKUFU.
A.H. 980-990. A.D. 1573-1582.

The twenty-sixth Sarki was Mohamma Shashere, son of Yakufu. His mother's name was Fasuma. He was unmatched for generosity among the Sarkis of Kano. He was the first to give a eunuch the title of Wombai (the eunuch was called Damu). He also gave to a eunuch called Dabba the title of Sarkin Dawaki. He gave to another eunuch called Mabaiyi the title of Dagachi.

He determined on an expedition against Katsina. He said to the Alkali Mohamma, the son of Tanko, the son of Jibril, the son of Mugumi: "Find me an Alkali to take with me to war with Katsina. When I go to the war, I shall not return alive unless I beat the Katsinawa." The Alkali gave him his pupil Musa, whose mother's name was Gero. The Sarki made Musa Alkali. Now when he came to Katsina, the men of Katsina came out to fight. The armies met at Kankia and fought there. The Katsinawa won because they were superior in numbers. The Kanawa ran away—deserting their Sarki—with the exception of San Turaki Mainya Narai, San Turaki Kuka Zuga and Dan Dumpki. Hence the songs "Narai the wall: ready to answer any challenge;" "Zuga does not run away."

These returned home together with their Sarki and entered Kano with him. The Sarki was very grieved. His men said to him, "Lay aside your grief, next year we will defeat the Katsinawa, if Allah wills." But meantime his brothers were treacherously planning to kill him. San Turaki Narai heard of their plans, and told the Sarki, saying, "Do not go outside your house, you or your Liman, to-day, or you will be killed." So the Sarki remained in his house, while San Turaki acted as Sarki. When the conspirators came in the evening, they found San Turaki with his slaves in the mosque, and, thinking he was the Sarki, attacked him. He had with him nine of his own slaves, and eighteen of the Sarki's household. The nine slaves were killed. Twelve of the others were killed and six captured. The names of the six were Burimah, Jigo, Adam Wukarka, Tukuki and Sarkin Wawayi. The new Sarki Mohamma Zaki intended to kill these six, but they prayed and begged him saying: "Spare us and we will be your slaves, we are your grandchildren." So the Sarki spared them, but each of them chose a task as a price of their lives.

San Turaki Narai was buried in the mosque* in which he was killed. For this reason Mohamma Zaki made Aderki build Serikin Jarmai a house inside the Sarki's compound. The " zowre " of Turaki Mainya was also built near the mosque, as also Yan Sintali's housse and the houses of Turaki Kuka and Mai-Shikashikai. The site of the mosque was changed. On account of this occurrence Turaki Mainya had the honour of acting for the Sarki, if he were absent, in the time of Mohamma Zaki, but afterwards the right lapsed. Shashere ruled nine years and four months and twenty-four days. Then he was deposed.

XXVII.—MOHAMMA ZAKI, SON OF KISOKI.

A.H. 990-1027.   A.D. 1582-1618.

The twenty-seventh Sarki was Mohamma Zaki, son of Kisoki. The name of his mother was Hausatu, the daughter of Tamma. When Mohamma became Sarki, Tamma came to live at Kano together with his men, the Kartukawa. In the time of Mohamma Zaki " Tchukana " and " Dirki "† were begun. The Sarki's men kept saying to him, " Sarkin Kano, if you leave the Katsinawa alone, they will become masters of all Kano and you will have nothing to rule but a little." The Sarki said, " I will conquer the Katsinawa if Allah wills." At this time the Sarkin Kwararafa came to attack Kano. The people of Kano left the city and went to Daura, with the result that the Kwararafawa ate up the whole country and Kano became very weak. The men of Katsina kept on harrying Kano. If it had not been for the sake of the mallams in Kano, they would have entered and destroyed the city. There was a great famine which lasted eleven years. The Sarki called all his men and mallams together and said, " I have called you together to take counsel with me. How are we to stay this calamity? " Shehu Abubakr the Maghrebine said: " If you wish to repel the men of Katsina, I will give you something to do it with, but if you do repel them, you will never return to Kano." The Sarki said " I agree." He gave Shehu great wealth and the mallams many gifts. Shehu did as he promised to do. The Sarki left Kano on the 22nd day of Ramadan and arrived beneath the walls of Katsina at daybreak on the day of the Salla. The men

---

* The mosque was not rebuilt till the time of Abdulahi Dan Dabo, a Fulani. The Turaki Mainya did not again have such prestige till the time of Mohammed Belo, who made his son Zacchari Turaki Mainya. History repeats itself.

† That is to say, the Koran covered with goat's skin. Afterwards cow hide was used for the purpose, as many as ten skins being used, and even forty in later times. In Alwali's time, the practice had gone to such a ridiculous length that he stopped it altogether. The people said " If you stop this practice, God will bring evil fortune upon you." Alwali replied, " Dirki is nothing but the Koran: I swear I will open it and expose its contents." So he ordered young men to take axes and open " Dirki." They did so. Alwali found the Koran inside, and took it to his house. The people said, " You will be expelled from this land even as you have expelled the Koran from Dirki." Alwali was afterwards driven out of Kano.

of Katsina came out to battle before the hour of the feast. The battle took place at Guraji. The men of Kano defeated the men of Katsina. The men of Katsina dispersed and fled, and the Kanawa took much spoil. They took four hundred horses, and sixty suits of horse armour. No one knows the amount of the spoil or the number of the slain. The Sarki returned to Karayi, where he died. His captains in war were eight in number: Madawaki Shaduka, Makama Babba, Jarumai Kaiotau, Atuman, Yanka Shaida, Burdi Hako, Dawaki Marku and Butali. He ruled Kano thirty-seven years and five months.

XXVIII.—MOHAMMA NAZAKI, SON OF ZAKI.

A.H. 1027-1032.   A.D. 1618-1623.

The twenty-eighth Sarki was Mohamma Nazaki. His mother's name was Kursu. When he became Sarki he sent messengers to make peace with Katsina. Sarkin Katsina refused his terms and invaded Kano. The Kanawa came out, and a battle took place at Karayi, in which the Kanawa defeated the Katsinawa. They then returned to Kano. Next year the Sarkin Kano went to Kalam. He left the Wombai Giwa behind at Kano because he was sick. When the Wombai recovered he said, "What can I do to please the Sarki?" His men said, "Add to the city." He said, "Very well." So he built a wall from the Kofan Dogo to the Kofan Gadonkaia, and from the Kofan Dakawuyia to the Kofan Kabuga, and to the Kofan Kansakali. He spent an enormous amount of money on this improvement. Every morning he brought a thousand calabashes of food and fifty oxen for the workmen till the work was finished. Every man in Kano went to work. No man surpassed the Wombai in benevolence to Moslems and the poor. The day when the work was to be finished the Wombai Giwa distributed among the workmen a thousand "tobes." He slaughtered three hundred cows at the Kofan Kansakali and gave the mallams many presents. When the Sarkin Kano returned from war, the Wombai gave him a hundred riding horses. Each horse had a mail coat. The Sarki was very pleased. He said, "What shall I do for this man, to make his heart glad?" His men said, "Give him a town." So the Sarki gave him Karayi. Hence the song:

"Elephant Lord of the town, Abdullah foe of the bull hippopotamus, whose chains for taking captive women are hoes and axes."

The Wombai left Kano and went to Karayi. Every day he fought the Katsinawa and took much spoil from them in war. He became master of a hundred mailed horsemen and a thousand horses. He was sung as "The Elephant who reduces his neighbours to servitude." He became so mighty that it was feared he would revolt. Hence he was turned out of his office in the time of Kutumbi. Mohamma Nazaki ruled Kano five years and one month.

XXIX.—KUTUMBI, SON OF MOHAMMA NAZAKI.
A.H. 1032-1058.   A.D. 1623-1648.

The twenty-ninth Sarki was Kutumbi, the son of Mohamma Nazaki, otherwise called Mohamma Alwali. His mother's name was Dada. He was a great Sarki. He had a friend whose name was Kalina Atuman, to whom he entrusted great power. No one would believe the extent of his power except one who saw it. He ruled over Kano town and country until his power equalled that of the Sarki, while the Sarki was like his Wazir. This Kalina Atuman was in power for twelve years. Then he died. After his death one of his men, Dawaki Kwoshi, came to the front. He too became so powerful that he seemed likely to revolt. He went to a place called Bakin Karre and was there for seven days. After this he went to Yankwosa, where he remained three days, and afterwards to Rimin Kwoshe, the Sarki's farm. All the chief men of the town flocked to his standard. He had been there nine days when the Sarki induced him to come back with fine words. Then he returned to Kano. He was celebrated in the song:

"See your prophet, ye Princes! You looked for a black dog, and did not find it at the hearth stones. Dawaki can put to flight a host with a shield of lotus. Dawaki the son of the great Dayi, the boaster."

Dawaki was the son of Turaki Kuka Allandayi. Thus it is that if the Sarki is sung, no one may be mentioned but him.

During the time of Kutumbi the saying, "O God great and loving! The great man hath the spleen," originated, because of Allandayi's anger when the Ungwa Kofan Kabagga was taken from him. No man of that time in Kano had accumulated such vast wealth, and so many eunuchs and ornaments. Hence he was sung in the song, "Great God, light of the town, O star!"

Kutumbi was the father of Bako. No prince could compare with him. In everything, in doing good, or doing ill, in courage, anger, and generosity he was like a Sarki, even while he was only a prince. He had six hundred horses and ninety mailed horsemen. He went to Kurmin Dan Ranko to war and took much spoil. When he returned to Kano he was given the title of Jarumai for this exploit. Afterwards he pray to die and died, for fear of civil war after his father's death. In the time of Kutumbi, Sarkin Dawaki Magara went to war with Bauchi and on his return built a town at Ganjua and settled there. He sent to Kano two thousand slaves. Kutumbi was very angry about this. Next year he mounted his horse and went off to war there. The people paid him *Jizia*. Then he returned to Kano leaving there five hundred slaves. The place was called Ibdabu since the people were all the slaves of the Sarki. The next year Kutumbi went to war with Katsina. He was victorious, and took much spoil. He camped at Dugazawa for nine months, during which time no one could venture out of Katsina. From this siege comes the song: "Alwali shutter of the great gate, Kimbirni, shutter of the great gate." Of Kutumbi's warriors the greatest was Madawaki Kimbirni. Then came

Makama Banki, Dan Maji Jartake, Jarmai Garaje, Berdi Kamoku, Goriba Babba, Dan Kanfache Zabarau, Dan Ataman Babakke, Gwoto, Kaderko, Dawaki Sun Kuche and Dan Maköo Makere (so called because he always fought with a *kere*). There were others beside, and they feared nothing but God. Kutumbi returned to Kano, and the next year went to fight with Gwombe, which he sacked. He was the first Sarki of Kano who collected the *Jizia* from the Fulani which is called *Jangali*. He collected a hundred cows from the Jafunawa, the chief clan of Fulani, seventy from the Baawa, sixty from Dindi Maji, fifty from the Danneji, and others too numerous to mention. When he had collected the cattle he said to his slave Ibo, " I make you Sarkin Shanu." Hence the latter was called " Ibo na Kutumbi." He said to Mandawali, " You are Sarkin Samri, because you have charge of all the youths among my slaves." He called the slaves Kirdua. He said to Gumki, "I make you Sarkin Dogare." He said to Buayi, " You are Sarkin Shamaki." This man was called Buayi because he was a " black sheep ". His name was Agurmaji. Kutumbi turned the Sarkin Surdi out of his house, and told him he had appointed another to his office. Sarkin Surdi built a house for himself. Whenever Kutumbi went to war or to Salla, he was followed by a hundred spare horses. Forty drums were in front of him, and twenty-five trumpets, and fifty kettle-drums. He was the first Sarki to create a " Berde Kererria." He was always followed by a hundred eunuchs who were handsomely dressed and had gold and silver ornaments. He built a house at Gandu, and another at Tokarawa. In the latter he lived when he went to war, and waited there until his army had assembled before setting out. When he returned from war he encamped at Gandu, where he would spend the night. Kutumbi was a very mighty Sarki in Hausaland. He went to war with Katsina and encamped close to the western gate of the city.

The Katsinawa came out in the night and a battle took place before daybreak. The Katsina army surprised the Kanawa; the whole of the Kanawa ran away. A man called Kumaza poised his spear and smote at Kutumbi, but Dan Maji Zartaki rushed in and killed him. Hence the song, " Rafter of iron, stronger than ' seri ' wood." Sarkin Kano mounted his horse and retreated together with the few men who were with him. The men of Katsina pursued the retreating Kanawa and harried them until they reached Yashi. As regards Sarkin Kano some people say he was killed in Katsina, others say that he died at Kano. The latter is the better account. In any case he died within three days of the battle. He ruled Kano twenty-six years.

XXX.—AL HAJJI, SON OF KUTUMBI.

A.H. 1058-1059. A.D. 1648-1649.

The thirtieth Sarki was Ali Hajji Dan Kutumbi. His mother's name was Fadima. He ruled Kano eight months and twenty-four days, then he was deposed—the reason, I do not remember. He went into the country to live at a place called Dan Zaki.

XXXI.—SHEKKARAU, SON OF AL HAJI.
A.H. 1059-1061.   A.D. 1649-1651.

The thirty-first Sarki was Shekkarau, the son of Alhaji and Fari. In his time peace was made between Kano and Katsina. The peacemakers were Shehu Ataman, Mallam Bawa and Liman Yandoiya. Shehu Ataman said: "In future, whoever is the aggressor between you shall never prevail, if Allah wills, till the day of judgment." About this time Dan Tamma Maji went out with Sarkin Gesu Sulimanu to Godia. Shekkarau ruled one year and seven months and twenty-four days.

XXXII. KUKUNA, SON OF AL HAJI.
A.H. 1061-1062.   A.D. 1651-1652.

The thirty-second Sarki was Mohamma Kukuna. His mother's name was Goro. After he became Sarki he ruled one year. The Madawaki Kuma turned him out, and gave the power to his sister Fasuma's son Soyaki.

XXXIII.—SOYAKI, SON OF SHEKKARAU.
A.H. 1062.   A.D. 1652.

Soyaki was the thirty-fourth Sarki. His mother was Fasuma. Kukuna fled to Zukzuk. Soyaki had been reigning three months when the chiefs of Kano met together and held a consultation about him. The chief of them were the Galadima Wari, the grandfather of Kofakani Dan Iya Babba, Makama Mukhtari and Sarkin Dawaki Gogori. They sent messengers secretly to Mohamma Kukuna, who at once set out for Gaiya. The Sarkin Gaiya joined him in his march to Kano. The Madawakin Kano heard of this, assembled the men of Kano, and told them the news. They said, "We hear." He said, "What do you propose?" They said, "Shall we not go out before they get close to the city." The Madawaki said, "Very well." A battle took place at Hotoro. The Kano men ran away and deserted the Madawaki Kuma. Kukuna attacked him with a spear. He feared to be killed, and tried to escape. Kukuna followed him. The Madawaki made for the Kofan Kawayi and shouted to the people to close the gate behind him, so that Mohomma Kukuna should not enter. Kukuna, however, got in before the gate was shut and reached the palace.

He found the Sarki Soyaki at the Giddan Ma-Shikashikai, together with his eunuchs. So he seized the sword from the hand of Soyaki and cried, "Allahu, Akbar, you, Sarki of a day! Go out! If you do not go I will cut your head off." The Sarki went out. A house was built for him at Dukarawa, where he lived and died.

XXXIV.—MOHAMMA KUKUNA (Restored).
A.H. 1062-1070.   A.D. 1652-1660.

Mohamma Kukuna then entered the Giddan Rumfa and lived sixty days there. After this he arrested the Madawakin Kano. Then he assembled many maidens, put the Madawaki on a donkey, and handed it over to the maidens, to drive round the town. They did as he commanded. The Madawaki died of chagrin. Kukuna drove away Tasuma, the wife of Shekkarau and mother of Soyaki, because of the grudge he bore her son. She built a house at Durumin Yer Madawaki. Next year Sarkin Kwararafa Adashu came to attack Kano. Sarkin Kano went to Yan Magada, where he stayed seven days, and then to Auyo and Abewa, where he remained forty days. On his return to Kano he found that the Kwararafa had battered down the Kofan Kawayi. He waited seven days, then marched round the city on a Saturday, entered his house, and stayed there two days. On a Monday he went to the Kofan Kawayi and built it up. From the first of these episodes he was called "Gewayer Garu," from the second "Na chin Kassa." On the same Monday he called all the Maguzawa to the city to salute him. They remained twenty-one days, and played a game in which they beat each other's heads with iron. The Sarki gave them many gifts, and asked them who was their chief. On their saying it was Zanku, the Sarki said to him, "Next year come again, and let all your men come with their 'hauyias' on their shoulders." "If you do so, Zanku," said Kukana, "God willing, no Sarkin Kano will be driven out again." Afterwards he sent for the Liman Yandoiya, and after giving him many presents said, "I want you to give me a charm which will prevent any Sarki from being again driven out of Kano." The Liman said, "Very well, but you must increase your presents." Kukuna did so, and gave him silver and gold. The Liman gave him what he gave him. The Liman told Kukuna to bury one charm in the Turaki Mainya's house, another in the house of Turakin Kuka, and another in the "Treasury" of Kano; and he further added that a fire must be kept burning every day above the charms, and assured the Sarki that if his instructions were carried out no Sarki would ever be again deposed. Kukuna did so, and ruled eight years and seven months in addition to the year that is mentioned above. Then he was deposed.

XXXV.—BAWA, SON OF MOHAMMA KUKUNA.

A.H. 1070-1081. A.D. 1660-1670.

The thirty-fifth Sarki was Bawa. His mother's name was Lamis. He was a learned, just, and good Sarki. In his time there was no war in Kano land, east and west, south and north. Goron Pugachi, which Abubakr Kado, the son of Mohamma Rimfa, had built for his sons, had fallen into ruins, so Bawa repaired it. Bawa fashioned the chair which is placed in the house of the great Turáki, that he might sit on it. He built Pugachin Kishi as a school. He had a friend who was called Dan Mallam Ali Diko. This Diko received such honour that a house for him was built in the palace called Soron Diko—in such honour was he held. He and the Sarki were inseparable. They rode together even at the Salla or elsewhere, since they had been the closest of friends from the time before Bawa had become Sarki. They had studied together. Diko always said his morning prayers at the Sarki's house and never returned home until after the evening prayer. In Bawa's time Abdulahi, a great student of the Koran, came to Kano with his friends. He had a wonderfully captivating voice when reading. He took a house near Diko's and preached after evening prayer. Diko asked, "Who is that man?" and was told it was Abdulahi, a stranger. The next morning Diko sent to Abdulahi, and when he came, took him to the Sarki and told him to read to the Sarki. So he read the appointed portion of the Koran. After the Sarki had listened he would not let him go away, but built him a house near to the gate of Turaki Mainya. He was wont to amuse the Sarki at night by reading. During Ramadan Abdulahi preached to the Sarki during the vigils. When Dan Lowan died the Sarki said to Abdulahi, "I make you Dan Lowan, and you will call to prayer." In Bawa's time there were many holy men. He ruled Kano ten years four months and twenty days.

XXXVI.—DADI, SON OF BAWA.

A.H. 1081-1114.   A.D. 1670-1703.

The thirty-sixth Sarki was Dadi. His mother's name was Iya Gari. He wished to enlarge the city of Kano, but Shehu Mohamma prevented him. The next year Sarkin Kwararafa came to fight with Kano. The Sarki wished to go out and fight him outside, but the chiefs of Kano demurred and he remained in his house. The Kwararafa entered Kano by Kofan Gadon Kaia, slaughtered the men of Kano, and reached Bakinrua. The Galadima Kofakani said to the Sarkin Kano, who was in the Pugachin Kishi with his Jarumai: "Establish 'Tchibiri' at Toji and 'Bundu' at Rimi Bundu." The Galadima said to the Sarki, "Rise up! The Kwararafa have destroyed the best part of your town and have killed many men! They have penetrated to the Kurmi, and will attack the 'palace.'" The Sarki mounted his horse and went out, and came to the Kofan Fada with the Galadima and eunuchs and Jarumai. There he met all the Kanawa. He went to Rimi Bundu, took the "Bundu" and gave it to Dan Durma Mazza Mazza, and thence hastened to Kofa Bai. He found the Kwararafa had come near the "Tchibiri," but every one of them who came close died at once. The Sarkin Kwararafa told his people to take away the "Tchibiri." The Kwararafa tried to charge, but they failed to seize it. The Sarkin Kano came to the "Tchibiri," and took it. On his right hand he had a hundred warriors, in front of him ninety-nine chiefs, all of them mallams, and on his left hand a hundred warriors. They were all slaughtered by the Kwararafa; only a few were left alive. Sarkin Kano fled to Daura. The Kwararafa followed him to Jelli and then returned. Of the men who were killed in this battle the chiefs were Dan Janbori, Dan Barra, Sarkin Buzza, Sarkin Durra, Dan Tanadi, Bundu, Sarkin Zabro, Magagi Bugaji, Sarkin Marua, Dan Garadu, Dan Raguma Giwa, Magaji Butachi, Dan Koamna, Magagi Sheggi, Dan Gamaji, Magaji Gantururu, Dan Dagazo, Magagi Tuntu, Sarkin Maguri, Dan Gauji, Magagi Garogi, Dan Tankaro, Dan Kargagi, Magaji Karfassa, Dan Kutuntu, Dan Toro, Dan Zaki Mazawa, Dan Bambawri, Kioto and others—in all ninety-seven Sarkis. In the time of Dadi the Sarkin Gaiya revolted. His name was Farin Dussi, the father of Mariamma. He was three years without paying the Sarkin Kano *Jizia*. Then the Sarkin Kano enticed him to an interview and killed him, some say with a razor, some at " Baura." In consequence of this revolt Sarkin Dawaki Debba (called Kamna) went out and became Sarkin Aujera. The Sarki said to him, " I am making you Sarkin Aujera because I am afraid of Miga, Dussi and Gaiya revolting." Dadi ruled Kano thirty-three years and eight months.

XXXVII.—MOHAMMA SHAREFA, SON OF DADI.

A.H. 1114-1143.   A.D. 1703-1731.

The thirty-seventh Sarki was Mohamma Sharefa, son of Dadi. His mother's name was Mariamma. She was the daughter of Sarkin Gaiya Farin-Dussi. In Sharefa's time, the men of Gaiya became very influential in Kano. Sharefa was a powerful Sarki. He introduced seven practices in Kano all of which were robbery, namely, Karo, Rinsua, Matafada, Yan Dawaki, Kuaru, Jizia of maidens on marriage, and Jizian Kasua Kurmi. He invented many other methods of extortion. Sharefa sent Wombai Debba to war. The Wombai left Kano for Kirru, and making war on it captured much spoil and many men. News came to Sharefa that the Womgai had sacked Kirru and that there was nothing in the town but ashes. Sharefa said nothing, but when the Wombai Debba returned to Kano asked him what he meant by such work. The Wombai said, " I like Kano," speaking in riddles. In Sharefa's time the Sarkin Jamfara, Yakubu Dan Mazura, came to make war on Kano. A battle was fought at Yergana in which the men of Jamfara defeated the men of Kano. The men of Kano fled and deserted the Sarki, who was left with Nasan Kanni, Kasheka Bugau, the Turaki Mainya Allah Nikimaiyi, Berdi Kereria Yashibka and Dogara Gateri. They all lost their heads. Sharefa said to them, " Does not a single one of you know the way back to Kano? " They said, " No." Nasan Kanni said, " I know the way to the city." The Sarki said to him, " Show me the road." So he showed the Sarki the road until they came to the Rimin Bugunsua. The Sarki entered the town and his house, and no one was allowed to see him, so great was his wrath. Nasan Kanni Bugau, Allah Nikimaiyi and Yashibka obtained great honour from the Sarki because of the fight at Yergana. After this the Sarki sent out Sarkin Gaiya Jan Hazo, and told him to put a wall round Gaiya. Walls were built, too, at Tarkai Tsokkua, Gano, Dawaki and many other towns. When Bugan became Turaki Kuka he sent messengers to Sarkin Yawuri to ask him for " Algaitas." The Sarkin Yawuri gave him ten Algaitas, and three " Kurra-Kurra." The messenger came with them to Turaki Bugau. Bugau kept them three months, and sent them to the Maidaki Mariamma, since she was a great personage. There was no woman like her in the seven Hausa states. In Sharefa's time cowries first came to Hausaland. The Sarki was a mighty warrior. Among his captains were Sarkin Dawaki Sodi, Dan Iya Maji Kudu, Dan Iya Mallam Shadu, Sarkin Jarumai, Mallam Bawa, Sarkin Jarumai Akwuria, Dan Iya Dashina, Sarkin Jarumai Ibrahim,

Limanin Beradai Dodo, Berde Ba Kuddu, Sarkin Jarumai Abdullah, Galadima Kofa-Kanni. These all fought under Dadi. There were also Maidawaki Magani, Dan Sudu Durraman, Ali Uban Dan Kurkuti, Yahaya Uban Dan Maji Babba, Sarkin Damargu Gabo, Sarkin Fulani Bebeji Abdua, Sarkin Fulani Dania, Sarkin Fulani Bugai Beriss, Sarkin Gaiya Alwali, Sarkin Fulani Sankara Dubai, Berde Alhaji, Madawakin Gawo Bajiddah and others. When they went to war they never ran away, but always were victorious, even though the Sarki were not present. Sharefa ruled Kano twenty-eight years and ten months.

XXXVIII.—KUMBARI, SON OF SHAREFA.
A.H. 1143-1156. A.D. 1731-1743.

The thirty-eighth Sarki was Mohamma Kumbari, the son of Sharefa and Luki. He was a liberal Sarki but quick to anger. His counsellors liked him, but the common people hated him. In his time there was fierce war between Kano and Gobir.

The name of Sarkin Gobir was Soba. If the Gobirawa defeated the Kanawa one day, the Kanawa defeated them the next. This state of affairs continued for a long time. In Kumbari's time Sarkin Bornu Mai Ali came to Kano to war. He encamped at Faggi for three nights without a battle being fought, since Shehu Tahiru and Shehu Bunduu prevented it. He returned to Bornu. Kumbari went to war with Dussi in the time of Sarkin Dussi Makuri and very nearly entered the town through the fierceness of his attack, but his advisers prevented him entering the town, saying to him, "Sarki Kano, you have won the day, go home." He listened to their advice and went home. In the Dussi war Sarkin Aujera Bugau was killed. Kumbari returned to Kano. In his time shields were first brought from Nupe, which was then ruled over by Sarkin Nupe Jibrila. Guns were also brought. Mohamma Kumbari was active in collecting *Jizia* from the Kasua Kurmi, so that the market was nearly killed. The next year he collected *Jizia* in Kano and made even the mallams pay. There was so much disturbance that the Arabs left the town and went back to Katsina, and most of the poorer people in the town fled to the country.

Turaki Kuka Tunku said to Kumbari, "Sarki, if you do not let this *Jizia* alone, there will be no one left in the town but yourself and your servants." The Sarki listened to him. Kumbari made war against Kuddu Baudam. When he went out to Zanga he was advised to make haste, for it was said, "If you do not make haste you will not conquer Baudam, because there are many warriors in the town." He said, "I hear." When he came near the gate of the town, an arrow was launched at him and a battle ensued between the Kanawa and Kudawa. When Kumbari saw that the battle was growing hot, he took a spear in his hand and attacked the wall of the town. The men of Kano followed him under a shower of arrows. The Kudawa slaughtered the Kanawa, and the Kanawa slaughtered the Kudawa, until Kumbari reached the gate of the town. Had not the gate been closed he would have got in. The Kudawa ran away in a body to their houses. Kumbari camped at Zongon Dan Ingarma. Afterwards terms of peace were arranged and Kunmbari returned to Kano. His captains were fifty-two men who knew no fear: Sarkin Jarumai Aidajika, Berde Duguru, Dan Iya Tefida, Dan Iya Gajigi, Sarkin Majia Dandawa, Dan Tama Dan Arkaya, the Maji Yakufawa called Kunkuru Dageza, Dan Berde Madawaki Yabo, Galadima Dan Faramu, Sarkin Dawaki Mallam Bawa, Berde Sokana, Sarkin Jarumai Akallam, Jarmai Tugwai, Dan Hamuda, Dan Tankari Hamadi, Dan Tara-Tara Abbas, Sarkin Gano Bako, Dandama Kanwa Chilaya, Makama Chikudu, Lifidi Sayadu, Dan Maskara, Maidawaki Berde Dan Ashifu, Sarkin Damargu Baji Dan Gaba, Sarkin Bebeji Zakkari, Dan Bugai Chusa, Dan Beras, Sarkin Ringim Ada, Al-Berka, Sarkin Tsekkia Atoro, Dan Farzaki, Sarkin Burku Muni, Dan Samayila Chikewa, Jarumai Raädu, Gashin Baki Tsofo, Makarma Della, Dan Ajibiji Kakwoshi Magani, Dan Shanono, Dan Ali Duka, and others. Each one of them had no fear in fight, but Kumbari thought there was no one equal to himself. He ruled thirteen years.

XXXIX.—ALHAJI KABE, SON OF KUMBARI.
A.H. 1156-1166. A.D. 1743-1753.

The thirty-ninth Sarki was Alhaji Kabe. His mother's name was Zama. She was also called Zenabu. He was a Sarki of many wars and terrible. From the time he obtained the kingdom he did not remain five months in his house without going to war or sending out Sarkis to fight. Sarkin Gobir sent to try and make peace with him but Kabe refused. He sent to Sarkin Gobir Barbari, saying, "I have a cap to fit anyone's head." Barbari said, "I hear." The next year Barbari came to Kano to war. a battle ensued between him and Kabe at Dami. The Kanawa ran away, because of the "magic" which Barbari possessed. The Kanawa left Kabe alone with the Dogarai and Kwinkele, and Sarkin Dawaki Kinku Ammi and Turaki Kuka Yadoka. The whole army of the Gobirawa came charging up to the Sarkin Kano. The Kwinkele withstood them until their chief was killed. Then Yakidoka said, "Sarkin Kano, all the men of Kano have run away and left you alone with your slaves." Sarkin Kano returned to the town together with his slaves (some say with the Kanawa) sick at heart. The Gobirawa went on slaughtering the Kanawa, and the Kanawa slaughtered the Gobirawa in frequent wars until Kabe's death. No record can be kept of the fighting between them in Kabe's time or the number of wars in which Kabe engaged or which he ordered. No one gave presents to the mallams so much as Kabe did, for he sought a reward in the next world. There was no man of his age who was so ruthless in killing men as Kabe. There was no peace in Kano, only trouble after trouble what with the war with Gobir and other wars. Sarikin Dawaki Ali, Jarumai Tugwai Dan Bajidda, Sarkin Jarumai Salihu, Lifidi Abubakr, Berdi Bakana, Makama Bagwinki, Lifidi Sawani, Ganda Faria, Magajin Kan-Kama, Doro, Lifidi Jedi Kwoma, Makama Almajir, Galadima Guraguri, Galadima Jarmawa Ali, Berde-Kunda, Burde Bakudu, Sarkin Damargu Buzu Dan Barii, Sarkin Ringim Kwirudu, Burdi Shahu, and others were Kumbari's warriors, and fought for Kabe. Kabe ruled nine years and seven months.

XL.—YAJI, SON OF DADI.
A.H. 1166-1182. A.D. 1753-1768.

The fortieth Sarki was Mohamma Yaji, son of Dadi. His mother's name was Mariamma. He was a just and good Sarki, and a man of mild disposition. On account of this his wives called him "Mallam Lafia." In his time there was no trouble.

He ruled in harmony with his brothers, the sons of Bauwo. There was no difficulty either with his Sarkis or his chief slaves, or his household, or any one. Many men came and settled in Kanoland in his reign. He reigned fifteen years and ten months.

XLI.—BABBA ZAKI, SON OF YAJI.
A.H. 1182-1190. A.D. 1768-1776.

The forty-first Sarki was the son of Yaji, called Babba Zaki. His mother's name was Yerduna. He was an able Sarki, of great strength, renowned for his memory and eloquence. He was called Babba Zaki. He made war on Birnin Auyau in the time of Sarki Abubakr. If it had not been for Madawaki Kano Dandawa, Sarkin Gaiya Gajigi and Sarkin Jafun Furtumi, the Kanawa would have entered the city of Auyan and destroyed the town. Yaji built a house at Takai and almost lived there, but the court refused to live there. He made war on Burumburum, and took the town by assault, capturing many of the inhabitants and cutting the throats of some, whilst the others fled. He curbed the power of the Sarkis and head slaves and plundered them every day. He forced them to give presents under compulsion, and to go to war unwillingly. Hence he was called "Jan Rano, well named the disturber of elephants." In war he forced them to fight against their judgment. He was the first Sarki, who had a guard of musketeers at Kano, a practice which has obtained ever since. He imitated the Arabs of Kano in almost everything. His war captains were five:—Sarkin Sankara Nagerki, Sarkin Bebeji Dembo, Sarkin Majia Kimfirmi Makama Bobawa, Sarkin Jarumai Achukur, Sarkin Dawaki Maina. The great men in his time were forty-two:—Dawaki Tokara, Bawa, Madawaki Dundurusu, Lifidi Gabjin, Galadiman Shamaki Alwali, Tunku, Yakufu, Berka Wuta, Bagalami, Berka. These were all slaves. Among the mallams were: Alkali Abbas, Alkali Makam, Limanin Kano Aburauf and his sons, Abubukr Dan Mallam Bohari from Yandoto, and Husani from Tarkai. The great men among the Arabs were: Sherif Hassan, Hajariki, Sherif Hamad, Sherif Dahab, and others. Among the Sarki's sons were: Dan Iya, Mallam Osuman, Choka, Daka and Nafata. Among his eunuchs were: Sarkin Dawaki Muradi, Turaki Mainya Munaga Allah, Turaki Kuka Kasan Allah, Turaki Kuka Ka-nem-Kiwo, Kwoninka Jephar, who was of the same people as Sherif Hassan and others. The chief of these were Dan Maji Babba, Hangaza and Dan Zanko Jibril. In all there were forty-two.

Each of them thought he was greater than the rest in the Sarki's eyes. Thus the Sarki planned, Babban Zarki ruled Kano eight years.

XLII.—DAUDA ABASAMA, SON OF YAJI.
A.H. 1190-1195. A.D. 1776-1781.

The forty-second Sarki was Dauda Abasama, the son of Yaji. His mother's name was Baiwa. He was a Sarki of good character, reticent and wise, generous and popular. He was prudent and at the same time warlike, and kept his word. He had a mind above favouritism or revenge, and took the Galadima Makama's advice in everything. The Galadima Makama was like a Sarki, while Dauda was like his Wazir, because he was so forbearing. There was no war in his reign or rebellion. He ruled Kano five years and four months.

XLIII.—MOHAMMA ALWALI, SON OF YAJI.
A.H. 1195-1222. A.D. 1781-1807.

The forty-third Sarki was Mohamma Alwali, son of Yaji. His mother's name was Baiwa. As soon as he became Sarki he collected stores of " Gero " and " Dawa " in case of war and famine. Nevertheless famine overtook him. His chiefs said to him. " Sarkin Kano, why do you refuse to give cattle to Dirki? " The Sarki said, " I cannot give you forty cattle for Dirki." They said, " What prevents you? If any Sarkin Kano does not allow us cattle for Dirki, we fear that he will come to some ill." Alwali was very angry and sent young men to beat " Dirki " with axes until that which was inside the skins came out. They found a beautiful Koran inside Dirki. Alwali said, " Is this Dirki? " they said, " Who does not know Dirki? Behold here is Dirki." Dirki is nothing but the Koran. In Alwali's time the Fulani conquered the seven Hausa States on the plea of reviving the Muhammadan religion. The Fulani attacked Alwali and drove him from Kano, whence he fled to Zaria. The men of Zaria said, " Why have you left Kano? " He said, " The same cause which drove me out of Kano will probably drive you out of Zaria." He said, " I saw the truth with my eyes, I left because I was afraid of my life, not to save my wives and property." The men of Zaria drove him out with curses. So he fled to Rano, but the Fulani followed him to Burum-Burum and killed him there. He ruled Kano twenty-seven years, three of which were spent in fighting the Fulani.

XLIV —SULIMANU, SON OF ABAHAMA.
A.H. 1222-1235. A.D. 1807-1819

The forty-fourth Sarki was Sulimanu, son of Abahama, a Fulani. His mother's name was Adama Modi. When he became Sarkin Kano, the Fulani prevented him from entering the palace. He went into the house of Sarkin Dawaki's mother. One of the remaining Kanawa said to Sulimanu, " If you do not enter the Giddan Rimfa, you will not really be the Sarki of city and country." When Sulimanu heard this he called the chief Fulani, but they refused to answer his summons, and said, " We will not come to you. You must come to us, though you be the Sarki. If you will come to Mallam Jibbrim's house we will assemble there." Sulimanu went to Jibbrim's house and called them there. When they had assembled, he asked them and said, "Why do you prevent me entering the Giddan Rimfa?" Mallam Jibbrim said, "If we enter the Habe's houses and we beget children, they will be like these Habes and do like them." Sulimanu said nothing but set off to Shehu-Osuman Dan Hodio asking to be allowed to enter the Giddan Rimfa. Shehu Dan Hodio gave him a sword and a knife* and gave him leave to enter the Kiddan Rimfa, telling him to kill all who opposed him. He entered the house, and lived there. All the Kano towns submitted to him, except Faggam, which he attacked. He took many spoils there. On his way back to Kano the chiefs of the Fulani said to him, "If you leave Faggam alone, it will revolt." So he divided it into two, and returned home. In his time Dabo Dan Bazzo raised a revolt. He dared to look for a wife in Sokoto and was given one. Sarkin Kano said, "What do you mean by looking for a wife at Sokoto?" So Dabo was caught and bound. His relations, the Danbazzawa, however, came by night and cut his bonds, and set him free. He ran to Sokoto with Sulimanu following him. At Sokoto they both went before Dan Hodio. Dabo Dan Bazzo said, "I do not wish to marry your daughters, but I wish for a reconciliation between myself and your Sarki Sulimanu." So a reconciliation was made and they returned to Kano. Sulimanu sent the Galadima Ibrahima to Zaria to make war. Ibrahima conquered Zaria and took many spoils. He returned to Kano. Sulimanu was angry because of the Galadima's success, and had sinister designs against him when he died himself without having an opportunity of carrying them out. He ruled thirteen years.

XLV.—IBRAHIM DABO, SON OF MOHAMMADU.

A.H. 1235-1262. A.D. 1819-1846.

The forty-fifth Sarki was the pious and learned Ibrahim Dabo, son of Mohammadu, protector of the orphan and the poor, a mighty conqueror—a Fulani.

His mother's name was Halimatu. When he became Sarki he entered the Giddan Rimfa. Dabo made Sani Galadima. He, however, immediately tried to raise a revolt and incite all the towns to disaffection. The country Sarkis assembled and became "Tawayi," from Ngogu to Damberta, from Jirima to Sankara, and from Dussi to Birnin Kudu and Karayi. Dabo said, "I will conquer them, if Allah wills." He entered his house and remained there forty days praying to Allah for victory. Allah heard his prayers. He went out to hasten his preparations for war, and made a camp on Dalla Hill. Because of this he got the name of "The man who encamped on Dalla." He spent many days on Dalla†, and then returned home. He sent Sarkin Dawaki Manu

---

* A flag was also given him as well as a knife and sword. He did not go to Sokoto, but sent a message. Had he gone himself, he would never have regained his position.

† Perhaps forty, I am not sure.

Maituta to fight with Karayi. When the Sarkin Dawaki reached Karayi he sacked the town and returned to Dabo. Dabo said, "Praise be to God," and prepared himself to go out to war. He went to Jirima and sacked that town and afterwards sacked Gasokoli and Jijita. Hence he was known as "Dabo, the sacker of towns." After he returned home he kept on sending out men to raid towns. He went in person to attack Dan Tunku and found him at Yan Yahiya. They fought. The Yerimawa ran away, and deserted Dan Tunku, who fled to Damberta, and thence, with Dabo following him, to Kazauri. When the Sarki reached the Koremma in pursuit he stopped, turned round again, and went back to Damberta, where he wrecked Dan Tunku's house. Dabo then returned home. Dabo was celebrated in the song:—

"The sacker of towns has come: Kano is your land, Bull Elephant, Dabo, sacker of towns."

When he went to war the trumpets played:—
"The sacker of towns is mounting."

He made war on Birnin Sankara and Birnin Rano, took the town of Rano, and lived in the house of Sarkin Rano. After this exploit he shaved his head. He never shaved his head except he sacked a town. When the Kano towns saw that Dabo would not leave any town unconquered, they all submitted to him, and his power exceeded all other Sarkis. He had a friend whose name was Ango. When the Galadima Sini died, he made Ango Galadima, and as Galadima the latter reached great power through his pleasant manner and his persuasiveness. In Dabo's time there was no foreign war and people had food in plenty. Dabo conquered and spoiled Yasko. He had many war captains, a few among whom may be mentioned as: Berde, Kano Buggali, Sarkin Dawaki Manu, Sarkin Jarumai Dumma, Sulimanu Gerkwarn Karifi (he it was who killed Tunari, the son of Sarkin Sankara), Juli Kuda, Lifidi, Maidawaki Gawo and many others. These warriors of Dabo's time had no fear in war. When Dabo mounted to go to war no such dust was ever seen, so many were his horses. The dust was like the Harmattan. Dabo was called "Majeka Hazo." His was a wonderful and brilliant reign, but we will not say any more for fear of "Balazi." He ruled Kano twenty-seven years and three months and nine days, his reign ending on the ninth of Safar.

XLVI.—OSUMANU, SON OF DABO.

A.H. 1262-1272.   A.D. 1846-1855.

The forty-sixth Sarki was Osumanu, son of Dabo. His mother was Shekara. The first act of his reign was to build a house for Shekara at Tafassa with a big room the like of which was never seen before. Shekara was called "the mistress of the big room." Osumanu was a learned and good man and generous. He was called "The skin of cold water." The Galadima Abdulahi obtained in his time almost as much power as the Sarki, while Osuman was like his Waziri. There was no war in his time except with Hadeijia. He built a house at Gogel and had a farm there. In his time mallams obtained great honour—among them Mallam Ba-Abseni, and others. In Osumanu's time Sarkin Dussi Bello revolted, but the Sarki enticed him to Kano and deposed him. Highway robbers were very numerous because Osuman was so good-tempered and merciful. He could not bring himself to cut a man's hand off nor, because he was so pitiful, could he cut a robber's throat. He was called " Jatau rabba kaya." There was no Sarki like him for generosity. He ruled Kano nine years and ten months.

XLVII.—ABDULAHI, SON OF DABO.

A.H. 1272-1300.   A.D. 1855-1883.

The forty-seventh Sarki was Abdulahi son of Dabo. His mother's name was Shekkara. When he became Sarki he set to work to kill all the robbers and cut off the hands of the thieves. He was called " Abdu Sarkin Yenka " because he was a strong-minded Sarki, ruthless, and victorious. He was quick to depose chiefs, but kept his word to his friends. He never stayed long in one place but went from town to town. In his time there was a very great famine, and the quarrel with Umbata grew big from small beginnings. The Sarkin Kano was eager to make war upon Umbatu. His first move was to attack Kuluki. Dan Iya Lowal of Kano died at Kuluki, whereupon the Sarki returned home himself, but sent Abdulahi Sarkin Dawaki Dan Ladan and his son Tafida to war in Zaria country. They went to Zaria together. This was in the time of Sarkin Zaria Abdulahi Dan Hamada. When they returned from Zaria it was not long before Dan Boskori made a descent upon Gworzo. The Sarkin Kano sent Sarkin Dawaki on ahead and followed himself personally to meet Dan Boskori Sarkin Maradi, west of Gworzo. A battle took place. The Kanawa ran away, deserting the Sarkin Dawaki Dan Ladan. Dan Boskori killed him. The Kanawa returned home in ones and twos. The Sarkin Kano was very angry. He gave orders that a house was to be built at Nassarawa for him to live in during the hot season; he also built a house at Tarkai for the war with Umbatu. He had a house at Keffin Bako where he lived almost two years because of Dan Maji the neighbour of Umbatu. He fought with Warji after the war with Kuluki, and took enormous spoil. No one knows the amount of the spoil that was taken at a town called Sir. The corpses of Warjawa, slaughtered round their camp, were about four hundred. The Sarki returned home. After a short time, the Sarki attacked Warji again, and once more took many spoils. Kano was filled with slaves. Abdulahi went to Sokoto, leaving his son Yusufu at Tarkai. While he was there Dan Maji came to attack Yusufu. A battle was fought at Dubaiya. The Kanawa fled and deserted Yusufu. Many men were slain and captured. After this Yusufu was made Galadima Kano, and hence acquired much power. Abdulahi sent him to Dal from Tarkai to capture Haruna, the son of Dan Maji. Yusufu met Haruna at Jambo, and a battle took

place. The Umbatawa ran away, deserting Haruna. Yusufu killed and took many men. It is said that about seven hundred were killed. Afterwards Yusufu tried to stir up rebellion and was deprived of his office and had to remain in chagrin and poverty till he was penniless. Abdulahi turned the Sarkin Dawaki Abdu out of his office and with him Makama Gadodamasu, Chiroma Diko, Dan Iya Alabirra, Galadima Abdul-Kadiri, and Galadima Yusufu. Abdulahi killed the Alkali Kano Ahmedu Rufaiyi, and degraded Maäji Sulimanu, Maji Gajere, and San Kurmi Musa. He deprived Mallam Dogo of his office of Waziri. The number of people that he turned out of office was countless. Hence the song—
"Son of Ibrahim, a pick-axe to physic hard ground."

He sacked many towns. He made a new gate, the Kofan Fada. In his father's time it had been built up. He rebuilt the mosque and house of the Turaki Mainya early in his reign. They had been in ruins for many years. In his time Soron Giwa was built. At Woso he met Dan Maji in war. It was towards evening when the battle was fought. Dan Maji retreated. If it had not been that the light failed he would have been killed. Abdulahi attacked Betu, but failed. Abdulahi used to have guns fired off when he mounted his horse, till it became a custom. His chief men were:— Sarkin Yaki, called Mallam Dogo, Mallam Isiaka, Mallam Garuba, Sarkin Gaiya, Mallam Abdu Ba-Danneji, Alhaji Nufu, his friend Mallam Masu, Tefida his son, Shamaki Naamu, Manassara, Jekada of Gerko, and Dan Tabshi. Mallam Ibrahim was his scribe, and was made a Galadima. This man was afterwards turned out of office in the time of Mohammed Belo. Others were the Alkali Zengi and Alkali Sulimanu, Abdulahi went to Zaria and sat down at Afira, and then at Zungonaiya. The Madawaki Ali of Zaria was in revolt against Sarkin Zaria. The Sarkin Kano made peace between them and returned home. In Abdulahi's time Salemma Berka became great. In the time of Mohammed Belo this man revolted and was degraded. In Abdulahi's time, too, the palace slaves became so great that they were like free men. They all rebelled in Mohammed Belo's time, but Allah helped Mohammed Belo to quell the rebellion. There were many great captains of war in Abdulahi's time, men without fear—so many of them that they could not be enumerated, but a few may be mentioned: Sarkin Yaki, Mallam Dogo and his son Düti, Jarumai Musa, Sarkin Bebeji Abubakr, Sarkin Rano Ali, Sarkin Gesu Osuman, Sarkin Ajura Jibbr. In this reign Sarkin Damagaram Babba came as far as Jirima and sacked Garun Allah. Sarkin Gummel Abdu Jatau came to Pogolawa to attack it. Sarkin Maradi Dan Boskori came to Katsina. Abdulahi went to meet him. They met at Kusada, but did not fight. For this reason the meeting was called "Algish Bigish Zuru Yakin Zuru," for they looked at each other and went back. There was also a fight between Barafia Sarkin Maridi and Sarkin Kano at Bichi. Barafia ran away and Abdulahi took all the spoils. It is not known how many men were killed and slain. We do not know much of what Abdulahi did in the early part of his reign. He ruled Kano twenty-seven years and eight days, and died at Karofi on his way to Sokoto.

XLVIII.—MOHAMMED BELO, SON OF IBRAHIM DABO.
A.H. 1300-1310.   A.D. 1883-1892.

The forty-eighth Sarki was Mohammad Belo, son of Ibrahim Dabo. His mother was Shekkara. He was a very generous Sarki. He said to his friend Sarkin Fada Dan Gatuma, " You are Waziri Kano; I place in your hands the management of Kano." The Sarkin Fada was unrivalled as a settler of disputes. Belo was like his Wazir, and Sarkin Fada was like Sarki. When Sarki Fada died Mohammed Belo stretched out his legs because he saw that now he must become Sarki in earnest. He expelled the Galadima Ibrahim from his office and banished him to Funkui in Zaria, whence his name, " Galadima na Funkui." Belo gave the post of Galadima to his son Tukr, and his son Zakari was made San Turaki. Another son, Abubakr, he made Chiroma in place of Chiroma Musa. . . .

LXI.—HISTORY OF DAURA.

Daura claims to be the earliest Hausa State in Nigeria. A written record called the Girgam appears to have been kept for many years, though it is not known at what period or by what King of Daura this writing was first undertaken.

About the middle of the nineteenth century the private property of Nuhu, Sarkin Zango, was seized by Damagaram, including all papers and ceremonial silver knife and horn. It is said that the Sarkin Dawaki of Damagaram opened the sacred horn in the hope of finding something of value and as a result suffered from dreams and visions, which caused him to return the knife and the horn to the Kings of Daura.

The papers were however not returned, and the Girgam was re-written from memory; it is from this that since the British occupation the early history of Daura has been taken.

Recently we have succeeded in obtaining a copy of the older Girgam, which was stolen from Sarki Nuhu by Tanimu Sarkin Damagaram and was placed in the keeping of Sulemanu Limamın Damagaram, whose son Hasan is now in charge of this and similar papers.

This Girgam runs as follows:—

" The people went up out of Canaan and settled in the land of Palestine. And a certain man among them named Najib the Canaanite went up out of Palestine with all his household and journeyed westwards into Libya, which is one of the Provinces of Egypt, and there they dwelt for many years. And a certain man among them named Abdul Dar, and he was a son of Najib, went up out of Libya and dwelt in the Province of Tripoli. And after a time he sought the kingship of Tripoli, but the people refused. Wherefore he arose with his people and journeyed to the south till he came to an oasis called Kusugu and dwelt there. And he begat children, and they were all daughters. Their names were

Bukainya and Gambo and Kafai and Waizamu and Daura, and she was the youngest. All these he begat before they came to Daura.

"And a certain man named Abuyazidu, son of Abdulahi, king of Bagdad, quarrelled with his father and the people of the city. And they were divided into forty companies. Then Abuyazidu with twenty companies journeyed until they came to Bornu, and they dwelt there. But the King of Bornu saw that Abuyazidu was stronger than he and was of a mightier house, so he took counsel with his people. And they counselled him that he should give Abuyazidu his daughter to wife, and become his father-in-law. And he did so and gave him his daughter Magira to wife, and he married her. Then the Sarkin Bornu said to Abuyazidu that he wished to go to war and prayed him to lend him his horsemen and warriors to aid him against his foe, and he gave him three thousand horses with their warriors, together with princes to the number of seventeen. And he said 'When we return from this war I will make them princes in my country'. And they went out to war and stayed for six months. Then Sarkin Bornu took counsel to kill Abuyazidu, but his wife Magira heard it and straightway told him. And when he saw all that had been done, that his horsemen had been taken from him and his princes, he saw that it was a plot to overcome him, and he spake unto his people and bade them flee to the north during the night. And they obeyed and left him, and he arose with his wife and journeyed to the west. And when they came to a place called Gabas ta Buram, his wife bare a son: and he left her there and passed on with his concubine and his mule, and his concubine also was with child. And they journeyed until they came to Daura at night and they alighted at the house of an old woman whose name was Waira and he asked her for water. But she answered that they could not get water except on Fridays. And he asked her what hindered them, and she told him there was a snake in the well. And he took the bucket which she gave him and went to the well and let the bucket down into the water. When the snake heard the bucket she lifted her head out of the well to kill him, but he drew his sword and cut off her head—and her head was like the head of a horse. And he drew water and took the head of the snake, and it was the night before Friday. And in the morning the people assembled at the well and they questioned one another who had done this thing to the snake, whose name was Sarki, and they marvelled at that part which lay outside the well and that which remained within it. And the news was brought to the Queen of Daura, and she mounted with all her princesses and came to the well, and she asked who had done this thing. And many people spake falsely and said that they had killed the snake, but when she asked to be shewn the head of the snake they were all dumb. Then spake the old woman at whose house Abuyazidu had alighted, and said that a man had come to her house during the night with an animal which was like a horse and yet was not a horse; and he asked me for a bucket and I gave it to him, and he drew water and watered his beast and gave me what remained, perchance it was he who has done this deed. And they summoned him and asked him, and he said he had done it, and shewed them the head of the snake. And the Queen said, ' I have promised that whosoever should do this thing, I will give him half my town.' But Abuyazidu said he wished rather to marry her, and she consented. And he dwelt in her house together with his concubine who was with child. And when the people came to the Queen to bring her news, she would bid them go to the house of Makassarki (the snake-killer). Then the concubine bare a son and she named him ' Mukarbigari '. Then the Queen of Daura also bare a son and she named him ' Bawogari '. Then Abuyazidu died and Bawo ruled in his stead. And Bawo begat six sons and these are their names:—

"*Gazaura* who became king of Daura,
"*Bagauda* who became king of Kano
"and these were sons of the same mother.
"*Gunguma* who became King of Zazzau,
"*Duma* who became King of Gobir
"and these two were sons of the same mother.
"*Kumayau* who became King of Katsina
"*Zamna Kogi* who became King of Rano; and these two were sons of the same mother."

This is the end of the book Girgam.

There are certain differences between this earlier Girgam and the one written from memory towards the end of the nineteenth century :—

(a) The traditional name of the stranger from Bagdad is Abayajidda, whereas the above gives Abuyazidu—presumably the same name as Bayezid, a famous holy man of Aïr.

(b) The newer writing states that before Abayajidda left Bornu his two brothers left him and became respectively kings of Kanem and Bagarmi. There is no mention of this in the older copy.

(c) The newer version refers to the stranger's animal as " like an ox and yet not an ox ", while the older copy has it " like a horse and yet not a horse " and elsewhere refers to a mule.

(d) The newer version states that it was the Queen of Daura who gave the stranger a Gwari concubine while the older copy states that he brought her with him from Bornu.

It is unfortunate that the written records of Gabas ta Buram—or Garun Gabas as it is now called Hadejia Emirate—were accidentally destroyed by fire in 1921, as a comparison with the Daura legend would have been interesting.

Among the burnt records was a list of Kings of the Town. Such as can be remembered will be found in Appendix "B".

The story as remembered by the present Chief of Garun Gabas, who claims to be a direct descendant of the early dynasty, is that the stranger from Bagdad came from Bornu with his wife and a mare, and that the soothsayers had said that where the mare did two things there he should build a town. He travelled westwards from Bornu and halted at a spot where is now the village of Zeni in Sarkin Arewa's District of Hadejia. There he found two huts occupied by hunters. He then moved on to the site of Garun Gabas, and as the mare fulfilled the two conditions as foretold by the soothsayers he built a town there and left his son, or brother, Biram as chief, while he passed on to Daura.

It is perhaps not generally known that the first town founded in this region was not Daura but what is now called Tsofon Birni. The site lies about six miles due north of Daura.

It would appear that the first nine Queens ruled in Tsofon Birni, the ninth named Daura founding the new town named after her. The name of her predecessor "Innagari" may possibly refer to some unrecorded detail of history which led to the removal to the new site. It would seem not improbable that "Daura" represents an invasion which destroyed the old town and founded a new one further down the river. The difference in style between the names of the first seven Queens and of the eight who follow Daura may perhaps support this theory.

It will be seen that the names of the daughters of Abduldar mentioned in the Girgam bear a close resemblance to those of the early Queens shewn in Appendix "A"

It will be observed that the "Girgam" states that Daura was the name of the Queen found by Abayajidda. The written list of Queens and Kings however shews that Magajiya Shawata was ruling at this period.

Presumably Daura was used as representing the female dynasty or the correct reading may be Daurama, *i.e.* Queen of Daura.

An interesting point is the difference in pronunciation of the name of the present town of Daura and the name of the legendary Queen. This may be represented as follows, the grave accent denoting a low tone and the acute accent a raised tone:—

Daù-rá—the name of the town.
Daúrà—the name of the Queen.

I have been unable to obtain any explanation of this curious but admitted difference.

As pointed out above the newer version of the Girgam, written from memory, lays stress on the animal "like an ox and yet not an ox". This has given rise to the theory that these strangers from the east introduced the horse into Hausaland, and also to the somewhat fanciful conjecture that the name "Hausa" is derived from two words "Hau" and "Sa", *i.e.* the riders of oxen. The definite mention of the mule in the earlier version rather interferes with these theories, and it may be that these eastern strangers were responsible for the introduction into Hausaland, not of the horse but of the perhaps more valuable donkey.

The tale of the snake—it will be noted that the snake is female—presumably has some religious significance, snake worship being one of the oldest forms of religion. Possibly reference is here made to the supplanting of the snake rites by others introduced by the strangers.

The Girgam gives the name of the snake as "Sarki". It is worth noting that the traditional name is "Ki" or "Kiye". From this it might be deduced that the title "Sarki" is derived from the words "Sare" and "Ki", *i.e.* the "beheader of the snake."

The connexion of the story with a well is at first sight rendered somewhat unintelligible by the fact that Daura town was built (as was Tsofon Birni and presumably all other early towns) on the banks of a river.

The explanation of this may perhaps be somewhat as follows. The town was surrounded by a wide stretch of dense thorn bush, which was no doubt infested by wild animals, so that the drawing of water from the river except in the day time, (note that the Girgam stresses the fact that the affair occurred at night) protected by a large concourse of people (*vide* the "Girgam") to frighten the beasts of prey, was too dangerous to be considered. The snake-killer, or introducer of the new worship, also introduced the art of making weapons more suitable to the killing of dangerous animals and also taught the people the art of digging a well through the solid rock of Daura. In other words an invasion by a more highly civilised people overcame the primitive aborigines, seized the power, and taught the new arts to a grateful people, while at the same time adapting themselves to and adopting many of the tribal customs of the conquered.

The legend contained in the Girgam therefore may perhaps be considered to be celebrating the following events:—

(*a*) The introduction of a new form of worship.

(*b*) The introduction of the art of well-digging in rock.

(*c*) The introduction of the horse or donkey into Hausaland.

(*d*) The substitution of patrilineal for matrilineal succession.

Whether this represents the work of one wave of invasion only or of several which occurred at different times it is beyond me to suggest. It would however seem clear that at some date unknown it was considered desirable to celebrate the benefits conferred by some tide or tides of immigration from the north-east, and accordingly the Girgam legend was written, adopting the name of some hero of fable and selecting a distant town in the east as the source of origin. This last point seems to have little significance, as a similar fabulous origin is claimed by many tribes in Nigeria and may possibly be due to Mahommedan influence.

The story of the two sons of Abuyazidu, Mukarbigari the son of the concubine and Bawogari the son of Daura, may possibly refer to an unsuccessful attempt by the aborigines to wrest the ruling power from the new-comers.

The connection of Daurawa with the Gwari appears to be a close one. The concubine of Abuyazidu is locally claimed to have been a Ba-Gwaria. The people of Zazzau before the Jihad were Gwari, and Sarkin Abuja still claims blood-relationship with Daura.

It is perhaps of passing interest to note that Sarkin Zazzau after being driven out by the Fillani, travelled southwards and on reaching the village of Kumboda left there the Magajiya who was unable to travel further. She became ruler of the town and until recently at any rate the ruler of this town was still a woman, appointed by Sarkin Abuja, though in a different Province. This tends to show that the founding of a town in this way as described in the " Girgam " in the case of Gabas ta Buram, is not only a legendary explanation of events but happens in fact.

The Daurawa and Gwari are " abokanen wasa " and easily recognise one another owing to their face marks being identical, namely two cuts down the side of the face.

It seems possible that some ethnological deductions might be made from the following points which occur in the legendary history of this part of Nigeria:—

(a) The Daura legend refers to the occupation of Bagarmi by a brother of Abuyazidu.

(b) The story of Abuyazidu apparently describes the substitution of patrilineal for matrilineal succession.

(c) The Auyo legend connects the Auyokawa with Bagarmi, stating that a woman of Kudigin married a Sarkin Bagarmi, but on his death the sarauta was refused to her three sons, Shira, Tashena and Auyo, and they moved southwards and founded other towns.

(d) The oldest inhabitant of Unuk (the oldest Auyokawa town) stated that they and the Bade were one race, but that the Auyokawa represented the female line, and the Bade the male line and hence were inferior. The Auyokawa migrated from their former home at Kunu before the Bade.

(e) Katagum History tells of Queens ruling at Tashena.

It may perhaps be that the stories of Daura, Garun-Gabas and Auyo all refer to approximately one period and deal with a movement of tribes from some part of Bornu or Bagarmi caused by an influx of a higher civilisation and resulting in the abolition of matrilineal succession.

It will be observed that in the Girgam six Hausa States only are mentioned and not the usually accepted seven. The Emir of Daura suggests that possibly Othman dan Fodio referred to seven States, including Bornu with the others. In support of this he mentions that up to the time of the Jihad representatives of the six States used to meet annually at Daura and thence proceed to Bornu to carry the news of the year to the Shehu, and presumably tribute.

With reference to "Duma, who became king of Gobir" Daura tradition has it that Duma founded the town of Alkalawa, north of Sokoto, and that it was only after being driven from thence by Songhay that his descendants founded Gobir.

A point that has always struck me as deserving of explanation is the reason why these early immigrants from the direction of Bornu followed this particular line to Daura. There would appear to be a simple explanation of this.

An ancient river rising to the south of Maradi used to flow past Tsofon Birni and Daura town eastwards along the northern border of what is now called Gumel Emirate, through Machina and the present District of Sarkin Arewa of Hadejia, thence to Aroro in the District of Galadiman Bornu and thence to a point near Adiani where it joined the Hadejia or Chalawa River, and so to Lake Chad. A list of towns and villages shewing the line followed by this river from Maradi to Adiani will be found in Appendix "C".

It is interesting to note that this river, though long extinct as a continuous stream, has in recent years occasionally flowed backwards, *i.e.* westwards from Adiani (now the Madum Swamp) for some distance through Sarkin Arewa Hadejia's district.

There was also a branch of the Chalawa River which broke off in the neighbourhood of Yalo in Jafun district (Kano) and flowed north eastwards past Garun Gabas, Zeni, Birniwa and Kakuri to Aroro. Until recently this branch, with the name of Kwondola, flowed across the Hadejia-Kano motor road, and in my own memory in one year reached Garun Gabas. The depression north of Garun Gabas is still known as "Kwarin Kogi" and an inhabitant of Birniwa informed me his father had told him of hippopotami in the river at that town.

My suggestion is therefore that these early immigrants followed the river from Lake Chad—it is obvious that they must have followed water—and on reaching Aroro probably divided into two parties, one following the southern branch to Garun Gabas and the other proceeding along the banks of the northern branch until they reached Daura.

It may be mentioned here that some say that this river does not rise at Maradi but that the old bed can still be traced as far north-west as Adir.

It is perhaps not impossible that this ancient river had its source in the southern hills of Aïr.

I would suggest that the following theory of the early history of this part of the country is plausible:—

  (a) That the aboriginal inhabitants of Daura and Aïr were of the same stock.
  (b) That the legend of Najib the Canaanite refers to an early immigration from Libya of a people similar to the Tuwareg.
  (c) That the later legend refers to the immigration from the north-east of the same people who drove the Tuwareg from Bornu and established patrilineal succession.

Story of the wanderings of the Habe Kings of Daura from their eviction by the Fillani to their restoration by the British Government.

Abdu, Sarkin Gwari, was king of Daura when the Fillani gained possession of the town after a siege by means of cutting off the corn supplies from the eastern villages. The leader of the Fillani was Mallam Isiaku, a pupil of Sheikh Othman, who had been given a flag and permission to occupy Daura.

Sarkin Gwari left the town by the gate called " Kidi da hauka " and marched northwards to Maiaduwar Kadai, thence to Dagura, thence to Shana. From there he sent a message to the King of Kwargwam to announce his approach, and Kwargwam came out to meet him and escorted him to the town. And the men of Daura remained six months in Kwargwam and then moved north to Kanche, thence to Barbarkiya and thence to Damagaram where twenty days were spent before moving to Murya, the daughter of whose king Ibil was the wife of Sarkin Gwari.

Then Sarkin Gwari determined to travel to Bornu, and he and his people marched through Goribi and Zarmu and Gijimu and the Lake called Gushika until they came to Nguru in the days of Galadima Umaru.

And Galadima told him that there was no king in Bornu for famine had scattered all the people, so Abdu Sarkin Gwari returned to Murya and spent nine years there. Then he left Murya and went to Falke and thence to the big river and so to Kalgo where he stayed four years. And afterwards he went to Sallewa ta Kuykuyo and spent six years and six months there, and from there he went to Yekuwa and collected his kingdom together, all but the city of Daura. And Sarki Abdu (Sarkin Gwari) died at Yekuwa and Lukudi his brother reigned in his stead.

When Lukudi became king he collected all his forces and destroyed Magariya. For Kitari his cousin had left Lukudi and had settled at Magariya so that he too might be a king. And another cousin Dan Shafunni also left Lukudi and settled at Dan Mairam so that he also might become a king. So Lukudi collected all his forces and destroyed the town and killed Dan Shafunni. For Lukudi said " we wish to collect in one place and be strong so that one day we may regain the home of our fathers, and you are causing dissension among us ".

Then Lukudi left Yekuwa and went to Yardaje and lived there with all his people for twenty years. Then Kaura Tamila began to intrigue and invited Sarkin Damagaram Ibram to come to them, and Ibram came and warred against them and defeated them at Yardaje. Then Kaura Tamila seized Kenkyari son of Sarkin Gwari Abdu and took him to Damagaram, and Umaru Shehu of Bornu, made him king. Kaura Tamila brought him back and they lived at Kudukudu. Then Tsofo, son of Dan Shafunni went out against them, and he killed Kenkyari and Kaura Tamila, and cut off the head of Kaura and sent it to Lukudi at Toka, who shewed it to his people and had it buried there. Then Lukudi left and went to Kaweri close to Kagare, and thence to Sandamu. And Dambo Emir of Kazaure sent to him and invited him to enter his country, for Lukudi had married Dambo's daughter, and Lukudi went south to Achilafia. But Dambo advised him to seek a place where he and his people could farm, so they left Achilafia and went to Toka, and they cut down the forest and built a town, where they lived after making peace with Damagaram.

Then Ibram, Sarkin Damagaram, sent to Lukudi and said " If you agree to live at peace with me, send me your son or brother and I will make him king, because you are now old ". And after taking counsel Lukudi agreed and sent Nuhu to him, and he was appointed king, and they remained at Toka five years.

But Nuhu and his brother Jiro hated Damagaram and revolted from it. Then Nuhu persuaded Lukudi to leave Toka and they went to Dan Ali. There the Damagaram horsemen attacked them but were driven off by Nuhu. Then they went to Zugai and afterwards returned to Toka, and there Damagaram twice raided and defeated them.

Then Kaura son of Dawambai suggested to Lukudi that they should persuade the Daura Talakawa to revolt from the Fillani and return to their old allegiance. And Lukudi agreed and when the people of Zango had driven out the Fillani, Lukudi went to Gurdo and had a house built for him in Zango in the Ungwa called Tsofon Kafi. Then Lukudi and his son Nuhu entered Zango and they spent their days in fighting the Fillani.

And Nuhu son of Lukudi deposed Kaura son of Dawambai and made Mazawaje Kaura in his place and the son of Dawambai fled to Maradi.

Then Lukudi died after four years at Zango and Nuhu became king.

Three years later Ibram Sarkin Damagaram came to Zango and spent nine months there. And the reason of this was that his cousin Tanimu had gone to Sokoto and obtained a flag from the Sultan Othman and had returned to Daura to collect forces to attack Damagaram. Then Ibram obtained the help of Sarkin Kano of Maradi and Sarkin Gobir and Dan Baura Sarkin Katsina and Sarkin Daura Nuhu and they prepared to attack Daura, though Nuhu warned them that no man would gain any good but only evil by attacking the town of Daura.

And Nuhu's warning was fulfilled, for the attack failed and they were scattered one by one. Ibram Sarkin Damagaram was wounded by a spear and died at Kiru twenty days later. Then Sarkin Gobir counselled Sarkin Maradi to fly. Sarkin Maradi answered that a king does not run away, but Sarkin Gobir replied that if the day is lost even a king runs, and so he fled. But Sarkin Maradi fought on and was killed to the east of the town, and the news was brought to Sarkin Gobir, who said " was that worth waiting for? ".

So Nuhu returned to Zango and Tanimu became king of Damagaram. But Tanimu hated Nuhu because he had helped Ibram, but peace remained for a time on payment of tribute of a thousand cowries per man.

But Kaura Mazawaje began to intrigue with the leading men of Zango to depose Nuhu. Then Tanimu sent to Nuhu telling him to send all his horsemen under the command of Kaura Mazawaje to help him in his wars. So Nuhu was left alone in Zango. And when Kaura came to Damagaram he brought Mahomman Sha, son of Sarkin Gwari, to Tanimu and he was appointed Sarkin Daura. Then Mahomman Sha sent to Nuhu and bade him leave Zango. Persuaded by his mother he left and went to Rafa and stayed there, and Mahomman Sha reigned at Zango.

After a time Tanimu persuaded Nuhu to leave Rafa and he went to Kandamka. And from there he was summoned to Damagaram alone, leaving all his family at Kandamka. Then Sarkin Damagaram sent to Kandamka and seized all his household and his property and had them brought to Damagaram. Sarkin Baka, Dan Giwa, told Nuhu this, and one of his servants suggested an assault on Damagaram that night. But Nuhu refused saying that it was he alone who was wanted, and he was in their hands. Then Sarkin Damagaram sent for Sarkin Zango Mahomman Sha and Kaura Mazawaje and handed Nuhu to them and Kaura had him murdered. Tanimu then seized Nuhu's son Tafida and had him bound, but Sarkin Dawaki Jan Damo advised him to spare him, and he consented and he kept him in his house for seven years. And Mahomman Sha was deposed by Damagaram and Haruna succeeded him, and he was followed by Dan Aro and Sule and Yusufu, all of whom were deposed in turn by Damagaram. Then Tafida was appointed Sarkin Zango, as compensation for the murder of his father, and he controlled some thirty-three towns until the arrival of the British.

The first Englishman to come to Zango was Captain H. C. Phillips (who died at Hadejia in September, 1906) and he had twelve Europeans with him and they encamped on the west of Zango. This visit was the cause of the separation from Damagaram and the independence of Zango. Captain Phillips gave to Tafida some 660 towns and villages. Three years later Tafida died and Mallam Musa succeeded him. He remained at Zango until he was summoned to Dutsi in Katsina by Mr. H. R. Palmer and was restored to Daura. Mallam Musa reigned for five years and on his death was succeeded by his son Abdurrahman, the present Emir.

APPENDIX "A".

LIST OF THE QUEENS AND KINGS OF DAURA.

Name.	Reign.			Name.	Reign.		
	Years.	Months.	Days.		Years.	Months.	Days.
1. Kufuru	At Tsofon Birni.			Yabau	—	—	10
Gino				Naji	7	—	—
Yakumo				Gani	33	—	—
Yakunya				Wake	15	—	—
Walzamu				Kamutu	40	—	—
Yanbamu				Rigo	1	—	—
Gizirgizir				20. Gaga	50	—	—
8. Innagari				Jabu	1	8	—
				Zamnau	4	—	1
Daura	150	—	—	Shashimi	9	—	½
Gamata	Title Magajiya.			Ada Inda	—	—	—
Shata				Doguma	109	—	—
Batatume				Ada Gamu	30	—	—
Sandamata				Ada Sunguma	—	7	—
Jamata				Shafau	5	—	—
Hamata				Ada	—	—	—
Zama				Sabau	8	—	—
17. Shawata				30. Ada Doki	99	—	—
1. Abayajidda (Sar)	150	—	—	Nagama	6	—	—
Bawo	90	3	7	Ada Kube	60	—	—
Gazaura	110	—	—	Hamama	6	—	—
Gakuma	71	—	2	Dagajirau	30	6	—
Jaaku	80	1	—	Kamu	—	—	3
Jaketake	50	—	10	Ada Guguwa	40	—	—
Yakama	201	—	—	Hamida	—	—	10
Jaka	30	—	—	Abdu 'Kawo	9	—	—
Ada Hamta	60	—	4	Nagama	6	—	—
10. Ada Jabu	20	—	—	40. Hanatari	Not	known.	
Dagamu	8	5	—	Rifau	80	—	—
Ada Yaki	106	—	—	Hazo	—	—	—
Hamdogu	210	4	1	Dango	—	—	—
				44. Bawan Allah	—	—	—

APPENDIX "A"—continued.

LIST OF THE QUEENS AND KINGS OF DAURA—Continued.

Name.	Reign.			Name.	Reign.		
	Years.	Months.	Days.		Years.	Months.	Days.
Kalifa	—	—	—	Dan Aro			
Tsofo	—	—	—	(son of 48)	6	7	—
Jiro	—	—	—	Sulemanu			
48. Sarkin Gwari				(son of 53)	2	—	—
				Yusufu			
Abdu Lukudi (brother)	30	—	—	(son of 49)	5	—	—
				Tafida (son of 50)	20	8	—
50. Nuhu (son)	15	—	—	Mallam Musa (son of 50)	7	—	—
Mahamman (son of 48)	3	3	—	58. Abdur-rahman			
Haruna (son of 49)	6	6	—	(son of 57)	appointed in 1912.		

It will be seen that the length of the reigns as given are not of much value. If they were accepted, Abayajidda would have reached Daura in the year 20 B.C. The History of Auyo gives the founding of the town about 1200 A.D.

It is claimed that the nine Magajiyas, from Daura to Shawata, and the first forty-seven Kings, were all buried in Daura Town.

No. 48, Sarkin Gwari was not, as has been stated, contemptuously so-called by the Fillani, but was so named by his people owing to his marriage with a Gwari woman. The title may be reminiscent of the fact that Gwari and Daurawa are in origin the same.

This Habe King was driven out by the Fillani and the next eight kings spent their lives wandering in exile until Mallam Musa was reinstated as Emir of Daura by the British Government.

In the names of the earlier kings the letters "Gam" frequently occur, e.g. Ada Gamu, Dagamu, Doguma, etc. It seems probable that these names or rather titles may be the same in origin and meaning as "Tagman" the equivalent of Sarki in Badanchi and Auyakanchi, the Ganata of Timbuktu, the Agwam or Gwom of the M'bum found in the name of the capital of Bornu N'gazargamu and the Kanta of the upper Niger.

Appendix "B".

LIST OF KINGS OF GARUN GABAS IN HADEJIA EMIRATE.

Biram.
Bomi.
Tumku.
Maji.
Kurada.
Yarima.
Kumari.
Dankwafan.
Jatau.
Amale.
Mamadu.
Dango.
Yahaya.
Dan Asan.
Abore.
Sakaina.
Musa.
Kujera.
Adam.
Ali.
Tagwai.
Jimami.
Barikurgu.
Gamajiya da yau.
Bako.
Burwai.
Gwarma.
Buri.
Usuman.
Gabdo.
Abdu.
Tukur.
Buba.
Kankarau.
Asawa.
Muhamman Bako.
Kawu.
Barwa.
Alhaji Abubakr.
Musa.

Appendix "C".

COURSE OF THE ANCIENT RIVER GIGIDE FROM ADIR TO ADIANI WHERE IT JOINS THE CHALAWA OR HADEJIA RIVER.

Adir*
Maradi.
Garin Tambari.
Gidan Boka.
Sabon Gero.
Gidan Dan Ja.
Kashasha.
Hali.
Maibulbuyo
Dan Tsofo.
Marande.
Mamu.
Maiyara.
Harbau.
Adangau.
Dan Kulare.
Mayayi.
Digaba.
Kanun Bakashe.
Dan Musa.
Kafin Kosau.
Sarkin Bai.
Takatsaba.
Iyatawa.
Kandamka
Dan Karo.
Gazawa.
Dan Damu.
Madawa.
Buguzawa.
Gurjiya.
Maifaru.
Gwalam.
Launi.
Kututure.
Madi.
Dan Dodo.
Rumaya.
Kwalmo.
Gartau.
Dabawa.
Tsigi.
Dan Yarima.
44. Danbarto.
Tsofon Birni.
Koza.
Rijiyar Kaura.
Isa.

* This Adir is evidently the same place or region which is mentioned in the Kano Chronicle in the account of the reign of Bogoda, and there called Adirani. From the fact that Adir is followed by Maradi, it is evident that Adir or Adirani means the Adar, Adrar, or steppe country of the southern Sahara, and refers to a Wadi or Wadis which flow south from the Asben *massif*. Adirani is simply the plural (Adiran) of Adir and equivalent to the ancient Saharan place name Deren. (H.R.P.)

APPENDIX "C"—*continued*.

Daura.	U. Liman.	Gawo.	90. Dogolimi.
Takyareji.	Kumajaja.	78. Gwanga.	Digimsa.
Kanyu.	Ruwan Sarki.	Galadi.	Muzba.
Kwasarawa.	Gangu.	Karaye.	Majanwa.
Arusu.	Kareka.	81. Takarda.	Gidan Dare.
Dargage.	Zanchen-wofl.	Karmashe.	Larai.
Kwajale.	Tabkin Sinyel.	Kugumi.	Digacheri.
Sara.	Soli.	Bago.	Maduwari.
Gaje.	Kaji.	Dole.	Machinamari.
Rogogo.	Burdiga.	Barambagori.	99. Matamu.
Kemo	Dogo.	Kagunsuwa.	100. Aroro.
U. Kaura.	Dan Burdodo.	Kurgele.	101. Nguru.
Tunfushi.	Maikashi.	Ramno.	Adiani.
62. Taramnawa.	Lalatakwari.		

  1–44 French Territory (Sahara).
  45–62 Daura Emirate.
  63–78 French Territory.
  79–81 Gumel Emirate.
  82–90 Machina District.
  91–99 Hadejia Emirate.
100–101 Bornu.
  102 Hadejia Emirate.

APPENDIX "D".

FEMALE TITLES OF DAURA WHICH DATE FROM EARLIEST TIMES AND ARE STILL MAINTAINED.

1. MAGAJIYA.—The title of the early Queens of Daura and hence the senior title.

2. IYA.—To this day at the Big Salla the Emir and all his people pay a ceremonial visit to the Iya's house to receive "mothers' milk". Iya produces two strips of Native White Cloth and presents it with the words "Ga nono".

The male title "Dan Iya" appears to be an adaptation of this early title, evolved after the substitution of male for female succession.

3. SARAKI.—The title of the "Sarkin Rawa" or leader of the dance for the youth of the Royal Family. The name of this lady's drum is "Turu".

4. GABSAI.—This woman has the right to carry on her back the infant children of the Emir. On the day the child is named this woman enters the mother's hut and bestows one of the ancient pagan names, apart from the Muhammadan name given by the Mallams.

5. DAKAMA.—The title of the musician attached to Gabsai. She drums on her calabash at the birth of a son to the Emir. She also has the right to sing first before a newly appointed Emir.

6. YARKUNTU,
7. MAGAJIYA KARYA, } Three minor titles of less importance than the preceding.
8. DAN GAWA.

When Emir's children are being prepared for marriage, the girls are put in Magajiya's care and the sons are handed over to Iya.

A. E. V. WALWYN.

NOTE ON ABU YAZID (ABUYAZIDU).

This legendary or semi-legendary hero appears also in the legends not only of Asben, but of Bornu. In those of Asben he is supposed to have introduced Islam, and his footprints on rocks are shown to the credulous, while in Bornu his name has become associated with that of the Masbarma family, a distinguished scion of which came to Bornu in the 14th or 15th century either from Fezzan or the Nile Valley, and was the ancestor of a long line of Bornu Muslim divines and Wazirs, who were constantly in power and office at N'gazargamu from at least 1500 A.D. and all called "Masbarma".

In the Asben region, at any rate, this hero Abu Yazid (Yazidu in Hausa) represents legends of the prowess of the great North African sectary Abu Yazid, who lived in the tenth century A.D. The presumption that the Bornu hero of the same name is derived ultimately from the same celebrity is almost irrebuttable.

We may assume that the Abu Yazidu of this Daura legend and the Abu Yazid of Asben, represent the same personage and are connected with the same events, though the connection of the historical Masbarma of Bornu with Abu Yazid can only be an anachronism.

The son of the "King of Baghdad" however of this Daura legend, is the Abu Yazid of the Bornu and Asben legends.

The question is, to what period and to what events in Hausaland and Bornu does this legend really refer, and to whom does it refer, if to a historic local personage at all?

It is, as has been seen, probable that it primarily refers to the period 900-1000 A.D., and that the name Abd-ul-Rahman or Abu-Yazid represents the Barbar sectary Abu Yazid whose great revolt in North Africa was crushed about 950 A.D., his followers scattering into the Sudan.

The reason that Baghdad is brought in, is no doubt due to the fact that these North African sectaries were Kharijites or Ibadities, and that the period corresponded roughly with the period 900-950 A.D., when first the Carmathians (who stole the Kaaba) harried and ravaged the Abbasid dominions; when the Fatimid Caliphate was set up first at Mahdiyya in Tunis and then at Cairo, and lastly when the Turkish General Tuzun at Baghdad even usurped the place of and blinded the Abbasid Caliph Muttaki (940-944.)

In some of the Daura accounts of Abu Yazid it is said that he left Baghdad because of a certain heathen called " Zi Tuwan." In a Bornu manuscript the same name is written Tuwi (or Tuzi) son of Butlus.

Probably the original was Tuzun, and Butlus is meant for Bitlis near Lake Van at the head of the Tigris which was in fact a starting point of Turkish and Tartar invasions of Baghdad, and a very famous place as the site of one of Alexander's " castles ".

The chronology and detail, however, must not be pressed too hard, but at about this period there was a good deal of migration from Baghdad to North Africa (*e.g.* the Barmecides or Baramik), and Fezzan (Zeila) was full of Kharijite slave traders, who traded with Kanem and Bornu, according to Yacubi.

The real " Abu Yazid " was killed in North Africa, but there is no reason why a Kharijite Barbar follower of his should not have done much as Abu Yazidu is supposed to have done in Bornu and Daura at a later date. The supposed connection of the famous Bornu family Masbarma, with these events is at least curious. The connection possibly bears some relation to the unorthodox Moslem community who live near Gumsa in Geidan, Masbarma's home, and are reputed to be Moslem sectaries of some kind even now.

It seems possible that in origin these Gumsa people, who worship in pits or caves, were some kind of Kharijites. There are still small communities of Carmathians in different parts of the Moslem world.

If this is so the legendary connection between Abu Yazid the sectary (950 A.D.) and the Masbarmas of Gumsa who lived much later (1300-1500 A.D.) would explain itself.

A Bornu account of Abu Yazid and the Masbarmas runs as follows:—

In the name of God, the Merciful, the Compassionate: May the blessings of God be upon the noble Prophet.

The Imam Sheikh Al Jalil Ahmad al Imam, the son of the Imam Muhammad the Fatimid, the son of the late Imam Muhammad Balyuma is reported as saying:—

" Now as concerning the history of Umr Masbarma the son of Othman, the son of Ibrahim: verily I am more learned in the Law than Mallam Umr Masbarma; more instructed than Sheikh Umr Masbarma; of greater understanding than Sheikh Al Waliu Masbarma; more eloquent than Al Mahiru Masbarma; and older than Mallam Umr Masbarma. But the learned and experienced Sheikh Al Wali Umr ibn Othman is of more exalted lineage than I, both on his father's and his mother's side, but it was I who found the book of his grandfather Ibrahim who came to the fortress of N'gazargamu.

" Now when he came to the fortress of N'gazargamu with his father Masbarma Othman, Umr was seventeen years old.

"When he reached twenty years of age, the Sultan of Bornu was Idris the father of Ali, who had given to his father Masbarma Othman his daughter Aisatami in marriage, Aisatami was the daughter of the Sultan Idris and the sister of the Sultan of Bornu, Ali.

"The following is the truth concerning his descent. The Sultan gave to his father Aisatami, the daughter of Idris, in marriage; she gave birth to Umr Masbarma and afterwards to his brother Ahmadu Bultami, who died when twenty-five years old, and left his elder brother Umr Masbarma ibn Othman, ibn Ibrahim, ibn Bukr, ibn Umar, ibn Sanyu, ibn Khalid Khalme, ibn Abd al Malik, ibn Muhammad the second, ibn Ahmad, ibn Muhammad At Tagi the Yamanite, ibn Abdulla Khalba Goni, ibn Muhammad Gana, ibn Ahmad Gana, ibn Muhammad Sanyu, ibn Muhammad Kande, ibn Hasan-at-Tagi the Yamanite, ibn Umar ibn Othman-al-Taisara, ibn Ibrahim Kanzaki, ibn Abd al Wahab the Arab, ibn Abd al Barbare, ibn Ahmad, ibn Al Hassan, the son of my lord Ali, the Emir of the Faithful, ibn Abu Talib (may God be gracious to them) so that he is of the descendants of Fatima, the Shining One, the daughter of Muhammad the Prophet of God, on whom be blessings and peace.

"This is Masbarma's genealogy and his origin, and thus did we find it in the book of his grandfather Ibrahim who came to us in the time of the Sultan of Bornu Idris, ibn Muhammad, ibn Ahmad, ibn Kadai, ibn Idris. ibn Muhammad. ibn Ibrahim. These are his ancestors on the side of his mother Aisatami the daughter of the Sultan Idris."

As for the number of his sons, Umr Masbarma ibn Othman begat male children. The first was Masbarma Ahmad Matalami. Then was born Masbarma Umr Gulgulma, then Masbarma Harun, then Masbarma Ali Dalagimi, then Masbarma Othman Aisatami, then Masbarma Umar Dabulemi, then Masbarma Muhammad Fasama Suyuma, then Muhammad al Imam Masbarma Nubami, then Masbarma Ahmadu Magaji, then Masbarma Othman Kulumi, then Masbarma Ibrahim Magaji Zarami, then Masbarma Ahmadu Ajimi who was in the council of the Sultan of Bornu Muhammad*, then Masbarma Muhammad Gambomi who was in the council of the Sheikh Muhammad al Amin, then Masbarma Muhammad Bosoma who was in the council of the Sheikh Umar ibn Sheikh Muhammad al Amin until the time of Sheikh Bukr the son of Sheikh Umar.

When Masbarma Muhammad Bosoma who lived to be 102 years and four months and was called Kiari Masbarma, died, at the beginning of the reign of Sheikh Abu Bakr†, his son was installed, but he did not function like his predecessors. They left the customs of the Bani Umr Masbarma ibn Othman and scattered owing to war, settling in the land of Bornu from time to time in diverse places and districts and towns.

---

* Who fought Gwoni Mukhtar, 1808.
† *i.e.*, the late Shehu Garubai, 1903-1922.

According to the Imam Muhammad ibn Al Imam Ahmad ibn Muhammad Fatimiye, the steadfast, learned, experienced, and noble Sheikh Umr Othmanmi ibn Ibrahim had female descendants from his daughters. His first daughter was Fatima Zahra. From her was born Mallam Bukr Gwoni and Fanta. Mallam Bukr Gwoni had a son named Abu Bakr and sons named Mallam Ahmadu and Muhammad. Also a son named Sheikh Umr Masbarma, and a son named Othman, also Ibrahim and Ahmadu, and two other sons Abu Bakr and Ibrahim. After these two no more were born till the end of thirteen years. Then God Almighty bestowed upon them a daughter Fatima Zahra, the daughter of Ibrahim who bore a daughter and four sons. This is all about eighty-two years ago from the present time. We know nothing further, but we have found in the book of Masbarma's grandfather Ibrahim that his father Bukr ibn Umr Saniyu had gone trading to Yaman and heard news that Mallam Adam had gone to the Sultan of Yaman Umr al Himyari. So he followed in his tracks until he found him, after which he returned home.

The next year he went to find him, and stayed with him for a year to profit from his learning, and was given Mallam Adam's daughter Zeinab in marriage. Bukr had two children by her, one Khalid Khalma, and the other Aisha Aiyame. For this reason some people trace the descent of Umr Masbarma from the people of Yaman, but he is not really of the people of Yaman, for though the people of Yaman are among the ancestry of his forebears they do not belong to his *nisba*.

His genealogy and origin are from Hassan the son of our Lord Ali ibn Abi Talib (may God be gracious to them and may God ennoble his face with light. Amen, and again, Amen.)

The Imam Ahmad ibn Muhammad said that his father Sheikh Muhammad al Imam made friends with the learned and noble Ibrahim the father of Othman, who begat Umr Masbarma Othmanmi at the time of Ibrahim's arrival from Egypt, which was in the time of the Sultan of Bornu Idris ibn Muhammad ibn Muhammad ibn Ahmad.

In his time there came a man, brave and masterly, whose name was the Said Abdurahman ibn Abdullahi, called Abu Yazid, ibn Abdullahi the Sultan of Baghdad. He and his people came with all his brothers through fear of an unbeliever named Tuzi ibn Butlus. When Tuzi ibn Butlus pressed the people of Baghdad in fight, in that night Abu Yazid Abdurahman, ibn Abdullahi Sultan of Baghdad, went out with three of his brethren and with many of the horsemen of his father. He advanced towards the country of Egypt with his force to wage Holy War. He stayed in Egypt three nights, and moved on from the land of Egypt towards the land of Kanem where a stay of two days was made. Then the host moved on from the land of Kanem making for the country of Bornu.

When they came within three days journey of Bornu, Abu Yazid sent a letter to the Sultan of Bornu which read as follows:—

" From Abdurahman, son of the Sultan of Baghdad Abdullahi, son of Sultan Othman son of Abd al'Aziz.

"After salutations verily I have come bringing peace: not with an army or to war but to see your land and what is in it. Perhaps we shall pass on towards the west."

The Sultan of Bornu Idris, ibn Muhammad, ibn Ahmad, sent a letter to find the grandfather of Umr Masbarma, and ordered him to read the letter from Abu Yazid. Sheikh Al Imam Ibrahim read it, saying "I hear and obey." When the morrow dawned the Sultan sent Kaigama Musa ibn Ahmad with the chief men of his kingdom, to the number of about 1,000 horsemen or over, to Abu Yazid. The Kaigama met Abu Yazid Abdurahman, ibn Abdullahi, Sultan of Baghdad, and was his conductor to the Sultan of Bornu, Idris. Abu Yazid then halted where he was and his people also halted out of respect to Abu Yazid. He refrained from entering the land of Bornu. His host camped by a mountain in the south as he ordered. Abu Yazid, the son of the Sultan of Baghdad, passed a night there, and sent his Wazir Hassan ibn Al Harith to the Sultan of Bornu after he had sent to him gifts of welcome, thousands of oxen and rams and numbers of different kinds of fruit one after the other. This continued for three days.

Abu Yazid sent greetings to the Sultan of Bornu Idris and said: "I have need of an eloquent scholar." The Sultan of Bornu Idris sent for the grandfather of Umr Masbarma, Mallam Ibrahim, and sent him together with my ancestor the Imam Muhammad to Abu Yazid. With them went seven men of the best of the Ulema of the council of the Sultan. They came to Abu Yazid the son of the Sultan of Baghdad, and saluted him. He ordered them to come into his presence. They came before him and found him to be unassuming, smiling and cheerful. He said to the grandfather of Masbarma Ibrahim: "Welcome to the good and eloquent-tongued Sheikh." Ibrahim answered "I thank you, O generous and brilliant Sultan."

Abu Yazid then said "O great Sheikh, I have need that you should read three books." He said to him, "Certainly." Abu Yazid brought the books to him and showed them to him so that he saw them and read all of them to him. Then Abu Yazid ordered Masbarma to be given a box full of coloured clothes and gave him two horses and two slave girls who had been presented to him by the Sultan of Kanem. When the Sheikh Mallam Ibrahim, the grandfather of Umr Masbarma, returned, he told all that had happened to the Sultan of Bornu Idris. The Sultan asked the Sheikh Ibrahim saying: "What is the purpose of his travelling? I do not think that the purpose of his visit is honourable and straightforward. From all I hear, his coming frightens me. What is his purpose? for his people and armies are greater than my armies. What do you think about it?" The Sheikh said to the Sultan of Bornu, "You must be patient, we will find out and tell you his purpose which is full of guile and craft."

Then the Sheikh Ibrahim, the grandfather of Umr Masbarma, rode in the darkness of the night and went to Abu Yazid. He dismounted among the soldiers and sent the doorkeeper to salute Abu Yazid and asked for an immediate audience, and that King

Abu Yazid should be informed concerning his coming that: "It is necessary for me to come secretly by night lest anyone of the people of Bornu recognise me." Abu Yazid ordered him to be admitted and lighted a large candle.

The Sheikh came in and they skook hands. Then Abu Yazid said: "What has brought you, O great and learned Sheikh, for I have not seen any one the like of you who would come to me at this time." The Sheikh said to him, "O king! Verily I came to this people and have tarried with them for years but have not found any of them who has entered upon the path of the Moslem 'Sunna', let alone the path of the 'Shari'a'; I am afraid of them. Now you have come amongst them and I have no knowledge of what you seek. If your desire is to stay here then I will stay with you; but if your desire is to wage Holy War against them and to fight them, because of the number of their sins and crimes, then I and my family and the people that are with me will leave them and go with you until your purpose is accomplished."

Abu Yazid, the son of the Sultan of Baghdad, answered him: "Are you an Arab or are you one of the people of this country? tell me and I will inform you of my purpose which I hope God Almighty will accomplish." Sheikh Ibrahim the grandfather of Umr said to him. "Verily I am an Arab and came from the East and the Sultan of this country befriended me; but now I am afraid of a change in their religion for they do not follow the path of the Moslem 'Sunna', let alone the 'Shari'a'. It is not becoming that a wise man like me should stay with a people until he has tested their characters. We have tested their characters, and they do not follow the perfect 'Sunna' let alone the Moslem 'Shari'a'. Now I would become your friend in truth: if you wish it we will be on your side, but if you do not wish it, then either we will stay with them or we will leave them."

Abu Yazid said: "Return to me tomorrow and come to me about this time and I will tell you my purpose."

Mallam Ibrahim left him and rode his horse back to the town and entered his house at morning time whilst the Sultan Idris was sitting down waiting for his return to give him information as he had promised.

When the morning prayer had been said, the Sheikh went to the Sultan. When the Sultan saw him he rose to take him into his pavilion and they entered it. The Sheikh said: "Be patient until tomorrow and we will bring you true news for we have not got anything definite from him but he has promised me and has undertaken to tell me tomorrow night." Then the two of them came out from the Sultan's pavilion and the people beheld them.

When the time came at which the Sheikh had promised to return, he went to Abu Yazid and found him and one of his brothers whose name was Mansur. Abu Yazid said to him in a friendly voice "I do not know what my desire is. Perchance we shall return to the East, perchance we shall go on to the West." He did not say one word more than this.

Mallam Ibrahim returned and gave the Sultan of Bornu Idris this news. The Sultan of Bornu said: "This is his guile. What see you concerning his strength? And what is the truth concerning him?" He said: "You will find me on the watch for what he is doing."

After two days the Sheikh returned to Abu Yazid to find out the truth. Abu Yazid, the son of the Sultan of Baghdad, Abd ul Lahi said to him, "What has brought you to us again?". Sheikh Ibrahim said to him, "The Sultan of Bornu, Idris, was angry with me because I had come to you, and he drove me from his gate. The alternatives to adhering to him are that, either we must stay here or leave the country because of my coming here. Such is the practice of his forefathers who were of the Banu Muhammad Saif of Mecca. For this reason I have returned to you: when you leave this place I will go with you in whatever direction you take." Abu Yazid said to him: "Return to your house and we will make a guileful plot with which we will kill the Sultan of Bornu Idris after thirty days, and I will make you my Wazir and helper." The Sheikh answered, "I hear and obey."

Mallam Ibrahim returned and informed the Sultan of Bornu of Abu Yazid's guile. That night the Sultan gave to Ibrahim the mother of Umar Masbarma, that he might give her in marriage to his son Othman, the father of Masbarma. She bore Othman two sons, one of whom died young. The other was Umr Masbarma, the son of Othman, the son of Ibrahim.

The Sultan treated Ibrahim with glory and honour and gave him much wealth. The Sultan of Bornu Idris of the Banu Saif took counsel with his people and said to them "Abu Yazid intends to kill me and to inherit my kingdom, and to gather the kingdom of this land to himself. What see you in it?"

Mallam Ibraham told him to send Kaigama Musa and Galadima Ali ibn Bukr and Chiroma Abba, and order them to say to Abu Yazid, "The Sultan of Bornu Idris intends to send his army to the West, and wishes you to give him of your people some of the greatest and bravest that they may help him with his army."

Abu Yazid gave the Sultan of Bornu three thousand warriors amongst whom were twenty-seven sons of the Sultan of Baghdad. The Sultan said to him "When they have returned from the expedition, we will return your people to you by God and His Prophet."

Abu Yazid ordered his people to go with the army of the Sultan of Bornu Idris. When they had been gone for seven days, Mallam Ibrahim (the grandfather of Umr Masbarma) came to the Sultan of Bornu Idris and said "You should play a trick on Abu Yazid. Take three of his brothers and give to each one of them the rule of a kingdom secretly and without the knowledge of Abu Yazid."

So the Sultan gave them each a dwelling place and said to each of them "Verily, my brother, I wish you to have a settled place like your brothers so that each one of you may be a great king." They replied that they would like this, and went to tell Abu Yazid the news.

Then Sheikh Ibrahim, the father of Othman, said to the Emir of Bornu Idris, " Make a present of your daughter Magira to Abu Yazid, even as you have given kingdoms to his brothers." The Sultan of Bornu was pleased with this advice of the noble Arab Sheikh Ibrahim, and said to him: " Thus should it be between friends and helpers." He was pleased with the great Sheikh.

So he gave his daughter Magira to Abu Yazid, and love and friendship reigned between them. The Sultan of Bornu Idris then gave to one of the brothers the country of Kanem, and to another the country of Bagarmi, and to the youngest he gave the land of the Tubus. To each one also he gave one of his daughters, and they went to their several countries. Thus was Abu Yazid left only with a small following of the foolish who were of no use to themselves, much less to any one else.

Not one of the raiders from the West returned for the people of Bornu killed them. These returned by another road secretly, and said to the Sultan of Bornu Idris, " We have made this raid and have killed Abu Yazid's people from the first to the last. Very few have escaped."

That night they laid their plot to kill Abdurahman, Abu Yazid, the son of the Sultan of Baghdad, but his wife Magira heard of it and said to him, " My father will kill you, our only plan is to depart to-night." So he fled with his wife, and his piebald horse, the winner of many races on the maidan. Magira was with child by Abu Yazid. They travelled on to the country of Gumsa but when they reached it, she was too weak to go further, so he left her in this country. She gave birth and called her son Burami, but for the rest of her days she heard no news of her husband.

In later days the people of Bornu heard that Abu Yazid had become Sultan of Daura. It is said there are kings of Daura to this day.

When the Sultan Idris of the Beni Saif saw what had happened, he assembled his brothers and sons to choose Sheikh Ibrahim (the father of Othman who begat Umr Masbarma) and his seed as their Wazirs and ministers, nobles and Governors, for the duration of his dynasty.

They did not cease being so until the time of the death of Muhammad Masbarma whose second name was Kiari, who lived for 102 years.

Sheikh Al Imam Ahmad ibn Muhammad says that when Othman begat Umr Masbarma Othmanmi it was at the age of nineteen. Umr Masbarma lived for 100 years less nine months.

The Sheikh Al Imam Ahmad ibn Muhammad writes: " I found a book amongst the books of Umr's grandfather, which his father Othman had inherited from his father Ibrahim, who came to the fortress of N'gazargamu in the time of the Sultan of Bornu Idris ibn Muhammad ibn Ahmad of the descendants of Muhammad Saif of Mecca. In this book were the names of the ancestors of Umr

Masbarma to the number of twenty-one from his grandfather, the noble, the generous Ibrahim ibn Bukr, to our master Hassan ibn Fatima, and our Lord Ali ibn Abu Talib, may God be gracious to them. Twenty-one in number were his ancestors."

The learned and truthful Sheikh, the Imam Ahmad ibn Muhammad writes: "I sat before Umr Masbarma Othmanmi and I was fourteen years old, when he was forty-one years old. We verified that he was the noble Arab from the stock of Hassan."

The learned Sheikh the Imam Ahmad ibn Muhammad writes: "As for the history of Umr Masbarma Othmanmi from the time of the Sultan of Bornu Idris to the time of his son Muhammad, to the time of his son Ali, to the time of his son Alhajj Idris, verily what happened in their days has been written until the last days of their kingdom and nothing has been left out. As for the date of the experienced, the learned, the noble, the Imam, the sage, the ruler, the Wazir Umr Masbarma ibn Othman ibn Ibrahim, his birthday was on a Monday after the midday prayer in the month Rabi'ul Awwal and the day of his death was on the 12th of Rabi'ul Awwal at the completion of 918 years A.H. or 919 according to the Indian calculation.

1512 A.D.

"The day of his birth is a day of splendour for the people of Bornu and a day of rejoicing for them. On this day the Sultan of Bornu and the Councillors, and the people of Bornu, both great and small, seek for blessings because of the birth of Umr Masbarma ibn Othman ibn Ibrahim.

"On that day and for seven days after his birth people came to the door of his father's house to salute. There were people who passed the night and people who passed the day at the door of his father Othman's house. So blessed was his mother Aisatami that verily she bore her blessed son on the great feast day. And all the people said 'Everyone who is born on this day in this month is blessed.'"

Sheikh Ahmad the Imam says that the people of Bornu keep the feast on the 12th day of Rabi'ul Awwal. That year this day was Monday. Thus the name Umr Masbarma brings blessing, and the day of his birth is a day of splendour to everyone as a day on which the Sultan leaves his city.

As for his birthday, verily it was winter time and the cold was unusually severe. It was a year of plenty for corn and stock and for this reason they called him "Bardi", *i.e.* the winter time, for the entry of winter was twenty-one days after his birth.

He grew up to be a youth and stayed in that place thirteen years and seven months. Then he went on a journey, he, and his parents, to the country of Machinna that he might read the works of Bukhari and the arts and sciences in the school of Sheikh Ahmad Fatumi whose second name was ibn Muhammad Balyuma, who was of the ancestry of the pious and learned Mallam Tahir, al Barnawi. Masbarma stayed with him for seven years and six months.

After he had understood and learned and become eloquent in speech and repetitions and set pieces and all legal knowledge and in the commentaries on the Kura'an, and the knowledge of the fear of God which he had learnt from Bukhari's works, he became a Sheikh, honoured, revered, great and pre-eminent in the sciences. He had understanding and learning in jurisprudence and Islamic practice, and was the greatest of the Sheikhs of Sultan Ali ibn Al Hajj Idris ibn Idris Al Awwal.

Then he went to "Umr's residence" which is a well-known town in the desert of the land of Bol, and the news of him reached the future Sultan of N'gazargamu, Ali ibn Muhammad Dunama, who was at that time the son of the reigning Sultan.

Now Ali the future Sultan of N'gazargamu was the son of Dunama ibn Abdullahi ibn Umr ibn Muhammad ibn Idris, and was at that time the son of the reigning Sultan of Bornu. Ali was a brave man and a courageous one, full of foresight, and he was to inherit the great kingdom. He was to be the most famous among all the children of his father's house.

But at that time there ruled his brother Ahmad Al Amin ibn Othman.

One night when he was sleeping, Ali saw in a dream a tree spring out of the ground with forty branches, and to every branch a thousand fruits. Of all the fruits some were gold and some were silver. Then he began plucking them with his hand and at times with his mouth. And he swallowed them down his throat.

Again he plucked the gold and silver fruit, and he hung them upon his shoulder and he took some of the fruit and divided it amongst the people. Some of it he gave to his friends, and some of it he put on the ground and carried it away.

He sent to all the learned men of N'gazargamu and told them of this. But they could not explain or make it clear and for the space of three days he found no explanation. He heard the news of one learned man and sought him out but did not get what he wanted.

Then he collected the chief men and the learned men and asked them: "Who is the most knowing and learned amongst you in this country who knows the news of the East and of the West?" And all of them said, "If that is what you wish for, —Sheikh Umr ibn Othman ibn Ibrahim. You will get an explanation from him."

So Ali ibn Muhammad Dunama sent to call Mallam Umr Masbarma ibn Othman to come to him to explain his dream to him, but Masbarma refused to come to him. Then Ali was angry, but afterwards repented, and when the night came he sent to his servant Musa ibn Bukr and told him about it and said to him: "What is our best plan to bring this Sheikh to us?" Musa said: "What need have you of a plan except of going to him? Perhaps he will reveal the dream to you and tell you what you need."

They rode forth and went to Masbarma and found him in the mosque praying in "the night hours." They stood still until he had finished. Then they saluted him and informed him about the dream saying: "Verily I saw this and this." Masbarma interpreted it as meaning such and such, as that he would rule over many kingdoms, and that his dynasty would last long; he said, "You will see this and this, a man will enter N'gazargamu who is a Mallam from a far distant country who will diminish your kingdom, and his kingdom will last for a long time. In that time will come a man, short, learned, of good memory, pious, eloquent, a Sheikh, full of guile and treachery, gross of face who will not look you in the eye, the most wrathful, and the sternest of men, and of great determination. And when he is angry exceeding great is his anger. He will take possession of this kingdom and it will remain with him for many years. In the time of his sons an Arab[*] will appear, the most evil and dissolute of men. Some will he keep alive, some will he kill. He will spare the women and will kill the men until they leave their dwelling places. For he is a brave man. The Sultans and Kings of the country will fear him, and he will rule the land for a short time. Then another people will kill him and they will take on the government in different places and countries. And they will inhabit a country in the desert and long will be their time there. And they will deal out justice among the people. They will imprison the evil doers and those who stir up trouble in the land so that long will be their time, until the end of the kingdoms of the world. And this is the finish of your dream."

Sultan Ali ibn Muhammad Dunama said to Masbarma: "After that will there be a king in our house or not?" Umar Masbarma answered, "I have no knowledge of that. I shall not live to that time. I have no knowledge of that time, God Almighty only knows." And he asked him again: and he said, "I will leave it at this, this news is sufficient for you, so thank you the one God."

Then Ali took leave of Mallam Umr ibn Othman and returned with his messenger Musa. When he had returned to his house, on the very night of his arrival his brother died. Ali then, young as he was, inherited the kingdom from his brother even as Sheikh Umr Masbarma had interpreted the dream to him. The people and councillors and his elder brothers all did obeisance to him although he was young. The kingdom was consolidated and became very wealthy in Ali's reign. He ruled for twenty-three years.

In the first days of his reign when his enemies and those who envied him were many, Ali sent to the learned Sheikh Umr ibn Othman to come to him quickly, so that he might give him power and honour, and so that perchance he might choose him as his judge and Wazir, charged with his commands, and might sit in council with him and become his friend even as he had been at first.

But Umr Masbarma refused to come and Ali sent to him a second time but he still refused. Then Ali sought out ten of the chief men of his kingdom and sent them to the Sheikh with honeyed words, asking him to come and straighten out his affairs, and then return to his house. Masbarma agreed to that.

He hastened to the Sultan of Bornu Ali ibn Muhammad Dunama. When he came Ali said to him: "Welcome to the

---

[*] *i.e.*, Rabih Zubeir.

Sheikh who truly told me my dream." He rejoiced and was glad at his coming, and caused him to enter his pavilion and talked with him all his affairs and gave undertakings and promises. Umr Masbarma agreed to his proposal.

Ali said to him: "If you desire it we will make you Kadi and Wazir until the end of my reign." Sheikh Umr said: "To God is the ordering of everything" but he was pleased, and took counsel with his father Othman and his grandfather Ibrahim. And it pleased them.

Then Umr returned home and brought with him his people and his fathers, and all who were of his house, and they came into the presence of the Sultan of N'gazargamu who took Masbarma with both hands and placed him near him and made him his ruler and chief Kadi, and chief Wazir. He took no action in anything except on the advice of Umr ibn Othman who took counsel with his father.

Ali would say "Masbarma" (for so was he nicknamed) "sit there", since Masbarma was the title of his father, and so his also during their epoch and even until now.

When the chief men of the countries of the Sultan of Bornu saw that he had chosen Umr Masbarma as his Wazir, they were envious of him and slandered him before the Sultan of Bornu Ali ibn Muhammad Dunama.

The people of the country came in a body to the Sultan of Bornu saying: "Either you choose Umr Masbarma and we leave you, or you choose us and drive away Masbarma, for we will not sit in council with him after to-day. If you wish, kill us—to this we agree."

When Masbarma Umr ibn Othman heard that, because his enemies had become many, he went out on Thursday the 27th of Jamada al Awwal, in the year 919 A.H. . . . . eighteen months . . . going to the town of Gumsa to till his farm and to prepare it, and to bury the corn in pits and turn it over.

1513 A.D.

He stayed at Gumsa for a time considering matters, and remained in that town for two months.

The Sultan of Bornu then sent for him to come to him but he did not go. The Sultan then assembled his chief men and informed them of the matter, and wrote Masbarma a letter and collected for him much wealth, silver and robes and linen stuffs and striped clothes and other articles and stuffs and shirts and bracelets and coloured clothes and silken clothes and shining robes and coloured sashes.

The Sultan wrote: "All this is my present to you;" he rejoiced and was exceeding glad, and wrote at the end of his letter, "If this my letter reaches you then make your preparations to come to the Sultan of Bornu that he may take you as a trusty and beloved brother to a greater degree than he did before."

Masbarma said to all his messengers: "Tell him I will not come to him until he has given me an assurance and has sworn by Almighty God that there shall be no enmity between us and his people." He sent this answer to the Sultan. The Sultan was pleased with it and sent to him a second time so that he made up his mind to leave his house and go to the Sultan of Bornu Ali ibn Dunama.

When he arrived, the Sultan was standing in front of his porch. He stopped Masbarma by the door in order to take the oath as he had arranged in his letter.

He washed his body and did his ablutions before the people and held the Kura'an on which he was to take the oath. But Masbarma stopped him saying "I do not agree unless you swear an oath to trust me." Then the Sultan accompanied Masbarma to his lodging and the people followed in their footsteps to see this marvellous sign of their love and trust.

The Sultan returned with the chief men of his kingdom, and that night he took counsel with the people and chief men of his kingdom as to how they should build for Masbarma a house greater and better than his first house.

They built for him a better and loftier house than his first house, and the Sultan of Bornu ibn Muhammad Dunama gave him his sister in marriage whose name was Mariam Hafsa. She was exceeding beautiful for no man had seen a greater beauty than her whose face shone with beauty and loveliness. She was well read, and no man knew the extent of her dowry. So she lived with him in his house.

The Sultan Ali ibn Muhammad Dunama went every day to Masbarma Othmanmi to hear him reading and explaining the Kura'an and the traditions until he became a true Moslem. Masbarma ordered him to marry four wives and to put away his other women. He did so.

Masbarma ordered him to place many slave girls in his house and told him that there would be no harm even if he had a thousand but that he must divorce the free women in excess of four. He also ordered the chief men of Bornu to do likewise which order some obeyed and some did not.

Those who disobeyed agreed upon a plan. They all went to the Sultan of Bornu Ali ibn Muhammad Dunama and said to him "Either you slay us or you send away your Wazir and Judge Umr ibn Othman, or if you do not do so we will kill him with an evil death." The Amir Ali held his peace and gave no opinion, but after a time he said "Either you kill me and Masbarma or you drive us both from your country."

After three days the Sultan arrested sixteen important men whose enmity to Masbarma was pronounced, and executed them. The chief among them were Kaigama Umr ibn Fatimami and Shettima Aba and Galadima Ari ibn Musa. These were among the sixteen men whose enmity was greatest to Masbarma ibn Othman ibn Ibrahim.

Ali the Sultan of N'gazargamu sent to his trusty friend and Wazir Masbarma in the night. The latter came to him secretly and sadly and finding Ali and his chamberlain together, said: "Be not sad and downcast and fear not for what they have done. Let your prayers be full of hope, and in submission to His will call on your Lord. Let not your sadness be long upon you as one who rebels against his Lord."

In that same night Masbarma and those who were with him went to Logone. The next morning the news of his going came to the Sultan Ali. He sent Yarima Musa ibn Umar to Logone after the Friday prayer, and sent with him forty-five men of his wisest and greatest. They hurried after Masbarma to Logone to raid and plunder but they were unable to do so, nor could they reach Logone. They spent the night upon the shores of the great Chad near the Wâdi Dûma. When day dawned they took possession of some booty and remained there for three days. Yerima Musa ibn Umar died there.

When the news of Yerima's death reached the Sultan Ali he rejoiced exceedingly. They remained there for two months and perhaps fifteen days.

On that night Masbarma with the remnants of his people returned. Sultan Ali rode out and met his Wazir and Chief and trusty friend with great joy. They returned together rejoicing and remained together for three months.

When Sultan Ali died, his reign had lasted for thirty-three years and seven months. His son Idris ibn Ali ibn Muhammad Dunama succeeded him. The death of Ali ibn Dunama took place on Thursday the fifteenth day of Dthul Ka'ada in the year 912 A.H.*   **1507 A.D.**

Sultan Ali was succeeded by Idris ibn Ali who treated Masbarma as his father had done. Then Idris died after a reign of twenty-three years, and was succeeded by his son Muhammad ibn Idris. When the people had installed him as Sultan, the chiefs of the people of his kingdom advised him to depose the Wazir Masbarma. The Sultan Muhammad agreed to this, and that either he should kill Masbarma or drive him to another country.

But no sooner was this plan settled than a pestilence fell upon them and forty-one men died in fourteen days. Even their Sultan died, he being the forty-first.

Muhammad was succeeded by his brother Abdullahi ibn Ali ibn Muhammad. Those that remained of the chiefs of the people then took counsel and sent to the country of Kanem. At that time Adam ibn Ahmad ibn Ibrahim, a grandson of the "royal house" was ruler of Kanem.

Alhajj Idris who then went with his army to Kanem was of the sons of Sultan Ali, son of Muhammad Dunama. He had three tribes of people under him; the first were called Bulala; they were the Beni Kadai and were amongst the bravest of warriors. They were wont to come to Bornu as allies on account of Mallam Umr ibn Othman ibn Ibrahim.

The Bornu people sent to Bagharmi and to its chiefs and to Mandara and all its chiefs that they should come to them quickly, under pretence that they were coming on a visit of condolence because of the death of the Sultan of Bornu, and that they might pay their respects to the Wazir Masbarma; but really in order that they should either kill him or imprison him until his death.

---

* *i.e.,* three years later than is generally supposed.

But Masbarma heard news of their guile, and when the Bornu people went out to meet the chief men of Kanem and Bagharmi and Mandara, he did not go out with them but appointed a substitute of the same appearance as himself. This substitute was named Ahmad ibn Ali Kachella. He clothed himself with a gown as if he were Masbarma.

When the Bulala and their allies saw him they took him and killed him thinking that he was Masbarma. But soon some of them returned and found Masbarma at the door of his house giving a lesson on theology and on the Kura'an. They marvelled at that for they had thought and believed that they had killed Masbarma. He thanked God and praised him exceedingly.

In due course this Sultan died but Masbarma meanwhile had become so trusty a friend that his rank was raised above that which it had been before. The Bornu people and Masbarma then made a covenant and swore on the mighty Kura'an. This covenant they kept by night and by day.

They compiled, with his help, many books amongst which were books on what is ordered and what is forbidden. This was at the time of the coming of Al Hajj Ibrahim ibn Ahmad the Arab.

After him came Ahmad Taram the Arab, and then the army of Abdu Salaam ibn Hadîm*, consisting of picked horsemen of the hosts of the " So ". As for the saying " Verily he will rule a kingdom between two ' Ms ' and an ' M ' ", the first M stands for Masr, and the other double M stands for Mulk Melle. So that the saying means, " He shall rule a kingdom from Masr to Melle ". But God Almighty caused his army to be defeated and he and his people perished by reason of the prayers of Umr Masbarma ibn Othman ibn Ibrahim.

Masbarma afterwards counselled the Sultan to go out to war towards the West.

1532 A.D. So he took his Wazir Masbarma, and his people, and marched west on the 7th day of Jamada al Awwal, in the year 939 A.H.†

He went in the direction of Agades which place he overcame. The people there are Tuwareg of four clans: Kelowi, and Atabasha (Iteseyen) and Agadasawa and Kel Giris Igidalen.

He made treaties of peace with many of the tribes and appointed as his representative his slave Ibrahim after the conquest of Agades. To this day the chiefs of Agades are of his seed and the people assemble before them and they rule. He overcame many fortresses. Then he returned home and died forty days later.

After the Sultan's (Abdullahi's) death, the government of the empire of Bornu changed because of the news of the coming of Al Hajj Idris, son of the Sultan Ali ibn Dunama, who had returned from the pilgrimage.

The chief men of Bornu sent to him to pay him their respects and made their obeisance to him. At this time the Sultan of Kanem Adam ibn Ahmad and Abdullahi ibn Abd ul Jalil, revolted, as also did the Sultan of Bagharmi and the Sultan of Mandara, owing to the fact that the King of Asben and the Kwararafa had defeated Bornu.

---

* King of Melle.
† In the reign of Muhammad ibn Idris according to accepted chronology.

When Hajj Idris the son of the Sultan Ali heard this, he sent to the chief men of Bornu, Kaigama Musa ibn Ali and Galadima Aba and Yerima Idris ibn Abdallah and Chiroma Bukr ibn Ali, and Yerima Ali Dalatu, and Ahmad ibn Muhammad, and Harun ibn Umar ibn Othman ibn Ibrahim.

At this time the Wazir Masbarma* died at the age of ninety-eight years and seven months in the year 1018 A.H.   1609 A.D.

Hajj Idris chose Harun as his Wazir. He refused on account of his age, but advised that his son Idris should be appointed to which Idris agreed. So the Sultan appointed as Wazir Idris ibn Harun ibn Umr ibn Othman ibn Ibrahim Masbarma, on the analogy of their respective ancestors.

Hajj Idris caused his Wazir Idris ibn Harun to write a letter to the Sultan Muhammad ibn Abdullahi to ask him for help in his war with the Sultan Abd ul Jalil, the Sultan of Kanem.

So they set out together. The Sultan Muhammad ibn Abdullahi camped in the north of the country of Kanem and Hajj Idris camped in the south. That day was Thursday the 22nd of Jumada al Awwal, in the year 1019 A.H.†   1610 A.D.

Abd ul Jalil, the Sultan of Kanem, set out to fight the Sultan Idris, but his brother the Sultan Muhammad ibn Abdullahi and Hajj Idris ibn Ali ibn Muhammad Dunama fell upon him with the chief men of the kingdom.

That a man should know his own side the armies put on respectively black and red signs. Hajj Idris ibn Ali put Abd ul Jalil to flight.

Hajj Idris camped by the gate of Abd ul Jalil's town for fourteen days and obtained dominion over it. God Almighty gave Sultan Idris ibn Ali Dunama victory in the flight of the Sultan Abd ul Jalil and his confederates.

Hajj Idris went on to conquer the land of Bagharmi and rule over it; likewise he conquered Mandara. He brought war to their Sultan and conquered them and then made terms after a fierce fight. Of the great men of Bornu who were killed in one day, were Galadima Aba, Yerima Idris ibn Abdallah ibn Umr, Kaigama Musa ibn Ali, Kaigama Ali ibn Dalatumi, Ahmad ibn Muhammad, and a very large number of others, great and small.

The total of the slain of the people of Mandara could not be counted nor reckoned, both of horsemen and foot soldiers.

Then they made terms with the Sultan Idris, as was done in the case of his father Sultan Ali ibn Muhammad ibn Dunama on the day when they shot him on the eye so that he became "one-eyed", though God Almighty gave him the victory.

Adam the son of Ahmad the Sultan of Kanem followed after him by night, not going out in the day time, and came to the Sultan Hajj Idris who appointed him successor to his father, and gave him his confidence.

---

* Not the first Wazir Masbarma.

† This and the date of Wazir Masbarma's death are both a good deal wrong.

But after three years Adam revolted and a battle was fought with him. He fled, he and his people. Many of the chief men of his kingdom were killed and he returned home.

Sultan Hajj Idris ibn Ali ibn Muhammad took counsel with his Wazir Idris ibn Harun ibn Umr ibn Othman ibn Ibrahim, that they should attack the Koyam and Barabar in that their king aforetime was Abd ul Jalil, and aforetime the father of Hajj Idris, had made a raid against them at Kuriyo, when his "maidugu" was wounded with a spear.

The Sultan Hajj Idris fought them. They are of the tribes of Kanem who came to the land of Bornu.

There advanced against Hajj Idris the Bulala host of Abd ul Jalil who are the Bani Kadai of the Bani Ismail ibn N'gazzar ibn Mudir ibn Abdu Kasim.

The Sultan fought with them and put them to flight and killed a vast multitude of them and conquered their kingdom.

Then he returned and determined to war against the Tubu. These are they who sought to slay the Sultan Muhammad Dunama in the time of our fathers. The Sultan Muhammad ibn Dunama made war against them and slew their king Abdu Salaam, and took possession of all their wealth and women; he ravaged their dwellings and ruled them by force and against their will.

Hajj Idris ruled over the countries and rulers of Kanem, Bagharmi, Mandara, the Tubus, Kirsala, and Kayala with the towns surrounding it, until the end of his reign.

When Hajj Idris ibn Ali died after a reign of twenty-seven years all the countries revolted and not one of them continue its allegiance to Bornu at the present day.

When Idris died his son Muhammad Dunama succeeded him for the space of fifteen years. When he died he was succeeded by his brother Idris-as-Saghir ibn Ali, the brother of Dunama al Kabir, who reigned for ten years and then died.

After him Muhammad Dunama ibn Ali reigned for nineteen years and died.

There succeeded Dunama the lesser, the son of Muhammad, for fifty years: Ali ibn Hajj Idris ibn Ali succeeded him for forty-six years, when he died.

Ahmad ibn Ali succeeded him for seventeen years and six months. Dunama ibn Ahmad succeeded him for four years and nine months. Then he died.

Muhammad Gulzumi ibn Ali succeeded him for seventeen years and three months.

Muhammad ibn Ahmad Dunama succeeded him. Muhammad Gwoni al Mukhtar fought with him and put him to flight and drove him and his people away for the space of a year and nine months. He sent to Muhammad al Amin ibn Muhammad ibn Ahmad Ningami el Kanemi to help him. Al Amin gave him his help and put to flight Gwoni al Mukhtar with his following.

Dunama returned to his kingdom but he died after two years. Then Muhammad al Amin made his son Ibrahim king for five years. When Ibrahim died, Sheikh Muhammad al Amin al Kanemi succeeded him for twenty-eight years and two months when he died, and was succeeded by his son by a slave maiden whom the Sultan of Bornu Muhammad ibn Ahmad had given him for his help in returning him to his kingdom. The name of the woman was Magira Baira, and her son's name was Sheikh Umr.

Sheikh Umr took possession of the kingdom of his father Muhammad al Amin al Kanemi. The time of his reign in the town of Kukawa was forty-six years and three months.

Sheikh Umr died and his son Sheikh Abu Bakr succeeded him for three years and two months when he died. Sheikh Ibrahim his brother succeeded him for a year and seven months.

Ibrahim's brother Muhammad al Hashimi succeeded for eight years less forty days when he died assassinated. Then his nephew Sheikh Kiari succeeded him for nine months when Muhammad Rabih, the oppressor, slew him.

Rabih the oppressor succeeded him for seven years and two months when the Europeans killed him.

Sheikh Abu Bakr succeeded Rabih for twenty-three years, and his elder brother Umr Sanda has succeeded him until the present time.

This history from the year 727 A.H. to 1346 A.H. is finished and also all the kings of N'gazargamu from Ali to Shehu Muhammad al Amin al Kanemi, and his dynasty.

1326 A.D to 1927 A.D

PEACE.

The above account sheds an interesting sidelight on the Masbarma family and Bornu history—even if its chronological sequence is not quite accurate or reliable.

H. R. PALMER.

For Product Safety Concerns and Information please contact our EU
representative GPSR@taylorandfrancis.com
Taylor & Francis Verlag GmbH, Kaufingerstraße 24, 80331 München, Germany

www.ingramcontent.com/pod-product-compliance
Lightning Source LLC
Chambersburg PA
CBHW081756300426
44116CB00014B/2138